Philosophical Interventions in the Unfinished Project of Enlightenment

Philosophical Interventions in the Unfinished Project of Enlightenment

edited by Axel Honneth, Thomas McCarthy, Claus Offe, and Albrecht Wellmer

translations by William Rehg

The MIT Press, Cambridge, Massachusetts, and London, England

This book was set in Baskerville by DEKR Corporation and was printed and bound in the United States of America.

Library of Congress Cataloging-in-Publication Data

Philosophical interventions in the unfinished project of enlightenment / edited by Axel Honneth . . . [et al.] ; translations by William Rehg.
p. cm. — (Studies in contemporary German social thought)
Includes bibliographical references and index.
ISBN 0-262-08208-X (hc). — ISBN 0-262-58109-4 (pbk).
1. Philosophy. 2. Critical theory. 3. Sociology—Philosophy. 4. Culture. I. Honneth, Axel. 1949– . II. Series.
B29.P46315 1992
190—dc20 91-23376
CIP

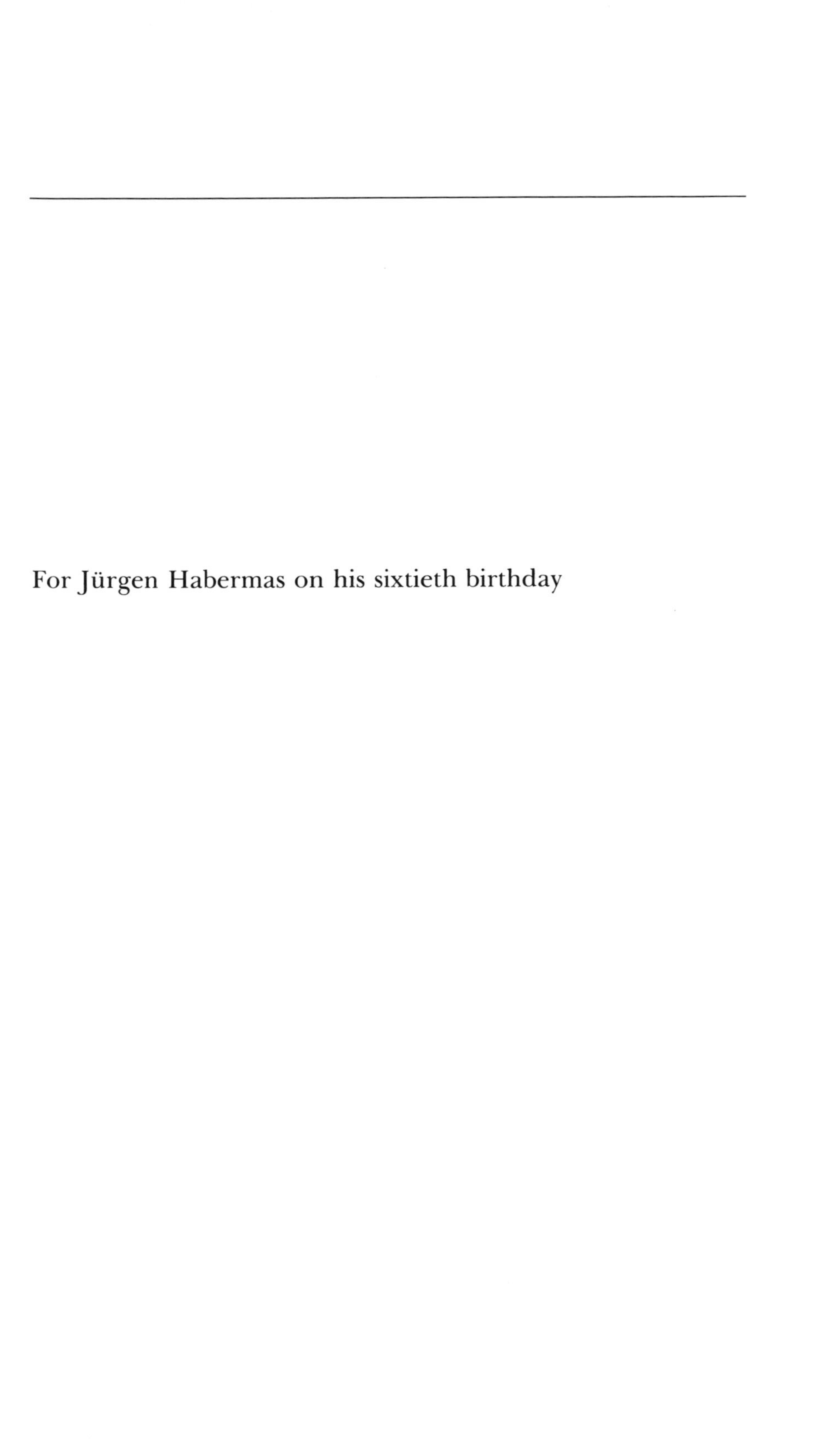

For Jürgen Habermas on his sixtieth birthday

Contents

Preface

In the welter of recent counterenlightenment and post-enlightenment theorizing, the work of Jürgen Habermas stands out for its unflinching defense of enlightenment rationality. His is, to be sure, a conception of reason informed by the critique of reason that has, from the start, accompanied enlightenment thought "like a shadow." And it is a conception that highlights the ongoing, unfinished nature of the project of enlightenment. The essays collected in this volume, which were dedicated to Habermas on the occasion of his sixtieth birthday, take up various, more or less "philosophical" aspects of that unfinished project. While the diversity of their topics reflects the multifaceted nature of his own work, it by no means exhausts it. A companion volume of essays, soon to follow, will deal with other, more "cultural" and "political" aspects of the project. Taken together, the studies collected in the two volumes attest to the immense variety and fertility of a life's work that has routinely transgressed the usual disciplinary and school boundaries.

This is not to say that all of the essays in this volume deal directly with Habermas's work. Some of them do engage with specific elements of it, for example, his attempt to establish the normative grounds of critical theory (Apel), his critique of wholesale critiques of reason (Jay), and his pragmatic approach to the theory of meaning (Wellmer). Others take his thought only as a reference point for developing variations on themes found within it, for instance, the origins of the theory of the modern subject (Henrich), the notion of critique as a philosophical ethos (Bernstein), the tensions between contextualism and universalism (McCarthy), and the widely proclaimed "death of man" (Schnädelbach). Still others simply take up key issues in the unfinished project of enlightenment: the forgetfulness of time in metaphysical thinking (Theunissen), the sources of modern identity (Taylor), the complexities of philosophical method (Tugendhat), and the relation of art to rationality (Bürger). None of the essays claims to be more than an intervention in an ongoing discussion.

Thomas McCarthy

I

Historical Perspectives

1

Metaphysics' Forgetfulness of Time: On the Controversy over Parmenides, Frag. 8, 5

Michael Theunissen

Translated by William Rehg

1

Among the achievements of Parmenides—the father of philosophy as rational argumentation, of logic and ultimately of all science—not least is that he also founded ontology, the theory of what *is,* which in his poem appears from the start as metaphysics, as the theory of what *in truth* is. After Parmenides, metaphysical ontology will constantly take on different shapes; in fact it already displays a new form in Plato's theory of Ideas. Despite its change, however, it still remains bound to the basic Parmenidean concept of Being.[1] With this concept Parmenides answers a question he was the first to raise. The peculiar shape of his ontology and metaphysics, his answer to this self-posed question, results from the opposite concept of Nonbeing. Parmenides even assigns every determination and hence every difference to the domain of Nonbeing. All determinations whatsoever must be kept away from Being, because as something determinate it could not be something else. Being is thus *only* Being [*das nur Seiende*]; indeed, it is Being as is just *existing* [*nur Existierendes*]. If, with all determinations, all predications as well belong to not-being, then, of the various ways of using the word "to be," only the existential usage remains for the Parmenidean "is."

The earliest answer to the question of what in truth is clearly becomes dubious as soon as one attempts, for instance, to make the concept of Being as what just exists the standard for interpreting fragment 3: *to gar auto noein estin te kai einai.*[2] In that case, this alone is obvious: the fragment does not proclaim an identity of being and thinking. The idealistically interpreted identity—hence the assumption that Parmenides dissolves being into thinking—is completely excluded. However, an identity in which the difference between being and thinking would be preserved also appears incompatible with that answer. Parmenides cannot give Being an identity with something external to it; rather, he can give it no more than self-identity, and that merely as a synonym for the pure positivity of what is only Being, a positivity that corresponds to the pure negativity of the nondeterminable.

Yet even if one is looking in fr. 3 for no identity whatsoever, one can hardly avoid a certain tension between this fragment and the reconstructed answer. To illustrate the difficulty, consider the translation proposed by Hölscher: "For the same can be thought and be." One could heighten the thrust of this translation by taking *noein* not as "thinking" but (with Tugendhat[3]) as "being aware of" [*Vernehmen*] in the sense of "perceiving" [*Wahrnehmens*]. Be that as it may, a translation such as Hölscher's can derive from two somewhat opposed interpretations. Zeller, who was the first to read "the same" as the subject of the sentence and not predicatively, as did proponents of the identity thesis, detected the following view in the text: "only what can be can be thought." Hölscher himself reverses the relationship: "only what can be thought can be."[4] One will probably have to reject Zeller's interpretation, not the least because it imputes a trivial statement to the text. Parmenidean philosophy is so far from trivial that any interpretation that reduces it to triviality disqualifies itself. On the other hand, Hölscher's style of interpretation collides with the concept of Being. For it proceeds on the assumption that thinking is, in any case, constitutive for being. Being conceived as what just exists, however, denies thinking any power to constitute being. The exclusion of all determinations excludes all predications and thus excludes predicating thought itself.

This contradiction is due not to the interpretation but to the interpreted text. Parmenidean thinking seems self-contradictory on its own terms. The key to a better understanding of this internal contradiction is its own conception of itself as a path. It pursues a path along which it changes. The concept of Being as only Being describes the path's goal. Its point of departure, on the other hand, is marked by a position that in fact still allows thinking a constitutive significance for being. This does not mean, however, that Parmenides abandons an initial intention somewhere between his starting point and his goal. Rather, the goal is a goal precisely because only there does the intention guiding from the start become documentable. This occurs where the concept of Being is given a stable meaning, i.e., in fr. 8.[5] As has often been pointed out, in fr. 2 "is" (*estin*) has no subject, or even if it has a logical subject, then at least it has no linguistic one; at the beginning of fr. 8, *estin* still lacks a subject. Only in the course of this fragment is the subject progressively revealed as "Being."[6] In fact, it is revealed there as Being taken specifically as "only Being," in the sense of what just exists. The *sēmata* (signs) put forward and explained in fr. 8, which mark the path of persuasive truth, are not features subsequently picked up from something that would already be accessible independent of them. Rather, they provide the right access to Being for the very first time.

2

In this chapter I would like to investigate the tension between the beginning and the end of Parmenidean ontology. I suspect this tension is grounded in the author's intention itself. If this suspicion is accurate, then fr. 8 deserves our attention. Here Parmenides attempts to show that the complete lack of determination and difference in Being is an absence of all temporal determinations and differences. His intention aims at an indifference to time. If it could be demonstrated that Parmenides nonetheless uses temporal determinations even in his quest for such absence, then a source springing up at the heart of this intention could be located. The long-lasting controversy over whether this is the case or not refers above all to fr. 8, 5–6a: *oude pot' ēn oud' estai, epei nun estin homou pan, hen, suneches.*

Any translation of this sentence perforce involves controversial interpretations. The first part has been especially discussed.

According to one reading, the sentence says, "It [Being] neither was nor will be, since it is now together as a whole, one, continuous." According to the other reading, the main clause means, "Neither was it at one time, nor will it be (at some time)." The apparently slight nuance in fact bears on the basic question at stake. According to the first reading, that is, Parmenides intends to negate the temporal difference between past and future; according to the second he is not at all interested in denying modal differences in time but merely wants to negate a passing away settled in the past and a coming to be located in the future. If the first reading credits the Eleatic with carrying through a conceptually adequate intention of timelessness, the second assumes he indeed aimed for timelessness but in fact achieved only unlimited duration.

To approach the controversy over fr. 8, 5–6a, from the perspective of my basic question, we have to bring the real point of controversy into still sharper focus. It probably cannot be denied that the Parmenidean concept of Being analytically implies timelessness. The only worthwhile point of contention is whether Parmenides saw this implication and drew the theoretical conclusions of his own concept. This is not only, nor is it primarily, a question of the linguistic realization of his intention. The *aporia* of his thinking could only be rooted in his intention itself if the undeniable inadequacies of his language indicated that he stopped somewhere in his thinking, that he omitted a step required by his conception. Leonardo Tarán, who has provided the most discriminating account of the option for duration and against timelessness, notes the stopping point most precisely.[7] Tarán begins with the observation that Parmenides speaks as though not at all aware of the difference between timelessness and unlimited duration. The contradiction between the timelessness intended and the duration actually put into words indicates first of all that awareness of the difference is lacking. Yet this lack of awareness in turn indicates that Parmenides proceeds from the negation of all differences to the negation of every process but not to the negation of time, even though there exists a logical connection between process and time. To investigate the contradiction in the intention of Parmenidean thinking means uncovering the ground of this blockage.

Now the full range of the controversy only comes into view when we identify it as a controversy over eternity. Both parties characterize the timelessness that the text implicitly affirms or denies as timeless eternity. However, since the concept of eternity admits of several meanings that the interpreters of the passage frequently do not differentiate, we must at least define it in a preliminary way before we adopt a position on the controversy itself. In so doing, we soon see that more is at stake than the notion of eternity qua timelessness.

We can speak of eternity either in a weak or a strong sense. In the weak sense, eternity could include unlimited duration. Inasmuch as duration, even without beginning or end, is admittedly a duration in time, it seems reasonable to restrict the concept of eternity to eternity in the strong sense. Below, then, I will use "eternity" only in a sense excluding mere duration. Yet "metaphysical eternity" is in turn merely a vague label for at least two notions of eternity. We only need to define one of these for starters, that of timeless (or atemporal) eternity. The reason is that, fundamentally, it alone is at issue in the question whether or not Parmenides sustained his intention of indifference to time. In contrast to this, the second metaphysical eternity is not atemporal insofar as one cannot abstractly separate it from time or oppose it to time as an absolute other. To be sure, it would not be eternity if time were not negated in it. But in its case the negation also positively sublates [*hebt . . . auf*] time.[8] Consequently, it cannot directly intend an indifference to time and thus cannot represent a position in the controversy over such indifference. To avoid confusion, the position holding that this latter view is already present in Parmenides will be examined separately in a later section. Until then we can also postpone its closer definition. For the moment, suffice it to note that it represents a position on eternity beyond the one thematized so far, i.e., it ascribes another eternity to fr. 8, 5–6a, than that of atemporality. The view that restricts the meaning of the sentence to temporal duration I shall designate as position D (duration, *Dauer*). I distinguish this from position E (eternity, *Ewigkeit*), which admits of two variants, E_1 and E_2.

If we focus now on the first eternity in the strong atemporal sense, then from a linguistic point of view it appears as the eternity implicit not only in genuinely metaphysical propositions but also in logical or mathematical ones and, more generally, in all propositions about necessary or allegedly necessary truths. This is the case inasmuch as such propositions detach the "is" from its connection with the "was" and the "will be," thereby detemporalizing themselves as well. Thus E_1 does not understand *oude pot' ēn oud' estai* in its objective literal sense, i.e., not as the statement "Being never was and never will be" but rather as a prohibition of a certain kind of talk about Being, namely, a manner of speaking that applies to Being the past and future forms of the verb "to be." In other words, E_1 already credits the Eleatic with the insight Plato unmistakably formulates this way in the *Timaeus*. Just this is what position D contests. In more precise terms that zero in on the real point of controversy, D by no means denies that Parmenides wrote "tenseless statements," sentences using the timeless "is." What it does contest is that, granting he actually wrote such statements, their semantic peculiarity was clear to him.[9]

In the rest of the article I shall proceed as follows. First of all, the controversy between D and E_1 must be recapitulated in enough detail to permit a preliminary assessment (section 3). This must focus especially on 5a, for the main object of dispute in that controversy is the first half of the line. To be sure, the disputants are anticipating the "is now" (*nun estin*) in the second half of the line. Still, they do not actually see it in that context. Next we must retrieve the eternity that is not atemporal without qualification and decide on the truth of E_2 (section 4). Since this position is essentially supported by 5b, it invites an alternative interpretation of 5b–6a, a phrase running over to the next line through an enjambment (section 5). It seems to me that a final assessment, even of position D, is possible only in view of 5b–6a. Finally, by way of conclusion just a few strokes will suffice to sketch the answer textual analysis gives to our basic question (section 6). My reason for hanging a picture of such breadth in the confined space provided by fr. 8, 5–6a, is that I find this text an interesting object in its own right, independent of its function for clarifying the framework of the broader problem. For this reason I shall review, with comparable detail, the relevant discussions conducted by other researchers. Naturally, in taking up these contributions I only want to further our effort to understand their argumentative value and supplement them by additional arguments.

3

Who is correct: the majority that celebrates Parmenides as the discoverer of timeless eternity (E_1) or the minority that finds his poem actually expresses a merely unlimited duration (D)? To make a reliable decision about which position we ought to side with, we would have to examine the sum total of arguments for and against E_1, as well as those for and against D. The examination of the reasons for and against E_1, however, we can accomplish rather briefly.

The arguments used to justify E_1 are largely irrelevant because they are based on a misunderstanding of the point of controversy. That is, they only work by bringing additional assumptions to the text, when the problem is just to show that Parmenides himself makes such assumptions. One can see this even in the strongest arguments for E_1, those of G. E. L. Owen and Charles Kahn. Owen draws for Parmenides the inference from the negation of change to the rejection of temporal verb forms; Kahn applies for him the exclusion of differences in general to temporal differences.[10] Yet the question is precisely whether Parmenides himself proceeds from the negation of change to the negation of time, whether he draws from his exclusion of differences the necessary conclusion for temporal differences.

To the extent that the arguments for E_1 are weak, so those against it are proportionately stronger. The arguments contra gain strength precisely because the burden of proof for E_1 looms so large. The latter would have to prove not simply that the idea of timelessness was possible for Parmenides but that he actually conceived it. In fr. 8, however, there is not a single sentence that would clearly betray an awareness of the logical connection between process and time. The thesis advanced by E_1 is indemonstrable.

We must, then, concentrate on the arguments pro and contra D, both the reasons D advances on its own behalf and the counterarguments that E_1 has us consider. I would like first to discuss D's statement of the temporal meaning of individual expressions. Then I shall examine the reference to time operating in the whole line of thought, focusing especially on the demonstration immediately following it (6b–21). I shall pick out only the most important of the temporally suspicious expressions, so to speak: the fundamental feature of Being and its explicans in the demonstration, as well as the words "at some time" (*pote*), "now" (*nun*), and "is" (*estin*), especially in 5–6a.

I understand the fundamental feature of Being as the first of the *sēmata* Parmenides wants to derive, the concept pair "ungenerated and imperishable" (line 3: *agenēton-anōlethron*); its explicans I take to be the concept pair "without beginning, endless" (line 27: *anarchon apauston*). Position D lays claim to both pairs of concepts in its defense. The negation of becoming and passing away, just as that of beginning and end, does in fact yield merely unlimited duration. The serious counterarguments are exposed to the objection of indemonstrability. One counterargument holds that Parmenides used negations in an "unrestricted" fashion.[11] The point here seems to be that Parmenides negates time itself through the negation of becoming and passing away, beginning and end. But this counterargument shows in no way that timelessness is necessarily conceived. The epistemological status of the other counterargument must be assessed in a similar fashion. This argument holds that Parmenides, like Wittgenstein, uses a ladder he throws away upon reaching his goal, and hence that he deletes time determinations retrospectively.[12] But this too cannot be verified. Nevertheless, we should hold on to this much: since the above is at least a *possibility,* a certain doubt still attaches to position D on this point.

Position D chiefly supports itself on the fact that in our model text Parmenides does not simply say, *oud' ēn oud' estai,* but adds "at some time" (or "ever," *pote*).[13] Proponents of D consider the use of this expression alone sufficient reason for assuming that Parmenides, far from negating past and future without qualification, merely denies that Being exists in a specific past or a specific future time. Such an interpretation has to supplement the text somewhat insofar as it, first, also refers *pote* to the future and, second, presumes a tacit implication we might explicate as follows: "In no way is it the case that being was at one time and now is no more, or that it will be at some time and now is not yet." One can hardly object to the first point, especially since Parmenides himself specifies the futurity he negates in line 20 with *pote.* Against the second point one might object that if Parmenides had been concerned with "at some time" in the sense of position D, he would have spelled out the "no longer" and "not yet."[14] But this is easily countered, for the amount of explication is a matter of individual style, and with a style as terse as Parmenides', explication will be slight in any case. A weightier doubt concerns how D reads the expression *pote* itself. It points out that in all of Greek literature the phrase *ou* (or *oude*) *pote* means "at no time."[15] Position D, however, claims the right to stress *oude* on its own rather than take it as the unstressed complement to *pote.* At the same time, even should one wish to deny D this right, one must admit that its reading is at least possible. O'Brien shows that the phrase *ou pote* is used in three ways and that the usage D requires is quite prevalent even in the non-Parmenidean literature.[16] In addition, Schofield points out that 5–6a abrogates the normal rules of usage anyhow.[17] Thus it is hard to avoid the conclusion that position D, while not entirely free of doubt, appears on balance tenable, even as a thesis about the temporal meaning of the expression "at some time."

At the heart of the debate is the controversy over the relevance of the word "now" (*nun*). For D this word demonstrates that we have to read the subsequent "is" as the temporal form of the verb "to be." For E_1 it represents nothing but an infelicitous expression that in no way prohibits us from understanding "is" as the linguistic sign for timelessness. To a certain extent this controversy is undecidable. Helene Weiss already saw the *nun* in our text as a temporal determination supporting Heidegger's thesis that ancient ontology interprets Being with a specific mode of time in mind, i.e., the present.[18] To this Beierwaltes replies that in Parmenides the "is" simply "follows the dictates of language" and thus only appears temporal. "On the basis of the subject matter," however, it is quite atemporal.[19] In a similar way Kahn excuses the temporal determination as due to the particular orientation of the Indoeuropean languages to temporal verb forms. The controversy is undecidable insofar as a textual statement can hardly tell us whether or not it reproduces the intended meaning. Nonetheless, we can at least narrow the problem down somewhat. Ultimately it is more than just a question of whether Parmenides inadequately formulated his intention. That is, the question is whether he intrinsically breaks off the intention itself. The means for its adequate formulation were at his disposal. Tarán in particular draws attention to the fact that Parmenides could have expressed a prohibition against applying temporal verb forms to Being in the same way his goddess expresses the prohibition against following the path of Nonbeing: "I do not allow you to say that Being was or will be, since it is." If, in possession of the requisite linguistic means, he nonetheless says "now," then the suspicion arises that he in fact does internally break off his intention of timelessness. So here too the balance tips towards position D, although again with some vacillation and certainly not unequivocally.

The ambivalence is even more striking if we turn to the "is" in line 20, which is closely related to line 5: "For if it (Being) came to be, it *is* not, nor [is it] if it will be at some time in the future." The first half of the sentence appears inconclusive, to begin with. True, we are inclined to draw the opposite conclusion: if something came to be, then it is. The *ouk est'* of the text is a non sequitur unless we understand the "is" as being in the absolute sense, as *pampan pelenai* (line 11), "to be all in all." Then we can lay out the meaning of the sentence in this way: "If something came to be, it *is* not, in the absolute sense in which Being is; therefore Being did not come to be." For a proponent of E_1 such as Mourelatos, this implies that one must read the "is" as a linguistic sign for timelessness. For Mourelatos the following assumption lurks behind the sentence: "What something becomes is not what it is in its timeless essence."[20] Thus E_1 is thought to offer the only interpretation freeing the first half of the sentence from the appearance of inconclusiveness. However, as much as this shows the ambiguity in the temporal qualification of the "is" in line 5, so on the other hand does the equation of absolute and timeless being remain premature. For Parmenides seems to conceive precisely absolute being as everlasting, enduring without limit. The "is" opposes the "came to be" and is thereby defined through its negation as ungenerated being. Because E_1 overlooks this, it tends rather quickly to reinterpret the "came to be" as a "was."[21]

This brings us to the question concerning the reference to time operative in the entire fragment, especially in the line of thought that essentially concludes with line 20. The question is this: Is Parmenides merely concerned with the negation of becoming and passing away, or is he concerned in addition with the negation of past and future? This is the concrete form the fundamental problem assumes in our fragment in relation to the programmatic negation of temporal differences. Position E_1 sees in 5a a negation of past and future; D the denial of both a passing away that would have occurred if Being were now no more and a coming to be one would have to assume if Being were now not yet. Position D supports its reading on the meaning and function of the subsequent text 6b–21. Its argument is that the "for" (*gar*) in 6b implies that the ensuing text is supposed to be a proof for the foregoing sentence; but in lines 6b–21 Parmenides demonstrates nothing other than the impossibility of becoming and passing away; therefore, the foregoing sentence only asserts their impossibility. E_1, of course, challenges just this premise, that lines 6b–21 merely justify the exclusion of becoming and passing away. In its view, these lines as well, especially line 20, aim at the negation of temporal differences.[22] However, such an interpretation strikes me as obviously false, since it simply generalizes the reinterpretation of "came to be" as "was." What in line 5 may be unclear with regard both to the past and the future, and what in line 20 is surely ambivalent with respect to the past, emerges quite clearly in the latter's statement on the future: for Parmenides, the not-being of Being would certainly not follow from its past or future but would follow from its coming to be—it is not if it first comes to be at some time in the future.

Thus the reference to time operative in the whole text more readily supports position D than does the temporal meaning of individual expressions. This time reference, however, confronts us with a problem. Anyone accepting the reading proposed by D must also acknowledge that Parmenides looks to the past for the passing away he wants to negate; coming to be he seeks to negate in the future. This must not only be acknowledged, it must be emphasized. Mourelatos errs when, in objection to that reading, he maintains that the whole text aims to reject a past coming to be and a future passing away. The demonstration Parmenides adduces merely adds the rejection of a past coming to be. But as line 20 shows, what Parmenides seeks to negate in the future is, as before, not passing away but coming to be. Naturally, it must appear strange that his entire exclusionary procedure focuses on future coming to be. At this point let us simply note that this oddity harbors the problem we must yet elucidate. Likewise in need of subsequent elucidation is the problem that arises when our attention turns to a past coming to be, namely, the fact that passing away diminishes in importance.

There is still another question we must leave open for the moment. It concerns the point at which one could unhinge position D most easily, assuming no better justification is available for it. Tarán asserts that our model text 5–6a contains no new predicates in relation to the characteristics "ungenerated-imperishable." This assertion possesses no evidential value whatever, because it already presupposes an option for D. If it cannot be proven as a statement about the entire sentence, it is downright counterintuitive in reference to the supporting clause. It rests on the premise that the demonstration for the first characteristic already begins with the sentence. This premise is also dubious, it seems to me. I find it more plausible to read the sentence as part of the thesis to be demonstrated, which is outlined in the programmatic enumeration of the *sēmata.* More specifically, the main clause explicates the first *sēma,* while the supporting clause reproduces the movement going through the additional *sēmata* in the immediately previous verse ("whole and unified and unshakable and complete"). Later I shall attempt to verify this specification of the sentence's context. Assuming this succeeds, it follows that at least the supporting clause expresses something quite new in relation to the characteristics of being ungenerated and imperishable. Only by acknowledging this can position D escape the objection that it renders the entire sentence trivial. In Mourelatos's eyes, the trivialization betrays its presence by weakening the "since" (*epei*) to a "but" (*alla*), thereby robbing the *epei* clause of its justificatory force. In order to counter this argument against D, I will have to carry the debate—fought out in the literature primarily over the interpretation of 5a—to the territory represented by the clause 5b–6a, which has been neglected by both of the positions treated thus far.

4

Before turning to the interpretation of 5b–6a, however, we need to examine the thus far omitted position E_2, which in fact relies on the supporting clause. The task of criticizing E_2 compels us, first of all, to define more exactly the eternity this position reads into 5b–6a. Thus we must specify the second notion of eternity in the strong sense. Among the proponents of E_2 this notion appears under various names, such as "absolute identity of the eternal present" (Calogero[23]), "pure presence" (Gigon[24]), or "the pure now of the epiphany in which everything is at the same time and in the One" (Picht[25]). In each case what is meant is the *aiōn* envisioned in the *Timaeus,* which the Latin tradition translates as *aeternitas,* setting it off against *sempiternitas,* unlimited duration. Just as E_1 finds in our Parmenides passage an early model of the *aidion ousia*—being, interpreted as timeless and, in Plato's *Timaeus,* set apart from the "was" and "will be"—so E_2 sees in this passage the kernel of the Aeon speculation beginning in the same dialogue. In contrast to the dominant opinion, however, I draw a sharp line between the *aidion ousia* and the *aiōn.* The former is the being of the Ideas, a being Plato conceives as at least everlasting if not timeless. As such it is not life; indeed, it is the very opposite of life, as one could easily show.[26] The Aeon, on the contrary, is the life on whose basis the *Timaeus* would like to bridge the cleft between the cosmos of Ideas and the sensuous world—at its highest, the life of the living God.

The philosophy of eternity stemming from the late Plato and extending all the way to Schelling's *Die Weltalter* (The Ages of the World) interprets this life from the standpoint of the historical life of human beings, a life that at each moment is leaving a past behind it and advancing into a future. More precisely, the philosophy of eternity recognizes in the Aeon a particularly excellent and indeed the perfect form of such life. The closer specification of the second metaphysical notion of eternity can only be a description of the aeonic form of life. The chief point of connection for this theory of eternity was Plato's explication of the divine Aeon as a *menontos aiōnos en heni* (37d6), as an abiding in the One. In terms of temporal modes, abiding in the One appears as the present's not flowing into the past and not merging into the future. Therein lies the negation of time characteristic of the second metaphysical notion of eternity, which, in contrast to the negation of time in timeless eternity, at the same time preserves what it negates. A present that neither flows into the past nor merges into the future negates time by negating itself as that temporal present characterized precisely by its flowing away and merging. At the same time, however, it affirms itself insofar as it concentrates itself on itself and in this way first comes to itself.

The possibility that eternity$_2$ has its roots in the Parmenidean fr. 8 is already given with the phrase "to abide in the One," cited from the *Timaeus*. Its roots apparently go back to lines 29–30: "Abiding (*menon*) as the Same and in the Same, it (Being) rests by itself and thus abides there fixed in place." If a Platonic abiding in the One sublates time [*ein zeitaufhebendes*], then lines 29–30 raise the following question: Do they intend an abiding that sublates time or merely a persistence in time?

The controversy over the *menein* in fr. 8, 29–30, boils down to this single question. For either way it denies timelessness. In response to this, E_1 has nothing to offer. In the final analysis, the only question is whether the sentence should be interpreted from the standpoint of E_2 or that of D. Whether one should be content with the traditional present tense (*ménei*) or like

Fränkel convert it to a future tense (*meneĩ*) is a question of secondary significance. Either option—that Being persists or that it will persist—would imply that, after all, Parmenides conceives Being as something persisting in time. This question is relevant only insofar as the decision for the future tense would automatically exclude the alternative of an abiding that sublates time. Yet the sentence provides no sufficient reason for actually excluding this alternative. The question of whether Parmenides presupposes a persistence in time or rather has a time-sublating abiding in mind can only be clarified through a more precise characterization of this abiding, i.e., only if we define it positively.

To this end Plotinus' further development of the concept of an Aeon abiding in the One deserves our attention. Not satisfied with simply citing the Platonic concept, Plotinus conceives it more profoundly by defining eternity in terms of abiding in the One: for Plotinus, eternity *is* abiding in the One. At the same time he transforms Plato's One into the Same, which is already familiar to us from Parmenides.[27] Turning to Parmenides, however, does not mean turning away from Plato; on the contrary, it only articulates what Plato intended. For Plato too understands abiding in the One as an abiding-in-itself. Only as such can it intimate eternity. The thought motif symbolizes in temporal terms a return to itself [*Rückkehr zu sich*] that has no need of a *recurrence* [*Wiederkehr*] for its completion but is completed as ever present and hence is eternal. Positively speaking, the abiding that sublates time signifies such an absolute abiding-in-itself.

Only as absolute abiding-in-itself is "abiding in the One" suitable for characterizing the Aeon on which Plato specifically confers this predicate. The assertion that such abiding is already discernible in the poem ultimately calls for an in-depth comparison, one going beyond lines 29–30, of this Aeon with Parmenides' notion of Being. Such a comparison would make it clear that E_2 is false in a far worse sense than E_1. Those casting their votes for E_1 may certainly point to the intention of the text as supporting their position and would even have a right to the entire line of thought, were the intention not blocked from within. E_2, on the contrary, overlooks the intention itself. Just this is what we learn from such a comparison. Parmenides' Being has nothing in common with the Aeon abiding in the One, and intentionally so. It is neither positively determined nor divine nor living. We need say no more about its lack of positive determination. As far as its nondivinity is concerned, I can only advance this here as a thesis whose full elaboration and justification exceed the scope of this chapter. In the space that remains, permit me simply to spell out its lifeless character a bit more thoroughly. For this characteristic touches on the nerve of the problem. Even at this point, however, the discussion over *menein* in lines 29–30 can be concluded with the following diagnosis: Parmenides can merely contemplate a persistence in time and not an abiding that sublates time, because the latter would have to be what in his view cannot be: an abiding-in-itself as the life of the divine intellect at its highest.

The Being of Parmenides is no more God than it is world. It necessarily excludes both of these from itself. For as *only* Being, it can have in itself neither the world's multiplicity nor God's fullness. Historical evidence supports this way of stating the case. Parmenides found before him a twofold tradition: on the one hand, Ionic cosmology, in particular that of Anaximander, and, on the other, the theology of his fellow Italian Xenophanes. He took a critical attitude to both sides. It has long been proven that precisely fr. 8 contains a critique of Anaximander.[28] E_2, however, gives the entire poem an affirmative attitude towards Xenophanes.[29] But Parmenides apparently wants to criticize his presumed teacher as well, in fact through a fundamental critique of theology. His approach is no less antitheological than anticosmological. The concept of Being as only Being excludes God and world in the precise sense that it is a title meant to replace both of these. Consequently, the critique of cosmology and that of theology go together. Their unity is attested to by the further determination of Being as the One. Again and again the suspicion arises in the literature that the concept of the One, which Plato certainly saw as essential to Parmenidean thinking, was not at all constitutive for Parmenides himself.[30] As convincing as the arguments are that dismiss such a suspicion, it is undeniable that the concept of the One justified by Parmenides' line of thought, as that concept must be defined in view of fr. 8, 5b–6a, takes on connotations its derivation cannot cover. In the layer of meaning accruing to it in its critical employment, it intends Being precisely as the substitute for the duality of God and world, for a reality polarized into divine and mundane spheres.

Yet the reality Parmenides replaces with Being is life, the life of God and life in the world. Accordingly, all the negations by which Parmenides would like to purify Being for what is only Being have the goal of saying no to life. In its lifelessness, Being is an *akinēton* (8, 38), something unmoved. The goal of removing life from Being casts a cruel light on some aspects of the text that have only indistinctly emerged in the history of its reception. From this standpoint the expressions for life, which from a logical point of view are superfluous, become comprehensible. "How, whence did it grow (*auxēthen*)?" (8, 7); and why should Being even have the natural urge "to develop (*phun*)?" (8, 10). The attack against life explains, then, the priority of coming to be over passing away. The much discussed question of whether Parmenides proves exclusively the impossibility of coming to be or also, somewhere and somehow, that of passing away is secondary. For even if the rejection of passing away does play a role on the side, the entire argumentation is still primarily oriented toward negating coming to be. The literature has provided ample grounds for this, some of which are quite plausible.[31] The deepest reason, however, probably lies in the will to annihilate life. Finally, bringing in this will to annihilation also throws light on why Parmenides locates coming to be in the future. Nothing is allowed to come into life. The result of the first demonstration—"Thus, becoming is extinguished and perishing unheard of" (8, 21)—betrays satisfaction over the fact that Being obeys this command. Because all becoming is extinguished, no one need fear that even a kernel of life will ever bestir itself again.

5

By viewing what is only Being in the perspective of the Aeon abiding in the One, E_2 imputes positive definition, divinity, and above all a living quality to such Being. This makes its interpretation of our main text, lines 5b–6a, seem perfectly obvious. Its interpretation concentrates on the words *homou pan.* It thereby presupposes that these two words form a self-enclosed complex, that they fuse together in a single phrase. Picht, for example, sees in *homou* an adverbial derivative of the One and reads the phrase as referring to the whole in the mode of the One. In this he carries on the Neoplatonic reading, which also had aimed to trace the Aeon abiding in the One back to our passage. In these supposedly connected words Neoplatonism already spotted a testimonial to the fullness of divine life. Plotinus calls the Aeon *hē zoē homou pasa,* which according to Picht's model translates as "the whole life in the mode of the One, befitting God alone."[32] Boethius, who was influenced by Plotinus, would derive from this the definition that expresses aeonic eternity in its perfect purity: *aeternitas est interminabilis vitae tota simul et perfecta possessio,* the complete and perfect possession of immeasurable life, a life that—especially for the Christian thinker—belongs exclusively to God.

Some peculiarities in the text's transmission through history, though, seem to show that the alleged meaning unit *homou pan* is a Neoplatonic construct. Within the scope of this article I must dispense with a justification of this "destructive" thesis.[33] Rather than lay out the historical material that compels the critical destruction of the reading favored by E2, I shall immediately start on the task of reconstructing 5b–6a. Beforehand, let me simply note Parmenides' usage of the word *homou* and its relation to the kindred *homōs,* which is likewise important for Parmenides: in Parmenides, *homou* and *homōs* both mean "together with" or "in the same way." While *homōs* carries a spatial accent, however, *homou* possesses besides the spatial meaning a temporal one peculiar to it, according to which it was equivalent as early as Homer to *hama.* Hence it means "together with" in the sense of "at the same time."

The linguistic evidence allows us, I think, to read fr. 8, 5 in the following manner: "Neither was it (Being) at one time, nor will it be (at some time), since it is now at the same time." According to this reading "was" and "will be" are the temporally different determinations that *homou,* taken as *hama,* synthesizes. According to this reading, "since" states why it is impossible that Being is no longer or not yet. It shows that "now," on the basis of its connection with past and future, refers to the present as temporal. Moreover, it unambiguously commits the "is" to an existential meaning. This is implied by the proposed reading insofar as the convergence between "at the same time" and "now" has for its flip side the separation of the problematic *homou* from the following words. This rules out an interpretation such as that of Mourelatos, who sees a predicate in *hen* and consequently must reinterpret *estin* as a predicative "to be."

This separation, however, is not only useful for dealing with *nun estin*. It also promotes an insight into the meaning of the sequence *pan, hen, suneches*. As long as one clings to the construct *homou pan* and understands it as the whole in the mode of the One, it is inexplicable why Parmenides still proceeds from the whole to the One. If one clears away this obstacle, one has a clear view of a series in which each subsequent concept explicates the one prior to it in a way that dispels the false impression that immediately arises. The word *pan* is open to the misunderstanding that it means *ta panta,* the universe as totality of all things. The word *hen* wards off this misunderstanding. Naturally, the use of the word *hen* may in turn arouse the false impression that it names a merely individual thing isolated by itself here and now. The last concept, that of *suneches,* corrects this misreading. It characterizes the One as a continuum of a temporal kind, if we follow its standard meaning. In accordance with Homer's usage, it makes it clear that Being as One is without interruption.[34] It thereby reveals that the whole series is temporally determinate: Being is the whole, whose unitary meaning consists in the fact that it exists in time without interruption. Thus it is justified only at the conclusion that it neither was at one time nor will be at another.

The proposed reading securely reinforces position D. To the extent that it does this, it also provides a certain evidence for the claim that our passage contains nothing new beyond the negation of coming to be and passing away. But an exhaustive interpretation cannot leave off with merely justifying position D. Something else is also obviously at work in the supporting clause, something new indeed. An element of truth in the construct *homou pan* apparently lies in the fact that Parmenides also wants to say, "Being, which always was and always will be, at the same time exists now in such a way that it is now everything it was and will be." By having the whole, one, and continuous appear in the light of *homou,* the passage explains the movement from the unified whole to the complete whole, sketched in line 4. The function of the forward-driving *epei* clauses in the subsequent line of thought is to elaborate this completion with increasing purity.[35] In this way it also becomes ever more clearly visible that the Eleatic, whose ontology is radically antiutopian, is principally concerned with warding off what is not yet Being. That everything is all there now primarily means for him that nothing more is still to come.

To this extent it makes sense for the advocates of eternity to claim that the determinate temporal character of Being's other predicates is overcome, at the very latest, with the "not incomplete" of line 32 and the "perfected" (or "completed") of line 42.[36] Yet in acknowledging the relative truth of *homou pan,* no concession is made to the E positions. For Parmenides was not capable of formulating being-now-together in terms of eternity. Put in positive terms, he can only conceive it spatially. Whenever he tries to lay hold of it, its temporal determinations suddenly change for him into a representation [*Vorstellung*] of space. This sudden mutation only brings out that spatiality implied in *homou* and likewise in the concepts following it. It is naive to think that a word such as *suneches* has nothing to do with spatiality simply because it is dominated in line 6 by the sense of time. Parmenides was not at all in a position to separate time from space. The increasing spatialization in the course of the fragment merely brings to light the sense of space operating from the very start. In other words, it executes the change already underway in our passage.

In view of this, going beyond a justification of position D can only lead in the direction of a position D_2. The above reflections basically move along lines opened by position D insofar as they impute past and future to Being, despite its being-now-together. The position they point to, D_2, differs from D_1 in that it takes this being-now-together into consideration. Nevertheless, it represents an extension of arguments that interpreters such as Fränkel and Tarán bring against the search for eternity in fr. 8, 5–6a. For the underlying spatial determination of Being still emphasizes the break in intention that leads Parmenidean thinking to assume that Being is temporally determinate.

6

Parmenides intended what is only Being, what is just existing. But there is nothing that just exists. Being is a Nonbeing, the very opposite of itself. The negativity of the nondeterminable denies the positivity of what is only Being, condemning it to not-being. The intrinsic not-being of Being manifests itself as not-living. Being, which also does not exist insofar as it is neither the world in its diversity nor God in his fullness, sinks into the nothingness of death; its perfection is the stillness of paralysis. At least in its initial form, metaphysics was actually what Nietzsche makes it out to be: nihilism. Plato inherited Parmenidean metaphysics only by way of a critical revision. The direct heir was Sophist philosophy, not least in its nihilistic variant. In his desire to invert Parmenides' intention, Gorgias expresses its truth. His proposition, "Nothing exists," deciphers Being as Nonbeing.

Nonbeing, which is the truth about Being, marks the limit on which the conclusions to be drawn from the analysis of fr. 8, 5–6a, converge. This analysis was guided by an interest in clarifying the break in the intention of Parmenidean metaphysics. Hoping to keep Being separate from all determinations, Parmenidean metaphysics in fact purifies it neither of conceptual nor of temporal and spatial determinations. Thus does it break off its intention. In the model text the nonnegation of space and time were especially evident. Explaining this break requires that we return to the ground of this nonnegation. At the same time, returning to this means going back to position D, thus not going beyond it but reinforcing it internally through reflection on its tacit presuppositions. Tarán describes the questionable nonnegation with these words: "Parmenides did not face the problem of time," to which he adds, "neither did he face the question of space."[37] Yet what does this mean? Fränkel concludes from his reading of the model text that "Parmenides has not gone as far as to deny the reality of passing time."[38] Or is he not conscious of time precisely in the sense that he denies it? Does he not squarely face time, perhaps, because he does not *want* to face it?

I believe the material reviewed above compels this conclusion. Parmenides not only denies the reality of passing time, he denies above all the time of passing reality—temporally constituted, living, unfinished reality itself, as a whole. This suspicion is fed by the circumstance that the unintentionally acknowledged determinate character of Being extends into spatiality. For space and time are forms for the intuition [*Anschauungsformen*] of reality. The suspicion is further reinforced by the fact that the tendency already at work in the self-forgetfulness [*Selbstvergessenheit*] of the knowing subject shows up in the forgetfulness of time and space. For the fact that Parmenides can so easily disregard the constitutive power of the thinking he starts with is grounded in his blindness for the reality possessed by his own knowing itself. The forgetfulness of time and space and the self-forgetfulness of thinking both stem from a forgetfulness of reality. And the nonnegation that blocks the intention in all this reveals itself as a negation of its own, the denial of reality.

Of course, denying reality must in turn have a reason. Delving into it means going behind the break in intention and even behind the intention itself in order to uncover their motive. In the end we would have to ask about the motivation behind the theory of what is only Being. Research on Parmenides is usually too preoccupied with internal problems to address this question of motivation, and where it does occasionally hunt for a motive, it does not dig deep enough. Klaus Heinrich decodes not-being as "the not-being in death and fate that threatens with the creature's perishing."[39] Uvo Hölscher answers the question "What, after all, induced Parmenides to conceive his notion of Being?" as follows: the need to be clear in his own mind that death is no less being [*seiend*] than life.[40] But in his heart of hearts Parmenides does not say "No" to the not-being coiled in death and even less to the not-being of death. In no way does he deny death in the name of life. On the contrary, he denies life in the name of death. This "no" comes from a "suffering from life [*Leiden am Leben*]."[41] Presumably, it is suffering from life that induced the Eleatic to formulate his concept of Being. Metaphysics will never entirely free itself from this experiential basis. As its motive, suffering from life also constitutes, despite everything, its warrant.

Appendix: Fragment 8, 1–50: Translation[42]

[1]A single story of a route still [2]is left: that [*it*] *is*; on this [route] there are signs [*sēmat'*] [3]very numerous: that what-is is ungenerated and imperishable; [4]whole, single-limbed, steadfast, and complete; [5]nor was [it] once, nor will [it] be, since [it] is, now, all together, [6]one, continuous; for what coming-to-be of it will you seek? [7]In what way, whence, did [it] grow [*auxēthen*]? Neither from what-is-not shall I allow [8]you to say or think; for it is not to be said or thought [9]that [*it*] *is not.* And what need could have impelled it [10]to grow [*phun*] later or sooner, if it began from nothing? [11]Thus [it] must either be completely [*pampan pelenai*] or not at all. [12]Nor will the strength of trust ever allow anything to come-to-be from what-is [13]besides it; therefore neither [its] coming-to-be [14]nor [its] perishing has Justice allowed, relaxing her shackles, [15]but she holds [it] fast; the decision about these matters depends on this: [16]*Is* [*it*] *or is* [*it*] *not*? but it has been decided, as is necessary, [17]to let go the one as unthinkable, unnameable (for it is no true [18]route), but to allow the other, so that it is, and is true. [19]And how could what-is be in the future; and how could [it] come-to-be? [20]For if [it] came-to-be, [it] is not [*ouk est'*], nor [is it] if at some time [it] is going to be. [21]Thus, coming-to-be is extinguished and perishing not to be heard of. [22]Nor is [it] divisible, since [it] all alike *is*; [23]nor is [it] somewhat more here, which would keep it from holding together, [24]nor is it somewhat less, but [it] is all full of what-is. [25]Therefore [it] is all continuous; for what-is is in contact with what-is. [26]Moreover, changeless in the limits of great chains [27][it] is un-beginning and unceasing [*anarchon apauston*], since coming-to-be and perishing [28]have been driven far off, and true trust has thrust them out. [29]Remaining [*menon*]

the same and in the same, [it] lies by itself [30]and remains [*menei*] thus firmly in place; for strong Necessity [31]holds it fast in the chains of a limit, which fences it about. [32]Wherefore it is not right for what-is to be incomplete; [33]for [it] is not lacking; but if [it] were, [it] would lack everything. [34]The same thing is for thinking and [is] that there is thought; [35]for not without what-is, on which [it] depends, having been declared, [36]will you find thinking; for nothing else ⟨either⟩ is or will be [37]besides what-is, since it was just this that Fate did shackle [38]to be whole and changeless [*akinēton*]; wherefore it has been named all things [39]that mortals have established, trusting them to be true, [40]to come-to-be and to perish, to be and not to be, [41]and to shift place and to exchange bright colour. [42]Since, then, there is a furthest limit, [it] is completed, [43]from every direction like the bulk of a well-rounded sphere, [44]everywhere from the centre equally matched; for [it] must not be any larger [45]or any smaller here or there; [46]for neither is there what-is-not, which could stop it from reaching [47][its] like; nor is there a way in which what-is could be [48]more here and less there, since [it] all inviolably *is*; [49]for equal to itself from every direction, [it] lies uniformly within limits. [50]Here I stop my trustworthy speech to you.

Notes

1. [The capitalized "Being" renders *das Seiende*; "Nonbeing," *Nichtseiende*; "being" is reserved for *Sein*; during the preparation of this translation Theunissen explained that the distinction between "Being" and "being" bears traces of Heidegger's "ontological difference."—Translator]

2. Fragments are numbered here and in what follows according to the arrangement in Hermann Diels and Walter Kranz, *Die Fragmente der Vorsokratiker*, vol. 1 (Zurich, 1951). For a recent English translation with facing Greek text, see Parmenides of Elea, *Fragments: A Text and Translation*, with Introduction by David Gallop (Toronto: University of Toronto Press, 1984). Gallop translates fr. 3 as "because the same thing is there for thinking and for being."

3. Ernst Tugendhat, "Das Sein und das Nichts," in Vittorio Klostermann, ed., *Durchblicke: Martin Heidegger zum 80. Geburtstag* (Frankfurt am Main, 1970), pp. 134–146.

4. Eduard Zeller, *Die Philosophie der Griechen in ihrer geschichtlichen Entwicklung*, 7th ed., ed. W. Nestle (Leipzig, 1923), vol. 1, p. 687, n. 1; Uvo Hölscher, *Anfängliches Fragen: Studien zur frühen griechischen Philosophie* (Göttingen, 1968), p. 97.

5. See the appendix for a translation of fr. 8, 1–50.

6. Here I skip over the complicated question concerning why and in what sense Being already shows up in fr. 6, 1.

7. Leonardo Tarán, *Parmenides: A Text with Translation, Commentary, and Critical Essays* (Princeton, 1965), pp. 175, 181; see also his "Perpetual Duration and Atemporal Eternity in Parmenides and Plato," *Monist* 62 (1979): 47.

8. ["Sublate" renders the Hegelian notion of *Aufhebung,* which is a kind of transcendence that both negates and preserves what is transcended; in checking the translation, Theunissen indicated that he had this meaning in mind.—Translator]

9. Tarán, *Parmenides,* pp. 183–188; also his "Perpetual Duration," pp. 43–49.

10. G. E. L. Owen, "Plato and Parmenides on the Timeless Present," *Monist* 50 (1966): 318 f.; Charles H. Kahn, "The Thesis of Parmenides," *Review of Metaphysics* 22 (1969): 716 ff.

11. A. P. D. Mourelatos, *The Route of Parmenides* (New Haven, 1970), pp. 107 f.

12. G. E. L. Owen, "Eleatic Questions," *Classical Quarterly,* n.s. 10 (1960): 100 f.; also Owen, "Plato and Parmenides," p. 321.

13. This point was already made by Hermann Fränkel, "Studies in Parmenides," in R. E. Allen and David J. Furley, eds., *Studies in Presocratic Philosophy,* vol. 2, *The Eleatics and Pluralists* (Atlantic Highlands, N.J., 1975), p. 46, n. 86.

14. Mourelatos, p. 106.

15. Besides Owen and Kahn, see also W. C. K. Guthrie, *A History of Greek Philosophy,* vol. 2 (Cambridge, 1969), p. 30, n. 1.

16. D. O'Brien, "Temps et intemporalité chez Parmenide," *Les études philosophiques* (1980), p. 262.

17. M. Schofield, "Did Parmenides Discover Eternity?" *Archiv für Geschichte der Philosophie* 52 (1970): 122 f.

18. Helene Weiss, "The Greek Conceptions of Time and Being in the Light of Heidegger's Philosophy," *Philosophy and Phenomenological Research* 2 (1941/1942): 178.

19. Werner Beierwaltes, *Plotin über Zeit und Ewigkeit (Enneade III 7),* 3rd ed. (Frankfurt am Main, 1981), p. 175.

20. Mourelatos, p. 106 f.

21. One can already find this in A. Patin, *Parmenides im Kampfe gegen Heraklit* (Leipzig, 1899), p. 555; G. Calogero, *Studi sull' eleatismo* (Rome, 1932), p. 62.

22. Calogero, pp. 61 ff.

23. Calogero, p. 23.

24. Olof Gigon, *Der Ursprung der griechischen Philosophie: Von Hesiod bis Parmenides,* 2nd ed. (Basel, 1968), p. 261.

25. Georg Picht, "Die Epiphanie der ewigen Gegenwart," in Helmut Höfling, ed., *Beiträge zu Philosophie und Wissenschaft: Wilhelm Szilasi zum 70. Geburtstag* (Munich, 1960), p. 243.

26. See my "Zeit des Lebens," in K. V. Bonin, ed., *Deutscher Evangelischer Kirchentag Frankfurt 1987* (Stuttgart, 1987), pp. 356–368.

27. *Enneads* III.7.6, 4–6; also 2, 34–35 and 3, 16–17.

28. Fränkel, pp. 25–36.

29. This is especially emphasized by Picht, pp. 215, 235.

30. Thus Mario Untersteiner, ed., *Parmenide: Testimonianze e frammenti,* trans. with Introduction and Commentary by M. Untersteiner (Florence, 1958), pp. xxvii–l.

31. See, among others, Hans-Georg Gadamer, "Retraktationen zum Lehrgedicht des Parmenides," in *Varia Variorum: Festgabe für Karl Reinhardt dargebracht von Freunden und Schülern zum 14. Februar 1951* (Münster, 1952), pp. 61 f.

32. Plotinus, *Enneads* III.7.3, 36–38.

33. See J. Whittaker, *God Time Being* (Oslo, 1971).

34. On Homer's usage, see, for example, *The Illiad* XII, 25–26: *hue d'ara Zeus suneches* ("Zeus had it rain without interruption").

35. Fr. 8, lines 22, 37–38, 48. I distinguish the "forward-driving" clauses from the backward-reaching lines 27–28 (line 42 has a special position insofar as it thematizes the possibility conditions for perfection). On the function of these clauses, see also J. Mansfeld, *Die Offenbarung des Parmenides und die menschliche Welt* (Assen, 1964), pp. 92–106.

36. Mourelatos, p. 102.

37. Tarán, *Parmenides,* pp. 188, 195.

38. Fränkel, p. 46, n. 86.

39. Klaus Heinrich, *Parmenides und Jona: 4 Studien über das Verhältnis von Philosophie und Mythologie,* 2nd ed. (Frankfurt am Main, 1982), p. 87.

40. Hölscher, pp. 126–129.

41. This is Hölscher's phrase. His commentary to fr. 12 reads, "Here there is now an undertone of an almost Empedoclean pessimism for which suffering from life becomes the *movens* of philosophical thinking" (p. 128).

42. [The English text is taken from David Gallop's translation of Parmenides' *Fragments,* pp. 64–75 (see note 2), reprinted with the permission of the University of Toronto Press. I have made one slight alteration, advancing the break between lines 9 and 10 so as to include "to grow" in line 10, since the Greek *phun* appears there and not in line 9. The corresponding Greek is noted where a reference from Theunissen's article might otherwise be unclear.—Translator]

2

The Origins of the Theory of the Subject

Dieter Henrich

Translated by William Rehg

1 "Paradigm Shifts"—Aids to Argument, Problems Lost

Sciences have always remembered their founders and their origins. They also recall the essential way stations along the path they have trodden. These are often marked by prominent achievements that at once summed up and reinvigorated the state of knowledge as a whole, namely through a reordering and deeper penetration of this knowledge that simultaneously gave rise to new questions and, along with these, new methods for seeking and securing answers. Such achievements account for enduring orientations in science, inasmuch as going back on them is out of the question. They continue to be necessary touchstones for every further reorganization of the body of knowledge, however far-reaching. Geometry, for example, still honors Euclid and medicine, Hippocrates.

With modern physics, with post-Cartesian philosophy and with historical consciousness, however, another relation between a body of science and its prehistory has become not only possible but even familiar to us. In contradistinction to the connection a science has to the essential way stations in its development—a development also quite capable of discontinuities—this relation neutralizes earlier epochs in the genesis of a body of knowledge as no longer relevant. This yields a new kind of discontinuity: past organizations of knowledge are now considered not only incorrect but fundamentally inappropriate and hence in no way authoritative for the present constitution of any genuine knowledge. The development of such distances and discontinuities presupposes the idea that knowledge as such can be captive to an illusion [*Schein*]. For the first time the charge of such an illusion, which was attributed to an anthropocentric way of looking at things, was brought against the Ptolemaic astronomy and, in addition, the concept formations of Aristotelian physics. The eighteenth-century critique of knowledge then sought to expose an even more deeply rooted illusion, one fixed in the very modes of inference practiced by a reason unbound from experience. The possibility and success of this form of critique were presupposed, once ways of knowing had finally come to be viewed not in terms of their truth claim but rather in relation to the de facto, hence transitory conditions of their development and acceptance. To this extent, the consciousness of the historical attachments intrinsic to all knowledge depends on the epistemological critique that—assuming just the contrary about itself, of course—sought to stop up every source of illusion seeping into methods for establishing knowledge of lasting reliability.

In the effort to understand [*Verständigung*] the contexts surrounding that basic mode of knowing called "philosophy," some ideas are in vogue today that derive from the forms of critique found in the more recent theory of knowledge, as well as from the historical analysis of forms of knowing. These ideas lend an air of plausibility—or even an authoritative status—to talk about "*paradigms*" of philosophical investigation and "discourses," which are understood at the same time in terms of the basic motives of historical epochs. The origin of the term "paradigm" in the historically oriented philosophy of science is well known. The idea underlying its application to philosophical epochs and traditions first of all comes from the critique of knowledge. This we can recognize in the way such critique refers to a "turn" (especially in regard to theoretical method), a phrase that enables it to wriggle free of the embarrassment caused by apparent problems [*Scheinprobleme*] that were previously quite significant but, at the same time, insoluble. We can also observe a historical consciousness at work in such talk, for this "turn" is supposed to occur in accord with changes in the state of collective consciousness and its wide-ranging tendencies, which are often effective for better life conditions as well.

Both assumptions can easily be supported by good reasons. Philosophical problematics can in fact be comprehended and advanced at a profound level only through newly conceived methods. Moreover, since these problematics cannot be isolated from the experiences of and needs for understanding emergent in pretheoretical thinking—the business of every human being, however inexpressedly—they are always connected with what one may call an age's "frame of consciousness," to employ an Hegelian manner of speaking. Yet such expressions can also provide one way of viewing such problematics with a headstart it could not gain from its investigatory powers alone. Hence this view encourages a theory development in which one dismisses as outmoded not only problems that really are illusory, but also those problems that always have to be pursued if a fundamental philosophical enlightenment [*Grundaufklärung*] is to be a reasonable prospect at all. This is to say nothing of the fact that promises of enlightenment accompanied by declarations of a paradigm shift fade especially quickly if they depend not only on a methodically new beginning but also on curtailing the problem. They actually invite proclamations of further paradigm shifts, shifts that today once again dilute and even inundate efforts at diagnosing the modern world. We thus do well to recall a proven durability test for whether a new beginning is in the position to know that it is, in fact, free of a problem condition that was decisive for thinkers one would relegate to a theoretical past: simply showing that the problem condition is based on assumptions incompatible with a new "paradigm" does not suffice. One must rather be able to show how the condition came about. And one can only dispel the problem condition by simultaneously reconstructing it in its entire breadth, a task demanding one provide a deeper and more reliable access to the facts at issue. Only in this way can one make sure this problem condition does not return to one's own theoretical project through the back door.

Jürgen Habermas extensively invokes a paradigm shift in order to make his project plausible. According to him, this shift took place in two stages. The first involved two different moves, already made by the Left Hegelians: they rigorously worked through a this-sided philosophical theory and, just as rigorously, made the sociopolitical nature of humanity the focus of their concern with the conditions of human life. Only through a second stage, however, was this paradigm shift theoretically secured: the fundamental inquiry formerly cast in transcendental-philosophical terms was redefined in terms of a theory of language use and the employment of signs. From this new theoretical perspective one could also develop the concepts of meaning and knowledge on an intersubjective basis secured by empirical science.

Both initiatives resulted from a turn away from the theory of the subject. Accordingly, Habermas sees his project as first of all directed against this theory. However, in contrast to paradigms that are postulated all too trendily, his project distinguishes itself by not immediately shying away from the aforementioned durability test. In fact, he has an interest in reconstructing the problematic around which the theory of the subject developed. One would expect this interest to be reinforced by the recent appearance of representatives of a paradigm shift in France. For them the difference between the theory of the subject and that of intersubjectivity boils down to two variants of the same illusion. In their view, Nietzsche casts a shadow large enough to cover not only Kant and Hegel, but also Bruno Bauer and Charles Sanders Peirce. A situation such as this must also remind Habermas that "intersubjectivity" is a corrective that presumes familiarity with a notion of the subject; so if theory may no longer make any use of such a notion, then "language" itself, taken as a dimension of fundamental enlightenment, may not even be intelligible. In this context it becomes all the more significant that the course of modern theoretical development brought subjectivity and intersubjectivity more or less simultaneously into view as theoretically relevant facts. In reaching back to the whole tradition of modernity in his lectures on its discourse Habermas has thus far been unwilling to take this circumstance into account.

It often happens that ideas that seem to distinguish epochs from one another can nearly coincide in their origin. This calls for some further remarks on arguments that seek to support theories by pointing to their present currency. Certainly those paradigms that are proclaimed on the basis of easily summoned stereotypes must be distinguished, before anything else, from an understanding of the relation between project and state of world affairs that really does issue from a diagnosis of historical processes in depth. Supposedly, it has already turned out that the recent proclamation of a "postmodern" epoch merely summarizes a bundle of artists' secessions; it does not reach, nor does it speak from, that point where transformations in the frame of consciousness occur. But even ideas that really could culminate in such a change are endangered when one comprehends this change according to a model that, though well entrenched and ready to hand, should be approached with caution. Not Herder and Hegel, but actually the Greek developmental doctrines began the practice of understanding the succession of epochs on the basis of a sequence of principles formative of overall conditions—thus in a succession governed by a one-to-one correlation at each point. However, if one then wishes to relate the principles of such epochs to philosophical ideas and problematics, it is anything but self-evident today that there exists between these "[underlying] reasons" [*Gründe*] the very sort of ordered relation that actually can hold for the epochs themselves, simply on the basis of the linearity of their temporal succession. Principles in thinking cannot be contrasted with each other in this way. Thus if one refrains from relegating past epochs once more to the mere prehistory of truth, then one has for starters the possibility of understanding them as stages in a process of increasing depth in the one entire truth. The difficulty simply in consistently conceiving an alternative to this model should be evident: so far only Heidegger has actually succeeded in this. His alternative is based on the idea that "being in the truth" can mean something different than grasping the truth. But then it follows that progress in the truth and based on the truth can also be conceived as its loss, intensifying in stages. This consequence, which necessarily leads to a critical rejection of civilization, is not the only reason we must shy away from Heidegger's concept, as we did the previous one. Like the concept from which it freed itself—whose logic Hegel thought through most profoundly—it cannot permit world-historical lines of development having *equal* right and nevertheless able to meet in a process amounting to more than a global loss in the essenceless [*Wesenlose*]. The epoch we have entered, however, forces us to consider the possibility of understanding history this way, taking our cue from philosophically conceived reasons as well.

Now what does philosophical investigation, taken purely in its own terms, have to say about the network of underlying reasons it arrives at? Much recommends the view that philosophy encourages, possibly even demands, a mode of understanding that approaches historical processes in exactly the manner just indicated. Namely, it does not arrive at a notion of unity that both absorbs all these underlying reasons and releases them from itself. Rather, it constructs an interrelationship whose basic form [*Grundform*] is constituted by "concepts" and "principles" that are just as irreducible to, as inseparable from, one another. This basic form is imbued with a further notion of unity embracing the form's cofunctionality. And this notion grounds [*begründet*] the task of interpreting that basic form in a way that reaches beyond its cofunctionality, but in such a way that none of these interpretations can settle into anything so stable as a theoretical conclusion. One thus has to expect that interpretive movements and world relations [*Weltverhältnisse*] oppose each other or are even incommensurable, although they proceed from the same ground [*Grund*]. This corresponds to the fact that the same rationality and dynamics of conscious life find expression in diverse frames of consciousness, which for that very reason do not have to remain eternally resistant to one another.

Taken a step further, this line of thought, which cannot be more closely argued here, raises the possibility that underlying reasons particularly resistant to philosophical explication can be at work in the basic network of relations [*Gefüge des Grundverhältnisses*] formative of rationality. In that case the assumption that all these reasons and factors are to be theoretically mastered in exactly the same way would rest on a preconception. This preconception might be explained in turn by the fact that a prenotion of analysis appropriate for particular areas of investigation somewhat removed from the center of rationality is carried over to issues coming under entirely different conditions of possible thematization. If one resists this tendency, which the phenomenological method, among others, is likewise based on, one is led to the further conjecture that difficulties in the analytic elucidation [*Aufklärung*] of factors in the basic relational network can be explained by the specific work these factors perform as well as by their position in the constitution of this network. For that reason, those factors conceptually organizing the world and structuring knowledge would have to be analyzed in another way than those preceding the formation of a world concept and not wholly involved in the constitution of this concept as such.

Considerations such as these can shed some light on the problems inevitably entangling a theory of subjectivity. Thus they can make the fortunes of this theory more comprehensible. In addition, however, we can also see why it is mistaken to think that a development that shifts the focus of efforts at understanding onto other factors in the basic relational network would amount to a destruction of the problematic known as "the theory of the subject." No doubt it makes sense to speak of an epoch in which subjectivity was discovered. No doubt too this discovery had significant consequences for the formation of a historical frame of consciousness. Yet surely this discovery must be very clearly distinguished from an invention. Moreover, if in this epoch the idea of a subject acquired the status of a principle, again this does not mean that the role of universal ground (or means of explication) had to accrue to it concomitantly. The latter view results only if one dispenses with more detailed inquiry and understands historical processes in terms of the succession of paradigms. As far as the actual history of subjectivity and its theory are concerned, such a leap [*Vorgriff*] also ends up directing attention to those modes of thinking that merely represent extreme positions, exceptions in the history of its discovery that actually did isolate the idea of the subject and give it the status of an absolute. Even these more extreme designs issued from considerations that, at the juncture where they arose, lent plausibility to such lines of thought. But this is not so evident for one enjoying an historical distance from this history of discovery and in possession of an overview of that epoch's entire problem condition. There are facts whose position in the constitution of our knowledge is such that they elude our attention for a long time, but when attention finally is concentrated on them, seem to encourage extreme theoretical paths and a kind of theoretical enthusiasm. But even this can be understood from the facts themselves and the conditions of access explained by these facts.

Now one can conceive the genesis of the theory of the subject as an "absolute" in the above fashion without certifying it as the one grand inference following from the discovery of the subject. In that case one of the most convincing reasons disappears for barring the subjectivity problematic from certain theory conceptions, i.e., those with focal points that were previously wholly subordinated to the theory of the subject or even entirely ignored by it.

It is very important not only to see the genesis of the theory of the subject clearly, but to grasp just as clearly the genesis of the motives for sealing oneself up in one's own theory conception, safe from the real problems the theory initially pursued. We look back today on an epoch of thinking that all but dominated our century and gave this motive a supremacy whose compulsive tendencies are now readily apparent. What is more, the subjectivity problematic has not evaporated, all the transformations in theory configuration notwithstanding; in fact, not even the onslaught of criticism leveled by literally all the new methods could dispel this problematic. Thus one can no longer look upon its critical destruction as a trailblazing project. Rather, every attempt at theorizing that would not be marked by long-exhausted urges to innovate must once again work its way into the subjectivity problematic. This task requires not only that one understand the special difficulties surrounding the problematic; in addition, one must order the multiform conditions for the constitution of subjectivity, situating these as much as possible in a larger picture that renders their position in the totality of knowledge-and-relation-to-the-world [*Wissen und Weltverhältnis*] comprehensible. In doing this an important goal has to be to clarify the fact that, and the extent to which, one must assign the relation of conscious life to itself a central position in this totality. And surely one can acknowledge such a position more readily if one understands why the subjectivity problematic should present special difficulties, though not such as would automatically force those involved with it to make subjectivity-in-relation-to-the world an all-inclusive ground disclosing everything.

Any such work today in the problem domain of subjectivity, however, must also affect our endeavor to understand the philosophical movement that first made subjectivity the most important theme and even a principle of theory: the classical period of German philosophy. The interpretations and receptions of the great theories of this epoch could fill libraries. Nevertheless, one must be clear about the conditions that gave rise to it. If it is true that the subjectivity problematic is an especially tangled one, mastered neither by normal theoretical models nor through brilliant tour de force, then we can hardly expect that its discoverers and first reconnaissance parties immediately saw with complete clarity what sort of terrain they would thenceforth have to traverse. When the influence of these explorers and the interpretation of their works was at its peak, however, one began with precisely this expectation, even with some emphasis, but also because of a lack of alternative starting points. But if in fact these reconnaissance parties could only gather blurred images of the problematic, then we must also reckon that, although they undoubtedly advanced with a clear and rigorous consistency, they nonetheless did not do so in a way corresponding to the makeup of the problematic and, consequently, not through a progressive, step-by-step enlightenment. Thus even the historiography of this period will only become instructive, at a careful philosophical level, when it has available to it versatile, differentiated means of orientation in the subjectivity problematic and can employ these in a practiced, flexible manner. Only this insightful approach to historical interrelationships could freshly inform efforts to understand the philosophical problematic and thereby lead to a collaboration of disciplines. Conceptions that arose in the founding age of the theory of the subject were worked out with high expectations and under equally high challenges. Thus they can easily have overshot what we now, in our sober detachment, consider justifiable limits. At the same time, they may have opened lines of thought that would never even have occurred to us without such extreme reconnoitering.

In such an investigation the historical interrelationships must not be missed by simply treating them as topics that have nothing new to teach us. This misfortune is best avoided if we take pains to describe the problem domain as it presented itself to the theories addressing that domain at the time. This requirement does not contradict the demand to interpret past thought on the basis of our own understanding [*Verstehen*] of the facts we wish to decipher. For we do not gain access to a problem domain simply by employing the conceptual forms and language of previous positions in that domain, nor even by relying on their results, perhaps out of theoretical cluelessness. If it is true that an overall view of this domain was denied them, then we can only inform ourselves of their viewpoints and evidence by not committing ourselves from the start to their self-presentation. In fact, such self-presentations can be adequately deciphered only at a distance—precisely that provided by the capacity for bringing one's own means of reaching understanding [*Verständigung*] into play.

2 Two Centuries of Revolution and Philosophy

Habermas's sixtieth birthday provides occasion for presenting him this study as a "specimen" of such an undertaking—an undertaking I hope will be carried out one day, although one could scarcely do this singlehandedly. It would be the centerpiece of a successor to Richard Kroner's *Von Kant bis Hegel*, a work based even then on scarcely acceptable presuppositions and yet without an equal since. Anniversaries such as these are the result of numerous circumstances, such as the use of the decimal system and the Gregorian Calendar, which are matters of indifference to our lives. Not so unimportant, especially for teachers, is the fact that we have to calculate the span of a generation at approximately thirty years. Thus someone at 60, who is also a distinguished teacher, can easily look back on the effects his ideas have had on those following him in the chain of generations. What is most important about anniversaries, however, is that they provide occasion for recollective overviews, an essential part of each one's life.

For such reminiscences, numbers too can have a certain external significance. So most will probably consider the constellation between Habermas's sixtieth and the two centuries gone by since the French Revolution an appropriate invitation to reflection. The distance from that event is quite short, only three times as great as the lived experience of a theoretician who got started after the Second World War. That alone makes it unlikely that the consequences of that event should already be fully realized and developed. The political project of modernity still continues to stand at the beginning phases of its formation, and of its fortunes as well.

In that case, however, we should also ask whether we ought not think of the classical period of German philosophy in a similar fashion. Cresting on the very waves of movements running counter to it, it appeared as a peculiar development in a provincial backwater of European intellectual life. Yet the contemporaries of the Revolution almost unanimously looked on the two foundational movements as interrelated. One can admit that this interrelationship exists and yet still adopt a defensive attitude, dismissing the ideas that governed the philosophical movement. Post-Kantian philosophy may then look like the masterly folly of powerless magicians of thought imitating the historical process with a highly abstract play in their provincial theater, bowling themselves over in phoney revolutionary somersaults. Perhaps in the "Secret *Consilium*" of the Weimar principality the local university at Jena was actually viewed this way. Yet that would have been simply a small principality's way of dismissing the potential of a profound understanding of reason and historical processes. The power these "magicians" had to intervene in these processes, even if indirectly, demonstrated itself straightaway.

In any case, we cannot understand the development of German philosophy as a mere reaction to the events in France. This is shown simply by the fact that the presuppositions in virtue of which this development got going, and had to get going, already appeared before the events in France released that enthusiastic sympathy Kant considered both incomparable and forever unforgettable. The following will supply this demonstration from sources that are generally accessible and yet continue to go unnoticed in this context.

3 Two Books from Spring 1789

About the middle of April 1789 two authors signed the prefaces to their books due to appear at the Leipzig Book Fair that spring. From these two books a development got started that led German philosophy along paths other than those envisioned in Kant's intentions and arguments. Carl Leonhard Reinhold published his *Versuch einer neuen Theorie des menschlichen Vorstellungsvermögens* (Attempt at a New Theory of the Human Faculty of Representation) and Friedrich Heinrich Jacobi the expanded edition of his *Über die Lehre des Spinoza* (The Philosophy of Spinoza).[1]

In these two books the authors developed philosophical conceptions which the younger of their contemporaries took as challenges for their own thinking. Each of the two conceptions could have produced such a challenge by itself, and thus independently of the fact that the other also found consideration or even a fruitful reception. The two conceptions are also set up in such a way that it is not easy to establish a material relationship between them, i.e., one constituted not by a critical distance but by a constellation of ideas bringing both conceptions into relation and thereby giving us the perspective of an internally unified thinking.[2]

Nevertheless, contemporaries sensitive to significant events in intellectual life could see immediately that these two works really did constitute such a constellation, even if they could not yet foresee how it should be understood and what ideas would be able to develop from it. What they could not doubt was that the treatment of philosophical themes in both works was laden with significance, their language resonant with tonalities unheard even in Kant. Moreover, wherever this appreciation is present we also find a growing awareness that both events demand a more than casual or forced response: one had to adopt a position integrating one's own ideas in a stable fashion and issuing from a profound sense of the problems actually at work in the new theoretical language.

Furthermore, across the great distances separating the approaches, messages and convictions of the two works a connection between them was discernible: both intended to have, and in fact immediately did have, far-reaching implications for a clarification [*Aufklärung*] of the crisis of traditional religious belief and the possibilities for a secure as well as free opening of life to the true God. Reinhold's theory aimed above all to safeguard Kantian truth, in this matter as well. In a single stroke Jacobi disclosed two possibilities for efforts to understand the last things: On the one hand, he sought to commit rational knowledge [*Vernunfterkenntnis*] to the fatalistic conclusion that God is nothing but the ground of order in the natural world. On the other hand, he tried to show that a belief in the reality of divine elements in human life takes root prior to every operation of reason. Not surprisingly, it was young theologians who carved their own way of thinking from the constellation between the two works. Of course, they were capable of doing this only as philosophers bent on transforming the intellectual situation again. By the time the first among them—Schelling and Hölderlin—produced the first fruits in this effort, an additional six years had passed. Hegel's work then grew out of exchanges with them and the theories they had brought together.

Reinhold's and Jacobi's books each had singular fortunes. These especially deserve mention in any investigation, such as the following, that would link these books with the origin of the theory of the subject. These fortunes affected how the theories put forth in the books were received—Reinhold's theory in his own lifetime, Jacobi's in the later history of interpretation.

Only in the 1789 edition do we find Reinhold's *Neue Theorie des menschlichen Vorstellungsvermögens* in complete form. His claim, that he set Kant's investigations for the first time on the foundation that the *Critique of Pure Reason* at most indicated without elaboration, found a predominantly unfavorable reception in the reviews of the day. The same reaction befell his proposal for a method of foundational science; reviewers found even less acceptable the derivations of definitions and theorems Reinhold himself worked out according to this method. Due to his great influence and his reputation, both as teacher and Kantian, he quickly got embroiled in controversies that elicited further methodological self-clarifications. Reinhold also realized that some of his deductions were not defensible and that he could still improve the layout of the entire deductive operation. Thus he undertook a new presentation of his "elementary philosophy," as he now called it. But this only got as far as the beginning of his theory of the faculty of knowledge, which had made up only the first half of his 1789 work. Then, under the pressure of further objections, he postponed an elaboration of the new version of the second half, finally dispensing with it altogether.[3] The fact is, these objections would have also forced him to rework the first half of the elementary philosophy once more, only now even more extensively than he had just done. In particular, the objections Reinhold encountered in the early summer of 1792 made it clear that he had to redefine the task of the elementary philosophy. And from that it followed that a good deal of its argumentation would also have to be altered.

The reception of Reinhold's theory, however, was predominantly based on the reading of its new version, which remained a fragment. This version had already appeared a year and a half after the *Versuch* of 1789, namely at the Fall 1790 Book Fair.[4] By then only a few persons had completely worked through the *Versuch.* And since the new presentation had to be considered from then on as the definitive version of the elementary philosophy, readers and critics alike concentrated on it. Thus its most influential critic, Gottlob Ernst Schulze, presented his critique following the paragraph numbering of the *Neue Darstellung.*[5] The result was that Fichte, whose Kantianism was thrown into crisis by Schulze's critique, also relied on the *Neue Darstellung* version as he got to work on his own version of an elementary philosophy.

As already mentioned, this presentation had been broken off in the middle of Reinhold's theory. Thus it did not contain the two components of the 1789 *Versuch,* which had to be of special interest both in themselves and for subsequent development: the theory of the understanding [*Verstandes*], which included the first theory of self-consciousness in general, and the theory of reason [*Vernunft*]. In addition, insofar as the theory of reason bears on the development of a theory of the subject, it must be accorded particular significance by anyone seeking to understand the deepest implications of Reinhold's ideas. This significance is twofold, for what Reinhold has to say about the constitution and role of the subject in the organization of knowledge can only be clarified in view of his theory of reason, which is also part of the theory of self-consciousness and, following the announcement of 1790, is even supposed to be grounded in a separate proposition on self-consciousness (see *Beytr,* 161). But when Reinhold reinterpreted and reorganized his entire position in 1792, it was again the theory of reason he called upon, henceforth maintaining it could provide the conceptual and theoretical means for such a reorganization.[6] For this theory, however, only the 1789 version was available—a version, moreover, bearing undeniable signs of a pressure to conclude the work and thus not so carefully worked out as the preceding chapters. Therefore, anyone wishing a direct acquaintance with Reinhold's position and its difficulties regarding the theory of the subject would have to rely on the 1789 work, which admittedly presents these theories in separate chapters and with uneven detail. In fact, it never received such attention, neither at the time of Reinhold's philosophical impact nor in interpretations of the development of classical German philosophy. All the same, the half found in the *Neue Darstellung,* refracted and shortened though it was, still contained so much information about Reinhold's theory that successors were able to learn of that theory, in particular Fichte.

The way in which Jacobi's "Little Spinoza Book" came to be disseminated following its publication in 1789 is quite another story. Well before Reinhold caused Kantianism to split between literalists and those "true" to Kant's principles, the shock wave generated by Jacobi's first edition of this volume, at the time still slim, had aroused a general sensation. This was due to several of its features and statements: the report that Lessing had declared himself a Spinozist; a fresh, textually innovative, yet quite attractive presentation of Spinozism; Jacobi's thesis that such Spinozism could only be escaped by admitting that the foundation of our true knowledge lies in something immediate, the certitude of belief, and not in rational demonstration. Moreover, the fact that Jacobi drew further support for his presentation of Spinozism by citing from the *Critique of Pure Reason* caused a sensation among the Kantians.[7] This use of Kant led to the conjecture that one could reconcile the Kantian doctrine of freedom with Spinoza's theory of the first cause. This view shaped the last decades of the century in a recognizably decisive manner. Kant was virtually compelled by his friend to protest.[8] Nevertheless, with Jacobi's first edition Spinozism began its rise to respectability in metaphysics. Even the "true" Kantians now considered it in a completely different light than the *Critique of Pure Reason* had cast on it. Moreover, as the *Critique of Judgment* attests, Kant himself did not remain unmoved by this transformation.[9]

Jacobi's way of thinking set these various effects in motion without arguing a philosophical approach of its own. The report of his conversation with Lessing certainly contained a few propositions that made a great impression, for example, that the researcher's highest service is "to uncover and reveal existence [*Dasein*]" (*Spin,* p. 42). And some of the pithiest images employed by Karl Marx go back, either directly or through Hegel, to Jacobi's "little book"—such as the idea that a philosophy can be "standing on its head" (*Spin,* p. 42) and the opening sentence of the *Communist Manifesto,* which says that a system of thought can haunt a country "as a specter" instead of circulating in its true form (*Spin,* p. 163). Yet Jacobi's theses are presented entirely as escape routes from the paradoxical character of Spinoza's convincingly grounded yet simply unacceptable ideas. Jacobi mainly focused his efforts on presenting Spinoza's system as the grand conclusion every consistent metaphysics must arrive at. In this he diverged from the critique of Spinoza shared by Leibniz, Wolff, and Kant, which reproached Spinoza for flaws in his analysis of basic concepts. At the same time, Jacobi reconstructed Spinoza's concepts and chain of justification in a way no one had done before. This prompted Mendelssohn, shortly before his death, to seek Jacobi out in order to show him that either way Spinoza really has no reply to the objections Wolff had already spelled out in detail.[10] One also could have shown that some of the ideas Jacobi used in his presentation of Spinozistic doctrine had seeped into his own ideas, ones he hoped would lead him out of the Spinoza he himself had rehabilitated. As a result, Jacobi could not avoid presenting a blurred, obscure profile in his double role of defending Spinoza against rationalist criticism while opposing certitude grounded on deductive inference.

In any case, he saw he could not avoid offering his own "positive" philosophy without the complications it had accumulated in discussions over the true Spinoza. This also became very clear in the debate he set off over Spinozism, which quickly intensified, spreading to a wide range of journals and books.

Jacobi implemented this by first publishing his *David Hume über den Glauben* (David Hume on Belief); this he followed with the "enlarged" edition of *Über die Lehre des Spinoza.* In *David Hume* he sought to ward off charges of obscurantism from his thesis that certitude is grounded on belief, turning for help to the Scottish empiricism from which the thesis was actually first derived. He drew further support from a thesis of his own on the origin of the concept of causality, which was intended to show that all causal deductions already rested on immediate certitudes. In the second edition of *Über die Lehre des Spinoza* he then introduced new texts and, more importantly, two treatises that may well be said to present Jacobi's chief philosophical work. For Jacobi intended these to outline his mode of thinking and conceptualization. Admittedly, his philosophical limitations became more obvious here than in the areas that displayed his real strengths, i.e., the analysis and critical penetration of modes of thought and forms of life. The experienced novelist apprehended their testimony just as surely as he grasped the dynamism of that life—weaknesses, aporias, and all—pulsing within them.

The expanded edition, however, no longer gained the same public attention as the "Little Spinoza Book" had at its first appearance. The mere indication that it was "enlarged" was hardly enough to arouse the expectation of any significantly new information beyond that in the first edition, which was already widely available. Moreover, it appeared just as the philosophical debate was shifting towards Kant's practical philosophy and, for the first time, towards its practical foundation of religion. With Reinhold's systematic work yet a further center of attraction immediately opened for debate. Attentive readers of Jacobi undoubtedly tried to draw public attention to the importance of the texts that were merely "inserted" in the little Spinoza book. In addition, students seeking to secure their independence in the force field defined by Kant, Spinoza, and Jacobi also took note of the new edition on its own terms.[11] But it first had a visible effect only in 1795, when the most prominent of the younger generation, now securely established, also took up Fichte's theory of scientific knowledge [*Wissenschaftslehre*] and attempted to reshape it. In their work it becomes evident for the first time how Jacobi's "inserted" texts can be related to the blossoming theory of the subject. Clear too is the nature of the theory of the subject we can and must draw from these texts.

The historians of classical German philosophy, however, have completely overlooked this interrelationship. This is evident from the fact that no really complete new edition of Jacobi's 1789 book has appeared to date. Thus we can hardly consider the ideas driving post-Kantian philosophy sufficiently elucidated. The following aims to contribute to this elucidation by spelling out how the problematic of a theory of the subject arose in the constellation constituted by the publications of Reinhold and Jacobi in spring 1789.

4 Kant's Analysis of "I think"

To accomplish this we must first of all recall the *Critique of Pure Reason* and the role Kant gave the "I think" in his analysis of the conditions of knowledge.[12] It is no secret that Kant used his so-called "transcendental unity of apperception" as the starting point for justifying the possibility of knowledge within the bounds of experience (*CPR* A); in addition, he declared it the "highest point" in the whole of transcendental philosophy (*CPR* B, 133–134 note). This transcendental unity finds expression in the "I think." For anyone who has tried to follow Kant's justification of his basic theory and is familiar with the history of its reception, it is a commonplace that elucidating the form and function of that starting point makes for the most formidable difficulties, taking one along widely divergent paths of thought.

That Kant gives such prominence to a thought through which self-consciousness arises obviously has its historical background in both Cartesian and Leibnizian modes of justification. For Descartes this thought displayed a certitude immune to skepticism, whereas Leibniz saw self-consciousness as the only case where the being-in-itself of substance can be displayed *in concreto*. But no one prior to Kant was willing to derive the formal constitution of knowledge as such from self-consciousness. In the Wolffian wing of Leibniz's school the practice had rather been to look at self-consciousness as derived knowledge, both in epistemological and psychological contexts. Of course, less prominent students had already disputed this. Moreover, the movement was long underway to investigate Locke's problem of personal identity in connection with the soul's perception and awareness of itself; the relation-to-self [*Selbstverhältnis*] here was taken as a source not further derivable.[13] Only in Kant's critique, however, did self-consciousness finally rise to the position of a first principle, not only of confirmation but also of the formal constitution of knowledge.

Kant has provided some clear statements about how he would have the "I think" understood: this consciousness should be distinguished from psychological self-observation; it corresponds to a Cartesian certitude independent of all experience; its form is not differentiated by anything further and lacks all individual features; and it is the way each individual stands in an epistemological relation to himself without knowing anything of what kind of existence [*Daseins*] he is, while nonetheless also being certain—precisely *in* the "I think"—that he exists as such an "I think." In addition, the "I think" does not merely happen from time to time but is produced by an act, just as its content also further indicates or presupposes an activity.

Yet the above theses and qualifications still leave the status of the "I think" somewhat unclear. They say even less about the conditions giving rise to it, or about what makes it a sufficiently determinate principle serviceable for philosophical investigation. In the *Critique of Pure Reason* Kant remained completely silent about the position one should adopt on these questions, questions that cannot be ignored by anyone using this principle. Kant's comportment is explained by the intentions governing his chief work, which was not meant to elaborate an exhaustive basic theory of the possibility conditions for knowledge. Its task was rather that of safeguarding knowledge inside the bounds of experience against justified doubt, expending in the process only as much theoretical capital as was suitable and not a penny more. Nor did Kant specify his task this way simply out of need for a justification that would be maximally accessible yet secure from controversies. Rather, he actually believed it was *impossible* to substantially elucidate the actual grounds of our knowledge—what underlies and gives rise to knowledge—any further than the account already given in the *Critique of Pure Reason.* For Kant distinguished between a theory that mastered a particular object domain and the fundamental philosophical elucidation that, its systematic efforts notwithstanding, can only be based on a "reflection" always already effected in actual knowing. What is disclosed through this pretheoretical reflection presents a threshold one cannot overstep even in the second-order reflection characteristic of philosophy, which is guided by theoretical interests but represents a theory in another sense than the knowledge it aims to justify. Returning to the first ground, then, is undoubtedly a path to first certitudes immune to correction through experience. But it is not the first step in a self-sufficient first science enjoying a sort of pure object domain made up of self-contained, transparent grounds of knowledge. Kant's conviction on this point explains the way he goes about writing the *Critique of Pure Reason.* Yet it was neither formulated nor justified there. Moreover, to the present day interpreters of the *Critique* have overlooked its significance for Kant's work, leaving both the conviction itself and its consequences unclarified.[14]

Contemporaries thus had to face not only the problematic as such, but also unmanageable problems of reception the nature of which was scarcely even clear to them. Yet even if Kant himself had made the background methodology of his *Critique* accessible, that would not have automatically dispelled all the difficulties surrounding any endeavor to understand his use of the "I think." Here I shall only mention two of these difficulties. I choose these because they were already evident in the first productive phase of the reception of Kant's problems and, beyond this, continued to affect classical German philosophy up to the last of its theoretical fruits. Both difficulties result from the fact that the "I think" involves a duplication that requires a distinction between the content of the thought and a subject who in thinking it knowingly relates to itself. The first difficulty issues from the mere relation existing between them, the second from the fact that the subject apparently must be conceived as the ground of this very relation.

Thoughts of "I think" are statements and thus affirmative clauses whose propositional contents are expressed by the formula "I think" irrespective of the further content of the particular thought I have just had at that point. Now such propositions cannot be examined [*erwogen*] for their truth or falsity without their already being true at the same time. This fact, which we may call "Cartesian," means not only that whatever may be designated with "I" has an existence concomitant with the proposition's consideration [*Erwogenseins*]. It also means that the one designated with the expression "I" is the very one considering the proposition. Therefore it must be said that he is the subject of this consideration of the proposition. And since the proposition is always true whenever it is considered, it further follows that someone considering the proposition does not merely entertain it and think it, but enjoys in that thinking a knowing of himself.[15] In addition, he knows not only that someone thinks but first and foremost that someone thinks of himself as thinking, and hence that this someone ascribes such a thought to himself. Furthermore, he knows that he himself is the one of whom it is true: in him such a thinking-of-himself is taking place. And this formula, which appears to express a multistage process of reflection, is still nothing more than an explication of what is executed in every simple "I think." It cannot be resolved into any sequence of thoughts, in which higher and more richly articulated thoughts rest on a still undifferentiated relation-to-self.

However, he who both entertains the "I think" and knows through it has a *superior* position vis-à-vis the content of this thought. It may well be that his existence cannot be separated from the fact that in such thoughts he relates to himself, indeed knowingly. Someone thinking *x* about himself would simply be designating some other entity if this *x* were never to entertain such an "I think." For to relate knowingly to oneself is not only more than an incidental or unimportant quality, it is the very ground for being able to possess or acquire a series of other qualities of the same kind. Nevertheless, it cannot be said that what is designated by the "I" in each such thought comes into existence in virtue of the fact that precisely this thought is being thought. For then it would no longer be possible to reconcile the thought's content with the notion that the thought is being entertained. After all, it makes no sense to have a thought be sustained [*unterhalten*] by the very thing that only comes into being at all by virtue of the content of this thought. Just this raises the question as to how one can characterize the relation of the subject of such thoughts to that which is thought in each "I think."

Although I have expounded these interrelationships by using distinctions Kant himself did not elaborate, I have not introduced anything incompatible with his mode of thinking. Now there are two places in the *Critique of Pure Reason* where the above question is addressed, each time from a different point of view. In one case Kant thematizes the subject of the "I think" as its ground; in the other he addresses the relation of the "I" component to what it designates. At the beginning of the transcendental deduction, where Kant first discusses and makes use of the "I think," he speaks of a self-consciousness that "generates" [*hervorbringt*] this thought (B 132). If one takes this formulation literally, one will have to explicate it something like this: The thought "I think" expresses a self-consciousness that constitutes in turn the *ground* for the fact that this thought—that I have (or think) this representation [*Vorstellung*]—arises in relation to every determinate representation. This self-consciousness would thus be something prior to every "I think" insofar as it, in contrast to each of these thoughts, exists independently of whether a representation (or a thought) is accompanied in any way by the (preceding) thought that I think it. Thus we could also call this an ever present consciousness vis-à-vis all such thoughts. That would explain why the ongoing persistence and thus identity of what is designated with "I" is implied in each "I think."[16] Still further, this self-consciousness also has priority in virtue of its being more than mere thought, which is to say it can *generate* something, namely, each of these thoughts.

The above explication certainly renders Kant's formulation more comprehensible. In the process, however, we have interpreted this formulation in terms of a thought that obviously creates difficulties of its own. Namely, if the "I think" is preceded by a ground that happens to be self-conscious, how is this self-consciousness in turn possible? Must not another thought having essentially the same constitution be entertained in that self-consciousness? Of course, one might distinguish these two thoughts by pointing out that the latter thought, dwelling in the grounding self-consciousness as such, is not an "I think" that accompanies other thoughts or representations in order to attribute them to the one who exists in that grounding self-consciousness. On the other hand, one cannot see how a self-consciousness could exist that does not arise in or through a thought having "I" as its prefix. But if a thought has this prefix, then precisely what should be considered essential for an "I think" is at hand. In that case, one must conclude that the "I think" presupposes a self-consciousness that for its part arises only through the thought "I think." This yields an infinite regress, from which it follows that the relation between self-consciousness and thoughts of "I think" has been understood in a circular fashion, and thus not understood at all.

Kant, of course, was quite reluctant to explain this relationship in any way. It was always consistent with his methodology for him to use that formulation without further elucidation. He thought it sufficient in the course of his deduction to secure the premise that thoughts of "I think" issue from a spontaneous achievement [or accomplishment: *Leistung*] that must, in virtue of the content of these thoughts, have an a priori identity transcending all individual thoughts of "I think." However, anyone given pause by Kant's formulation will recall other passages in the *Critique of Pure Reason* that likewise call for serious study.

One of these passages is found in his critique of rational psychology, where Kant himself refers to a *circle* present in the representation "I" (*CPR,* A 345–346). Thus, seeing how easily Kant's explanation of the genesis of the "I think" gets into a circle, it is tempting to transform what looks like a reef threatening certain shipwreck into safe anchorage: one need only call upon the above-cited passage, already available in the first edition of the *Critique.* The intrinsically circular constitution of a self-consciousness mediated by the thought "I" is, one can then maintain, exactly what Kant had in mind for a theory of self-consciousness.

The stopgap provided by this textual combination, however, overlooks the difference between the two points of view from which each of the two passages was written. While the first aims to thematize the ground of the "I think," the second focuses on how the prefix in this its content relates to what it designates. For if each "I think" designates something that supports this thought, it would seem one could, on the basis of such thoughts, specify more closely what this subject is. Kant, however, wants to exhibit the merely illusory status of this prospect by demonstrating that one cannot make this subject designated by "I" present in a way that would allow the ascription of any properties to it. Its position is such that "I" can never step out of the role of being a prefix. If we want to say what such an "I" is, we must yet again make use of the "I" as a prefix in the very attempt to express this. Thus it always slips away at the very moment it is submitted to the conditions that alone make an objective characterization possible.[17] Precisely this yields the circle Kant described with well-chosen vividness as compelling us to "revolve in a perpetual circle" (*CPR,* A 346): the attempt at thematically fixing the "I" sets it in motion, swinging it into the position from whose standpoint the thematization would have to be carried out.

This circle, therefore, is by no means a circle in the explanation of self-consciousness, nor should it be taken as necessarily leading to a circular explanation. Adverting to it does nothing more than emphasize the fact that one cannot start with the constitution and Cartesian status of the "I think" in order to derive a priori knowledge of an object constituted as a subject. To be sure, this circumstance deserves consideration in any projected investigation into the constitution of the "I think." It would also have to be taken into account in an elucidation of how self-consciousness, which is supposed to precede the "I think" as its ground, relates to these "its" thoughts. But again, Kant stopped short of the first step that would have headed toward an elucidation and thence to a theory of the subject, a subject that would have to be conceived as nothing but a further, albeit prominent, object among objects.

Kant's strategy, therefore, was one of theory avoidance regarding both self-consciousness and the idea of a subject, which he considered the only means by which self-consciousness could have been conceptually characterized. Yet this strategy was spun from threads all too delicate: from the methodology behind the strategy, from the special role he still gave self-consciousness in his deduction, from his tendency to say as little as possible on questions of principle. Anyone who appears on the scene with a completely novel mode of justification and seeks to attract attention, yet strives to direct that attention exclusively to the consequences of this justification, cannot but provoke freely roaming reflections, as it were, on the very themes he wanted to keep out of the discussion (even though he himself was also the one who first disclosed these themes).

We can now get some sense of the two difficulties such reflections managed to run into before anything else. The first difficulty arises when one does not recognize that Kant's strategy aims to avoid a theory of the subject. As a result, his remarks about the relation between the "I think" and its subject become suggestions deliberately hinting at a Kantian theory, be it one he actually possessed but did not communicate or one his critique has need of and invites. Once one understands Kant in this way, one will want to examine the "I think," the most basic thought in the justification of knowledge, in order to find out how a subject stands and is capable of standing in a knowing relation to itself through it. Then one cannot but notice immediately that this relation threatens to resist all but circular attempts at comprehension. Once again that leads one to take Kant's remarks about the circle in the "I think" as suggesting a way to transfigure a mere difficulty into a proposed solution. Consequently, one takes these remarks as real theoretical content, the result of an analysis that has arrived at a positive explanation of the relation-to-self arising through the "I think."

The second difficulty arises in connection with the first as follows: Kant expressly declared that the "I think" issues from a subject's spontaneity. Now if one grants that a positive explanation of this subject's constitution would require the subject itself to already enjoy some kind of "I think," which yields the circle, one must then ask whether this subject's actual constitution is rightly characterized at all by the information that the subject is related to its "I think" as the active ground of this thought. Doubts in this regard by no means force one to deny that every thought with a determinate content is entertained by the subject and that, at least to this extent, this active relation actually exists. But to the extent that the subject sustains a relation-to-self *in* each "I think," this thought is rather less likely to be explained simply in terms of its being generated. For the relation between ground and effect is univocal and asymmetrical, and all the more so when it is taken as that of a producer to his product. Such a relation, if it is to be conceived as a real relation at all, cannot be translated into a circle. It is conceivable, then, that the ground of the "I think"-with-its-particular-content already stands, as such, in a knowing relation-to-self that *precisely cannot* be described as a product but that still comes about through thoughts that must be next of kin to the "I think." For they enter into particular thoughts of "I think" insofar as their prefix, the "I," cannot be simply a product of the actually productive relation-to-self but must also give expression to this relation.

The above shows how both difficulties arise in succession, and directly in the wake of Kant's development of the problem, assuming one does not clearly see the methodology explaining Kant's strategy of theory avoidance in matters of self-consciousness. In fact, without getting into a close reading of Kant's texts and mode of thinking, we can also see why the problematic was transformed in the subsequent reception of the *Critique of Pure Reason:* it was evident that Kant sought to accomplish the justification of knowledge claims in a new theoretical form. The concept formations and fundamental distinctions of this theory grew up hand in hand with a new way of talking about self-consciousness. And the subject of knowledge, to whom self-consciousness is ascribed, was assigned a key role in the construction of this theory. This alone has to arouse the expectation that a theory of the subject and its relation-to-self confronts problems of a kind that earlier philosophical theories had not reckoned with at all. This expectation will then grow into the idea that such a theory has need of a characteristic language and mode of justification, which also throw a new light on other, long familiar philosophical problems. If one follows this orientation, the first task confronting a theory of the self-conscious subject is to investigate the two properties Kant had ascribed to the subject in relation to its thoughts; more specifically, one must relate these to each other in a way at once transparent and credible. These properties are its status as a principle, which is connected with its property of being active, and its relation-to-self. It is to be expected that explaining the relation-to-self will make for special difficulties. For Kant too described in passing its constitution as circular, though he was not willing to say that this constitution could only be defined in a circle, which would render it wholly inconceivable. In any case, reflections guided by this orientation would eventually have to extend what Kant presented.

It is also possible, however, to look at Kant's problematic from a still greater distance, aiming not simply to extend it, but to criticize it as well. Thus one might consider the tension between the subject's activity and relation-to-self as irresolvable inside a theoretical framework thoroughly oriented by Kantian premisses. This conclusion is an easy one to reach: if its relation-to-self precedes all of the subject's activity, then this relation must be comprehended in a language and conceptual form that contrasts with the concepts through which activities and productive achievements can be comprehended; in addition, such a language must also clearly articulate this very contrast. In that case it seems reasonable to understand the subject's relation-to-self on the basis of conditions that are not in its power and in no way its products. However, if one does not want to thereby cast doubt on the foundational role of the subject's achievements in the organization of knowledge, then self-consciousness must be understood both as something that does not make itself possible and as the ground of the possibility of that organizing activity emanating from it. This yields a dual notion of knowing. But if one gives self-consciousness that foundational role in all knowing, this duplication will also have to be applied to all modes of knowing, producing a fundamental distinction between them—albeit in such a way that the special difficulties in the explication of the subject's self-consciousness are also taken into account.[18]

Thus both the extension of Kant's conception as well as its revision can be derived from motives rooted in the conception itself. To this extent, these motives internally resist an integration with any of the conceptions developed before the appearance of critical philosophy. In 1789 this dual possibility of a connection was actualized in a real constellation of mature theoretical projects. What is more, their interplay opened up the space for further conceptual development. Reinhold's theory contained the first attempt at a theory of the subject that understood itself as extending Kant's own line of thought. It was with a view to revising this thought that Jacobi presented a first sketch of his own theory of relation-to-self [*Selbstverhältnisses*], which uses an antithesis to reciprocally determine activity and self-relationship [*Selbstbeziehung*].

5 Reinhold's Theory of the Subject

Considering for how long, how widely and industriously, the classical epoch of German philosophy has been researched, it is surprising that Reinhold's attempts at a theory of subject and self-consciousness have been completely ignored. Yet this is only one of the many deficits that together show how much an analysis situating the formative period of post-Kantian philosophy in its context still remains to be done. Certainly we know Reinhold attempted to rebuild the entire conceptual apparatus of critical philosophy as a process of derivation starting from foundational justifications and definitions; we know too that this made a new theoretical model available for discussion. In this framework, however, he also created a new theoretical climate for a possible theory of the subject. His attempts at this would have attained an even greater influence on subsequent developments had his contemporaries studied them more carefully. As it is, the fact that such influence is not evident has kept interpreters from taking notice of Reinhold's theoretical initiatives.

Reinhold's attempts at a theory of the subject result almost of necessity from the general approach of his theory, which is based on a clarification of a concept of representation [*Vorstellung*]. For the definition of representation already contains the idea of a subject as one of its constitutive components. Moreover, the thesis that a basic form of representation underlies every manner of having representations ultimately implies that even the subject's representation of itself must be comprehensible in terms of this basic form. As a result, the problem immediately arises as to how a subject's representation of itself, i.e., self-consciousness, is possible. Thus Reinhold was also the very first to raise, in a fully explicit way, the question about the conditions of possibility for a knowing relation-to-self. Nevertheless, his theory of the subject bore all the marks of provisionality; in addition, there were signs of an insufficient intellectual penetration of the problematic. Just this, however, makes it all the more suitable for helping us understand the difficulties complicating the issue it addressed.

Reinhold's theory was constructed in three stages, whose relation to one another he did not sharply elucidate. These stages correspond to aspects of the problematic, albeit ones treated in widely separated subsections of the theory of representation. These are (1) the definition of the concept of subject in the context of a clarification of the "original concept of representation" (*Beytr,* 169; compare *TVV,* 200 ff.); (2) the theory of consciousness, the introductory piece to a theory of knowledge that attempts to explain self-consciousness (*TVV,* 333 ff.; *Beytr,* 222, compare 246); (3) the theory of reason in whose framework Reinhold deals with the "spontaneous" [*selbstthätige*] activity of representing on the one hand and the idea of a subject on the other, which, as an "absolute subject" (*TVV,* 533), underlies the whole human faculty of representation and in particular its a priori constitution.

Only in the 1789 book are all three subsections of the theory of the subject actually treated. In the *Neue Darstellung* of 1790 (*Beytr,* 165–254) the theory of reason is completely absent. Moreover, the theory of self-consciousness is no longer developed within the framework of the theory of consciousness (*Beytr,* 222). The idea on which the theory of self-consciousness was grounded in the 1789 book is present only in concealed form, in a place suggesting that Reinhold thenceforth intended to forge a tighter connection between the theory of self-consciousness and that of reason (*Beytr,* 253–254). In mid 1792 Reinhold made this explicit, declaring that those aspects of subject and self-consciousness essential for philosophy itself, as well as for its grounding, could only be investigated and understood within a theory of reason.[19] Yet with that he also switched positions. In treating the origin of the theory of the subject we shall have to leave this switch out of consideration, although it is partly explained by the tensions evident in the 1789 attempt and its new presentation from the following year. Let us turn, then, to a more detailed discussion of the three subsections of the theory of the subject found only in this 1789 attempt. For our purposes it is good to order these according to the three Reinholdian catchwords: subject, self-consciousness, and absolute subject.

Subject

As is well known, Reinhold's theory takes its starting point in an attempt to provide a structural characterization of the concept of representation, which for Kant was merely a universal feature of classification. From this characterization, so Reinhold hoped, additional properties of particular forms of representation, as well as further facts and achievements pertaining to the faculty of representation, would be derived and defined by their position in the construction of the representative faculty [*Vorstellungsvermögens*]. Reinhold strives, albeit unconvincingly, to spell out the method of such derivations with as much clarity and detail as possible. However, not only the method but, even more, his individual deductions drew criticism, to which he then attempted to respond as well. We cannot go into these details here, nor can we deal with the difference between Reinhold's and Kant's procedures. That difference rules out any chance of presenting Reinhold's method as a deeper grounding of Kant's.

For as a matter of fact, the concept of the subject is already one of the components in the first simple definition of representation as such. In 1789 Reinhold declared that "the characteristic feature of the concept of representation . . . meant to supply the foundation of my theory" is the following: "Every representation [involves] a representing subject and a represented object . . . both of which must be *distinguished* from the *representation* in which they are involved" (*TVV*, 200). In 1790 this characterization is honed into the "Proposition on Consciousness": "In consciousness the representation is distinguished by the subject from subject and object and related to both" (*Beytr,* 167).

With this definition Reinhold gives representation an independence vis-à-vis the events or execution in virtue of which it materializes and is sustained. Others have already demonstrated that many developments in subsequent philosophy, beginning with Herbart, can be related to this step.[20] Given its position in a system making a universal claim, this definition leads to a doctrine of strict representationalism: nothing can be known or perceived or meant except through the vehicle of some representation.

But in Reinhold's definition this dominance of representation in consciousness competes with the role this very same definition gives the subject. Reinhold rejected every form of Platonism that would ascribe to representation something like a separate existence or at least a dynamic independent of the grounds located in the "faculty" of representation. On the other hand, of course, he is willing to speak of this faculty only insofar as it grounds the properties of representation displayed in the representation itself and, consequently, in consciousness. Since the relation to and distinction from a subject is only one of the properties of representation, it would, strictly speaking, be possible to ascribe the representative faculty to a real substrate other than a subject. One could even imagine that this substrate and its faculty themselves underlie the subject that, insofar as it appears in consciousness, is also merely an aspect of representation. Nonetheless, Reinhold quickly identifies this substrate with the subject in consciousness. As a result, this subject must be characterized as the "one representing" [or representing agency: *das 'Vorstellende'*] (e.g., *TVV,* 250 ff.; *Beytr,* 204), now taken in a wholly unrestricted sense. Its "predicate [is] the entire faculty of representation" (*TVV,* 270).

We can already foresee this development in light of the basic definition of representation. For it assigns the subject *in* the representation the simultaneous role of being that *through which* the representation is at once distinguished from and related to what is represented and the one representing. Already in the definition of representation, therefore, the subject is that to which the distinguishing and relating of the representation is attributed. Hence the subject is that in virtue of which the representation has its characteristic relations; to this extent it is also responsible for the independence and dominance of representation vis-à-vis the other two relations. The result is that Reinhold's elementary definition has, so to speak, a double foundation. We shall soon see even more clearly how much this is the case. To begin with, though, we should note an additional effect of the representing subject's presence in the definition. This subject supplies the basic constitution of every representation whatsoever, which means that a uniform notion of the subject must be employed throughout the entire course of theoretical developments regarding the constitution of representations. Also enlisted along with this notion, however, is the unity of each individual subject, which will be awarded a wealth of additional and particular functions while remaining nonetheless one and the same throughout all the achievements that further characterize representations.

That such a subject has to be brought in at all is something Reinhold finds self-evident. Just as he sees his definition of representation as taken immediately from a "fact" of consciousness, indeed, from the fact comprising consciousness itself, so too the fact that each representation has a subject seems to him irrefutably given with the fact of such consciousness. Nevertheless, one can easily see that this supposedly simple evidence results from a whole bundle of primarily conceptual interrelationships. Reinhold cannot elucidate these precisely because he methodologically commits himself—and as founder of a philosophy based on a first principle must commit himself—to expound in detail with this principle only what is already given in the most original fact of consciousness itself. Here we need pursue only a few of these conceptual interrelationships.

If one assumes that each representation represents something—that which is represented in it—then this immediately suggests allocating this *passivum* ("what is represented") to an *activum,* which then comprises that which represents something by means of the representation and hence is the one representing. The apparent reasons for doing this actually do not get beyond the surface grammar. "To represent" is an active verb, while "representation" is a substantive that, like "action," designates an achievement that must be produced by someone or something. Yet one could avoid such reasoning if one were not already inclined to ascribe representations to a bearer or subject, rather than consider them independent mental events.

If one further assumes that each representation in consciousness is distinguished from and related to that which it represents and if, sticking to the above methodological commitment, one also locates the representing [agency] in consciousness as such, it then becomes reasonable to take a further step, going beyond the mere fact of being related and distinguished. One then takes both relating and distinguishing as something like achievements to be ascribed to the representing [agency] as such. In this way the representing [agency] becomes something to be grasped as "subject" on a double basis: as he who *has* a representation, and to this extent subsists beneath the representation, and as he who *produces* achievements that simultaneously take place in and constitute the representation. In fact, this dual function already makes it inevitable that the subject, which is still actually supposed to be lifted into consciousness through the representation, is taken not merely as one of its moments but as the subject of all that comprises and makes possible the representation as constituted, from which it follows that the faculty of representation can and must be assigned to the subject itself. Far from excluding further capabilities, this in fact demands that they be ascribed to this subject over and above the capacity to have and—as we can now add—to structure representations. Reinhold even introduced some of these straightaway as inferences following from the simple concept of representation itself.

When Reinhold defined the simple concept of representation to already include a rather strong notion of "subject," he was undoubtedly motivated by the memory of Kant as well. For, starting with a new foundation, he wanted to arrive at a specification of the subject in which spontaneity "of soul" or "mind" [*Spontanteität 'des Gemüts'*] has a constitutive role for each representation just become conscious. But his meticulous clutching after Kant's reflections and definitions, which Kant had always presented in a merely ad hoc fashion, finally had the result that even the simple definition of representation required a highly complex structure, and not just for each representation. This complexity is also structured in such a way that a close reading of it threatens to explode the meaning of representation envisioned in the definition. That is, if the representation is that in virtue of which a subject is found in consciousness at all, then one cannot also say, at the same time, that essential traits in the representation's constitution issue from performances of something found in the subject insofar as that subject is factually present in consciousness through the representation.

Thus Reinhold created a situation where persistence in such questions—such as that concerning the grounds for assuming a subject and that concerning the manner of its functioning in consciousness—leads to reflections necessarily taking one beyond the problem condition as Reinhold defined it. It was Fichte who really entered into such reflections. The situation at which Fichte arrived, however, for the most part simply repeats at a higher level of reflection the one created by Reinhold. In fact, the relations Reinhold thought he could manage on the basis of the evidence of the simplest fact of consciousness together with a first definition still coalesce into problems clogging the philosophical analyses of our own day, problems for which there are no solutions free of controversy. We have come to realize, moreover, that these problems do not disappear when we trade the starting point labeled "representation" for the actually more appropriate one of sentence form and sentence truth conditions.

In further developing his theory Reinhold makes explicit use of the fact that the subject has been understood from the start as the active principle in consciousness. He thus attempts to show that one must assume each representation contains two "components" through which it can be related to the object on the one hand and the subject on the other (*TVV,* 235 ff.). The component correlated with the subject is supposed to be the form of the representation. Furthermore, in contrast to the matter [*Stoff*], this form is seen as generated, indeed, by the subject to which this form is related; this latter relation in turn must take place through the subject as well, according to the definition of representation (*TVV,* 255ff). Now the proofs Reinhold outlined for this are the most criticized of his theorems. Reinhold himself finally had to give them up, which led to the 1792 reversal of positions that most of his contemporaries did not even notice. However, while developing this proof in 1789 he attributed to the subject the achievement of "actively" [*thätig*] producing in each representation the form of that representation (*TVV,* 269). This spontaneous activity [*Selbsttätigkeit*] (*TVV,* 536) is not an absolute. For it ensues in relation to a material content [*Stoff*] that must be given. And the latter's givenness is explained by another faculty that is likewise ascribed to the subject as its receptivity, à la Kant. All in all, however, a double structural characterization results when the relating and distinguishing, allotted to the subject's jurisdiction by the definition of representation, is taken in combination with the "spontaneously active" production of forms by which the representation can be related to the subject. If one does not keep both these moments separate, but sees in them a single, complex basic fact of the elementary representational act [*Vorstellens*], one is just a hair's breadth from simultaneously ascribing a self-relationship to the subject generating the form. This would enrich the idea of the subject by yet another essential component. Other than this, the particular occasion for assembling both components results from the fact that the form Reinhold speaks of is not meant as a particular albeit formal content of representation, but rather as that form the representation has simply as a representation. However, since something qualifies as a representation only if the relation and distinction with respect to object and subject ensues in it, it follows that a generating that produces the representation as such can no longer be conceived as at all separate from a generating of that which is related and distinguished. Inasmuch as this relation includes that to a subject, one must say that with the generating of form the relation to the subject enters as well.

If one takes this as a self-relationship, it must be added at once that Reinhold cannot also view it as self-*consciousness.* For his definition of representation makes it necessary to mobilize a further, special representation for such a conscious self-relationship. That is, there is no mode of being conscious that is not also a representation. But in each representation object and subject, and hence matter and form, must again be distinguishable (*TVV,* 256; *Beytr,* 181). Thus Reinhold can only begin to speak of self-consciousness when, in relation to the subject, he has reached a representation that for its part represents the subject as an object as well and in which, therefore, the subject must be present through a material content. Such a thought at least satisfies a necessary condition for defining and understanding self-consciousness. What is more, this insight into a condition given with Reinhold's principle, a condition he actually took quite seriously, can lead us to his treatment of the "self-consciousness" problem.

6 Reinhold on Self-Consciousness and Reason

Reinhold's theory of the subject is instructive, the possible starting point for profound reflections, even if this is largely because of the complications entangling it. These complications, however, issue from the attempt at elucidation in a thoroughly systematic context. Reinhold's theory of self-consciousness, on the contrary, deserves special notice and even esteem for a different reason. For it was first to recognize and display a difficulty every attempt at elucidating self-consciousness must sooner or later confront and either evade or overcome. It is necessary too to see the conditions that give rise to this difficulty and perhaps allow one to get around it. Beyond this Reinhold also gets tangled up in new difficulties in the course of working out this theory proposal. These are connected with the fact that the endeavor to completely understand self-consciousness must in his opinion make use of a justification of the idea of *spontaneous* activity.[21] In fact, this idea had already been of service in the preceding theory of the subject. According to Reinhold's program, however, the place where it can first be defined is the third theoretical component in a complete theory of the subject, the "theory of reason." As already mentioned, only a sketch of it was given in 1789, and later too Reinhold failed to take it up again, let alone really argue it in detail.

Self-Consciousness

Self-consciousness is the "consciousness of the one who represents as such" [*TVV*, 326]. The *relation* to [*Beziehung auf*] the one who represents is a constitutive component of every representation; thus it occurs in any consciousness. Self-consciousness, however, is a consciousness that distinguishes itself from simple representation first of all by the fact that it does not also involve a relation to an object different from the representing [agency]. Accordingly, Reinhold proceeds on the assumption that self-consciousness is a higher level consciousness, indeed in a twofold sense: (1) the representation, insofar as it always refers [*sich . . . bezieht*] primarily to an object distinct from the subject, must be sharply separated from self-consciousness; (2) self-consciousness must come about in virtue of a representation whose object is the very one who represents. To this extent, Reinhold sees self-consciousness as a mode of consciousness having its *genesis* inside consciousness itself (*TVV*, 336). In order to attain the isolation of the subject's conscious relation to itself, the representation as such must first of all have come to consciousness. This in turn is separate from the particular representation through which all self-consciousness internally arises insofar as it too is a mode of consciousness and thus a mode of representing.

The content [*Gehalt*] of this representation must be one that can be ascribed to the one representing and only to him. For this reason Reinhold links his elucidation of self-consciousness to a theorem taken from the analysis of the bare faculty of representation—the thesis that in all representation forms can be distinguished that, precisely because they are not grounded through a *given* matter, can also themselves be represented a priori (*TVV,* 304). The derivation of this thesis is one of the many weak points in the theory of representation. However, neither this nor the role it played in Reinhold's reversal of 1792 concern us here.

Reinhold's outline for a theory of self-consciousness (*TVV,* 332–338), on the other hand, belongs among those passages in his work destined to secure him a lasting memory. For it carefully distinguishes a series of steps that an elucidation of self-consciousness within the framework of Reinhold's theory would actually have to follow. Moreover, even a contemporary theory of self-consciousness must at least take these steps into consideration. In the first place, the bilevel character of self-consciousness leads Reinhold to the conclusion that self-consciousness must represent the representing subject *as* representing. He interprets this "as" in such a way (*TVV,* 334) that we have to take it as propositional: the *features* distinguishing the bare [act of] representing [*Vorstellen*] must be *ascribed* to the one representing if that one is to enjoy a relation-to-self within the [act of] representing. Reinhold understands these distinguishing features as those of the representation and not of the one representing. All the same, they indirectly fall to the subject. The reason is that for all representations Reinhold has already ascribed the forms of representation, which he has in mind as the features of the [act of] representing, to the one representing qua subject of the faculty of representations. The content represented in these features is "an a priori material content." Its very materiality, moreover, allows this matter to mediate a representation that grounds a relation-to-self in the representational act. For a representation without a represented material content is inconceivable. Only through such a material content does any representation refer to an object. In the case of self-consciousness, however, this object must be the one representing as such (*TVV*, 334–335).

It is worth noticing now that Reinhold, having come this far in his reflections, does not stop with an inquiry into the possibility of a relation-to-self. With the following step he becomes the very first to ask what it means that not only one who represents is represented as such, but that one who represents relates knowingly *to himself*. "Self-consciousness alone contains not merely the representation of the *one representing*, but of the one representing as the *one who* is representing in this very [act of] representing" (*TVV*, 335). With this Reinhold draws none other than the distinction between the representational act of one representing who objectively is in a representational relation-to-self and one representing who entertains such a relation to himself.[22] Above all else it is the latter that comprises the subject's relation-to-self. This relation, one must add, is presupposed if a relation-to-self in an objective attitude is understood as a knowing relation-to-self. In fact, Reinhold immediately arrives at the formulation that would subsequently be used to express the peculiarity of this knowing relation-to-self from the internal perspective: "In self-consciousness the object of consciousness is represented as identical with the subject" (*TVV*, 335). As can be gathered from the preceding sentence, he evidently meant that what is actually known in self-consciousness is not only a subject's identity with the object, but its identity with the subject who is the very one representing.

One can see that Reinhold gained an appreciation of this problem and its formulation precisely because he had located the content of self-consciousness-engendering representations in the pure matter and hence in the forms of the representative faculty. For these forms are really only indirectly ascribed to the one representing. This inevitably raises the question as to how a knowing relation-to-self could possibly arise through them. As it turns out, he was also thinking of Kant's theory about a kind of inner knowledge: Reinhold sought to use this for developing his own explanation of the possibility of a knowing relation-to-self. But all that in no way alters the fact that

Reinhold posed the task of explaining this possibility with surprising exactitude, in view of how completely unexplored this territory was.

The actual explanation, however, does not do justice to the program that was framed so precisely. As mentioned, Reinhold takes the content of the representation by which the subject apprehends itself as the "pure matter" of the forms of representation. He thinks these are allocated to the knowing subject by virtue of the fact that in order to apprehend them as such forms, this subject must "affect" the forms, a process that must "occur through *nothing other* than the representative faculty, but only through the activity of the representative faculty itself" (*TVV,* 335). Through this activity "this representation of the object, which is represented as representing, also represents the subject in the quality of an object" (*TVV,* 336). One can easily see that all the conditions that Reinhold's general concept of representation prescribes for a self-representation are indeed taken into consideration in his proposed solution, but for all that he does not solve the problem in self-identification he himself posed so precisely, and hence the problem in the subject's knowledge of itself. For the question clearly repeats itself in relation to the activity of the one representing: How does he know it is his *own* activity that is exercised in the forms of representation? If he was already supposed to know that as well, then any information about the possibility of self-consciousness is thereby either denied or deferred to the question concerning the constitution of this henceforth primary knowledge grounding a relation-to-self inside the activity itself. Reinhold himself, by the way, can no longer raise this second question at all, because the prospects for answering it in line with his concept of representation are nil. In fact, he would have to enlist a "matter" all over again as mediator of the self-representation. Yet how could this matter be procured and made conscious in the interiority, so to speak, of the subject's pure activity?

Absolute Subject

Thus far Reinhold's theory of self-consciousness has passed through four stages: the specification of the starting point, according to which the subject has to apprehend itself *as* the one representing; the propositional interpretation of this "as"; the exact formulation of the question concerning the knowing self-relation a subject has to itself, which is in each case its own; and the proposed solution, which finally proves inadequate. Yet Reinhold takes the overview of the problems besetting the theory of self-consciousness a further step forward.

His theory of consciousness, with which the theory of self-consciousness is associated, forms a kind of opening foray into his theory of knowledge. However, it cannot yet lay claim to a concept of knowledge. This circumstance also keeps Reinhold from developing in any clear fashion his propositional interpretation of the relation-to-self and its possible implications. Reinhold himself noticed how his theory could give the impression that a knowing relation-to-self could and would be granted without qualification to every faculty of representation. Yet such a relation-to-self is rather obviously connected with what one may call "rationality," not to mention their close association in Kant. Reinhold, however, does not concern himself with this connection as it implies the faculty of judgment and the thoughts of "I think" associated with its exercise, thoughts that played the key role in Kant's theory. Rather, he makes the connection between relation-to-self and rationality via that a priori knowledge occupying—not just according to Reinhold's explanation but also in fact—the key position in the internal possibility of a knowing self-relationship: via the activity affecting the "pure" matter the subject becomes conscious of the fact that it, the subject, is the one of whom it has a representation in the matter of its representation. Now according to Kant too thoughts of "I think" deserve a Cartesian status: such thoughts are possible in relation to *each* case of knowing or thinking something. Moreover, their possibility is not determined by or dependent on what this something happens to be in virtue of which an "I think" is one thought among others.[23] And just as the content of the specific thought can be neither a basis for, nor a restriction of the possibility that an "I think" arises, so also *what* is thought in such a thought is independent of all the specific conditions under which the thought occurs. It may not always be de facto possible to apprehend an "I think." But that can only be due to a state of consciousness being so composed as to exclude such a thought from entering it. The fact that such a psychological blockage can exist, however, does not mean that the internal possibility of an "I think" must depend on some other content for its own content and realization. To this extent, therefore, it is both self-sufficient and a priori.

Reinhold, however, strives in his theory construction to avoid relying on a thought that has an autonomous position vis-à-vis the sequence controlling the development of the concept and modes of representational action—autonomous, that is, in the sense that one must take its possibility as a starting point without being able to give it a specific place in that sequence of development. Thus he considers Kant's principle, which relies on the form of the "I think," both capable of and in need of further elucidation. This elucidation is supposed to assign the consciousness of "I think" a place in the system, in fact, within the theory of reason, which is taken à la Kant as the faculty of "unconditioned or absolute" unity (*TVV,* 502). This should yield the result that self-consciousness itself is possible only in rational beings capable of representation and precisely in virtue of what their reason specifically makes possible: "Insofar as it is shown in the theory of reason that every pure a priori representation is possible as such only through reason, we will be able to clearly conceive that and why the representation of the I, on which the consciousness of personality depends, is an exclusive privilege of rational beings" (*TVV,* 338). Without this part of the theory, then, the analysis of subject and self-consciousness remains incomplete. And the dependence of the intelligibility of self-consciousness on that which reason makes possible is understood through the following simple two-step chain: (1) there is no self-consciousness without a representation of what is determined a priori in the representative faculty, but (2) each pure a priori representation is enabled and determined by reason.

His theory of reason is also the site where Reinhold penetrates most deeply into the entire network of theorems that Kant had developed in the *Critique of Pure Reason.* He preceded this with a theory of understanding [*Verstandes*] that already contained a derivation of categories deviating from Kant's. In the theory of reason Reinhold picks up those achievements Kant ascribed to reason and thoroughly reworks them into a fully new arrangement. He thereby lays the foundation for a doctrine of ideas [*Ideenlehre*] that simultaneously exhibits the fundamental concepts for practical philosophy insofar as such philosophy includes a doctrine of ideas. This part of the theory of the representative faculty, if it was noticed at all, was thus able to provide subsequent theoretical developments with a starting point that could hardly be further removed from the architectonic construction found in Kant's texts.

Only the following need be reported here of this attempt: Reinhold sees unconditioned unity as formed on the one hand in relation to judgments of understanding [*Verstandesurteile*] and on the other in relation to forms of inference. In their first application they yield laws of reason [*Vernunftgesetze*] governing the systematic unity of experience, in the other, three special ideas, namely those of an absolute subject, an absolute cause, and an absolute community. These three ideas each have in turn a twofold application, that is, to the external and internal senses. The absolute subject resulting from the application to internal sense is the "subject of the a priori represented faculty of representation" (*TVV,* 530). Now this unconditioned unity is also that element whose services had long been necessary in the theory of self-consciousness for understanding how the one representing should be able to relate knowingly to himself as subject of the faculty of representation. According to Reinhold's construction, this relation-to-self arises through the self-ascription of the a priori forms of the faculty of representation. This self-ascription, however, presupposes for its part the idea of an "absolute" subject (*TVV,* 530).

Through these additional operations Reinhold accounts for some traits of a self-consciousness one must call "pure": it is a unitary subject in relation to all possible representations; moreover, it can be apprehended *only* in thoughts, not through any intuition [*Anschauung*] or through some other mode of knowing. Finally, in the broader context of the theory of reason Reinhold realizes that spontaneity [*Spontaneität*] can and must be ascribed to this subject nonetheless. This spontaneity follows from the idea of the absolute ground (*TVV*, 522, 536–537), which as the second idea is immediately linked with the idea of the absolute subject. Such spontaneity, which is "self-activity" [*Selbstthätigkeit*], must enter into the constitution of self-consciousness in a twofold respect: (1) it is what allows the internal affection of a priori matter to occur; through this affection the self-ascription of the representative faculty ensues. (2) At another level, this spontaneity is also what produces the ideas themselves.

Reinhold has no hesitation in ascribing the predicate "free" to this highest order of spontaneous activity (*TVV*, 537). In this way he is able to understand it as the ground both of the theoretical unity of reason and of the "moral aspect of acts of will" (*TVV*, 537). This last step is of considerable consequence for subsequent philosophical developments: Reinhold finally has the third of the ideas, that of the absolute community, rest on "absolute spontaneity" [*Selbstthätigkeit*] in the same way that this spontaneous activity rested on the idea of the absolute subject and was apprehended as that subject's activity. From this it follows that the idea of the absolute community is immediately represented by the subject as "the *moral world*" (*TVV*, 538).

On the one hand, Reinhold's theory of reason distinguishes itself in its conceptual richness and will to lucid order. On the other hand, however, it is also characterized by traces of haste and carelessness. The territory Reinhold frequents Kant had opened through decades of effort, populating it with theorems that had been examined from all sides and in all kinds of applications and consequences. He had left important questions open in this area; in fact he had referred only to a few of them, such as the question concerning the unity of theoretical and practical reason. Relying on Kant's achievement and on his own power to order and define, and aware of what he had already achieved (or so it seemed) in the analysis of the faculty of representation, Reinhold wove his youthful flights and raptures into an arrangement replete with instabilities. One notices this, for example, in the fact that he must, on the one hand, introduce the spontaneous activity of an absolute subject as an actual achievement enabling the self-relationship of self-consciousness; on the other hand, insofar as this spontaneous activity is an idea, he has to view it as itself a product of spontaneous activity. This yields a circle he did not further pursue. This alone, however, would have led him to question the tenability of his artifice of collapsing into one the consciousness of "I think" and the idea of an unconditioned and absolute that is the subject. Then he would have seen that Kant had good reason to allocate the "I think" to a pretheoretical knowledge, which he called "reflection," and to view the ideas strictly as concepts of objects, concepts that could not cast any light on the internal constitution of knowledge as such.[24] To this extent anyone who surveys Reinhold's strategy as a whole must conclude it is not possible to stay essentially within the basic structure of Kant's critique and at the same time come up with a theory answering the questions that Kant's way of speaking about subjectivity in fact raises (although Kant had quite consciously left this notion theory-free).

In hindsight, the inherent weak spots clearly stand out in the entire systematic formation Reinhold employed in his search for a theory of the subject. Already in the theory of representation he made use of the idea of the subject's spontaneous activity. Through this same spontaneity he then attempted to render self-consciousness comprehensible as such. In the process he put off grounding this spontaneity to a third part of the theory, the theory of reason. Yet when he finally got to this part he lost sight of the task this necessarily entailed, namely, how it is possible to start with two levels of presuppositions, each of which encompasses a highly complex state of affairs, and then arrive at an analysis of a basic fact that is still intrinsically constituted as a unity and that can also be immediately realized as a unity in the way this actually takes place in the case of simple self-consciousness. No doubt Reinhold is correct in assuming that this realization is intrinsically complex. Yet he is so absorbed in the task of introducing via definitions the components of the intrinsically complex, knowing self-relationship that he remains, as theoretician, wholly unconcerned with the understandability and realizability of this self-relation in its internal unity. Once he became familiar with reservations of this sort, it was inevitable that he would be compelled to rethink the very formation that gave him his theory of the subject. Such reflection could not be satisfied simply with a new interpretation of this one interrelationship he had set up. It had to reach into the theory's very substance.

Reinhold actually found himself in this position. The attempt to reorganize his theory, however, remained programmatic, never getting beyond the initial stages. Moreover, this initial attempt was not the sort that could ever have led to an outline of a theory of the subject with the conceptual power its earlier version achieved in Reinhold's theory of the representative faculty.[25] Soon after starting his second attempt, he was confronted with Fichte's *Wissenschaftslehre.* Although the kind of theory this represents derives from Reinhold, it is also grounded in a mode of thinking developed through the critique of Reinhold's approach. So in any case Reinhold would not have had the opportunity and leisure to rectify the deficits of his first theory of the subject while sticking to its perspective on the problem and how it should be solved. Any attempt at that had to give way to the task of adopting a reasonable position to Fichte's theory of the subject, which had just aroused a general sensation. Inasmuch as we have not, even today, arrived at a detached and complete analysis of Fichte's theoretical language of subjectivity, it can scarcely surprise us that Reinhold was not in a position to solve both tasks at once: mastering Fichte's theory and setting his own theory once again on a more reliable track.

At their very point of origin, then, the endeavors toward a theory of the subject displayed great acumen in getting hold of and developing a problematic that they nonetheless could not bring under control. No doubt this can be partly explained by the conditions of the time. These infused the business of philosophical theorizing with both an urgency and effervescent productivity that permitted none of the contemporaries a detached overview. Yet we must not overlook the peculiarities built into the problematic itself. Subjectivity is not one theme among others. Once brought up, it raises problems that can only be treated by securing an overall view of various theoretical paths and examining questions having to do with the relation of philosophical investigation to basic facts that constitute all knowing, indeed the human life of reason itself. For this very reason, however, the theory of the subject cannot be considered an affair that has been exhausted by one period of philosophical thinking. Nor does the treatment it received in that epoch justify our dismissing it as something obsolete, so that we would merely need to find a new theoretical language capable of ferreting out and clearly displaying the reasons for its mistakenness. The course taken by the historical origins of the theory of the subject, as well as the fact that its problematic deserves reconsideration in ever new ways, are both explained by one and the same set of objective interrelationships.

7 A New Form of Thinking: Friedrich Heinrich Jacobi

Jacobi's position in the historical origins of the theory of the subject, in contrast to Reinhold's, is not grounded in an original and definitive theoretical proposal. Nor did his efforts contribute to the growing clarity over what such a theory would really have to accomplish. To this extent what he actually did contribute on this issue can only be appreciated in the context shaped by the work of Kant and Reinhold. Nevertheless, he prepared the foundation and motives whose power to form a context extended beyond Kant and Reinhold both, remaining effective through the entire epoch of classical German philosophy and finally shaping the mature theories of Fichte, Schelling, and Hegel.

If, to begin with, we wish to get a general sense of the fundamental contours of the conceptual catalyst supplied by Jacobi—effective for the theory of the subject as well—we should direct our attention to two basic features of his mode of thinking: (1) Jacobi thought in terms of contrasts in modes of knowing and confirmation. (2) In grappling with Spinoza's thinking he came to the conviction that in the dimension foundational for acquiring an understanding of ourselves, one must reckon with relations that cannot be mastered in the conceptual structure underlying the knowledge of finite objects. If such contrasts are not simply those separating true and false theories but are also definitive for the investigation of modes of knowing itself, then a perspective emerges in which two oppositely constituted modes of knowing account for the internal organization of our knowing. If one adds to this contrast the second basic feature of Jacobi's mode of thinking, it follows that one side of this two-sided knowing, indeed the foundational one, has a constitution surprising our expectations of what can be understood with familiar theoretical tools and reconstructed in explanations.

Within the above contours the problematic of the theory of the subject can be registered as follows: Our knowing relation-to-self will be part of that basic dimension as well, at least in its elementary foundational form. One can then see that this relation cannot be known as an object and analyzed according to models provided by the conceptual structures of normal knowledge. Moreover, it is to be expected that once this fact and the reasons for it are appreciated, one is free to give the relation-to-self a constitution hitherto unimaginable, even by those who had recognized the singular, disclosive significance of this relation and the difficulties entangling attempts to master it theoretically.

Yet this characterizes Jacobi's position at the founding of the theory of the subject in merely formal terms, which are still a long way from his own manner of expression. As the next order of business we must get a closer look at Jacobi's total conception, which must be drawn from the short texts he inserted in the second edition of *Über die Lehre des Spinoza* in 1789.

It is well-known that in 1785 Jacobi had already presented Spinoza's system as the result to which every rational metaphysics is finally led. This metaphysics aims at a final, comprehensive explanation of all reality. It is impossible to give such an explanation on the basis of reasons that, while intrinsically independent, simply precede the likewise independent explanandum. From this follows the immanence of the finite in the "absolute." Yet this conclusion has consequences Jacobi considered either absurd or at least unacceptable: a fatalism regarding all our actions and the separation between the idea of the absolute and that of personality. For this reason he countered Spinozism with a conviction he himself had to admit could not be further demonstrated: the immediate certitude of our freedom and the existence [*Dasein*] of a living God.

Still, he had to establish more than just a critical relation between the certitude he clung to and the paths of thinking leading to Spinozism. He had to attempt to explain which logical principles in such thinking in fact yield the Spinozistic result, and precisely in that human knowing that, as he himself argued, was in fact grounded ultimately in immediate certitude. It seemed reasonable to employ a type of argument he actually had begun to develop in his 1787 work, *David Hume über den Glauben:* Underlying the conclusion to a first cause is a mode of inference we have for controlling events in the finite, temporal world. It cannot be extended beyond this sphere of application, a misstep that occurs whenever the path leading into Spinozistic consequences is taken. Where it is legitimately employed, however, it rests in turn on a primary certitude that precisely cannot be obtained through deductive inference: the certitude of our own existence and of the existence of finite, temporal realities; the existence of the "I" and the "Thou," which originally is "Not-I" (*Hume,* 175–176, 278). These cannot be deduced because both emerge for us as inseparable from one another "in the same indivisible moment" (*Hume,* 175, see also 143). To explain the illusion nonetheless attaching to Spinoza's mode of inference, Jacobi turned to a mixture of two basic concepts: causality and the relation of logical cause and effect. The concept of causality is tied by its very meaning to finite, temporal relations; moreover, its intelligibility involves the consciousness of acting had only (and immediately) by beings "revealed to themselves." The cause-effect relation, while free of such ties, is by itself incapable of supporting any real knowledge. With this theory sketch, which bore on the central point of his Spinoza thesis, Jacobi advanced from a contrast between incompatible philosophical doctrines to an explanation of a contrast that arises in the grounds of knowledge and also underlies the contrast between doctrines.

Now when Jacobi sought to demonstrate the inevitability of the Spinozistic result for explanatory thinking aimed at a first cause, he had reconstructed Spinoza's position in a way that widely deviated from Spinoza's own line of justification, employing other basic concepts than Spinoza himself. Rational explanation aims at a first cause, which is the ground. However, since such a ground can be neither temporarily nor temporally nor really separated from what is grounded, anyone reasoning with Spinoza arrives at an immanent first cause. Jacobi, now, explicates the idea of this first and absolute cause not as substance or *causa sui* but in purely modal terms—an operation he was led to by the main text of the precritical Kant (*Hume,* 189). This first cause is "being" [*Sein*], which must be thought prior to all finite "existence" [*Dasein*]—being as such, which must be thought as preceding all merely determinate, limited beings [*Seiendes*].

How this idea arises and how it could be justified as the basic theorem of Spinozism cannot be discussed here. I do want to point out, though, that Jacobi's own mode of thinking no longer defines itself simply by its critical stance to the idea of the being in all existence. Rather, one must see that, precisely to the contrary, Jacobi arrived at his reconstruction of Spinoza because this idea had a disclosive significance for his own convictions as well. For the idea that underlying all existence is a being conceived purely as modality, and hence as all-encompassing, can just as easily fit into a conceptual approach that considers the absolutely underivable as already, indeed immediately, underlying each idea of something finite, in relation to which one may then seek a derivation, albeit only from other finite things. Existence as such is not derivable. Only from such a finite thing that itself exists can another finite thing be derived. Nor do such derivables allow one to resolve existence into comprehensible parts. The derivation yields no more than conditions and lines of impact affecting what for its part simply is, what one may therefore also say is preceded and inhabited by being *simpliciter.* This allows Jacobi to clarify his own approach with that powerful expression to the effect that "the researcher's greatest service" is "to uncover and reveal existence," for "his ultimate purpose" is not explanation but "what does not admit of explanation—the insoluble, immediate, simple" (*Spin,* 42). This also explains the physiognomic similarity between Jacobi's own doctrine on the one hand and his reconstruction of the Spinoza he rejected, on the other. The tangled reception of Jacobi's work was the result of this similarity. The fact that even later interpreters have difficulties in getting a trustworthy overview of Jacobi's mode of thinking and theorems also contributes to the opacity of this similarity.

Already after the publication of *David Hume,* Jacobi felt himself under increasing pressure to present a fully worked out version of his own conception. The additions he inserted into the second edition of *Über die Lehre des Spinoza* were an attempt to correspond to such a demand where possible. In these texts, and in them *alone,* we find Jacobi's theory in the form in which it worked its way into the formative phase of post-Kantian philosophy. The texts at issue are primarily the following: the preface, which was never again reprinted in its entirety; an introductory treatise "on human freedom"; and Supplement 7 on the "natural history of speculative philosophy" and the objects connected with it. In these texts Jacobi was able for the first time to give an account of his doctrine from a point of detached reflection and with thoroughgoing coherence. Of course, the account still remained a sketch in need of clarification and open to objections at many points. Jacobi distinguished explanatory knowledge from the immediate knowledge beyond the reach of all explanation. The dynamic of self-assertion operative in the practical domain corresponds to explanation in the domain of theory. This dynamic, together with all formalistic ethical conduct [*formelle Sittlichkeit*], belongs to nature, where freedom has no place (*Spin,* xxvii ff.). The causal mode of explanation too Jacobi sees connected with self-assertion: it is what first allows the stabilization of dependent existence in its world (*Spin,* 402). We have to understand immediate knowing both as contrasting with this and as foundational for all knowing in the world of finite things. It is, moreover, always characterized by a self-certitude, certitude of other existents and certitude of that being in all existence, which Jacobi wished to equate straightaway with the essence [*Wesen*] of the living God. Whereas explanatory knowledge is constituted by the distance between the derived and that rendering it intelligible, the mode of knowledge in which nothing is explained has the quality of simultaneously taking in the real distance between ground and what is grounded. In the consciousness of freedom my action is at the same time an acting that flows from an energy exceeding that of the finite creature [*Wesen*] (*Spin,* xlvi-xlvii). Corresponding to this in the domain of knowing is the fact that consciousness of our own existence is not self-sufficient and absolutely primary but depends in itself on the representation of an unconditioned and the certitude of its existence (*Spin,* 423–424).

From this point on, the foundation of Jacobi's thinking involves the operation of two pairs of concepts. The first of these is "conditioned/unconditioned" [*bedingt/unbedingt*], the second, "mediated/immediate" [*vermittelt/unmittelbar*]. Jacobi himself sees the central significance of their operation, though it remains somewhat opaque for him: already in the preface he draws attention to the first term of the second pair, taken as the idea of a "mediation," through the use of capital letters, which are employed only in this case (*Spin,* xxii). We might note in passing that this operation obviously played a significant role in the genesis of the conceptual structure of Hegel's logic, a role still hardly elucidated at all.

The logic of Jacobi's operation can now be clarified as follows. Knowing in the realm of finite things is mediate knowledge, insofar as it is a knowing through explanations. As a knowledge of grounds, these explanations accomplish a mediation. This contrasts with knowledge that is *un*mediated as such, i.e., knowledge that neither mediates nor is mediated in any way. However, since explanations are drawn from the conditions of the conditioned in an ever unfinished regress to further conditioning factors, and if the classification mediated/immediate can and should be taken as the fundamental order underlying all modes of knowing, it follows that immediate knowing, and hence knowing determined by its contrast to all mediated knowing, must also be conceived as unconditioned and as knowledge of the unconditioned. In this way, merely through an ordering of concepts, Jacobi identified immediate knowing with a knowledge whose basic feature was defined by the unconditioned. Certainly this operation is not, taken by itself, a conclusive justification for the truth of the idea it intends. But it convincingly summarizes Jacobi's reflections and theses, and in a manner doing justice to their contents. Moreover, it clearly shows that Jacobi's reasoning, at least in its basic tendency, is based on a critique of the conceptual structure that both makes finite knowledge possible and reaches toward the development and justification of another, contrasting conceptual structure, one displaying what Jacobi terms "unconditioned" knowing, and hence the immediate knowing that as such is fundamentally knowledge of the unconditioned. As mentioned above, this kind of argument, which attempts to limit the validity of conceptual structures not by restrictions on their spheres of application but by reason of their internal constitution, was most significant for the genesis of Hegel's science of logic.

8 Lessons from Jacobi for a Theory of the Subject

Only against this background can we begin to understand how Jacobi's thinking could have such a significant impact on the development of the theory of the subject. In addition, we can now see what position he occupied in the constellation announcing that theory's birth. In fact, Jacobi contributed nothing to the internal elucidation of knowing self-relationship. Yet the possibilities for articulating such a theory were essentially enriched through his ideas, as well as through the initiatives he directed toward the development of a conceptual structure designed to contrast with its normal countertype.

For Jacobi self-certitude is also one of the modes of knowing that is neither reducible nor explicable, though it nonetheless provides information about the grounds of other kinds of knowledge. To this extent it is "immediate" knowledge in the sense elucidated above. Furthermore, however, it is a knowledge connected internally as well as immediately with knowledge of the unconditioned. Jacobi finds that one can know oneself only in conjunction with knowing oneself as enabled by an unconditioned: "Thus we do not need to seek the unconditioned at all, but have the same, yea an even greater certitude of its existence than we have of our own *conditioned* existence" (*Spin,* 423–424)—so Jacobi writes in a passage marking both the high point of his reasoning and the birth of the essential positions of post-Kantian thinking.[26] It follows from the connection between self-certitude and certitude of the unconditioned that if self-certitude should be explained theoretically, the form of knowledge pertaining to the unconditioned would have to be pressed into service, together with its exceptional conceptual structure.

As already mentioned, Jacobi does not engage in such an attempt. Nor can he, for the reason that doing so would have led him to doubt the thesis that immediate knowledge as well as knowledge of the unmediated cannot be explained. However, he does make a statement about the relation between knowledge of the unconditioned and our knowledge of ourselves, although this statement is restricted to the formal relation between the unconditioned and the conditioned, which means that it stays more or less within the limits set by his form of thinking. The significance of this statement is understood in terms of what Jacobi calls his anti-Cartesianism: he considers not the *cogito* but the *sum* as the fact of consciousness foundational to self-certitude (*Spin,* xxiv–xxv).[27] The key text cited above from the second edition of the Little Spinoza Book is also situated in this same context: I know of my *existence,* which is a conditioned one, only in relation to the knowledge of the *un*conditioned. But such knowledge is precisely the internal ground making possible that certitude Descartes had affirmed in his proposition *Cogito, ergo sum.*

Thus the knowledge that Jacobi thematized simply as certitude of (one's own) existence is essentially self-certitude, not merely in the sense of an ontological relation that also happens to be the object of knowing but also in the sense of an exceptional epistemic fact, a knowing of oneself. Now when a theory of the subject and subjectivity actually gets in gear, it confronts the task of investigating whether an unconditioned and a consciousness of such an unconditioned conceptually cohere with a knowing self-relationship, especially when this unconditioned is considered the ground of that relationship's own internal possibility. Such an idea would not categorically deny that self-certitude necessarily includes a consciousness of what Reinhold had called "spontaneous activity." But it would imply that such self-certitude, for its part, can no longer be conceptualized on the basis of spontaneous activity. Moreover, even the spontaneous activity that is grounded in self-certitude would have to be understood as a founded [*fundierte*] spontaneity made possible on the basis of the unconditioned, albeit made possible by an unconditioned that does not confront it as an Other but is rather present and operative in it.

Clearly, an idea meant to bring such things together immediately collides in several ways with implications of the conceptual structure by which world relations are ordered for thought and opened to rational explanation. One must even expect such incommensurability, given the way Jacobi sets things up. Nothing in this incommensurability, then, prohibits one from assuming a certain basic state of affairs in all self-conscious knowledge of this sort. Rather, one is enjoined to go beyond the task already tackled by Jacobi, i.e., beyond merely asserting this incommensurability and situating it in a systematic overview. Thus the prospect is now open for spelling out the internal constitution of the knowing self-relationship in a conceptual structure based first of all on the insight into the incommensurability of this basic fact vis-à-vis all world-related knowledge. At the same time, however, one would have to develop this conceptual structure in light of an expanded formulation of the problematic connected with the basic fact—a connection visible even for someone who, like Reinhold, has attempted to focus on an investigation of the constitution and possibility of knowing self-relationship.

This, then, is the constellation that appeared with the publication of Reinhold's first theory of the subject and the simultaneous publication of Jacobi's theory sketch. Beyond the conclusion that was actually drawn by those involved at the time, three pertinent points can be made:

1. It had become a basic and unavoidable requirement of theoretical reason that one adopt a position in this constellation. On account of the weaknesses of Reinhold's theory and, in addition, because Jacobi did not work out a theory of the subject at all, this position could only be reached through a new and productive conceptual endeavor.

2. It was to be anticipated that in the course of this attempt, extreme possibilities had to be reconnoitered and theoretically

elaborated. The complications that Reinhold had consciously introduced into the problematic, together with the reasonable presumption, going back to Jacobi, that a theory of the subject must rely on exceptional conceptual structures, allowed such attempts to mobilize good reasons in their support. They were encouraged by the example provided by Fichte's theory, which independently developed such a conceptual structure in order to reach solid ground inside a theory of knowing self-relationship, all without instructions along the way from Jacobi. The integration of Reinhold's manner of treating the problem and Jacobi's mode of access was set in motion in 1795 by Schelling and Hölderlin.

3. The third point concerning the constellation of 1789 has to do once more with the orientation in contemporary theory: it is neither correct nor philosophically sound to hold that a paradigm shift has henceforth released us from the problematic of subjectivity and the constellation arising in 1789. Anyone propagating this view would, at the very least, first have to submit a theoretical proposal of his own coming to terms with this problematic without shortcuts. However, this proposal also ought to be suitable for rendering a historically significant constellation comprehensible in light of all its consequences. Nothing in contemporary thinking is cause for the summary statement that this has already been accomplished or that we can do it in some easy fashion.[28]

Therefore, just as the revolution in France first provided the grounds for the problematics of the present political world, so the subjectivity problematic numbers among the catalysts of present thinking, catalysts that are by no means exhausted. Exhausted, rather, is a thinking that simply tries to evade this problematic. Let us continue, then, to follow both paths, however arduous that may be!

Notes

1. Hereafter the following works will be cited as indicated:

C. L. Reinhold. *Versuch einer neuen Theorie des menschlichen Vorstellungsvermögens*, original edition (Prague, Jena, 1789) (cited as *TVV*).

C. L. Reinhold. *Beyträge zur Berichtigung bisheriger Mißverständnisse der Philosophen,* original ed. (Jena, 1790) (cited as *Beytr*; all citations of this work refer to vol. 1).

F. H. Jacobi. *David Hume über den Glauben,* 1787, in *Werke,* ed. F. Roth and F. Köppen, vol. 2 (Leipzig, 1815) (cited as *Hume*).

F. H. Jacobi. *Über die Lehre des Spinoza in Briefen an den Herrn Moses Mendelssohn,* original 2nd ed. (Breslau, 1789) (cited as *Spin*).

A reprint of *TVV* (Darmstadt, 1963) is available, likewise of Jacobi's collected works (Darmstadt, 1968). A new but not complete edition of *Spin* is available in *Neudrucken seltener philosophischer Werke,* ed. Kantgesellschaft, vol. 6, *Die Hauptlinien zum Pantheismussstreit zwischen Jacobi und Mendelssohn,* ed. Heinrich Scholz (Berlin, 1916). Other editions contain even larger gaps.

2. One cannot render the development of post-Kantian philosophy at all comprehensible in terms of the successive achievements of individual theories. It is necessary at the start to secure the problem constellations they had to react against. I have elaborated this methodological postulate in greater detail in "Konstellationen," in Lothar Berthold, ed., *Architektonik der Vernunft* (East Berlin, 1987), pp. 11 ff. This text, which is not readily available, will be republished soon in the journal *Dialektik.*

3. In an unpublished letter to J. B. Erhard (June 18, 1792) Reinhold attested that the most important of these objections was made by C. I. Diez, who had just left his teaching assistantship in Tübingen and come to Jena to study medicine. Between April and August of 1792 Reinhold rearranged his entire philosophical position. The only public indication of this was the first essay in his *Beyträge,* vol. 2, written in the summer of 1792 but first published at the beginning of 1794.

4. This new version is found in *Beytr* under the title *Neue Darstellung der Hauptmomente der Elementarphilosophie* (A New Presentation of the Main Aspects of Elementary Philosophy).

5. G. E. Schulze's *Aenesidemus oder über die Fundamente der von dem Herrn Professor Reinhold in Jena gelieferten Elementarphilosophie* (in *Neudrucken seltener philosophischer Werke,* vol. 1 [Berlin, 1911]) had no influence on Reinhold himself, however much impact this book had on the public and subsequent systematic thought.

6. In the letter cited in note 3 above. In documentation issuing from a Munich "Jena Program," Marcelo Stamm will present an essay over the motives and resources for this reorganization.

7. See *Spin* 173–174 and above all 193–194, also with respect to the transcendental unity of apperception.

8. The result was Kant's 1786 essay "What Does It Mean to Orientate Oneself in Thinking?" in Gabriele Rabel, *Kant* (Oxford, 1963), pp. 168–170.

9. See *Critique of Judgment,* sec. 73, the beginning of B 327.

10. See H. Scholz's edition of the writings on the pantheism dispute, *Die Hauptlinien zum Panteismusstreit,* pp. 283 ff., 110 ff. (see note 1 above).

11. See my "Philosophisch-theologische Problemlagen im Tübinger Stift zur Studienzeit Hegels, Hölderlins und Schellings," *Hölderlin-Jahrbuch* 25 (1986/1987): 60–92, here pp. 83 ff.

12. Quotations are taken from the Norman Kemp Smith translation, unabridged ed. (New York, 1965), hereafter referred to as *CPR,* followed by the pagination in the original German editions (1781 ed. = A, 1787 ed. = B).

13. See my "Die Identität des Subjekts in der transzendentalen Deduktion," in Hariolf Oberer and Gerhard Seel, eds., *Kant, Analysen, Probleme, Kritik* (Würzburg, 1988), p. 64 and note.

14. I treat these interrelationships in "Kant's Notion of a Deduction and the Methodological Background of the First Critique," in Eckart Förster, ed., *Kant's Transcendental Deductions* (Stanford, 1989), pp. 29 ff.

15. ["Entertain" renders the German *unterhalten,* which can also have the sense of "maintain" (a relationship) or "keep (an institution or business) going." Thus I shall sometimes use "sustain" to bring out these latter connotations.—Translator]

16. See note 13.

17. To this extent one can know the "I" and the "me" not as an object but only through reflection; moreover, this knowledge extends only to the mode of functioning and not to the real substrate.

18. The double notion of knowing spoken of here is taken, on the one hand, from Kant's concept of knowing as "making" (or constructing) and, on the other hand, from knowing as a quasi "awareness" [*Innesein*]. This difference is introduced here with a view to Jacobi, who explicitly stated it.

19. See note 3 above.

20. Alfred Klemmt, *Karl Leonhard Reinholds Elementarphilosophie* (Hamburg, 1958).

21. [Here Henrich emphasizes the *Selbst* in *Selbsttätigkeit,* so that the literal sense is that of "*self*-activity."—Translator]

22. In *Fichtes ursprüngliche Einsicht* (Frankfurt am Main, 1967), earlier available in *Subjectivität und Metaphysik: Festschrift für Wolfgang Cramer,* ed. Dieter Henrich and Hans Wagner (Frankfurt am Main, 1966), I first pointed out the central significance of this distinction for a theory of self-consciousness. H. N. Castañeda has simultaneously worked out this thesis, taking the semantic approach of analytic philosophy. At the time neither of us knew of Reinhold's antecedent achievements in this matter.

23. See pp. 51–53.

24. See the second half of my "Kant's Notion of a Deduction."

25. See notes 3 and 6 above.

26. See note 11 above.

27. It is not yet clear whether the function actually fulfilled by the proposition "I am" in sec. 1 of Fichte's *Wissenschaftslehre* (1794) and in the preceding *Eigenen Meditationen zur Elementarphilosophie* (*Gesamtausgabe,* series 2, *Nachgelassene Schriften,* vol. 3, ed. Reinhard Lauth and Hans Jacob [Stuttgart, 1971], p. 144 and passim) goes back to a suggestion Fichte gained through Jacobi. In any case, it led those who had read Jacobi carefully to see a significant objective relationship between Fichte and Jacobi. No doubt Fichte himself took his orientation first of all from Spinoza and then from the new

edition of Ernst Platner's *Philosophische Aphorismen,* part 1 (Leipzig, 1793). In secs. 142 ff. of this work the proposition "I am," in contrast to "I think," stands for the consciousness of the unity, existence, and identity that is always one's own.

28. Jürgen Habermas bases his conviction that this result has essentially been achieved on G. H. Mead. When it comes to a problematic directly connected with so many basic philosophical questions, I would find it difficult to place such trust precisely in this author. Habermas, however, also finds confirmation in Ernst Tugendhat's critique of my endeavors in the theory of self-consciousness (*Self-Consciousness and Self-Determination,* trans. Paul Stern [Cambridge, Mass., 1986]), a critique he implicitly refers to many times. I reply to this critique in "Noch einmal in Zirkeln," in Clemens Bellut and Ulrich Müller-Schöll, eds., *Mensch und Moderne* (Würzburg, 1989).

3

Inwardness and the Culture of Modernity

Charles Taylor

I want to distinguish, and start a debate, between two kinds of theories of modernity. I will call them "cultural" and "acultural" respectively. I'm leaning on a use of the word "culture" here which is analogous to the sense it often has in anthropology. I am evoking the picture of a plurality of human cultures, each of which has a language and a set of practices which defines specific understandings of personhood, social relations, states of mind/soul, goods and bads, virtues and vices, and the like. These languages are often mutually untranslatable.

With this model in mind, a "cultural" theory of modernity is one that characterizes the transformations which have issued in the modern West mainly in terms of the rise of a new culture. The contemporary Atlantic world is seen as a culture (or group of cultures) among others, with its own specific understandings, e.g., of person, nature, the good, to be contrasted to all others, including its own predecessor civilization (with which it obviously also has a lot in common).

By contrast, an "acultural" theory is one that describes these transformations in terms of some culture-neutral operation. By this I mean an operation which is not defined in terms of the specific cultures which it carries us from and to, but is rather seen as of a type which any traditional culture could undergo.

An example of an acultural type of theory, indeed a paradigm case, would be one which conceives of modernity as the growth in reason, defined in various ways, e.g., as the growth of scientific consciousness or the development of a secular outlook or the rise of instrumental rationality or an ever clearer distinction between fact-finding and evaluation. Or else modernity might be defined in terms of social, as well as intellectual changes: mobility, concentration, industrialization, and the like. In all these cases modernity is conceived as a set of transformations that any and every culture can go through and that all will probably be forced to undergo. The changes are not defined by their end point in a specific constellation of understandings of, say, person, society, good; they are rather described as a type of transformation, to which any culture could in principle serve as "input." For instance, any culture could suffer the impact of growing scientific consciousness, any religion could undergo secularization, any set of ultimate ends could be challenged by a growth of instrumental thinking, any metaphysic be dislocated by the split between fact and value, and so on.

Modernity in this kind of theory is defined by a rational or social operation which is culture-neutral. This is not in the sense that there may not be good historical reasons why this transformation arose first in one civilization rather than another, why some may undergo it more easily than others. The point rather is that the operation is defined not in terms of its specific point of arrival but as a general function that can take any specific culture as its input.

To grasp the difference from another angle, the operation is not seen as supposing or reflecting an option for one specific set of human values or understandings among others; rather it is seen as the exercise of a general capacity, which was awaiting its proper conditions to unfold. Under certain conditions, human beings will just come to see that scientific thinking is valid, that instrumental rationality pays off, that religious beliefs involve unwarranted leaps, that facts and values are separate. These transformations may be facilitated by our having certain values and understandings, just as they are hampered by the dominance of others, but they aren't *defined* as the espousal of some such constellation. They are defined rather by something we come to see concerning the whole context in which values and understandings are espoused.

It should be evident that the dominant theories of modernity over the last two centuries have been of the acultural sort. Many have explained the development at least partly by our "coming to see" something like the range mentioned above. Or else the changes have been partly explained by culture-neutral social developments, such as Durkheim's move from mechanical to differentiated, "organic" forms of social cohesion, or Toqueville's assumption of creeping "democracy" (by which he meant a push towards equality). On one understanding, "rationalization" was for Weber a steady process, occurring within all cultures over time. But above all, the explanation of modernity in terms of "reason" seems to be most popular.

Jürgen Habermas himself seems to have adopted a Weber-derived variant of this, in laying great weight on the differentiation of the three "validity-spheres," which is central to modern culture as he reads it.[1]

But, one might object, how about the very widespread and popular *negative* theories of modernity, those that see it not as gain but as loss or decline? Curiously enough, they too have been acultural in their own way. To see this, we have to enlarge somewhat the description above. Instead of seeing the transformations as the unfolding of capacities, negative theories have often interpreted them as falling prey to dangers. But these have often been just as aculturally conceived. Modernity is characterized by the loss of the horizon, by a loss of roots, by the hubris which denies human limits, our dependence on history or God, which places unlimited confidence in the powers of frail human reason, by a trivializing self-indulgence which has no more stomach for the heroic dimension of life, and so on.

The overwhelming weight of interpretation in our culture, positive and negative, tends to the acultural. On the other side, the voices are fewer if powerful. Nietzsche, for instance, offers a reading of modern scientific culture which paints it as actuated by a specific constellation of values. And Max Weber, besides offering a theory of rationalization which can at any rate be taken as a steady, culture-independent force, also gave a reading of the Protestant ethic, as defined by a very particular set of religiomoral concerns, and which in turn helped to define modern culture. What are the reasons for this preponderance of acultural theory?

Before we begin to judge which view is right, some grounds stand out. Acultural theories in defining the crucial operation generally build in an evaluation. Modernity arises because we "come to see" something, or for the negative cases, because we lose something from view. Cultural theories by their very nature describe the change in terms of a contrast between constellations, before and after, which will not normally be *defined* evaluatively. This is not to say that any ulterior judgement of value between cultures is ruled out. Quite the contrary, I believe. But the transformation is not defined in these terms.

Now we Westerners have been living the transition to modernity for some centuries out of the civilization we used to call Christendom. It is hard to live through a change of this moment without being partisan, and in this spirit we quite naturally reach for explanations that are immediately evaluative, on one side or the other.

Indeed, since a cultural theory supposes the point of view in which we see our own culture as one among others, and this is at best a recent acquisition in our civilization, it is not at all surprising that the first accounts of revolutionary change were acultural. For the most part our ancestors looked on other civilizations as made up of barbarians, or infidels, or savages. It would have been absurd to expect the contemporaries of the French Revolution, on either side of the political divide, to have seen this as a cultural shift, when the very idea of cultural pluralism was just dawning in the writings of, e.g., Herder.

But even when this standpoint becomes more easily available, we are drawn by our partisan attachments to neglect it. This is partly because an immediately evaluative explanation (on the right side) is more satisfying: we tend to want to glorify modernity, or vilify it. And it is partly because we fear that a cultural theory might make value judgements impossible. This latter notion is, I believe, a mistake, as I mentioned above. Full understanding may not be incompatible with judgement. We don't need to agree with Cortés and the Conquistadores and conclude that the Aztecs served the devil; we can come to a deeper and fairer understanding of what underlay their practice of human sacrifice, and still judge that it is well that that practice has ceased.[2] But still the belief that understanding impedes judgement is widespread, and this is grist to the acultural mill.

Which view is right? I don't think one can make an exclusive choice between them. Just relying on a cultural theory would make us neglect certain important facets of the transformation. For instance, modern science *has* a validity, and the accompanying technology an efficacy, that we have "come to see"; and all societies are sooner or later forced to acquire this efficacy, or be dominated by others (and hence have it imposed on them anyway).

But it would be equally wrong to think that we can make do with an acultural theory alone. It is not just that other facets of what we identify as modern, such as the tendency to try to split fact from value, or the decline of religious practice, are far from reposing on uncontestable truths which have finally been discovered—something one can claim, I would argue, for modern physics, for example. It is also that science itself has grown in the West in close symbiosis with a certain culture in my sense, i.e., a constellation of understandings of person, nature, society, and the good.

To rely on a purely acultural theory is to miss all this. One gets a distorted understanding of Western modernity in one of two ways: on one side, we misclassify certain changes, which ultimately reflect the culture peculiar to the modern West, as the product of an unproblematic discovery or the ineluctable consequence of some social change, like the introduction of technology. The decline in religious practice has frequently been seen in this light. This is the error of seeing everything modern as belonging to one Enlightenment package.

On the other side, we fail altogether to examine certain facets of the modern constellation, closely interwoven with our understandings of science and religion, that don't strike us as being part of the transformation to modernity. We don't identify them as among the spectacular changes which have produced contemporary civilization, and we often fail to see even that there have been changes, reading these facets falsely as perennial. Such is the usual fate of those, largely implicit, understandings of human agency that I want to group under the term "modern identity," such as, e.g., the various forms of modern inwardness. We all too easily imagine that people have always seen themselves as we do, e.g., in respect of dichotomies like inward/outward. And we thus utterly miss the role these new understandings have played in the rise of Western modernity.

And so a purely acultural theory distorts and impoverishes our understanding of ourselves, both through misclassification (the Enlightenment package error), and through too narrow a focus. But its effects on our understanding of other cultures is even more devastating. The belief that modernity comes from one single universally applicable operation imposes a falsely uniform pattern on the multiple encounters of non-Western cultures with the exigencies of science, technology, and industrialization. As long as we are bemused by the Enlightenment package, we will believe that they all *have* to undergo a certain range of cultural changes, drawn from our experience, e.g., "secularization" or the growth of atomistic forms of self-identification. As long as we leave our own notions of identity unexamined, we will fail to see how theirs differ and how this difference crucially conditions the way in which they integrate the universal features of "modernity."

In short, exclusive reliance on an acultural theory unfits us for what is perhaps the most important task of social sciences in our day: understanding the full gamut of alternative modernities that are in the making in different parts of the world. It locks us into an ethnocentric prison, condemned to project our own forms onto everyone else, and blissfully unaware of what we are doing.

I realize that there are a lot of far-reaching claims in the above paragraphs. I can't hope to redeem them all here (or perhaps anywhere). All I shall try to do is illustrate them with an example I mentioned above: the facet of the modern identity concerned with inwardness.[3]

In our languages of self-understanding, the opposition "inside/outside" plays an important role. We think of our thoughts and feelings as "within" us. Or else we think of our capacities or potentialities as "inner," awaiting the development which will manifest them or realize them in the public world. The unconscious is for us within, and we think of the depths of the unsaid, the unsayable, the powerful inchoate feelings and affinities and fears that fight for the control of our lives, as inner. We are creatures with inner depths, with partly unexplored and dark interiors. We all feel the force of Conrad's master image in *Heart of Darkness*.

People didn't always think of themselves in this way. In particular, the notion of inner depths would have been strange to many other cultures, including those of the premodern West. Our inwardness is connected, I believe, to another feature, that we think of ourselves as "selves." This is to say not that others didn't have and use the reflexive pronoun but that there is a peculiar usage involved in describing the human agent as "a" self or "the" self, with the definite or indefinite article. This seemingly insignificant linguistic shift, which is peculiar to modernity, reflects something rather important about us.

Why is this expression so important for us? I think this is of a piece with our use of the "I" and the "ego" (our latinate translation of what for Freud was simply "das Ich"). We use the reflexive expression, or the term for self-reference, because this brings out what for us are the essential powers of human agency. These in our conception are connected to reflexivity or the first-person stance.

A person's perspective on himself is different from that of an observer. This banality is central to human life. Things look different from the first-person perspective, and not just in this or that case but systematically. The issue I'm pointing to between modern and, e.g., ancient civilization concerns what you make of this. We make a lot of it because we have come to believe that the important human capacities can only be realized by cultivating this perspective, by focusing on and developing features that become salient only in this perspective. And this in more than one way. I want to examine two here which I think are important to my main theme: self-control and self-exploration.

Self-control is a basic theme of our whole moral tradition. Plato speaks of the good man as being "master of himself."[4] He remarks himself how paradoxical this can sound. Mastery is a two-place relation. So mastery of oneself must mean that something higher in one controls the lower, in fact, that reason controls the desires. From Plato through the Stoics into the Renaissance and right to the modern day, this mastery of reason remains a recognizable ideal, even though it is contested in modern civilization in a way it doesn't seem to have been among the ancients.

But something very important happens to this tradition during the seventeenth century that alters it quite fundamentally. The understanding of what it is for reason to be master shifts. For Plato, reason in us is the capacity which enables us to see the order of things, to grasp the Ideas, and their ordering for the best, which latter insight he captures with the famous image of the Idea of the Good. For reason to rule in us is for us to be moved by this vision, to want to imitate and realize the good which it reveals to us—something that Plato thinks we cannot help but want once we see it. In a sense, we are always moved by the Good. Only when desire is on top do we have only a dim and confused perception of it. To be ruled by reason, in contrast, is to have a clear vision; it is to be ruled by that vision. One might almost say that on this view one's action is under the hegemony of the order of things itself.

Reason, considered as a property of human thoughts and desires is understood substantively. That is, our being rational just *is* our having the substantively correct vision of things. The latter is criterial of the former. From Plato's point of view, it makes no sense to imagine a perfectly rational person who would nevertheless have quite erroneous views about the order of things or the morally good; for instance, who might believe in a kind of Democritan universe of accidentally concatenating atoms or might believe that the end of life was accumulating power or wealth.

The Stoics challenged many aspects of the Platonic philosophy, notably the prime importance it gives to the theoretic vision of the truth and its soul/body dualism. But they retain the view that the mastery of reason involves the mastery of a certain vision. Here it is a vision of the order of goods we can seek; it is one that concerns purely practical reason. Which is not to say that the grasp of a cosmic order didn't also play an important role for the Stoics. The wise man sees all things as disposed by the providence of God, and for that reason is perfectly consenting to the order of events however they fall out. But in the end, the key practical insights concern what is worth desiring and what isn't. And just as with Plato, for reason to rule desire is for desire to be reshaped by the vision of order. As Plato puts it in the *Symposium,* the love which impels us toward perfection ceases to focus on imperfect copies of its real goal and comes to center on the unchanging and true. In the Stoic version, our passions disappear altogether, because at base they are nothing but false opinions couched in affect, as it were, to the effect that things are to be loved and feared that reason shows to be worthless.

Now to show the contrast with the modern age, we can look at what Descartes did with a doctrine and language which was drawn from the Stoics. Descartes's conception of the mastery of reason, as he develops it in his correspondence with Elisabeth and his *Traité des Passions* (1649), is radically altered. It is not the hegemony of a certain vision but the direct domination of one faculty over another: reason instrumentalizes the passions.

Thus Descartes gives a quite novel theory of the passions of his famous treatise. They are not understood in the Stoic way as opinions but are explained purely functionally in terms of their role in the maintenance of the substantial union of soul and body that God has designed for us. Rational mastery consists simply in our being able to control them so that they serve only these proper functions, so that they function, in other words, as instruments of our purposes as soul/body unions and don't escape from our power and subvert these ends. Rational mastery is instrumental control.

So Descartes, in contrast to the Stoics, doesn't call on us to get rid of our passions. On the contrary, he admires "les grandes âmes" who "ont des raisonnements si forts et si puissants que, bien qu'elles aient aussi des passions et même souvent de plus violentes que celles du commun, leur raison demeure néanmoins la maîtresse."[5] The idea that our passions might not only be strong but even "violent" is not only unthinkable from a Stoic perspective but shocking even for those other strands of traditional ethical thought which didn't accept the extreme Stoic goal of a complete liberation from passion. But it makes sense from the new Cartesian perspective, where what matters is instrumental control. If this is what mastery means then the strength of the subordinate element is no problem; indeed, the stronger it is, the better, as long as it is properly steered by reason.

This new idea of the mastery of reason went along with a changed conception of reason itself. Descartes no longer accepts the substantive notion of Plato. Reason is now defined procedurally. The goal of theoretical reason is science, and science is defined by Descartes in terms of certainty. But certainty is generated by a certain procedure. We have to organize our thoughts so as to achieve clarity and distinctness in our ideas.

The Platonic notion of an order of Ideas in the cosmos is utterly abandoned. This couldn't survive the Galilean revolution that Descartes espoused. But Descartes puts in its place, as it were, the goal of an order of representations in the mind. On the order of deployment of our ideas hangs their certainty and thus science. This order, however, is constructed. One of the instructions in the *Discours* tells us to conduct our thoughts so as to build from the simpler to the more complex, "et supposant même de l'ordre entre ceux qui ne se précédent pas les uns les autres."[6]

Rationality is here being defined by a certain manner of thinking, regardless of the substantive beliefs which emerge from it. Of course, Descartes holds that this procedure will result in substantively true beliefs about the world. But this is something which has to be established. Indeed, it is one of the most important goals of Descartes's philosophy to establish it. We make the link between procedure and truth with the proof that we are the creatures of a veracious God. The procedure is not *defined* as the one which leads to substantive truth. It could have been leading us entirely astray if we had been victims of a malicious demon. Rationality is now an internal property of subjective thinking, rather than consisting in its vision of reality. In making this shift, of course, Descartes is articulating what has become the standard modern view. Despite the wide disagreements over the nature of the procedure and despite all the scorn that has been heaped on him from the dominant empiricist trend in modern scentific culture, the conception of reason remains procedural.

Now this shift, at once in the conception of mastery and in that of reason, bespeaks a quite different notion of the human agent. And once more, what is involved comes out very clearly in Descartes. Reason and human excellence requires a stance of disengagement. "Disengagement" here is a term of art, meaning a stance toward something which might otherwise serve to define our identity or purposes, whereby we separate ourselves from it by defining it as at best of instrumental significance.

In this sense Descartes calls on the enquiring mind to disengage from the cosmos. This can no longer be considered a meaningful order, in relation to which our paradigm purposes are to be defined, as with Plato. It is a neutral domain of mechanical movement, whose laws have to be adequately represented in the mind. But we have to disengage also from our own bodily nature, not just because the body is another part of the "external" universe but also because in order to achieve the proper rational mastery, the soul must instrumentalize the passions, as we have seen. The proper stance to self and nature is one of disengagement.

Descartes's disengaged subject, like his procedural notion of rationality, is not just an idiosyncratic conception. For all the challenges and disagreements to his dualism in modern thought, with the central idea of disengagement he was articulating one of the most important developments of the modern era. Recent research has shown the tremendous importance of the mode of thinking roughly designated "neo-Stoic" in the late sixteenth and early seventeenth centuries, associated with Justus Lipsius and in France with Guillaume duVair. As the name implies, these thinkers were inspired by classical Stoicism, but with a number of important differences. These included not only soul/body dualism, but also an increasing emphasis on a model of self-mastery that prepares the Cartesian transposition to the model of instrumental control.

More significantly, neo-Stoicism was bound up with a broad movement among political and military elites toward a wider and more rigorous application of new forms of discipline in a host of fields: in first place the military, of course, as one sees with the reforms of William of Orange, which had world-historical consequences in the Netherlands' revolt against Spain, but also later in various dimensions of the civil administration, which grew with the new aspirations and the capacities of the "absolutist" state, regulating labor, health conditions, mores.[7] The rise and spread of these new forms of discipline has been described in very evocative terms by Michel Foucault in his *Surveiller et Punir.*[8]

What one finds running through all the aspects of this constellation—the new philosophy, the methods of administration and military organization, the new spirit of government, and methods of discipline—is the growing ideal of a human agent who is able to remake himself by methodical and disciplined action. What this calls for is the ability to take an instrumental stance to one's given properties, desires, inclinations, tendencies, habits of thought, and feeling so that they can be *worked on,* doing away with some and strengthening others, until one meets the desired specifications. My suggestion is that Descartes's picture of the disengaged subject articulates the understanding of agency that is most congenial to this whole movement and is part of the grounds for its great impact in his century and beyond.

Where it was heading beyond can perhaps be seen if we consider Locke's views as representing the next stage. Locke develops a view of the subject and his formation in which in principle everything is as it were up for grabs, susceptible in principle of being shaped in the direction desired. The mind is a tabula rasa. There are no innate ideas, and morality cannot be grounded on an inborn tendency to the good. We have to be shaped by education, and this means that we can also become, at least to a certain degree, self-shapers. The ideal stance of the rational subject is thus not to identify with any of the tendencies he finds in himself, which can only be the deposits of tradition and authority, but to be ready to break and remake these habitual responses according to his own goals, as far as this is possible.[9]

The Lockean subject is in this respect something quite new, and deeply unsettling from a traditional perspective. He *is* essentially none of his properties. What defines him is the abstract power to remake these properties. There are empirical limits, of course, to this remaking in any given case, but there are none set by his identity. What does essentially define him is self-consciousness. And that is why Locke can define the issue of identity in the peculiar (but immensely influential) way that he does, in terms of my awareness of my continuity.[10]

Once again, many people have taken issue with Locke's philosophy, but this picture of what we might call the punctual subject has been of immense importance way beyond the ranks of those Enlightenment reformers and their spiritual heirs who believe in the total malleability of man. Its strength comes from the central place of the disengaged, disciplinary stance to the self in our culture. So that even those who reject many of Locke's doctrines feel the power of this model. We can see it in one way in some contemporary discussions of identity.[11] It is the basis, I believe, of the mature Freudian conception of the ego, which belongs to the "structural" model. This ego is in essence a pure steering mechanism, devoid of instinctual force of its own (though it must draw power from the id to function). Its job is to maneuver through the all but unnavigable obstacle course set by id, superego, and external reality. Its powers are incomparably less than Locke's punctual self, but like its ancestor, it is fundamentally a disengaged agent of instrumental reason.

Thus, if we follow the theme of self-control through the vicissitudes of our Western tradition, we find a very profound transmutation, all the way from the hegemony of reason as a vision of cosmic order to the notion of a punctual disengaged subject exercising instrumental control. And this, I would argue, helps explain why we think of ourselves as "selves" today.

The crucial capacity for the great ancient moralists was that of seeing the order in the cosmos (for Plato) or in the priority of human goals (for the Stoics). Introspection had no significance for the first and wasn't thought to be crucial for the second. The Stoics give us an argument about reason, nature, self-sufficiency to convince us that we shouldn't put any store by ordinary satisfactions; they don't ask us to examine ourselves.

By contrast, the modern ideal of disengagement requires a reflexive stance. We have to turn inward and become aware of our own activity and of the processes that form us. We have to take charge of constructing our own representation of the world, which otherwise goes on without order and consequently without science; we have to take charge of the processes by which associations form and shape our character and outlook. Disengagement demands that we stop simply living in the body or within our traditions or habits and, by making them objects for us, subject them to radical scrutiny and remaking.

Of course, the great classical moralists also call on us to stop living in unreflecting habit and usage. But their reflection turns us toward an objective order. Modern disengagement by contrast calls us to a separation from ourselves through self-objectification. This is an operation which can only be carried out in the first-person perspective. It doesn't tell us, like Stoicism, to be aware of what is worth while for humans as such or, like Plato, to focus on the properties of reason and desire, and their relation to what we know about the happy life. It calls on me to be aware of *my* activity of thinking or *my* processes of habituation so as to disengage from them and objectify them. Indeed, the whole (strange and ultimately questionable) picture of myself as objectified nature which this modern turn has made familiar to us only became available through that special kind of reflexive stance I am calling disengagement. We had to be trained (and bullied) into making it not only, of course, through imbibing doctrines but much more through all the disciplines that have been inseparable from our modern way of life, the disciplines of self-control in the economic, moral, and sexual fields. This vision is the child of a peculiar reflexive stance, and that is why we who have been formed to understand and judge ourselves in its terms naturally describe ourselves with the reflexive expressions that belong to this stance: the "self," the "I," the "ego."

That at least is part of the story. Another is that this self, which emerges from the objectification of and separation from our given nature cannot be identified with anything in this given. It can't be easily conceived as just another piece of the natural world. It is hard for us simply to *list* souls or minds *alongside* whatever else there is. This is the source of a continuing philosophical discomfort in modern times for which there is naturally no analogue among the ancients. Various solutions have been tried—reductionism, "transcendental" theories, returns to dualism—but the problem continues to nag us as unsolved. I don't want to try to tackle this problem here. My point is rather that this ungrounded "extraworldly" status of the objectifying subject accentuates the existing motivation to describe it as a self. All other appellations seem to place it somewhere in the roster of things, as one among others. The punctual agent seems to be nothing else but a "self," an "I."

Here we see the origin of one of the great paradoxes of modern philosophy. The philosophy of disengagement and objectification has helped to create a picture of man, at its most extreme in certain forms of materialism, from which the last vestiges of subjectivity seem to have been expelled. It is a picture of man from a completely third-person perspective. The paradox is that this severe outlook is connected with, indeed, based on, according a central place to the first-person stance. Radical objectivity is only intelligible and accessible through radical subjectivity. This paradox has, of course, been much commented on by Heidegger, for instance, in his critique of subjectivism, and by Merleau-Ponty. Modern naturalism can never be the same once one sees this connection, as both these philosophers argue. But for those who haven't seen it, the problem of the "I" returns, like a repressed thought, as a seemingly insoluble puzzle.[12]

Thus for us the subject is a self in a way he couldn't be for the ancients. To see the difference, we have to distinguish between ordinary reflexivity and a more radical kind. Ancient moralists frequently formulated the injunction "take care of yourself," as Foucault has recently reminded us.[13] And Epictetus reminds us that all that really matters to us is the state of our own hegemonikon, or ruling part, sometimes translated "mind" or "will." And, of course, what underlies all these admonitions is the basic fact that only I can cure my own soul or bring myself to virtue.

But this reflexivity of concern was not radical, in the sense I want to use that word here. By that I mean that what we are called upon to take heed of and concern ourselves with is not those features of ourselves that are available only in the first-person perspective. The ancient call to take care of oneself is in this analogous to an appeal someone might make today in the same terms to a busy executive to stop killing himself with overwork. The factors the addressee would have to heed to obey this injunction are all within the scope of a discipline, namely medicine, which doesn't give any special place to the first-person perspective. Similarly, the lore that an ancient would have to turn to if he wanted to obey the injunction addressed to him would be wisdom about the soul, available in Plato, Aristotle, Chrysippus, without any special reliance on the first-person standpoint.

That's what makes the striking difference with the follower of Descartes, Locke, Kant, or just about anyone in the modern world. The turn to oneself is now also and inescapably a turn to oneself in the first-person perspective, a turn to the self as a self. That is what I mean by radical reflexivity. Because we are so deeply embedded in it, we cannot but reach for reflexive language.[14]

But this is also what underlies modern inwardness. What we turn to in radical reflexivity seems to demand description as something "inner." This spatial metaphor is irresistible to describe the "space" opened by self-scrutiny. The stance of radical reflexivity opens up, we might say, a certain kind of inwardness, which comes to play a role in our lives it didn't before.

The transition from Plato to Augustine illustrates this.[15] Plato has no use for the language of inwardness. True, he speaks of our capacities as being "in" us. And the obvious distinction between thoughts and feelings that I express and those I keep to myself was carried in ancient cultures, as in most others, by the contrast inner/outer. But the suggestion, which seems so obvious to us, that in turning away from bodily things to those of the soul we are turning inward seems to be absent. Plato doesn't speak that way.

In part this connects with what we were looking at in the previous section: that the lore of the soul gave no special status to the first-person perspective and that the moral sources were external. The turning is captured in the powerful image that Plato uses in the *Republic,* where the soul swivels around to direct its gaze toward the illuminated reality, the Ideas.[16] It is not self-focus but attention to true reality that makes for wisdom and justice.

The turn to a language of inwardness comes with Augustine. Although he shares much of the same metaphysical beliefs as Plato, he does constantly speak of turning inward. "Noli foras ire; in interiore homine habitat veritas."[17] Why this shift of language occurs is a difficult and deep question, but I believe that it has a lot to do with the fact that Augustine found a crucial use for the first-person perspective.

Augustine holds that we discover God within ourselves. God is the "light which lighteth every man that cometh into the world," as he quotes from John's Gospel (1.9). But what he means by "within" is that one encounters God in one's own presence to self. That is because God is not only the maker of heaven and earth, whose work can be seen in the cosmos; he is also the power that continually sustains me as a spiritual being. He is at the foundation of my power to think, know, and love. God vivifies the soul, as the soul does the body.[18] But just as to see the evidence of God's creative work in the universe, we have to turn our thoughts to the frame of the world, so to become aware of God as the foundation of our own powers, we have to focus reflexively on these powers. We don't discover God through this route by considering human powers as such impersonally. Rather, each in the awareness of his own can come to see that they draw on a higher power. Radical reflexivity is essential to this path toward God.

And that is the point of saying that God is found within. He is found in the intimacy of self-presence. He is "intimior intimo meo et superior summo meo."[19] That is why Augustine begins so many of his arguments for the existence of God with the cogito, anticipating Descartes. The cogito is the argument that essentially has to be made in the first-person perspective. It is an argument that only goes through (if it does) because it is about myself.[20]

Augustine's inward turn was tremendously influential in the West. At first it inaugurated a family of forms of Christian spirituality, which continued throughout the Middle Ages and flourished again in the Renaissance. But then later this turn takes on secularized forms. We go inward, but not necessarily to find God; we go to discover or impart some order, some meaning, or some justification to our lives. In retrospect, we can see Augustine's *Confessions* as the first great work in a genre that includes Rousseau's work of the same title, Goethe's *Dichtung und Wahrheit,* Wordsworth's *Prelude*—except that the Bishop of Hippo antedates his followers by more than a millennium.

Augustine's turn was obviously built on by Descartes, so that the Church father helped to lay the distant groundwork for modern disengaged self-control. But it is clear from what I have just been saying that he is also the origin point of another kind of inwardness, that of self-exploration.

To the extent that this form of self-exploration becomes central to our culture, another stance of radical reflexivity becomes of crucial importance to us alongside that of disengagement. It is different and in some ways antithetical to disengagement. Rather than objectifying our own nature, and hence classing it as irrelevant to our identity, it consists in exploring what we are in order to establish this identity. Because the assumption behind modern self-exploration is that we don't already know who we are.

There is a turning point here whose representative figure is perhaps Montaigne. There is some evidence that when he embarked on his reflections, he shared the traditional view that these should serve to recover contact with the permanent, stable, unchanging core of being in each of us. This is the virtually unanimous direction of ancient thought: beneath the changing and shifting desires in the unwise soul and over against the fluctuating fortunes of the external world, our true nature, reason, provides a foundation, unwavering and constant.

For someone who holds this, the modern problem of identity remains unintelligible. Our only search can be to discover within us the one universal human nature. But things didn't work out this way for Montaigne. There is some evidence that when he sat down to write and turned to himself, he experienced a terrifying inner instability. "Mon esprit . . . faisant le cheval échappé . . . m'enfante tant de chimères et monstres fantasques les uns sur les autres, sans ordre et sans propos."[21] His response was to observe and catalogue his thoughts, feelings, responses ("j'ai commencé de les mettre en rolle").[22] And from this emerged a quite different stand toward the impermanence and uncertainty of human life, an acceptance of limits, which drew on both Epicurean and Christian sources.

It is not that the aspiration to stability is altogether abandoned. Rather, Montaigne comes to a certain equilibrium even within the ever changing by identifying and coming to terms with the patterns which represent his own particular way of living in flux. So although "nous n'avons aucune communication à l'estre,"[23] Montaigne sought, and found some inner peace in, his "forme maistresse."[24] Self-knowledge is the indispensable key to self-acceptance. Coming to be at home within the limits of our condition presupposes that we grasp these limits, that we learn to draw their contours from within, as it were.

But self-knowledge can't mean here just impersonal lore about human nature, as it could for Plato. Each of us has to discover his own form. We are not looking for the universal nature, but each for his own being. "Il n'est personne, s'il s'escoute, qui ne descouvre en soy une forme sienne, une forme maistresse."[25] So Montaigne's study has to be essentially reflexive in a strong sense. "Le monde regarde tousjours vis à vis; moy, je replie ma veue au dedans, je la plante, je l'amuse là. Chacun regarde devant soy; moy, je regarde dedans moy."[26]

The search for the self in order to come to terms with oneself, which Montaigne inaugurates, has become one of the fundamental themes of our modern culture, or so I would claim. His goal still resonates with us: "C'est une absolue perfection, et comme divine, de sçavoir jouyr loiallement de son estre."[27] And this gives us another reason to think of ourselves in reflexive terms. There is a question about ourselves, which we roughly gesture at with the term "identity" and which cannot be sufficiently answered with any general doctrine of human nature. The search for identity can be seen as the search for what I essentially am. But this can no longer be sufficiently defined in terms of some universal description of human agency as such, as soul or reason or will. There still remains a question about me, and that is why I think of myself as a self. This word now circumscribes an area of questioning. It designates the kind of being of which this question of identity can be asked.

I have been exploring a facet of the modern identity, our senses of inwardness and the self. I have been trying to offer a "cultural" account of them, in the terms of this paper. That is, I have connected their development to a skein of particular conceptions of the human good and the corresponding notions of human agency. In a nutshell, I have been arguing that our modern ideas of inwardness and the self are connected with views of human excellence and fulfilment which privilege activities inseparable from radical reflexivity, specifically those of disengaged self-objectification and self-control on one hand and the range of forms of self-exploration on the other, which have ramified through the Romantic period and beyond and have become deeply intricated with our notions of personal fulfilment, of artistic originality, and of the creative imagination.

I hope that the advantages of such a theory begin to suggest themselves even if mine may be wrong in detail. In looking at Western modernity not as the result of a culture-neutral operation but in terms of the specific cultural constellation it is organized around, we see it from a different angle, so to speak. And from this angle, things come to light which are otherwise cast in shadow. Modern inwardness is not a simple phenomenon but at least double. Modern self-exploration is in some senses at odds with self-control. Self-objectification tends to occlude what self-control tries to articulate. The one seeks to grasp us in the general categories of science, the other to allow our particularity to find expression. The difference was already prefigured in diverging uses of "I" in Montaigne and Descartes.

The latter's "I" is anyone's; the former is speaking about "moi, Michel de Montaigne."

There is a struggle in our civilization between different variants of these two orientations, between the protagonists of objectifying control and those who protest at the price it exacts in occluding and silencing particularity, our inner nature, and hence also our responses to nature without. This struggle is often identified as that between the proponents of modernity and its critics. That is how it looks from the perspective of an acultural theory. But what stands out from my perspective is the connections and affinities between the two sides, their common roots and kinship as forms of modern inwardness. The idea of lining up behind some global judgement about modernity, for or against, begins to seem much less plausible from this cultural perspective. And this, I would argue, is one mark of its superiority. A more rounded view of our culture shows the deeper connections between rival spiritual outlooks, which the partisan views ignore or tear apart. Above all, these partisan acultural views fail to measure how inescapable this modern identity is for us, how much of it is involved even in what is seen as the most radical opposition to it. But at the same time it shows that the unreserved partisans of modernity who define it just in terms of disengaged control are far from an adequate understanding of what they're involved in.

At the same time, a better understanding of our Western modernity should enable us better to recognize the alternative modernities which are developing in other parts of the world, to free them from the distorting grid of a bogus universality and us from our ethnocentric prison.

Notes

1. See *Theorie des kommunikativen Handelns* (Frankfurt, 1981), vol. 1, chapters 1 and 2. See especially pp. 254 ff. for Habermas's arguments against a nonevaluative theory of rationalization. English transl., *The Theory of Communicative Action* (Boston, 1984), vol. 1, pp. 180 ff.

2. I have argued this point further in "Understanding and Ethnocentricity," in *Philosophy and the Human Sciences* (Cambridge, 1985), and also in "Explanation and Practical Reason" (forthcoming).

3. I have developed this discussion more extensively in my book *Sources of the Self* (Cambridge, Mass., 1989), part 2.

4. *The Republic,* 430e.

5. "Those great souls whose reasoning is so strong and powerful that, although they also have passions, and often even more violent passions than the common sort, their reason remains nevertheless master." Letter to Elisabeth of 18 May 1645.

6. *Discours,* part 2, pp. 18 f. "And by supposing some order even among objects that have no natural order of precedence," *The Philosophical Writings of Descartes,* trans. John Cottingham, Robert Stoothoff, and Dugald Murdoch (Cambridge, 1988), vol. 1, p. 120. See also the *Regulae,* rule 10, which enjoins on us the method of "constantly following an order, whether it is actually present in the matter in question or is ingeniously read into it," *Philosophical Writings,* vol. 1, p. 35.

7. This whole development is very well described in Gerhard Oestreich, *Neo-Stoicism and the Early Modern State* (Cambridge, 1983).

8. Paris, 1975.

9. See James Tully, "Governing Conduct," in E. Leites, ed., *Conscience and Casuistry in Early Modern Europe* (Cambridge, 1986). I am indebted to James Tully's work for much of my understanding not only of Locke but of the whole movement of modern politics and thought that starts with the neo-Stoics and lays the groundwork for Locke.

10. Tully, "Governing Conduct."

11. See, e.g., Derek Parfit, *Reasons and Persons* (Oxford, 1984).

12. See, e.g., D. Hofstadter and D. Dennett, *The Mind's I* (New York, 1981).

13. "Epimeleia heautou." See *Le Souci de Soi* (Paris, 1984).

14. Of course, ours is not the only civilization which has found a use for reflexive words. Hindu and Buddhist thought also is concerned with the self, at least if the majority of translations from Sanscrit, Pali, and other relevant languages are not wholly misleading. And in relation to the fundamental ideas of these religious traditions, this is perhaps understandable. If the aim is to go beyond self, to take us beyond where we usually understand ourselves to be in virtue of our having a first-person perspective, either by showing the self to be illusory (Buddhism) or by looking for an identification of the "I" with some greater reality (as we see in at least some versions of Hinduism), then plainly reflexive language is going to be indispensable. It defines here what we're negating, and in the nature of things there is no alternative way to say what we aspire to. It goes without saying, of course, that these terms will be used in very different ways from the modern West.

15. I have dealt with this at greater length in my "Humanismus und moderne Identität," in Krzysztof Michalski, ed., *Der Mensch in den modernen Wissenschaften* (Stuttgart, 1985).

16. 518e.

17. "Do not go outwards; return within yourself. In the inward man dwells truth." *De vera Religione,* 39.72.

18. "Ut vita carnis anima est, ita beata vita hominis Deus est," *De Civitate Dei,* XIX.26; "as the life of the flesh is the soul, so the blessed life of man is God," *The City of God,* trans. Marcus Dods (New York, 1950), p. 707. See also *The Confessions of St. Augustine,* trans. John K. Ryan (Garden City, N.Y., 1960), VII.1.2, where God is described as "the life of my life" [vita vitae mei].

19. "More inward than my inmost self, and superior to my highest being," *Confessions,* III.6.11.

20. For Augustine's frequent invocations of the cogito argument, see E. Gilson, *The Christian Philosophy of Saint Augustine* (London, 1961), pp. 41–43. I have discussed the inward turn in Augustine at greater length in my "Humanismus und moderne Identität."

21. *Essais,* I.8. "My spirit . . . playing the skittish and loosebroken jade . . . begets in me so many extravagant Chimeraes, and fantasticall monsters, so orderlesse, and without any reason, one hudling upon an other," *The Essays of Montaigne,* Florio translation (New York, 1933), p. 24. I have drawn on the interesting discussion in M. Screech, *Montaigne and Melancholy* (London, 1984).

22. *Essais,* I.8. "I have begun to keepe a register of them."

23. *Essais,* II.12. "We have no communication with being," Florio translation, p. 545.

24. *Essais,* I.50. "My Mistris forme," Florio translation, p. 261.

25. *Essais,* III.2. "There is no man (if he listen to himselfe) that doth not discover in himselfe a peculiar forme, a sawying forme," Florio translation, p. 731.

26. *Essais,* II.17. "The world lookes ever for-right, I turne my sight inward, there I fix it, there I ammuse it. Every man lookes before himselfe, I looke within my selfe," Florio translation, p. 597.

27. *Essais,* III.13. "It is an absolute perfection, and as it were divine for a man to know how to enjoy his being loyally," Florio translation, p. 1013.

II

Theoretical Issues

4

Reflections on Philosophical Method from an Analytic Point of View

Ernst Tugendhat

Translated by William Rehg

Does philosophy have a method? If we cast about in the history of philosophy or even in current philosophy, we find very little by way of answer to this question. Perhaps this is because in philosophy one is always on the lookout for new territory, and thus considers it ill-advised to slip into a methodological corset in advance. On the other hand, one's own conduct must then remain peculiarly opaque. Yet just as philosophical procedure is itself always provisional, so it should likewise be possible to reflect on that procedure in a provisional way. In the present essay I would like to present a few reflections on how this question might be approached from the perspective of analytic philosophy.

The question concerning philosophy's method undoubtedly presupposes a definite idea about what philosophy is, and that alone could already appear overly ambitious and controversial. However, I think one can name two aspects that were largely, if never exclusively, constitutive for philosophy and its difference from the sciences since Socrates and Plato. First, philosophy has always been concerned with conceptual clarifications. As classic examples I can mention the Platonic dialogues, Aristotelian metaphysics, and Hegel's logic. In contradistinction to the sciences, which aim at statements (and mostly generalizing ones) about the world, these clarifications do not have a merely secondary, preparatory character. Second, philosophy was always concerned with the whole, the totality, where this is not the totality of beings or objects but the whole of our understanding.

If we put these two aspects together, the second yields the particular concepts philosophy would like to clarify. In contrast to "empirical" concepts, these concepts belong to the whole of our understanding. We can also distinguish with Kant between the empirical questions of science and concepts belonging to the "conditions for the possibility" of experience. This suggests that we view scientific experience as in turn embedded in the whole of prescientific experience. Husserl introduced the term "lifeworld" to designate this whole. The concepts in which philosophy is interested would then be those that are constitutive for the lifeworld as such, which is to say the concepts that are constitutive for our understanding as a whole, and hence those we must "always already" understand, whatever else we understand.

Still and all, this explanation is typically vague. One might well doubt whether it provides a criterion for distinguishing philosophical from empirical concepts. This becomes clear when we start to look for examples. We could, say, begin as Kant does: all the experiences we have occur in *space* and *time.* And we might go on to note, for example, how we also understand what it means that something has *existence* in space and time; we have a concept of *objects* that exist in this way. At that point we could continue further in different directions. To mention just one of these, we might say we form *opinions* about these objects. We understand what it means that an opinion is *true* or *false.* We have a *language* with a determinate structure. We *judge, assert, question.* Yet we also *want* and *desire.* We *act* and *reflect.* We also understand what it means to speak with *others* or, to take more particular examples, to *request* something from someone or to *promise* someone something.

Must we not hesitate here? Does the concept of promising belong among philosophical concepts? According to the above approach, that would mean this concept is constitutive for our understanding as a whole. Is it true that we cannot understand ourselves without this concept? That evidently depends on how broadly we understand the "we" in "ourselves."

Now one could propose along with Kant that philosophical concepts be designated as those "given *a priori*."[1] Indeed, for individual cases even this criterion will not be able to dispel uncertainty about whether or not a concept such as that of promising should be included among philosophical concepts. Besides this, the concept of the a priori could prejudge the issue in certain respects in a way that is not self-evident. I shall return to this point later. Since my first concern is simply to gain some understanding of those criteria whose authority has largely dominated the history of philosophy since Socrates, the viewpoint of a priori givenness seems helpful. Connecting this with the above would then imply that those concepts conditioning our understanding as a whole are at the same time those one can designate in some sense as "given a priori." Indeed, this simply seems to explicate what was already presupposed when I contrasted these concepts with those that are empirically given.

The concept of the a priori has also always been connected with that of necessity. This aspect of necessity I likewise presupposed when I located the criterion for determining whether a concept is philosophical in the question whether we *can* conceive ourselves or our understanding without this concept. A priori concepts seem to be those that are *indispensable* for our understanding.

I can now take a first step toward the question concerning philosophical method by recalling Augustine's dictum about time, a passage Wittgenstein also took up in his *Philosophical Investigations* (sec. 89): "What, then, is time? If no one asks me, I know; if I want to explain it to someone who does ask me, I do not know."[2] The same seems to hold for all other a priori concepts, though not for empirical concepts. For all empirical concepts it seems to be characteristic, first, that someone can also not have them, i.e., not know what is meant by the corresponding word. Second, however, if someone knows what the word means, he can also always explain it without difficulty. For example, I do not know what is meant by the color word "sepia"; I know indeed there is this concept but am not familiar with it. I would not be able to recognize something as sepia-colored. However, whoever possesses this concept, which is to say, can recognize something of this color, can also explain it to someone else. This is not due to the particular circumstance that something directly recognizable in perception is involved. The one who knows what chess is can also explain the game to someone else. Or take a scientific concept such as gold. One cannot explain what gold is by presenting it to perception. Gold has a structure, and only those familiar with the corresponding systematic and causal relationships have the concept of gold. But if someone does have the concept, which is to say, can apply it, then he can also, when questioned, answer without difficulty. Just the reverse is true with the concept of time, as also with all the other concepts listed earlier. We understand what is meant by the word "time," we can readily and correctly employ the concepts of before and after to which this word refers, but when asked to explain it, we can answer only with difficulty.

The peculiarity Augustine pointed out does not, of course, consist in a paradox that one can both know and not know something. For Augustine employs the word "know" equivocally. In the first sense, knowing [*Wissen*] means being familiar with [*Kennen*], i.e., understanding or being able to employ the corresponding word. In the second sense, knowing means being able to give an account or explain. The difficulty Augustine pointed out consists in the fact that from the perspective of our usual empirical concepts, it appears surprising that there are concepts we can indeed understand but cannot easily explain, so that in such cases a separate investigation becomes necessary, to be exact, a specifically philosophical one.

The first philosopher to become aware of this was Socrates, that is to say, the young Plato. He raises questions about things we evidently "already" know (and thus know a priori) and that we apparently cannot explain simply because they have become too self-evident to us. Ever since then it has been clear that these peculiar concepts must be clarified in reflection, in the reflection on what has already been given us.

I can now turn to the question concerning philosophical method. The understanding of reflection, or philosophical method, will vary according to how one comprehends what is "already given" to us in our understanding. Aside from the quasi-deductive constructive method we find in the late Plato and German Idealism, there have been two answers to this question. The first, already represented in Plato and most extensively explicated by Husserl, is that of intuition. A priori concepts, like all concepts, are understood as essences that must be inwardly perceived. Now, to begin with, no one has succeeded in giving his metaphor of intellectual intuition a concrete sense and showing how such an inward perception supposedly occurs. Second, even if there were something like it, it could not be mediated intersubjectively. For philosophy as a communicative undertaking, therefore, the intuitive method would be altogether worthless.

The only alternative seems to be that of language analysis, especially as it has been developed by Wittgenstein. This approach begins with the assumption that every concept consists in the way a linguistic expression is used. The two ways of knowing that Augustine had in view, then, have the senses already anticipated above: the first stands for the ability to use the corresponding expression correctly, the second for the ability to explain its use to someone else. By stating how I would explain a conceptual term to someone who was not yet familiar with this word and also had nothing corresponding to it in another language, I give myself and others an account of what we "always already" know inexplicitly when we use the word without reflection. The explanation counts as successful only if it enables the one to whom we explain the word to use it correctly himself.

In the special case of the concept of time Wittgenstein described language games by which the words "before" and "after," as well as the series of words "now," "future," and "past" might be explained to a child.[3] The question as to how one might teach these words to a child is not based on any particular interest in learning psychology, and it is also unimportant whether children actually do learn these words in precisely this way. In these language games children are merely the placeholders for anyone who does not yet possess these concepts. It might be added in passing that children will naturally only be able to learn time words, for example, if they already have the ability for it, but that does not mean that this ability consists in an inner time consciousness. Analogously, a child will first be able to learn to count at a specific age, but that does not mean that this child then has a prelinguistic number consciousness, and thus a corresponding nonliguistic concept.

This notion of philosophical method—that the clarification of concepts consists in an explanation of how linguistic expressions are employed—is viewed by nonanalytic philosophers as a superficial conception of philosophy. A first objection holds that we cannot be concerned with mere words but, to speak with Husserl, with the things themselves. But what can be meant here by "things"? If we were dealing with scientific concepts the objection would be justified. In fact it would be absurd if one wanted to answer the question of what gold is by saying one must reflect on how we use the word. Here it is necessary to carry out empirical investigations, which is just what the demand to return to the things themselves means. But what sense could the analogous demand have in the case of a priori concepts? Evidently such a demand would have to lead us to postulate an internal-intellectual analogue to experience, and hence an inner experience, which is precisely what happened with Husserl.

A second objection holds that philosophy would perforce be mired in a peculiar conservatism if it merely stayed with what is linguistically given. However, it would be a misunderstanding to believe that the analytic conception of philosophy binds it to the accidents and limits of one's own language. Later I will briefly go into the hermeneutical character of analytic philosophy, which will show that this conception of philosophy is quite open to the recognition of one's own language as relative and limited, although the authority allowing one to recognize this can only be in each case another linguistic entity and not something extralinguistic.

A further objection charges that philosophy, so understood, seemingly becomes part of linguistics. Even apart from this objection, the question as to how philosophical semantics differs from linguistic semantics is important for bringing out the specifically philosophical character of this investigation of linguistic meaning. The difference can be elucidated with the help of the two aspects we have already seen are constitutive for philosophical method in general, whether one understands it as language analysis or not: first, the fact that philosophical method is reflective [or reflexive: *reflexiv*] and, second, the fact that it has to do with a clarification of concepts. The reflective character of the philosophical thematization of language resides first of all in its taking as theme the language "we" speak, and not *a* language we approach in an objectivating attitude as the language of *a* community of speakers. The objectivating linguistic attitude characteristically approaches one's own language as just one more language that can be thematized like any other. The hallmark of this objectivating semantics is that it answers the question concerning the meaning of the linguistic expressions of the given thematized language by using another language, normally its own, which then functions as a so-called metalanguage. But that means the language theorist must already have available the concept represented by the word in need of explanation. Hence the language theorist does not satisfy the requirement I established above for a philosophical explanation of a word, i.e., that such an explanation must proceed in a way that makes the use of the word comprehensible to someone who does not yet have available a corresponding word or group of words from another language. Hence the above-required move from the explanation of concepts back to that of words does not mean that the explanation (and consequently any explanation) of words now takes the *place* of concept clarification. Rather, it is always the concept that must be clarified by means of the ways of using the word. This fact, that the explanation of a word aims at the clarification of the corresponding concept, restricts what is conceived here as a theory of meaning. To be precise, it means that the use of a metalanguage is ruled out and the clarification of the meaning of a word of one's own language can no longer take place in a manner analogous to the clarification of foreign terms but merely amounts to making what one "already" understands explicable and thereby explicit. Later we will see that the reflective philosophical approach also differs from the objectivating linguistic one in how it thematizes foreign words.

A further difference between philosophical and linguistic semantics results from the fact that one must invent new words in philosophy, terminological expressions. Admittedly, this could be taken as an objection against the analytic approach as a whole, for why must philosophy invent new words if it does not have a language-independent thematic? In the first place, however, the concepts constitutive of our linguistic understanding can sometimes be apprehended not in individual words but only in linguistic structures. Thus the words "subject" and "object" were philosophical inventions that Aristotle needed in order to thematize the predicative structure of our understanding.

Yet a further circumstance, one I have so far neglected, is at least as important. Concepts are interdependent. This is especially true of those concepts thematized in philosophy, the very ones I first took as constitutive of our understanding as a whole. The use of the corresponding linguistic expressions thus forms a network. It is actually this network that philosophy has the task of clarifying. Moreover, in order to bring out such interconnections between concepts, philosophy must often construct artificial expressions, the explanation of which is then subject, of course, to the same conditions as hold for that of all other expressions.

Perhaps a further reason behind the low regard for analytic method is the fact that it appears so simple. In reality, it is an extraordinarily laborious undertaking that has brought even moderately definite results only in rare cases. The reason for the difficulty lies in the fact that the question about the meaning of a philosophically interesting word can be answered through a definition only in exceptional cases. An example of such a straightforward case is the explanation Plato worked out in the *Theaetetus* in response to the question of what we mean by knowledge. According to this explanation we say of a person *S* that *S* knows *p* if three conditions are satisfied: *S* believes that *p*, *p* is true, and *S* has sufficient grounds for *p*. Although this answer that Plato reached by the end of the dialogue appeared unsatisfactory in his own eyes, it remained nonetheless definitive up to Russell and did not become problematic again until very recently.[4] In any event, even to reach an answer in this simple case, Plato had to write a longer dialogue. What makes this case so simple and at the same time allows it to appear so untypical is the fact that it rests on another concept, that of opinion—a concept that has yet to receive a satisfactory explanation—which the case merely modifies through two simple additional qualifications.

Why is it in general so difficult to adequately explain a philosophically relevant word? That I can only give an unsatisfactory answer to this indicates how little this philosophical method has so far progressed. The fundamental problems one confronts here can only be seen through the further clarification of individual concepts.

An important aspect that generally excludes a definitional explanation is the previously mentioned fact that a priori concepts represent points of connection in a complex network. Thus if one wants to give an adequate explanation of "morality," one must consider a range of word groups such as "good"/"bad," "ought"/"must," "guilt"/"indignation," and so on. On the one hand, these groups display certain interrelationships with each other; on the other hand, they are part of yet further interrelationships. Naturally one could give a simple definition of morality, but that would then prove inadequate and unproductive for dealing with further possible questions.

A further reason why definitions are not possible in most cases is that we run into limits where a word simply can no longer be explained through further words. As Wittgenstein has shown for "before" and "after," recourse to a language game can help in many cases. However, in other cases this difficulty reinforces the one mentioned earlier, which makes matters worse. What do we mean, for example, by "identity"? We can show that understanding "is the same as" is connected with the understanding of singular terms and other linguistic forms, none of which is simpler than the others. Apparently the child must learn these all at once ("in one mad scramble," as Quine once put it[5]).

With the example of morality I have indicated that we expect the proposed explanation to be adequate. The same holds for all other philosophical explanations of words. Only if an explanation is adequate can it serve as a clarification. Adequacy

[*Angemessenheit*] concerns the character of the truth we demand of philosophical clarifications. To speak in this way might once again suggest some sort of phenomena to which the adequacy of philosophical clarification would have to be related. One might say, for example, that we do not so much expect an adequate philosophical clarification of "morality" to correspond to the given use of this word as to our "moral consciousness." Although basically correct, this claim is nonetheless misleading. It is true the adequacy of a philosophical explication does not depend on exactly hitting the meaning of this one corresponding word. Moreover, if this word has several nuances—as is the case with "morality," for example—we can be quite justified in excluding certain of these precisely in order to find an explanation as adequate as possible for our "moral consciousness." At the same time, this moral consciousness is not something that has a prelinguistic status; rather, we get hold of it only by grasping other words that make up the environment for understanding the word "morality." This, however, implies that what we have to measure [*anzumessen*] our philosophical clarification against is not necessarily the corresponding word but is indeed the given linguistic understanding. A philosophical clarification of a word is fruitful if it succeeds in elucidating a feature (or aspect) of our actual understanding.

Our actual understanding, however, is something empirically given. But in that case the truth philosophy strives for is also an empirical one. Although this truth indeed concerns our understanding as a whole, and this understanding is not observed but rather reflectively explicated, still it is *we* who are at issue here: not a transcendental or somehow preworldly consciousness but an empirically available language community.

This means I can no longer characterize philosophical concepts as "given a priori," a term I introduced more as a way to link up with the philosophical tradition. Were this retained, philosophical statements too would have to raise a supraempirical truth claim. It would imply that we speak not only for our own language community but for a supraempirical subjectivity.

I introduced the concept of a priori concepts as a natural criterion for distinguishing those concepts belonging to the whole of our understanding from empirical concepts. If the former now are also empirical in a broader sense, then the latter might perhaps be designated as concepts that are accidental for us, ones that do not affect our very understanding. As a criterion for distinguishing between the two kinds of concept, we should hold on to the methodological difference garnered from our discussion of Augustine's proposition on time. With the one kind, we can imagine ourselves not having them, but if we have them, we can always explain them as well. With the other kind, we cannot imagine ourselves not having them (although we know we acquired them in our childhood), but because they are concepts that we have "always already" had in this sense (although they are not a priori), we cannot readily explain them.

Of course, if we cannot imagine ourselves not having these concepts, then they still seem to deserve the characteristic that was connected with apriority in the first place: that of necessity. Yet even when I first introduced this concept, I described it in this way: these concepts are indispensable *for us*. Now that means such necessity is relative to us, to this language community.

This, however, makes a progressive derelativization possible. What at present appears to us as indispensable can later prove to be merely one of several alternatives. At the same time, it now makes positive sense to leave open the range of "we": by being confronted with the understanding of other language communities, we can learn new possibilities for understanding, which we can then incorporate into an expanded "We."

This casts a new light on the problem of the possible relativism of our philosophical concepts. Since our propositions still only concern what is indispensable for *our* understanding, they do not imply any claims about consciousness in general or about all human beings or all languages. If we say, for example, that our language is essentially predicative, this does not involve an anticipation [*Vorgriff*] of all possible languages. It has sometimes been claimed that languages lacking a predicative structure have been discovered. This seems to have been based on confusing syntactic with semantic predicative structure. In fact, it would be surprising if a human language should be found that had no semantic predicative structure, hence one in which conclusions according to predicate logic would be impossible. But if such a language should nonetheless turn up, that would not mean that something formerly asserted would prove false. Rather, our comprehension [*Verständnis*] of the possibilities of human understanding [*Verstehens*] would expand, similarly to how our understanding of "space" has expanded through the discovery of non-Euclidean spaces.

The potential expansion of horizons that can result from the encounter with other language communities shows the latently hermeneutical character of the analytic method. The way in which the philosopher deals with foreign languages remains reflective and to this extent differs from the objectivating methods of the linguist, just as it always did. He thematizes the foreign language not in the third person but in the second, i.e., in the same attitude he uses in dealing with other members of his own language community: he speaks with them and not about them. The foreign language is a potential expansion of one's own language. Just as we can make the already familiar "a priori" concepts clear only by showing how we might explain them to someone who did not yet possess them, so also we can appropriate new modes of understanding only by learning the corresponding concepts for ourselves.

Notes

1. *Critique of Pure Reason,* trans. Norman Kemp Smith (New York, 1929), B 756.

2. *The Confessions of St. Augustine,* trans. John K. Ryan (New York, 1960), XI.14.

3. Ludwig Wittgenstein, *The Blue and Brown Books* (New York, 1958), secs. 50 ff.

4. See E. L. Gettier, "Is Justified True Belief Knowledge?" *Analysis* 23 (1963): 121–123.

5. W. V. O. Quine, *Word and Object* (Cambridge, Mass., 1960), p. 102.

5

Normatively Grounding "Critical Theory" through Recourse to the Lifeworld? A Transcendental-Pragmatic Attempt to Think with Habermas against Habermas

Karl-Otto Apel

Translated by William Rehg

1 The Central Point of Contention within the Horizon of a Common Aim

This contribution aims directly at the central disagreement that has apparently developed between Habermas and myself over the years. Of course, I should note that this point of contention indicates not so much a difference in our philosophical aims as in our strategies of argument and concept formation. That being said, I would like to propose the thesis that the point at issue concerns a feature of Habermas's thought that threatens its coherence and even its consistency. How then can we get at this point of contention as directly as possible?

We can arrive at an answer to this question most quickly, perhaps, by reflecting on the significance of my sidestepping a reconstruction and confrontation of our two "architectonics." What I mean is that, so far as I can see, this maneuver cannot prevent me in what follows from continually presupposing and making use of a vague idea of the horizon of preunderstanding in need of reconstruction. One might say this horizon supplies the specific "background resources" of the "lifeworld" that every coming to an understanding [*Verständigung*] depends on, as Habermas shows in *The Theory of Communicative Action.*[1] (According to Heidegger and Gadamer, this has to do with the "forestructure" of the facticity of being-in-the-world with understanding, which precedes every actual mutual understanding [*Verständigung*] and makes it possible.) Such "background resources" of mutual understanding are constantly presupposed not only in everyday life but also at the level of the argumentative discourse of philosophy. Let me emphasize that on this point there exists a de facto consensus between Habermas's universal, or formal, pragmatics and my own *transcendental* pragmatics. To this extent we are both heirs of the "hermeneutic-linguistic-pragmatic turn" taken by contemporary philosophy, finding ourselves in agreement with thinkers such as Wittgenstein, Heidegger, Gadamer, Searle,[2] and even with Richard Rorty.[3]

The point of unclarity and contention between Habermas and myself is most likely to be found in the answer to the following question: Is it sufficient (or at any rate necessary) for *philosophical discourse* to rely on those background resources of mutual understanding that are already drawn upon in every coming to an understanding in the lifeworld, to wit, those factually indubitable,[4] indeed not even fully objectifiable, certainties that in *everyday life* cannot be circumvented? In the final analysis, these certainties of a "form of life" (in Wittgenstein's sense[5]) are what make concrete doubts about this or that conviction possible, as well as enabling the formation of concrete, theoretically or practically sound convictions (consensuses, agreements) on controversial questions. Or to the contrary, can and must "argumentative discourse," which both formal and transcendental pragmatics consider the "reflective form" of lifeworld communication, recur not only to the above described background resources of sociocultural forms of life but also to reflexively confirmable background presuppositions that make such argumentative discourse possible and distinguish it from all other forms of lifeworld communication? Inasmuch as philosophical discourse was made psychologically and historically possible through critical reflection on the historical contingency of the background certainties of all sociocultural forms of life, cannot and must not that discourse, with its relativizing insight, also simultaneously lay claim to a new sort of background presupposition, to wit, presuppositions of mutual understanding that are not historically contingent but are rather incontestably *universal?* Such presuppositions provide the grounds for doubt and mark the limits of possible doubt, and to this extent they provide the grounds—in the sense of a philosophical *ultimate justification*[6]—of validity claims. In providing such grounds, however, are not such presuppositions *transcendental* insofar as they transcend in principle the relative background resources of historically contingent forms of life?

In my estimation most of today's leading philosophers hold the position suggested in the first of the above questions. They see therein a plausible and sufficient mediation or synthesis of the principled fallibilism of Peirce and Popper with the Wittgensteinian and philosophicohermeneutical insight, also had by Peirce, into the indispensability of a factual basis of certitude for actually attending to problems and potentially solving them. For if everything were simultaneously or equally dubitable, raising concrete doubts and formulating questions could not even begin. Nowadays this is clear to anyone schooled in Peirce and Wittgenstein. By contrast, most will have great difficulties simply in understanding the exact sense and rational motive behind the alternative transcendental-pragmatic position indicated in the second of the above questions. To the extent they think they understand its sense and motive, they are inclined to see therein a tendency to fall back not only behind the principle of fallibilism but also behind the conceptual enlightenment achieved by those linguistic-pragmatic and historicohermeneutical advances that brought an appreciation of the facticity, historicity, and contingency of everything belonging to the "preunderstanding" and "prior agreement" of any situation in which participants seek to arrive at an understanding.

How then does the core Habermasian position—i.e., the conception of the formal pragmatics of human speech or "communicative action" as supplemented in *TCA* by the concept of the "lifeworld"—how does this relate to the alternative I have set forth? In my opinion this question is not easy to answer, for Habermas would like precisely to avoid the alternatives I am driving at. On the one hand, he wants to maintain the *universalism* of the validity claims connected with human speech (the claims to intelligibility, truth, sincerity, and normative rightness); moreover, he insists on the moments of "unconditionedness" and "ideality" in the counterfactual presupposition, which is also an actually effective anticipation, of the possible consensus of all conceivable partners to an argument over the justification of validity claims. In this vein he has thus far spoken of "quasi-transcendental" structures and, in line with this, laid claim to a "weak version" of the transcendental-pragmatic approach.[7] On the other hand, Habermas nevertheless continues to reject, as impossible and unnecessary, the demand for an a priori valid *ultimate justification* of the philosophical validity claim made in universal-pragmatic statements about the necessary presuppositions of argumentative discourse just mentioned above.

For example, he has disputed an epistemologically and methodologically relevant distinction in principle between the possible statements of the empiricoreconstructive social sciences (e.g., the hypothetical statements made by Chomsky's linguistics about grammatical universals) and the, in my view, a priori valid universal statements of philosophy (e.g., the above-mentioned statements of universal pragmatics).[8] Instead, he makes unrestricted use of the principle of fallibilism, extending it to the statements of universal pragmatics (thus also to statements about the principle of fallibilism and its necessary presuppositions), which in his view are valid only because they are *factually without alternatives*. With this he has, in spite of apparent reservations,[9] de facto accepted the unrestricted and thus self-applicable principle of fallibilism held by the late Popperians (Bartley, Albert, Radnitzky).[10] He has likewise acknowledged the assumption held by Gadamer and the Wittgensteinians that the preunderstanding of the world is tied to the factual commonality of a particular form of life. This is especially clear in what he has said since *TCA* about the rational potential of the background resources of the lifeworld.[11] Apparently for Habermas too this fact that all the resources of mutual understanding are tied to the background of an already concretized lifeworld, one that is "in each case our own," as Heidegger put it, stipulates the principled contextuality, historicity, and contingency of the necessary conditions of communication (and to this extent, of argumentative discourse too). Evidently these are *necessary* and *universally valid* only insofar as they have proven themselves up to now to be without alternatives.

I interpret Habermas this way primarily because of his demand that even the presuppositions of argument be empirically tested as widely as possible, in analogy to Chomsky's universals.[12] From the viewpoint of transcendental pragmatics, of course, this raises the question as to what possible sense it can have to empirically test presuppositions of a concept such as testing (qua falsification attempt), as these are explicated in the discourse principle. Indeed, even in the event of their falsification they would have to be simultaneously confirmed as transcendental-pragmatic presuppositions of falsification. Thus it can at most be a matter here of correcting the *explication* of the *meaning* of these presuppositions. In the process, however, the truth of the presuppositions must also be once again presupposed. Thus the *transcendental difference* between empirically testable hypotheses and statements about the presuppositions of testing is always preserved.

The question, then, is how the "antifoundationalist" assumptions just sketched allow Habermas to maintain his normative-universalistic, ultimately ethical claims to justification regarding the conditions of possibility for a critical theory. How can he be so sure that the *critical evaluation* of forms of sociocultural life, forms that determine in each case the specific contents of the lifeworld background resources, does not elevate *merely other* background assumptions but also such normative standards as are able to justify the critique?

At the end of his review of *TCA*, Herbert Schnädelbach pinpoints the problem I have sketched thus far:

> It may well be the case that unconditioned claims are raised in communicative action, but this does not yet qualify them to found critical theory. For this they would themselves have to be open to critical evaluation, i.e., the theoretician would already have to have the *unconditioned standards of critique* unconditionally available to him, and he will never be able to derive these from his subject matter via hypothetical rule construction. . . . Critical unconditionality without foundationalism—this is a goal Habermas has set for himself; it is doubtful whether he has reached it.[13] [Emphasis added by Apel.]

As far as I can tell, two characteristic argument motifs identify Habermas's strategy for an antifoundational grounding of the normative standards of critical theory qua reconstructive science. I consider the first of these to be incomplete but capable of completion; the second, on the other hand, I consider merely a result of the first's incompletion, i.e., it represents the central symptom of the inconsistency in Habermas's strategy of justification.

Argument motif 1

The first argument or thought motif concerns the impossibility of a *normatively neutral understanding*. One can, I think, explicate it in the following steps: One cannot even *understand* most human utterances (and to this extent, the symbolically structured reality that makes up the domain of the human and social sciences) without also at least implicitly understanding universal validity claims and critically assessing the reasons speaking for or against those claims. To this extent, mutual understanding is oriented from the start toward the dynamic of a learning process that has to issue in a rationalization of the processes of mutual understanding within the lifeworld. This rationalization must extend even to the lifeworld itself, insofar as background resources can also be called into question. The long-term *goal* of this rationalization process (or more precisely, of the self-differentiating rationalization processes, which are related to the three validity claims of truth, truthfulness, and normative rightness distinguished according to linguistic functions and world relations) can only be explicated through the regulative idea of an absolute, universally valid redemption or justification of validity claims capable of universal consensus. For the ethically relevant validity claim to the *normative rightness* of actions or action norms, as well as for the speech acts related to these, such as requests, demands, proposals, and the like, this means that every speech act implicitly and every regulative speech act explicitly always already anticipates the counterfactual structures of equal rights and solidarity (or coresponsibility) given with an "ideal speech situation" or "ideal communication community." This anticipation operates in such a way that it must be presumed to constitute, in addition, an actually effective motive driving long-term learning processes, i.e., rationalization processes.

I can fully accept this first argument motif, which is meant in some way to succeed the speculative philosophies of history, and in what follows I would like to defend it against objections. I can only do this, however, by completing the argument with a transcendental-pragmatic ultimate grounding, which means that I must reject, as a somewhat unacknowledged or unrecognized relic of the speculative philosophy of history, Habermas's apparent implication that this argument motif itself already contains its sufficient justification. This leads me to the second argument motif, which I find typical of Habermas.

Argument motif 2
Habermas evidently believes that there is no need to justify the presumption that the (unavoidable) background resources for coming to an understanding in the lifeworld supply lifeworld communication with the rational potentials that also fix the long-term goals of learning (or rationalization) processes. The attainment of these goals is thereby supposedly proven to be possible in principle and, at least in the ethically relevant dimension of rationalization, deontologically required, so that a fundamental denial of the immanent learning goals of the rationalization processes would have to end up in a pathological process of self-destruction. On the basis of this presupposition Habermas, if I understand him correctly, thinks he can draw the following conclusions for grounding ethics:

• A weak version of the transcendental-pragmatic grounding of the fundamental principles of morality has already been attained with the insight into the necessary normative conditions of all lifeworld communication, and thus into the necessary conditions of ethical life [*Sittlichkeit*].[14]

• Any further ultimate grounding of the principles of morality, say by reflexively ascertaining the presuppositions of argumentative discourse as the reflective form of lifeworld communication, is in the last analysis impossible and unnecessary.[15] (Habermas draws this conclusion even though he too holds it is not the ethical life current at a given time but the principles of morality, in the sense of Kant or of the discourse-ethical transformation of Kant, that represent the formal and to this extent sole universal standards of the "ought." For such standards necessarily abstract from all particular evaluations of the good life and hence "cut into" the ethical life of concrete forms of life, thus producing the complementary problem of the individual realization of the good life under the limiting conditions of morality.[16])

• What must fill in for the ultimate grounding of morality is a recourse to the ethical lifeworld [*lebensweltliche Sittlichkeit*] that is always already attested to in the structure of communicative action and without which social life would have to collapse and the individual destroy himself.

It seems to me that Habermas himself underlines the point of the above three-step thought motif, and displays the *aporia* infecting this form of argument, when he marshals the following quasi-Wittgensteinian argument against all philosophers challenging the rationality or binding character of morality in general:

> Nor need moral philosophy maintain the claim to ultimate justification because of its presumed relevance for the lifeworld. The *moral* intuitions of everyday life are not in need of clarification by the philosopher. In this case, the therapeutic self-perception of philosophy, as initiated by Wittgenstein, is, for once, I think, appropriate. Moral philosophy does have an enlightening or clarificatory role to play vis-à-vis the confusions it has created in the minds of the educated—that is, to the extent to which value skepticism and legal positivism have established themselves as professional ideologies and have infiltrated everyday consciousness by way of the educational system. Together, skepticism and positivism have misinterpreted and thus neutralized the intuitions people acquire in a quasi-natural manner through socialization. Under extreme conditions they further the moral disarmament of the academic strata, whose skepticism is already rampant.[17]

In this passage, which shocked and mystified me and many others familiar with Habermas, I would not criticize the thesis that philosophy has created confusions in the minds of the educated through the positions Habermas indicates (not to mention Nietzsche's "explanation" of moral conscience). As a matter of fact, this phenomenon can be observed since the philosophical enlightenment and, I think, be understood without too much trouble as the confusion occurring at Kohlberg's crisis stage 4½, where the transition from the conventional to a rationally grounded postconventional morality has not yet been mastered.[18] Such an explanation is entirely in line with the developmental logic of moral consciousness elaborated by Piaget and Kohlberg and then taken up by Habermas himself as "reconstructive science" (thus as critical theory), which he has tentatively applied to phylogenesis.

But how should precisely this reconstructive understanding be reconciled with the idea that the unselfconscious substantial *Sittlichkeit* (Hegel) of the *lifeworld prior to philosophical enlightenment* was, so to speak, a world untouched by moral problems? This world displayed what Kohlberg terms the conventional in-group morality of stages 3 and 4, roughly speaking, the morality of tribal societies and early societies organized around states.[19] Or how should this reconstruction come to terms with a current version of the same idea: that the orientation to conventional morality, which according to Kohlberg is still the standard for approximately 80 percent of Western industrialized societies,[20] represents a basis of "*moral* intuitions of everyday life" that in principle do not have need of philosophical enlightenment? In Kohlberg's terms, this means that such intuitions do not have need of universalistic orientations found in utilitarian contract theory and, beyond this, in the "completely reversible" reciprocity of role-taking or in justice as fairness. For did not philosophical enlightenment, dawning in the West since Socrates and, in a broader sense, since what Jaspers called the "pivotal age" [*Achsenzeit*] of ancient civilizations, first create the metainstitutions of argumentative discourse, without which one cannot even conceive a radical rational redemption or rejection of validity claims, i.e., a redemption or rejection free of all open and concealed solutions by force and thus going beyond rituals and even negotiations? And on the other hand, was not the National Socialist challenge to, indeed ridicule of, universalist humanitarian ideas of law and morality able to appeal with great success to the prephilosophical and hence conventional feelings of solidarity found in a people's in-group morality?

It seems to me that only the particular context provided by the justification problem explains the cited passage, which is inconsistent in every respect with the basic tenor of Habermasian thinking. In context it manifestly appears as a kind of defiant reaction in view of the lack of prospects Habermas alleges for an ultimate justification of ethics. To this extent the passage admittedly fits into one of Habermas's established thought motifs, which can be characterized in logical terms as a *circulus vitiosus* or *petitio principii,* in deontological terms as a *naturalistic* or *substantialistic fallacy.* I would like to describe it as follows: Although the Habermasian reconstruction of cultural evolution also assumes that prephilosophical lifeworld communication, given its background resources, was *not* in a position to justify the claims to normative rightness raised by conventional morality; thus although the level of discourse we can and must carry out today always already crosses the cultural threshold to philosophical argumentation so that the post-conventional situation of argumentative discourse always already belongs to the "forestructure" of our reaching agreement [*Verständigung*] over norms or, more precisely, over principles of norm justification; although all of this must be presupposed in every discussion, the philosophical justification of a principled ethics (including discourse ethics) is nevertheless supposed to be replaced by *a recourse to the factually functioning ethical life of communicative action in the lifeworld.*

In my view, this is the "architectonic" structure of the point at issue. In what follows I will try to lay out my own position on the issue more precisely. To this end I will come back once more to the first argument motif—that of the impossibility of a normatively neutral understanding of human speech acts—which I consider in need of completion and which, as I will try to show through critical reconstruction, does not suffice for a normative justification of critical theory (section 2). I will then attempt to show that the kind of argument provided by a transcendental-pragmatic ultimate justification of the discourse principle—together with its historical implication, the principle of the self-appropriation [*Selbsteinholungsprinzips*] of the reconstructive sciences—supplements the project of critical-reconstructive science with far greater consistency and coherence than does the thought motif preferred by Habermas, in which a recourse to the ethical lifeworld replaces an ultimate justification (section 3). Finally, I would like to indicate that an ultimate justification does not comprise a relapse into dogmatic metaphysics but, on the contrary, contains a standard able to unmask those types of cryptometaphysics most influential today: the scientistic reductionism of the "nothing but" explanations and the historicist ersatz arguments suggesting that this or that is obsolete today (section 4).

2 Why Can and Must the Scientific Understanding of Communicative Actions Be Guided by the Regulative Idea of Critically-Reconstructible Rationalization Processes? The Rights and Limits of the Methodological Approach of *TCA*

In his review of *TCA* Herbert Schnädelbach thematized anew a problem up for discussion since Max Weber and, in my opinion, still unresolved: the question of the possible value freedom or normative neutrality attaching to the rational understanding of human actions. I consider this appropriate, since the issue at stake in *TCA*, as earlier in Max Weber, concerns the rational understanding operative in a reconstruction of the rationalization processes of cultural evolution. Yet Schnädelbach calls into question the basic presupposition of every rational reconstruction: that the sought-after rationality of human actions, or of the corresponding dispositions of the acting subjects one strives to understand, must be presumed to set the normative standards for both the subject and the (subject-)object of the reconstruction, and hence to be identical for both sides. He asks whether one might not view the "normativity of the rational" as something one "can put entirely on the 'side of the object,' in the sense that one would mean by such normativity only that pertaining to the behavioral regulations or action orientations of observed persons or social systems, and nothing more."[21] Schnädelbach argues further against Habermas that it is "not clear why those who attempt to understand others by calling to mind their grounds for action and interpreting them rationally are 'drawn into the process of assessing validity claims.'" To this Schnädelbach replies, "To interpret something *rationally,* i.e., on the basis of reasons, does not yet mean to interpret it *as rational.*"[22] What can we say to this? Can we affirm Schnädelbach's suspicion and view the presumption of an identical rationality for both the subject and the (subject-)object of understanding as perhaps one of those metaphysical remnants of German Idealism refuted by analytical philosophy?

In my opinion the opposite is true. The lengthy discussions between the proponents of scientistic reductionism (the reduction of understanding, as taken above, to causal or nomological *explanation*) and those of a "rational explanation" mediated by the understanding of reasons (W. Dray, C. Taylor, G. H. von Wright, and others) have, so far as I can see, produced the following answer to Schnädelbach's question.[23] Every attempt to apply the nomological (subsumption-theoretic) schema of explanation to the understanding of reasons or motives for human actions requires that one first of all insert into the explanatory schema an additional, quite specific premise to the effect *that the actor is or was rational.* Without this presupposition even the most intuitively obvious explanatory schema could be challenged with the objection that possibly the actor is (or was) not rational. To this extent it has been shown that explanations of human behavior, which are mediated by the rational understanding of reasons, must in fact presume rationality not only on the side of the subject of knowledge but also on that of the object of knowledge. But must we presume this rationality *sets identical standards* for both sides?

If the normativity of the rational should be put "entirely on the side of the object," then it ought to be possible to satisfy the above requirement, i.e., to insert a rationality premise into the schema of "rational explanation" so as to exclude the objection of the actor's possible irrationality. That could in fact be achieved if and only if the meaning of rationality could be defined independently of the possible self-understanding of the subject of the rationally interpretive explanation, say in the way that disposition predicates of the natural sciences, such as "is water-soluble," can be empirically operationalized. Precisely this, however, is not possible with respect to the predicate "is rational." No list of empirically operationalizable characteristics inserted in an explanatory schema is capable of so defining the predicate "is rational" as to exclude the rejoinder to a disappointed prognosis "but perhaps the actor is (or was) not rational." To this extent a "rational explanation," taken as a *nomological explanation,* is in principle immune from possible falsification. By comparison, if one conceives it, in my opinion rightly, primarily as an achievement of *rational understanding* along the lines of Weber, Dray, C. Taylor, and von Wright, then the answer to our problem is at hand: in the form assumed by Schnädelbach the "normativity of the rational" cannot be put "entirely on the side of the object"; one must rather reckon with the possibility both that the rationality concept of the understanding subject will be corrected by the factually attested rationality of the investigated agents and, conversely, that the factual rationality disposition of the latter will be corrected through the rationality presupposition of the understanding subject. However, precisely this sort of learning, which functions as a "hermeneutic circle" and is characteristic of rational understanding and reconstructive science, presupposes that rationality is taken from the start as in principle identical and normative for both sides.

With this the answer to Schnädelbach's second thesis as well is already sketched out: to interpret something rationally, i.e., on the basis of reasons, without interpreting it *as rational* in principle, can at most mean interpreting something (such as inorganic nature) that is *not understandable* in Dilthey's sense through *causes* that are grounds of rational knowledge only for human beings. To stay with Dilthey's terminology, this is to *explain* from the outside. But all rational understanding, including the "purposive-rational understanding" assumed by Max Weber as a minimal presupposition for "interpretive [*verstehende*] sociology," necessarily supposes that the thematized action of human beings can be interpreted *as rational,* namely, by positing a normative rationality that sets standards for the subject and the (subject-)object of understanding. To this extent there is no normative neutrality of understanding even for Max Weber, at least regarding "purposive-rational understanding." Rather, understanding here reaches just as far as the possibility of rendering the other's action comprehensible through a "good-reason essay" (W. Dray[24]) that is also normatively plausible for the understanding subject, i.e., one that could be applied to the latter's own action in sufficiently similar situations. With magical practices such as the use of amulets, purposive-rational understanding consists in the fact that even though we can no longer rationally share a belief in the effectiveness of the amulet, we can, under the hypothetical presupposition of such belief on the agent's part, nonetheless understand the instrumental use of the amulet in a sense rationally binding for ourselves as well.

According to Weber, even the *choice of goals,* whose presupposition makes possible purposive-rational understanding as a good-reason essay, can still be reconstructed as normatively right for both the (subject-)object and the subject doing the reconstruction, provided the latter succeeds in hypothetically positing a "value relation" that rationally grounds an understanding of the setting of ends. For Weber, only the "value relation" itself, which grounds "value-rational action" and its comprehension, can no longer be grounded or evaluated as rationally binding; it serves only to *constitute* the *rationality* that necessarily has to be presupposed for all (further) understanding and that binds both subject and (subject-)object. Since in Weber's view, however, the setting or choice of values no longer admits of a rationally binding justification, the enterprise of rational understanding made possible by this choice also becomes a *value-neutral* undertaking, both as carried on by the cultural sciences themselves and as a whole.

Here it is a matter of the *normative-analytic* and thus value-neutral reconstruction of rationally grounded forms of behavior, a reconstruction made possible by hypothetically presupposing "value relations" of various types. For example, a normative-analytic reconstruction of action is possible for modern decision theory and strategic game theory under the hypothetical presupposition of a formal-egoistic value relation to the actors' respective self-interests.[25] The reconstruction of the "Occidental process of rationalization" forming the encompassing horizon of Weber's "interpretive sociology" also follows a similar methodology, for certainly the goals of the rationalization process are hypothetically given ahead of time.

Of course, it amounts to a substantive evaluation when Weber, presupposing the *irrationality* and *antagonistic plurality* of decisions about ultimate values, takes as the highest form of rationality, including that given in the Occidental rationalization process, not "value rationality" but rather "purposive rationality." (The former is displayed, for example, in choosing one's ends on the basis of the unconditioned value of a form of behavior; the latter in the choice of means to the end *and* the analogous assessment of ends as possibly giving rise to secondary effects.[26]) This leads him to single out the "ethics of responsibility" as rationally superior to the "ethics of conviction." Like Karl Popper after him, Weber simply presupposes in his "ethics of responsibility" that human beings are capable of distinguishing desirable from undesirable consequences and, what is more, that their diverging evaluations of consequences do not produce any fundamental problem for a rational foundation of ethics.[27] In my opinion, this is where a transcendental-pragmatic grounding of ethics (and of the reconstruction of science) has to come in.

A further unexamined ultimate valuation at work in Weber's conception of the rationalization process follows from the postulate of the value freedom of science itself. Certainly this postulate is itself not value-neutral. Rather, it is easy to see that its justification presupposes the highest value of *objectivity* as a condition of possibility for the truth and falsity of scientific statements. To this extent, therefore, it turns out that Weber, in addition to presupposing purposive rationality as a condition of possibility for a moral responsibility for consequences, also at least implicitly presupposes the highest value of *truth* (and hence that of *logical consistency*) in his concept of reconstructible Occidental rationalization processes.

Now this is where a conception of rationality along the lines taken by Habermas and myself and going beyond the idea of purposive rationality can set to work at correcting or supplementing Max Weber's presuppositions, in something like the following way:[28]

First, it can show that the rationality of argumentation, as well as that of an ethics of responsibility, are not exhausted in the fact that each individual, employing a means-end rationality and independently of everyone else, weighs the foreseeable consequences of actions and then relates these consequences to his finally irrational value decisions. Rather, the rationality of argumentation actually consists in the fact that those who argue in communicative discourse follow rules that also enable them to reach a consensus on a generally binding evaluation of the ascertained consequences.

In addition, this broader concept of rationality can also provide the formal-procedural principle that must undergird the rules of consensus-formation on the evaluation of action consequences and the consequences of a rule's observance. This is to say, it can provide the principle of a two-level discourse ethics, which does not itself justify concrete, situation-specific norms but does ground the regulative idea for the revisable justification of such norms in practical discourses involving those affected (or representatives who substitute for them).

However, in order now to *ground* such a discourse ethics, I believe we must turn to an ultimate transcendental-pragmatic justification. That is, such a justification is required if we want to demonstrate by compelling argument not only that universal moral validity *claims* are to be found in the ethical lifeworlds of every sociocultural variety—this much Max Weber could accept—but that these claims, rather than retreating before rational questioning (or "enlightenment") as illusions, can on the contrary be definitively justified by the reflective awareness such questioning brings to bear on its own normative conditions of possibility. In doing this, such a justification recurs not simply to the background resources of the lifeworld—precisely these have been called into question by the "enlightenment"—but to the *presuppositions of argumentation,* which are no longer rationally contestable inasmuch as the very attempt to do so actually brings them into play.

In short, an ultimate transcendental-pragmatic justification has to show the following: to vindicate in argument the truth claim of science presupposed even by Max Weber in his postulate of value-freedom, one must in turn draw upon ethical presuppositions of the communicative rationality of discourse. This means that owing to the dependence of all thinking qua argumentation on linguistic interpretation and monitored rule following, one must necessarily enter the field of argumentative discourse and thus also recognize the norms given with the ethics of an unlimited ideal communication community. These basic norms include not only the *equal rights* of all conceivable argumentation partners but also their fundamentally equal *duty to share responsibility* for the solution of all problems open to discussion. In my opinion, the recognition of this obligation in the form of a transcendental-pragmatic care [*Sorge*] is attested to in each *question* qua contribution to a discourse.[29]

How, then, does Habermas's envisioned rational reconstruction of communicative action and societal rationalization relate to this critical reconstruction of Weber? For his undertaking too involves a critique of Weber. As I intend this question in the present context, it focuses not so much on how the notion of action rationality can be expanded along the lines of "communicative rationality"—this Habermas presumes just as much as I do—as on the new appraisal that this expansion entails for the relation between rational understanding and values.

Like most readers of Habermas, Schnädelbach has the impression that Habermas's interest in his intended renewal of critical theory has led him to replace the Weberian postulate of value freedom with one positing an *internal interdependence of rational understanding* (of validity claims) *and values* (of reasons). Schnädelbach, however, rejects this shift by calling on Max Weber and on the usual formal-semantic explication of the meaning of sentences in terms of the knowable *possible* conditions of truth (but not of the known factual existence of these conditions). Presupposing one can generalize from an understanding of truth claims to the understanding of validity claims of all sorts, Schnädelbach paraphrases Davidson: "Someone can understand [the communicative action of another] if he knows under which circumstances the validity claim at stake *could* be discursively redeemed, i.e., how the consensus then reached would appear."[30] Now how does the Habermasian position relate to this?

Habermas's position is so complex that one cannot simply ignore the possibility of its being unclear, indeed ambivalent. Permit me first to clear up from my own point of view a confusion that I find in Schnädelbach but that I suspect goes back to Habermas's tendency to disregard the distinction between a concrete, empirically testable reconstructive understanding and the philosophical theory of this understanding, be it the theory found in *TCA* or that underlying formal pragmatics.

In the first place, then, it seems clear to me that *TCA* itself, say in its formal-pragmatic core and its distinctions between types of action rationality and between "system" and "lifeworld," is *not* "drawn into" the *concrete understanding and assessment* (or evaluation) of reasons for action. Rather *TCA* treats such understanding and assessment as the object of statements claiming a *formal universal validity*. It avoids a concrete assessment because the analysis is located at a fundamentally higher reflective level of the claim to universality.[31] But at the same time *TCA* is not, at least in its formal-pragmatic core, a normatively neutral, empirically generalizing theory propounding hypothetical "universals" in the way Chomsky's linguistics does for innate grammatical presuppositions, which should or could be empirically tested by "as wide a range as possible" of experiments or observations of competent speakers. For in its core *TCA* contains statements that are already presupposed for every conceivable testing of hypotheses. Examples of such statements are those dealing with the four validity claims necessarily implied in human acts of communication and open to further reflection in argumentative discourse, those dealing with the necessarily presupposed consensual redeemability of validity claims, or those having to do with the primacy of communicative rationality vis-à-vis instrumental and strategic-purposive rationality (i.e., the important thesis regarding the "parasitic" relationship a "success-oriented" use of language has to that "oriented to reaching understanding"). In summary, one could say that the *discourse principle,* which includes everything pertaining to validity claims and their redemption, is a *transcendental-pragmatic presupposition of the falsification principle.*[32] The discourse principle can possibly be explicated in a mistaken or incomplete fashion, as is trivially true of every theory or statement subject to human finitude. But as a transcendental-pragmatic *condition for the meaning of the falsification principle,* and hence as a condition for the principle of fallibilism as well, it cannot be empirically testable, falsifiable, or fallible. Nor would this cease to be the case at the metalevel of a principled fallibilistic proviso, for there too the transcendental-pragmatic conditions of meaning would remain unchanged.

Instead of extending the requirement of empirical testing to the central statements of universal pragmatics, something Habermas has called for since his 1971 extrapolation of the Chomsky paradigm of reconstructive theory formation, the transcendental-pragmatic interpretation offers the following alternative mode of testing: all candidates for the status of genuine *universal*-pragmatic statements must be tested according to whether they can be disputed without *performative self-contradiction.* If such dispute is not possible, then one is dealing with a transcendental-pragmatic statement enjoying a philosophically ultimate justification insofar as it cannot be circumvented in any argumentation. Of course, to this extent such statements also cannot be "grounded" by derivation from something else without circularity. An example of such an indisputable claim, Lyotard notwithstanding,[33] is the a priori claim made with every theoretical truth claim: that the latter is in principle capable of universal consensus.[34]

In this case, then, what is the relationship—quite relevant for the renewal of critical theory—between the universal-pragmatic statements of *TCA* and the statements represented by the concrete, empirically testable understanding of the reconstructive social sciences, an understanding that Habermas postulates is drawn into the process of an evaluative assessment of the validity claims it seeks to understand?

In the first place, it seems to me that *TCA* necessarily contains such formal-universal statements, which explicate the internal relation between the possible understanding of speech acts and the knowledge this presupposes with regard to the conditions for the possible redeemability of the validity claims raised in such speech acts. This type of statement is represented in Habermas by the summary formulation "We understand a speech act when we know what makes it acceptable."[35] As Schnädelbach rightly maintains, however, this does not yet imply any divergence whatsoever from the usual appraisal of the relation between understanding and evaluation, for the Habermasian formulation does not imply that understanding depends on our knowing *whether* the conditions of acceptability are satisfied. One can compare this with Wittgenstein's dictum "To understand a proposition means to know what is the case if it is true. (One can understand it, therefore, without knowing whether it is true.)"[36]

Hence the possibility of *abstaining from evaluation*—in the way practiced by Max Weber and empirical-analytic theorizing—is well provided for here. Indeed, the distinction between presenting the *possible* conditions for redemption and determining *whether these hold* is the philosophical sleight of hand that actually enables the historicohermeneutical sciences to employ such abstention as a fixed methodological abstraction. Of course, one should not confuse this methodological commitment to abstaining from evaluation with the principled value neutrality demanded in the natural sciences with respect to their object. After all, the object of natural science does not present any validity claims or reasons that could be understood and assessed. In distinction to the principled value-free subject-object relation necessarily presumed for a nomological explanation, understanding [*Verstehen*] is a moment in virtually coming to an understanding [*Verständigung*] with cosubjects and thus has always already commenced with a virtual assessment of validity claims and reasons. However, precisely in the interest of an unprejudiced evaluation considering all the possibly relevant criteria, understanding is able to abstain from evaluation, even establishing this as the methodological abstraction just explicated.

However, the methodological attitude established with this does not suffice to make something like *critical theory* possible. By the latter I mean a critically reconstructive science that enables a normative assessment of reasons good and bad—say, with respect to the historically understandable validity claims of law or ethical life or even of philosophers' moral theories, as belonging to a particular epoch or form of sociocultural life. Such assessment makes claims like those brought to bear in the reconstruction of the "internal history of science," such as that of Imre Lakatos.[37]

I have already indicated in the foregoing that Habermas de facto assumes that such a normatively evaluative reconstruction is possible for the rationalization processes he distinguishes, which correspond to the three quasi-Kantian dimensions of validity claims and hence to the dimensions of reason. This assumption makes it understandable that he would go beyond the usual explication of the relation between understanding and evaluation and, striking out from this well-trodden path, strive to demonstrate an internal relationship between these two operations. Such a relationship implies that reconstructive science, which is critically tied to and reflects on prescientific mutual understanding, is also more or less subject to the progressive learning dynamic that mutual understanding both enables and drives on. On this presupposition, and only on its basis, do those statements about the necessity of evaluation, which astonished Schnädelbach (and others) and whose exact significance is so difficult to appraise, become somewhat comprehensible.

Consider, for example, the following:

But if, in order to understand an expression, the interpreter must *bring to mind the reasons* with which a speaker would if necessary and under suitable conditions defend its validity, [thus far everything still accords with the usual explication that makes a factual abstention from evaluation quite possible, indeed, builds it in] he is *himself* drawn into the process of assessing validity claims. [Here the reader's ears start to perk up! And now comes the justification.] For reasons are of such a nature that they cannot be described in the attitude of a third person, that is, without reactions of affirmation or negation or abstention. [That's new!] The interpreter would not have understood what a "reason" is if he did not reconstruct it with its claim to provide grounds; that is, if he did not give it a *rational interpretation* in Max Weber's sense. The *description* of reasons demands *eo ipso* an *evaluation,* even when the one providing the description feels that he is not at the moment in a position to judge their soundness. One can understand reasons only to the extent that one understands *why* they are or are not sound—[a bewildering claim, for the usual explication would read, "to the extent that one understands under which existent or nonexistent conditions they would be sound," yet something like an answer to the reader's bewilderment follows]—or why in a given case a decision as to whether reasons are good or bad is not (yet) possible. An interpreter cannot, therefore, interpret expressions connected through criticizable validity claims with a potential of reasons (and thus represent knowledge) without taking a position of his own. And he cannot take a position without applying his *own* standards of judgment, at any rate standards that he has made his own. [This speaks unequivocally for critical theory's basic attitude, which differs from value-neutral social science. The following brings in the connection to the theory of communicative rationality.] . . . In this respect, a merely virtual participation does not free the interpreter of the obligations of one who is immediately involved; on this point, which is decisive for the objectivity of understanding, the same kind of interpretive accomplishment is required of both the social-scientific observer and the layman. [This introduces a new concept of the *objectivity* of understanding and, along with it, of the hermeneutically mediated social sciences. It differs from the concept of objectivity oriented by the natural sciences, as well as from Max Weber's, insofar as it understands understanding not as a subject-object relation but as the subject-cosubject relation of reaching a communicative understanding about something in the world.][38]

The upshot of the cited passage, taken as a tentative formulation of the methodological attitude of an understanding that is not value-neutral, consists in the following point: The abstention from evaluation that the usual explication brings into the relation between understanding and evaluation as the *normal attitude* of methodological abstraction in the service of the ideal of objectivity is not tossed aside by Habermas. In fact, this attitude can be indispensable for an unbiased understanding of the validity claims or reasons of others. Rather, it is taken as a *deficient mode* of the evaluative understanding that would be part of reaching an understanding qua consensus building—as a *reflective not yet being in the position* to definitively assess the soundness of the arguments and counterarguments speaking for and against a validity claim. Accordingly, the way in which the senses of utterances are usually explicated in terms of the conditions for the *possible* redemption of their validity, and that sets up a more or less enduring methodicoabstractive abstention from definitive evaluation, significantly differs from the Habermasian position but is not logically incompatible with it. This usual approach would merely have to be critically reinterpreted as a *methodicoabstractive fixation of a mode of understanding, in itself still deficient,* which then must be "sublated" [*aufgehoben*], so to speak, into critical theory. As a matter of fact, the usual abstention-oriented explication also aims to determine as unequivocally as possible what the methodological access to the still outstanding definitive judgment would consist in. This reference to the possibility of definitive judgment was already the point of the verification principle, conceived as a criterion of meaning.

I would like to express my support for the above position as an appropriate explication of the methodological attitude of critical-reconstructive science. Of course, I must immediately raise the following question: Where does the social sciences' critical-reconstructive understanding, insofar as this is to be in a position for evaluative assessment, get its standards for rationally assessing reasons, in particular, the standards of assessment for the critical reconstruction of rationalization processes assumed to correspond to the three validity claims of human speech?

I have already indicated Habermas's answer to this question in the opening section of this article. It proceeds on the assumption that the three types of validity claims raised in speaking (the claims to truth, truthfulness, and rightness), which correspond to three different relations the speaker takes to the world, are *as understandable claims already* related to *universal validity* and that therefore the process of reaching understanding can have the regulative principle of its teleological progress only in a universal consensus (or as I would put it, in the consensus of an unlimited ideal communication community). Taking Peirce and Royce as a point of departure, I proposed this myself in my contribution to the 1970 Gadamer festschrift. The proposal was intended as a normative alternative—at that time still without an ultimate transcendental-pragmatic justification—to the Heidegger-inspired Gadamerian conception of the "happening of truth," which has it appear that only an always context-dependent "understanding otherwise" is possible.[39] In his conception of "universal pragmatics" Habermas then fleshed out the postulate of consensus formation by partially assimilating the analyses of speech act theory, Karl Bühler's trichotomy of linguistic functions, and the concept of validity claims redeemable, when challenged, in argumentative discourse.[40]

Yet how can this concept be grounded without giving the impression of a dogmatically posited teleological philosophy of history? By declaring the regulative idea of a required progressive rationalization to be a hypothetical goal assumption that one does not justify any further? This, in fact, is what it comes to when Habermas treats the consensus-oriented presuppositions of argumentative discourse merely as empirically testable hypotheses. If that is the case, his conception would not differ in principle from Max Weber's approach, which is ultimately considered value neutral. But then expanding the Weberian conception of the rationalization process in the direction of communicative rationality and discourse ethics becomes especially problematic. For how is one to conceive a *deontological* ethic that supposedly traces the "unconditional moment" of its validity ultimately back to an hypothesis in need of empirical testing?

According to Kant, this would necessarily amount to relativizing the binding character of the ethical principle. Moreover, as far as the supposition of a corresponding rationalization process in morality goes, for example, as structured with the help of the Piagetian-Kohlbergian developmental logic of moral judgment competence, we could at most point to the empirical performability of empiricogenetic theory in answer to the nowadays ready objection that the entire conception of progress is *Eurocentric*. We could not, however, provide a genuinely philosophical justification for the "superiority of the higher stage," nor could we justify in particular the selection of the highest stage of moral judgment competence.[41] Still less would we have an ethical justification of the moral progress required of us, the binding character of which would be independent in principle, as Kant postulated, of the de facto course of history.[42] How, therefore, can we strengthen the *normative grounding of critical theory* intended by Habermas so that it can lay claim to a binding ethical character?

3 Which Argument Motif Is More Suited for Grounding the Reconstructive Science of Critical Theory: Ultimate Transcendental-Pragmatic Justification plus the Principle of Self-Appropriation or Recourse to the Ethical Lifeworld?

In all his contributions to the "normative grounding" of critical theory—which for Horkheimer and Adorno, in any case, had overtones of a philosophy of history that, in my opinion, ultimately amounted to a metaphysics if not a quasi-theological eschatology—Habermas has de facto laid claim to much stronger presuppositions than those of a "strong theory" à la Popper and Chomsky (with empirically testable hypotheses about "universals"). In the theoretical "architectonic" Habermas actually presumes, empirically testable hypotheses of the reconstructive social sciences always function as merely "complementary" constituents in a *combination* of philosophical and empiricoscientific methods. One can already see this, for example, in his earliest attempt at a critical reconstruction of Marx.[43] One sees it above all in the suggestion, accepted by Kohlberg, to ground the cooperation and possible mutual support and correction between philosophical justification and empiricopsychological hypothesis formation and testing in the domain of genetic-structural theories of the evolution of moral judgment competence.[44] Yet how could philosophical and empirically testable theory formations ever mutually support and correct each other if they could not recur to autonomous, methodologically different, and thus "complementary" procedures of justification that can be systematically related to each other?[45] There must already be two different classes of statements here from the start, inasmuch as one either provides for their empirical testing and possible falsification or, on the contrary, considers them justified insofar as their validity is a presupposition simply for understanding the requirements and meaning of empirical testing and falsification. Naturally it makes no sense at all to require empirical testing in the latter case.

In his Reply to criticisms of *TCA* in *Communicative Action,* Habermas has, on the one hand, straightaway rejected Kuhlmann's arguments (and mine as well) for the distinction between empirically testable and transcendental-pragmatic statements.[46] On the other hand, in his reply to the numerous objections that maintain, not without reason, that he more or less smuggled strong but unjustified *normative* premisses into a quasi-descriptive theory of the lifeworld, of factual communicative action, and of language use, he has nevertheless referred repeatedly to the difference his readers overlook between the *philosophical* and the *empiricosociological* levels of his theory.[47]

Furthermore, one should recall that, like myself,[48] Habermas wants to distinguish between the basic formal-procedural principle of discourse morality and the justification or legitimation of concrete, situation-related norms. The latter task is delegated to those affected or representatives substituting for them and produces results that are obviously revisable.[49] In addition, he likewise wants to distinguish between the standard of morality as it cuts into the ethical lifeworld and the latter's settled, concrete norms, which are more or less receptive to such morality. Now what sense can these distinctions possibly have if, in the final analysis, the formal principle of discourse morality is also supposed to stem from a historically contingent presupposition of communicative action in the lifeworld—a presupposition that one must constantly check by submitting it to widespread empirical testing? On the other hand, if one takes these distinctions seriously, in the sense of the transcendental difference, then one can easily concede that substantive, situation-specific justifications of norms, such as Rawls's "principles of justice," can never be based *solely* on the formal a priori principle of discourse morality but must always also link up with a "contingent" basis of consensus (Rorty), for example, as Rawls does with the American constitutional tradition.[50]

In the exemplary cases just indicated the Habermasian strategy of avoiding a methodological distinction between philosophy and empirically testable reconstructive science seems to me openly inconsistent: I suspect Habermas will have to make up his mind one day whether he wants to persist in the inconsistency or give back to philosophy its genuine *justificatory function,* together with its a priori universal and self-referential validity claims. Later I will say something about the rather timely motives for disavowing these claims.

The strongest argument for the view that Habermas de facto follows a stronger justification strategy than he himself would like to admit is found in the absence of empirical or quasi-empirical arguments at decisive points in his own most recent works, for example, in *The Philosophical Discourse of Modernity.*[51] Rather, his procedure involves probative attempts to derive performative self-contradictions, just what I set forth above as a genuinely philosophical alternative for testing arguments. Naturally, everything depends here on the insight that one cannot employ this procedure at all except at the highest epistemological and argumentation-theoretic level of reflection. That is, as an ultimate transcendental-reflexive justification involving the reductio ad absurdum of attempts to dispute statements of principles, this procedure works only at the level of the self-reflection of argumentative discourse and not at the level of theoretical statements about lifeworld communication. Only for the one engaged in philosophizing, who reflects on the incontestable presuppositions of argumentation as such and thereby grasps the first move, so to speak, in the transcendental-pragmatic language game, are the necessary presuppositions of communication qua argumentation *methodologically inescapable.*[52] This is not the case, by contrast, with those normative presuppositions that the subject of lifeworld communication may possibly find *practically inescapable.* The latter can, for example, be found in a conventional morality (of an unselfconscious substantial *Sittlichkeit*) and are connected with the subject's role and status within the framework of a "form of life" (Wittgenstein). If one wanted to recur to these presuppositions (or "background" resources) as methodologically inescapable, one would most likely arrive, with Gethmann and Hegselmann, at the result that the norms of an aristocratic morality are, for an aristocrat, "ultimately grounded."[53] Or one might even reach Rossvaer's macabre though perhaps consistent Wittgenstein interpretation, according to which the SS at Auschwitz could have followed Kant's "categorical imperative" *in their own way,* i.e., according to the application rules of their "form of life" and "customs."[54] This implies a complete and quite up to date devaluation of philosophical "principles" and their relevance for praxis in favor of whatever conventions happen to be "customary." It amounts to fundamentally the same thing when Richard Rorty refuses to assess (and probably justify) the American form of life and its institutions with philosophical principles, recommending instead the opposite procedure.[55]

I think it is sufficiently clear that the above consequences of a neopragmatic "commonsense" philosophy oriented by the factually given form of life are incompatible with the Habermasian aim of renewing and normatively grounding critical theory. But it still needs to be made clear that the tempting suggestions of this commonsense approach, which appear together with Wittgensteinian promises to dissolve problems and neo-Aristotelian dismissals of anyone out to improve the world, cannot really be overcome unless it is shown that the postconventional reconstruction and grounding of lifeworld rationalization processes can call on background resources of reason that are not identical with the historically conditioned, contingent background resources of "a lifeworld in each case our own," i.e., one happening to be one of many forms of life. Here, I think, is precisely where there is the possibility of a consistent and coherent solution to the problematic of a normative grounding for critical theory, and not in the currently widespread assurance that one should and will find the way to a solution this side of or beyond the foundationalism-relativism polarity (whatever that might mean). And as a matter of fact, it is just at this point that I detect the deepest ambiguity of the Habermasian strategy of justification.

The ambiguity lies in this. In the preceding I have already touched several times on a theorem I call Habermas's "discourse principle," which I understand as positing four validity claims necessary to speech, whose consensual redemption in argumentative discourse must be counterfactually anticipated as possible in principle. On the one hand, with this principle Habermas has, in my opinion, laid bare the "Archimedean point"—a term he would reject, of course—for an ultimate justification of philosophy that is no longer ontological and no longer based in the philosophy of consciousness but is rather *transcendental-pragmatic* (again, this is my terminology). On the other hand, he nonetheless fails to make any architectonically appropriate use of what he has uncovered, for he does not rest content with tracing back the *constitution of meaning*—conditioned by interests among other things—to the background resources of lifeworld communication. While I too would go that far, in the final analysis Habermas also reduces the *justi-*

fication of validity, such as the grounding of moral validity, to such lifeworld resources, apparently for fear of otherwise losing contact with lifeworld praxis as the material basis of philosophy. One might call this a "reconstructivistic naturalism" with respect to the justification of validity.

Rather than pursue an immanent critique of the Habermasian strategy of justification any further, I would like to propose instead a positive alternative aimed at making good on my earlier promise to complete the first argument motif. According to this proposal, an incontestable grounding of the validity of a normatively engaged reconstructive science as a renewed critical theory should start not with existent lifeworld claims and resources but with the standpoint of discussion always already reached in science and philosophy insofar as these place lifeworld claims and background resources *in question,* the standpoint of argumentative discourse that cannot be methodologically circumvented.

Now this does not mean uncoupling discourse from the lifeworld.[56] My proposal is rather the following. To begin with, recall the fact that argumentative discourse is precisely not an undertaking one has the freedom to chose or turn down, since by nature of its structure it is already presupposed even for the solitary thinking—coming to an understanding with oneself—carried out by *anyone making an understandable choice.*[57] This *inescapability* provides the representative of reconstructive science with the a priori legitimation to assume a process of lifeworld rationalization and then reconstruct it along normative-critical lines in such a way that argumentative discourse and its presuppositions, as the incontestable starting point of the reconstruction, must at the same time be supposed *as historical fact* as well, and therewith *as an already achieved and* (according to the possibilities) [*still*] *achievable telos* of lifeworld rationalization processes. I have called this the self-appropriation principle of reconstructive science.[58] And I see in it the transcendental-pragmatic, i.e., metaphysics-free, grounding of critical theory.

The principle of self-appropriation results from the *principle of avoiding performative self-contradiction* in combination with the presupposition just sketched: that the inescapable discourse principle must also, as condition for the possibility of reconstructing history, be at once the fact and telos of the history one seeks to reconstruct. I believe the principle of self-appropriation shows incontrovertibly that the rational reconstruction of rationalization processes must always take precedence over strategies of external explanation and unmasking (such as externally explanatory sociology, base-superstructure theories, and other types of ideology critique; psychoanalysis; "genealogies" à la Nietzsche or Foucault; structuralistic, system-functionalistic, or Being-historical explanations of the present era; deconstruction; and so on). Naturally this in no way says that the above external explanations cannot be more or less appropriate supplements to a "maximally internal" (Lakatos) reconstruction. It does mean, though, that the *reductionism* of the "nothing but" explanations—the really influential and mostly scientistic antimetaphysics of modernity and seemingly of "postmodernity" as well—is definitively finished off by the self-appropriation principle of the reconstructive sciences. The "happy total demystifiers of human rationality" either get caught in performative self-contradictions or immunize themselves against possible criticism by refusing to argue (e.g., totally freeing themselves from rules). It must also be emphasized that fully grounding the reconstruction of rationalization processes in the self-appropriation principle allows the charge of Eurocentrism to be avoided, in contrast to Max Weber's hypothetically grounded reconstruction, which has to appear obviously one-sided and incomplete in light of the discourse principle. The charge of Eurocentrism can be leveled only if one considers it possible to criticize the very reason one demonstrably makes use of, on the basis of the "Other of reason" or, what amounts to the same thing, "another reason" that later could become the standard.

In his three-dimensional discourse principle spelling out the three world relations and validity claims of speech, Habermas has set out a rather complete point of departure for the reconstruction of possible rationalization processes, where these are taken as the self-appropriation of the *logos* of reconstruction.[59] This allows one to show incontestably, by transcendental-pragmatic means, that the reconstructive sciences—just as Habermas supposes hypothetically—are entitled to single out communicative rationality (i.e., to separate it analytically from instrumental and strategic rationality and from so-called "system rationality"). In addition, one is able to show that reconstructive science can and must proceed on the assumption that universal validity claims, which are already linked to speech acts used in lifeworld communication, in principle can and must be vindicated in a discursive-consensual manner, and not simply through strategic negotiations, in contrast to mere power claims. To this extent one is also able to demonstrate, I believe, the parasitic dependence of the use of language "oriented toward success" on that "oriented toward coming to an understanding," not only with respect to the *concealed* strategic use of language but also with respect to its *openly* strategic use (which includes not just such imperatives as "Hands up!" but, more important, offers and threats used as reasons for coming to terms in hard negotiations). For anyone who seriously argues realizes and must admit that by playing out a power claim he necessarily blocks the process of reaching agreement on validity claims, an agreement whose consummation he has at the same time always already acknowledged as necessary for the redemption of those validity claims.

Yet the above transcendental-pragmatic justification, which begins with the inescapable self-reflection of argumentative discourse, is not identical with Habermas's appeal to those lifeworld communicative relations demonstrable through descriptive analyses of language. That is, by reference to the latter one can indeed demonstrate that someone using language in a "concealed strategic" manner in order to *talk* another *into* something has in himself always already acknowledged the parasitic dependence of this use of language on that (virtually argumentative) use "oriented to reaching understanding." Just this is what his speaking behavior *shows*. Nonetheless, at the level where *TCA* presents a reconstructive, empirically testable theory, one can no longer take the further step of showing that those who negotiate in an openly strategic fashion from a position of power (as the Athenians did against the inhabitants of Melos in Thucydides' account) would also have acknowledged, in their very use of language, that the standpoint of power has a parasitic relation to that of reaching agreement on validity claims through argument. One can show this in a "strictly reflective" manner only if one seriously argues, i.e., wants to find out who is right.[60]

Once again, though, it does not follow from this that the willful refusal to enter into argumentative discourse (e.g., by the skeptic not wishing to be refuted) would make an ultimate justification impossible, for at the level of philosophical discussion we may and indeed must presuppose the will to argumentation (which is precisely the will to *reach a complete agreement* on moral validity claims too—something we may not presuppose at the level of lifeworld communication such as occurs in negotiations). Now anyone who does not go along with this simply cannot argue for any point of view whatsoever. He and his possible motives can figure only as an *object* of the theorizing of those who argue, but not as a subject of arguing.[61] And if one makes the *principled* refuser of discourse an object of theorizing (disregarding for the moment the harmless case of the strategic refuser, who has already basically admitted the superiority of the opponent's arguments), one must necessarily assume that he even refuses the [internal] discourse aimed at reaching self-understanding. To that extent, one has reason to suppose that a pathological process of self-destruction is at work in such a skeptic.

I have only lately observed that Habermas often employs this or a similar argument in a fundamentally different sense. Namely, he supposes, in my view incorrectly, that the skeptic can indeed escape refutation at the level of discourse but as a human being existing in the lifeworld he cannot deny, upon pain of self-destruction, that principle of discourse, and hence of morality as well, built into linguistic communication and communicative action.[62] That strikes me as at least not a *sufficient* argument. To be sure, the *conventional* morals or the unselfconscious substantial *Sittlichkeit* that is *factually* built into the communicative action of the lifeworld (as opposed to one *virtually* present and redeemable in discourse) differs in principle from the moral questioning of the radical skeptic or principled cynic. Moreover, it is not reducible in principle to the motives of purely strategic action in a Hobbesian state of nature. Nevertheless, it also differs from the *morality* of one who has seen through the compromise every conventional in-group morality makes with the imperatives of self-assertive social systems and with strategic rationality and who is capable of affirming through rational insight the universal validity claim of a postconventional discourse ethics of responsibility. For this person, who moves at the postenlightenment level of the radical skeptical challenge and demand for rational grounding and who poses the question "Why ought I be moral at all?"—a question that means, among other things, why ought I accept coresponsibility for the consequences of the industrial society's collective activities and not rather live by the motto "What's that to me?" or "After me the deluge!"—for such a person the reference to the *unavoidable ethical lifeworld* is not a relevant answer at all. For our [more skeptical] questioner can also comfortably make do with this ethical lifeworld, conceived as it is without the incisive standard of postconventional morality, should he not be up to answering the above decisive question about the rational grounding of morality. (In my view, that would then be to remain stuck at Kohlberg's crisis level 4½.)

4 Is the Ultimate Transcendental-Pragmatic Grounding a Relapse into Dogmatic Metaphysics or Can It Rather Unmask Cryptometaphysical Tendencies, Such as Insinuations of the Historically Necessary Eclipse of Positions?

The reader—as well as the jubilarian to whom my arguments are directed above all—will have noticed that once again it is, after all, a question of rejecting the *vicious circle of the substantialistic fallacy.* In fact, the chief aim of this investigation was to spell out how something like a "naturalistic reconstructivism" or a grounding of validity "from below" is inadmissable. In my opinion, such approaches are necessarily connected with an unrealistic assessment of lifeworld circumstances that endows these with an idealistic radiance. On the other hand, the scope of the present investigation unfortunately does not allow me to fully demonstrate that my architectonic alternative of a transcendental-pragmatic strategy of justification is, after all is said and done, feasible. That is, the alternative of a reflexive ultimate justification has been able to disarm all the objections brought against it so far. This alternative grounds validity "from above," looking down from the reflexive angle of an ultimate justification of argumentation while simultaneously recognizing that the constitution of meaning (e.g., the disclosure of a meaningful world through language) depends on the historically conditioned form of sociocultural life. In what follows, I shall content myself with some remarks on the objections to it, objections Habermas apparently has made his own.

In the present context, I think the most important and most astonishing of these is the objection that questions the possibility of a participant in an argument *reflecting* on the performative knowledge of his actions [or knowledge-in-action: *Handlungswissen*], or in other words, the possibility of discursively transforming such reflexive knowledge-in-action into *propositional* knowledge (for example, reflecting on the act of making an assertion so as to arrive at the statement, "This was an assertion with a truth claim"). Habermas seems to consider the recourse to a reflexive knowledge-in-action to be a priori illegitimate. In fact, I have to draw upon such knowledge in the language game of the transcendental-pragmatic self-justification of argumentative discourse. In any case, he equates it with the recourse to a prelinguistic "experience of certainty" available "only under the conditions of a philosophy of consciousness" (such as Fichte's), from which I too have distanced myself.[63]

I must limit my reply here to the following remarks. I have never called upon a prelinguistic "experience of certainty" in the sense given this phrase by Descartes, Fichte, or Husserl. Rather, I have laid claim first and foremost to the "paradigmatic certainty" belonging to a language game in Wittgenstein's sense. Such certainty is already linguistically interpreted and constitutes in Wittgenstein's view a condition for meaningful speech.[64] To be sure, I consider it the greatest achievement of Austin's and Searle's speech act theory to have shown that one can also apply the latter sort of certainty—in a certain analogy to Fichte's prelinguistic confirmation of the evidence of "deeds" [*Tathandlungen*]—to the performative knowledge of speech acts. Habermas himself has formulated this insight in his talk of the "double structure" of speech acts.[65] With this mobilization of performative, propositionally transformable reflexive knowledge, analytic philosophy of language has entered the (transcendental-)pragmatic dimension of language use and is finally in a position to find its way back to the problematic of the subject found in the philosophy of consciousness. Analytic philosophy can then be transformed along lines informed by the primacy of *communicative intersubjectivity* (e.g., Mead's reciprocity of self-reflection and understanding of the alter ego). On the other hand, refusing the transcendental-pragmatic claim to a reflexive knowledge pertaining to speech acts would undoubtedly throw back "post-linguistic-turn" philosophy to the *abstractive deficit* of the semantistic or behavioristic-pragmatic phase of Morris and Carnap.[66] In that case, reflecting on the "validity claims" that the communicating subject performatively brings forward, perhaps Habermas's most important discovery, would not be possible at all.

Habermas also clearly agrees with still other objections against the possibility of an ultimate justification. These include the argument that it is possible for the *skeptic to refuse discourse.* I have already indicated that I consider this argument wholly untenable.[67] In addition, the *particularity* argument is likewise quite popular today. The latter seems to me identical with the objection that all the presuppositions of argumentation that *we* have to consider without alternatives and that thus are necessary *now* are perhaps in fact not *universally* valid but will at some later time prove to be unnecessary or replaceable.[68]

Permit me first to respond briefly to the last of these arguments. As far as the *categorial* presuppositions of our understanding of the world go, I would concede this argument a certain legitimacy in principle, albeit a quite esoteric one. For example, with great difficulty but at least without performative self-contradiction, it is possible for us to conceive a possible world in which one could no longer bring about an effect *b* by doing *a, ceteris paribus.* To this extent one could not presume the causal necessity of a sequence of events as a condition of possibility for action-related experience in the lifeworld and in experimental physics.[69] Yet even in this thought experiment—

as in every other attempt at mentally abrogating our categorial understanding of the world—we must still precisely presuppose the necessary presuppositions of the *discourse principle of argumentation* (the four validity claims and the presupposition of their consensual vindication in principle). Should we to try to conceive these presuppositions too as falsifiable, we would no longer be in the position to make any sense at all of the concept of falsification, nor of the fictitiously posited replacement of presuppositions corresponding to it.

The fundamental reflexive deficit found in the particularity argument, however, can be elucidated in yet another form. As with most of the other objections against a reflexive ultimate justification, this argument cannot be advanced without thereby producing a philosophical statement that precisely has to credit itself with a universal validity.[70] This shows the *reflexive inescapability* of the universal validity claims connected with specifically philosophical statements.

Only by ignoring this reflexively inescapable character of the language game that forms the context for philosophical argumentation does one arrive at the further objection raised by G. Schönrich, and apparently taken over by Habermas, that equates ultimate justification with a *petitio tollendi.* As H. Lenk uses the term, it means that the transcendental-pragmatic argument amounts to a *formal-logical* demonstration of the *irresistibility* [*Nichtverwerfbarkeit*] of a validity claim within a language game that, as a *factually given* whole, can indeed be called into question.[71] However, precisely this is not possible in relation to the language game—used by Schönrich as well—in which one is able to talk about *language games in general* and relativize their paradigmatic certainties as merely factual presuppositions. As presuppositions that cannot be disputed without performative self-contradiction and, for that very reason, cannot be deductively justified without a *petitio principii,* the reflexively ascertained presuppositions of this language game are not simply the *formally irresistible* aspects of a merely factually presupposed language game. Rather, in conjunction with the transcendental-pragmatic language game whose pragmatic presupposition is not contingent, such presuppositions must also be acknowledged as unavoidable presuppositions of philosophy.

It seems to me that Schönrich and many other critics of transcendental pragmatics have not really taken seriously what Kuhlmann and I have repeatedly emphasized: that the *logico-semantic* concept of *deductive* justification—or more generally, that of deriving one thing from another via deduction, induction, abduction, or even "transcendental deduction"—is replaced here by the *pragmatic* one of the reflexive return to what cannot be circumvented in philosophical argumentation and thus is not in need of justification. This consideration leads me to conclude with an attempt at characterizing, from a greater distance, the significance of the transcendental-pragmatic strategy of justification as this bears in particular on the philosophical grounding of ethics. Three points must suffice here.

• A logical dilemma is often invoked to the effect that one cannot rationally justify the obligation to be moral or rational because this would already presuppose what has to be justified. Here this dilemma has no force whatever, since the ultimate transcendental-pragmatic justification consists in the *reflexive* confirmation of the principles of reason that have necessarily already been acknowledged. (As shown earlier, the one who seriously argues has also, by his serious questioning, already in principle acknowledged a coresponsibility, in the practical-rational sense.)

• By avoiding the traditional concepts of justification (whether that of the deductive, inductive, or abductive derivation of one thing from another), a transcendental-pragmatic justification has also left *foundationalism* behind, where the latter term has the sense of a dogmatic metaphysics recurring to axioms assumed as evident. The strictly reflective ultimate justification in no way includes *metaphysical assumptions*. It is open to self-critique and constant self-revision insofar as it continually readjusts the necessary explication of the discourse principle in light of the presuppositions that are already necessarily presupposed—in the sense this principle intends—for each *revision* and are to that extent ultimately grounded. Of course, in contrast to Habermas, I believe such *self-correction* is something essentially different from testing the hypotheses of empirical-reconstructive science against evidence *external to argumentation,* as this is done, for example, by linguists when they gather evidence from the rule intuitions of as many and diverse competent speakers as possible.

• As a metaphysics-free, transcendental-reflexive confirmation of the inescapable presuppositions of philosophical argumentation, the transcendental-pragmatic justification of the standpoint of reason also contains the standards able to unmask cryptometaphysical theorizing, such as that already pointed out in variants of scientistic reductionism. One of the most exquisite of such tendencies to backslide into cryptometaphysics, however, is the currently widespread attempt to replace argued philosophical refutations with the mere insinuation that this or that approach—e.g., "ultimate justification" or "transcendental philosophy," possibly even philosophy as a discipline of justification in general—has now become obsolete, been surpassed by history, etc. In my opinion, this reflects an inability to shake off the motif of historical necessity bound up with the speculative philosophy of history (what Karl Popper called "historicism"). And this danger of cryptometaphysics is greatest when one tries to avoid a transcendental-reflexive justification, which alone guarantees a standpoint of reason independent of history.[72] In that case it gets to the point of the peculiar arrogance of a philosophy wanting to conceive its own end as necessary. Critical-reflexive philosophy will, I think, survive this, unless the barbarity of reflection (Vico) in fact leads to a regression of human culture back to primitive conditions.

Notes

1. Two vols., trans. Thomas McCarthy (Boston, 1984, 1987); hereafter cited as *TCA.*

2. See John Searle, *Intentionality* (Cambridge, 1983), chap. 5, "The Background."

3. Of course, in my opinion that does not mean one would have to accept the thesis defining Rorty's *historicism,* which holds that there is only a "contingent basis for consensus." Compare my discussion of Rorty's essay "The Priority of Democracy to Philosophy" (in M. Peterson and R. Vaughan, eds., *The Virginia Statute for Religious Freedom* [Cambridge, 1988], pp. 257–282) in "Zurück zur Normalität? Oder könnten

wir aus der nationalen Katastrophe etwas Besonderes gelernt haben?" in Apel, *Diskurs und Verantwortung: Das Problem des Übergangs zur postkonventionellen Moral* (Frankfurt am Main, 1988), pp. 370–474.

4. See C. S. Peirce on the "paper doubt" in his critique of Descartes: *Collected Papers of Charles Sanders Peirce,* 8 vols., ed. Charles Hartshorne, Paul Weiss and Arthur W. Banks (Cambridge, Mass., 1931–1935, 1958), 5.265. Admittedly, Peirce later made it clear in his essay "Fallibilism, Continuity and Evolution" (*Collected Papers* 1.141–175) that a *principled fallibilism* can be maintained at the methodological metalevel, regardless of currently indubitable certainties.

5. See Ludwig Wittgenstein, *On Certainty,* ed. G. E. M. Anscombe and G. H. von Wright, trans. Denis Paul and G. E. M. Anscombe (New York, 1969).

6. [Apel's concept of ultimate justification (or ultimate grounding: *Letztbegründung*) involves some terminology of which the reader should be aware. Inasmuch as an ultimate justification relies on what Kuhlmann has termed "strict reflection," it is sometimes designated as a "reflexive ultimate justification" (*reflexive Letztbegründung*); see notes 34 and 52 below. This latter designation stems from the fact that such justification turns on one's being reflexively aware *in actu* of what one is doing when one raises and questions claims in argument. Thus the propositions that thematize such awareness cannot be treated with the same detachment with which one treats hypotheses or theories that could prove false. For this reason I will often prefer the term "reflexive" over "reflective." Finally, what this reflexive grasp reveals are those presuppositions of argument that "cannot be gotten behind" (*nicht hintergehbar*). This last term has been variously translated. Although the German contains traces of "nontranscendable," the basic idea seems to be the same as that expressed by "inescapable" in Anglo-American discussions of self-referential claims. Thus I shall use either the latter term or circumlocutions such as "cannot be circumvented."—Translator]

7. See especially Jürgen Habermas, "Discourse Ethics: Notes on a Program of Philosophical Justification," in Habermas, *Moral Consciousness and Communicative Action,* trans. Christian Lenhardt and Shierry Weber Nicholsen (Cambridge, Mass., 1990), pp. 43–115.

8. This first occurs in "What Is Universal Pragmatics?" in Jürgen Habermas, *Communication and the Evolution of Society,* trans. Thomas McCarthy (Boston, 1979), pp. 1–68.

9. In my opinion, Habermas's explication of the problematic of the fallibilism proviso remains unclear in his Reply that appeared in Axel Honneth and Hans Joas, eds., *Communicative Action: Essays on Jürgen Habermas's "The Theory of Communicative Action,"* trans. Jeremy Gaines and Doris L. Jones (Cambridge, Mass., 1990), pp. 214–264. There Habermas highlights the pragmatically incontestable fact that we no longer *speak* of "hypotheses" in those cases where the lack of opposing criteria leads us to be "convinced of the definitive truth of 'p' as a statement the validity of which is accepted" (p. 232). Yet this point is completely irrelevant for the Peircean and Popperian principle of fallibilism. Precisely the argument, also advanced by Habermas, that even "reasons which are sufficiently convincing today *could* tomorrow be devastated by criticism" (p. 232) lead Peirce and Popper to declare truth claims that are *factually* considered certain or final to be also in principle hypotheses subject to the fallibilistic proviso. Habermas too reaches this result when he defends the principled "openness" of all discourses (p. 231). The difference is that Peirce and Popper also realize that one can put forward a definitive truth claim—in the sense of the grammatical role of the expression "true"—while simultaneously being aware, at the critical-philosophical

level, of the possible fallibility of one's truth claim. Along with Hans Albert (whether he is so aware or not), I see this principled reflective distinction between *truth* claims and *certainty* claims as an achievement of philosophical enlightenment.

But with this, of course, the reflective enlightenment is not yet finished. The question brought up by Kuhlmann and myself still has to be answered: whether it makes sense to expect that those philosophical statements spelling out fallibilism and its call for ongoing attempts at falsification will themselves one day prove to be fallible. The decisive, meaning-critical argument against this possibility runs as follows: If, or the extent to which, this would occur, one could no longer *understand* what "fallible" or "falsification" mean at all, since the statements at issue here explicate the principle of fallibilism, that is, the presuppositions necessarily implied by it (which are precisely the necessary presuppositions of argumentation that Habermas himself has explicated in the postulates of discourse and consensus). To be sure, these statements can, *as explications of meaning, be corrected under the presupposition they are true.* But they are infallible precisely insofar as they state necessary presuppositions of the principle of fallibilism.

Kuhlmann has, in my view rightly, inferred from this a difference in principle between classes of statements. As I read it, this distinction corresponds to the one Peirce and Popper had already drawn between statements that formulate a *truth claim,* such as those of empirical science, and the reflective statements that pertain to philosophical methodology or scientific logic and formulate the fallibility proviso, i.e., one's reservation regarding the *certainty* attaching to each empirical truth claim. One must undoubtedly add, however, that the transcendental-pragmatic statements of philosophical-methodological reflection take such reflection even further beyond the limits of meaningful fallibilism to the point of a reflexive self-confirmation [*Selbstvergewisserung*] of the inescapable truth claims of philosophy.

Habermas dismissed Kuhlmann's argument with the following assertion: "There are no meta-discourses in the sense that a higher discourse is able to prescribe rules for a subordinate discourse. Argumentation games do not form a hierarchy" (p. 231). Might he have noticed that this sentence claims exactly what he denies and thus that he falls into a *performative self-contradiction?* It is simply not so easy, in my view it is impossible, for philosophers to renounce formulations at the highest conceivable level of reflection and generality, which state what in general is the case. On this point see Wolfgang Kuhlmann, "Philosophie und rekonstruktive Wissenschaft," *Zeitschrift für philosophische Forschung* 40 (1986): 224–234, and also Karl-Otto Apel, "Fallibilismus, Konsenstheorie der Wahrheit und Letztbegründung," in Forum für Philosophie Bad Homburg (Wolfgang R. Köhler, Wolfgang Kuhlmann, and Peter Rohs), ed., *Philosophie und Begründung* (Frankfurt am Main, 1987), pp. 116–211.

10. See G. Radnitzky, "In Defense of Self-Applicable Critical Rationalism," in International Cultural Foundation, ed., *Absolute Values and the Creation of the New World* (New York, 1983), vol. 2, 1025–1069.

11. See Habermas's more recent Reply, in Honneth and Joas, eds., *Communicative Action,* pp. 245 f. and 248 f.

12. See Habermas, "What Is Universal Pragmatics?" (see note 8), and also his "Discourse Ethics," (see note 7), pp. 97 f. and passim.

13. Herbert Schnädelbach, "The Transformation of Critical Theory," in Honneth and Joas, eds., *Communicative Action,* pp. 7–22, here p. 22 [I have altered the translation of this and subsequent quotations from this text.—Translator]

14. See Habermas, "Discourse ethics," pp. 99 f., 102. In answer to Habermas's summary, "In a word, the skeptic may reject morality but he cannot reject the ethical substance [*Sittlichkeit*]" (p. 100), I would like to reply as follows: The skeptic, as

representative of philosophical enlightenment, can, with apparently and/or genuinely good reasons, challenge every form of *factual* ethical life and even, at great existential risk, reject it. But if he succeeds in thinking this through to the end—in Kohlberg's terms, if he gets past the crisis stage 4½ of "sophistical" enlightenment—he realizes that he cannot rationally reject (i.e., not without committing a performative self-contradiction) the principle of morality elaborated by discourse ethics. He has then arrived at that rational standard [*Vernunftmaßstab*] of morality that Habermas himself defended so convincingly, in his exchange with Bubner, against the substantialistic temptation (see "Über Moralität und Sittlichkeit—Was macht eine Lebensform rational?" in Herbert Schnädelbach, ed., *Rationalität* [Frankfurt am Main, 1984], pp. 218–235). I would like to argue with this Habermas against the Habermas of "Discourse Ethics." See also note 48 below.

15. Habermas, "Discourse Ethics," pp. 99 ff.

16. Habermas, "Discourse Ethics," p. 104; also Habermas, "Über Moralität und Sittlichkeit," in Schnädelbach, ed., *Rationalität,* pp. 218–235 (see note 14 above).

17. Habermas, "Discourse Ethics," p. 98.

18. See the last two essays in Apel, *Diskurs und Verantwortung:* "Die transzendentalpragmatische Begründung der Kommunikationsethik und das Problem der höchsten Stufe einer Entwicklungslogik des moralischen Bewußtseins," pp. 306–369, and "Zurück zur Normalität?" pp. 370–474.

19. See Klaus Eder, *Die Entstehung staatlich organisierter Gesellschaften* (Frankfurt am Main, 1976).

20. Lawrence Kohlberg, Charles Levine, and Alexandra Hewer, *Moral Stages: A Current Formulation and a Response to My Critics* (Basel, 1983).

21. Schnädelbach, "Transformation," in *Communicative Action,* p. 12.

22. Schnädelbach, "Transformation," p. 14; citing also Habermas, *TCA* 1:115.

23. See Karl-Otto Apel, *Understanding and Explanation: A Transcendental-Pragmatic Perspective,* trans. Georgia Warneke (Cambridge, Mass., 1984), pp. 162 ff.

24. See William Dray, *Laws and Explanation in History* (Oxford, 1957).

25. See Otfried Höffe, *Strategien der Humanität* (Freiburg/Munich, 1975).

26. See Max Weber, *Economy and Society,* 2 vols., ed. Guenther Roth and Claus Wittich (Berkeley, 1978), 1:24–25. Also on this point, see Habermas, *TCA* 1:281 f.

27. See Karl-Otto Apel, "Das Problem der Begründung einer Verantwortungsethik im Zeitalter der Wissenschaft," in Edmund Braun, ed., *Wissenschaft und Ethik* (Frankfurt am Main, 1986), pp. 11–52.

28. See Karl-Otto Apel, "The Common Presuppositions of Hermeneutics and Ethics: Types of Rationality beyond Science and Technology," in Jan Baermark, ed., *Perspectives in Metascience* (Goeteborg, 1979), pp. 39–55.

29. I think this consideration contains the answer a transcendental-pragmatic discourse ethics can give to the objections that can be raised from the perspective of an

ethics of responsibility or *care* against a pure *justice ethics.* Naturally I cannot pursue this here, but see the subject index to Apel, *Diskurs und Verantwortung.*

30. Schnädelbach, "Transformation," *Communicative Action,* p. 16.

31. On this point and the following, see note 9.

32. In my essays "Die Logosauszeichnung der menschlichen Sprache," in Hans-Georg Bosshardt, ed., *Perspektiven auf Sprache: Interdisziplinäre Beiträge zum Gedenken an Hans Hörmann* (Berlin, 1986), pp. 45–87, and "Die Herausforderung der totalen Vernunftkritik und das Programm einer philosophischen Theorie der Rationalitätstypen," *Concordia* 11 (1987): 2–23, I explicated the discourse principle as a *logos* principle that should be opposed to the proposition-oriented logos concept employed in logical semantics, the Heideggerian notion of "enframing" [*Gestells*] and Derrida's "logocentrism."

33. See Jean-Francois Lyotard, *The Postmodern Condition: A Report on Knowledge,* trans. Geoff Bennington and Brian Massumi (Minneapolis, 1984); see also Manfred Frank, *Die Grenzen der Verständigung* (Frankfurt am Main, 1988).

34. See my formula for ultimate grounding in "Das Problem der philosophischen Letztbegründung im Lichte einer transzendentalen Sprachpramatik," in Bernulf Kanitschheider, ed., *Sprache und Erkenntnis: Festschrift für Gerhard Frey zum 60. Geburtstag* (Innsbruck, 1976), pp. 55–82; see also Wolfgang Kuhlmann, *Reflexive Letztbegründung: Untersuchungen zur Transzendentalpragmatik* (Freiburg, 1985).

35. *TCA* 1:297.

36. *Tractatus Logico-philosophicus,* trans. D. F. Pears and B. F. McGuinness (New York, 1961), see 4.024.

37. See Imre Lakatos, "Die Geschichte der Wissenschaft und ihre rationalen Rekonstruktionen," trans. Paul Feyerabend, in Werner Diederich, ed., *Theorien der Wissenschaftsgeschichte: Beiträge zur diachronen Wissenschaftstheorie* (Frankfurt am Main, 1974), pp. 55–119.

38. Habermas, *TCA* 1:115 f.

39. See Karl-Otto Apel, "Scientism or Transcendental Hermeneutics? On the Question of the Subject of the Interpretation of Signs in the Semiotics of Pragmatism," in Apel, *Towards a Transformation of Philosophy,* trans. Glyn Adey and David Frisby (London, 1980), pp. 93–135.

40. See above all Habermas, "What Is Universal Pragmatics?" and *TCA,* vol. 1, chapter 3.

41. Lawrence Kohlberg sees this quite clearly in his late essay "Justice as Reversibility: The Claim to Moral Adequacy of the Highest Stage of Moral Judgment," in Kohlberg, *The Philosophy of Moral Development* (San Francisco, 1984), pp. 191 ff.

42. See Immanuel Kant, *What Real Progress Has Metaphysics Made in Germany since the Time of Leibniz and Wolff?* trans. Ted Humphrey (New York, 1983), "Solution to the Academy's Problem, II: Purported Theoretical-Dogmatic Progress in Moral Theology during the Epoch of Leibniz and Wolff," pp. 147–151; see also his *On the Old Saw: It May Be Right in Theory, but It Won't Work in Practice,* trans. E. B. Ashton (Philadelphia, 1974), chapter 3, pp. 75–81.

43. Jürgen Habermas, "Zur Philosophischen Diskussion um Marx und den Marxismus," in Habermas, *Theorie und Praxis* (Neuwied, 1963), pp. 261–335.

44. See Jürgen Habermas, "Reconstruction and Interpretation in the Social Sciences," in his *Moral Consciousness and Communicative Action,* p. 39. See also Kohlberg, *Moral Stages* (see note 20), pp. 15 ff.

45. See Karl-Otto Apel, "Die transzendentalpragmatische Begründung der Kommunikationsethik und das Problem der höchsten Stufe einer Entwicklungslogik des moralischen Bewußtseins," in *Diskurs und Verantwortung,* pp. 306–369.

46. On this, see note 9 above.

47. See Habermas, Reply, pp. 230 ff. and, on the other hand, pp. 243 ff., where Habermas once again confuses the transcendental-pragmatical inescapability of the formal-pragmatic presuppositions of communication—and thus of argumentative discourse in cases of disagreement—with that of the "*massive preunderstanding* of those who communicatively share the culturally habituated and internalized self-evident assumptions of an intuitively present, prereflexively known lifeworld presupposed as unproblematic" [p. 244; translation altered—Translator]. The latter assumptions have an inescapability relevant for everyday life but certainly not for methodological reflection. See also p. 249, where the "advantage of arriving at one's conceptualization of society from philosophical premises" cannot be effectively clarified because the conceptualization merely recurs to the "factual recognition of counterfactual validity claims" in the lifeworld and not, as would be necessary to refute the objections, to a demonstration that anyone who argues must acknowledge certain universal and formal-procedural basic norms of a discourse ethics—and this in distinction to the factual ethical substance [*Sittlichkeit*] of the lifeworld, which is always more or less limited to meeting the formal standard of discourse morality "halfway."

48. See Karl-Otto Apel, "Ist die philosophische Letztbegründung moralischer Normen auf die reale Praxis anwendbar?" in *Funkkolleg Praktische Philosophie/Ethik: Dialogue* (Frankfurt am Main, 1984), vol. 2, pp. 123–146, and *Studientexte* (Weinheim, n.d.), vol. 2, pp. 606–634.

49. See Jürgen Habermas, "Morality and Ethical Life: Does Hegel's Critique of Kant Apply to Discourse Ethics?" in Habermas, *Moral Consciousness and Communicative Action,* pp. 195–215. Here Habermas ultimately defends (against neo-Aristotelian and neo-Hegelian objections) the primacy of morality's function of setting universalistic standards, while rightly acknowledging the complementary necessity to realize the "good life" at the level of ethical life. In my opinion, this line of argument is quite inconsistent with the strategy Habermas summons against an ultimate justification of morality, i.e., his attempt to ultimately ground the universally valid standard of morality in the ethical lifeworld.

50. See note 3.

51. Trans. Frederick Lawrence (Cambridge, Mass., 1987). Even here, though, he is not consistent when it comes to grounding ethics; see note 60 below.

52. See my argument and Habermas's quite typical objection in Willi Oelmüller, ed., *Transzendentalphilosophische Normenbegründungen* (Paderborn, 1978), p. 227. The insight into methodological inescapability is tied to the self-reflection of participants engaged in argumentation *as* those who are so engaged. Hence it is tied to philosophizing as that reflective form of lifeworld communication in general, which can without confusion distinguish between, on the one hand, the merely factually necessary but none-

theless historically contingent and culturally specific "background" presuppositions of communication and, on the other, the a priori necessary presuppositions of every argumentative communication and thus of all thinking with validity claims. "Objective" theories about necessary rule following, e.g., in the sense of grammar, are in principle unable to make this analytical separation between contingent and a priori presuppositions, since such theories, which are not self-referential, tend to relativize the objectively ascertained rule-oriented necessity as contingent at the very moment they explain this necessity. (This is what happens, for example, with Chomsky's theory of an innate grammatical competence, a theory that expressly does not concern all the grammatical rules constructible by linguists. The same thing even happens with Kant's "transcendental deduction" of the categories and principles of knowledge insofar as this theory too, which as transcendental must also be self-referential, cannot justify its claiming for itself another sort of knowledge of the existence and function of the thing in itself, a knowledge that, strictly speaking, is "transcendent.")

Wolfgang Kuhlmann has formulated this point using the term "strict reflection" (on the performative certainties of arguing). He argues that for argumentation to have any sense at all we have to suppose ourselves capable, at any point in a discourse, of transposing performative certainties, e.g., that we now assert something or pose a question, into propositional certainty. See Wolfgang Kuhlmann, "Reflexive Letztbegründung" *Zeitschrift für philosophische Forschung* 35 (1981): 4–26.

53. C. F. Gethmann and R. Hegselmann, "Das Problem der Begründung zwischen Dezisionismus und Fundamentalismus," *Zeitschrift für Allgemeine Wissenschaften* 8 (1977): 342–368.

54. Viggo Rossvaer, "Transzendentalpragmatik, transzendentale Hermeneutik und die Möglichkeit, Auschwitz zu verstehen," in Dietrich Böhler, Tore Nordenstam, and Gunnar Skribekk, eds., *Die pragmatische Wende: Sprachspielpragmatik oder Transzendentalpragmatik?* (Frankfurt am Main, 1986), pp. 187–201.

55. See note 3.

56. A caricature of discourse ethics along these lines can be found in the idea of a strategically expedient morality merely set up for conducting an argumentative discourse when it happens to be useful for all those participating. I have dealt in detail with this view, which is especially represented by Karl-Heinz Ilting, in "Faktische Anerkennung oder einsehbar notwendige Anerkennung? Beruht der Ansatz der transzendentalpragmatischen Diskursethik auf einem intellektualistischen Fehlschluß?" in K.-O. Apel and R. Pozzo, eds., *Zur Rekonstruktion der praktischen Philosophie: Gedenkschrift für Karl-Heinz Ilting* (Stuttgart, 1990).

57. See my argument against Popper's supposition of a prerational decision for reason in "Sprache als Thema und Medium der transzendentalen Reflexion," in *Transformation der Philosophie,* vol. 2 (Frankfurt am Main, 1973), pp. 311–329, but also see my argument in note 61 below against Habermas's assumption that the skeptic in principle could refuse to argue.

58. See the subject index in Apel, *Diskurs und Verantwortung.*

59. As Habermas realizes, difficulties persist in the attempt to base the claim involved in authentic artistic expression, a claim one could correlate with a rationalization process, on the expressive claim to truthfulness. It also seems to me unlikely that the fundamental validity claim to intelligibility, which has to precede the three validity claims differentiated by world relations, may be reduced to the claim to grammatical well-formedness. For in my opinion one of the greatest achievements of the post-Peircean and post-Wittgensteinian critique of meaning lies in the demonstration that

not only syntactically well-formed sentences but even sentences ostensibly above semantic suspicion disqualify themselves a priori as bearers of truth claims because they destroy their own meaning (e.g., the sentence, "In the end, *everything* considered real is *merely my dream*"). Finally, the claim to intelligibility would from the start have to be related to the historically conditioned lifeworld constitution of a meaningful world (e.g., the linguistic disclosure of meaning), without once again reducing the independent *justification of validity* to the lifeworld in the process. See Karl-Otto Apel, "Sinnkonstitution und Geltungsrechtfertigung," in Forum für Philosophie, ed., *Martin Heidegger: Innen- und Außenansichten* (Frankfurt am Main, 1989), pp. 107–151.

60. See Karl-Otto Apel, "Sprachliche Bedeutung, Wahrheit und normative Gültigkeit: Die soziale Bindekraft der Rede im Lichte einer transzendentalen Sprachpragmatik," *Archivio di filosofia* 55 (1987): 51–88. One might be able to object that even in hard negotiations such as those the Athenians conducted with the Melians, those parties taking the standpoint of power would still at least have to raise truth claims (e.g., in order to support rhetorically effective threats by referring to the existing power relations). To this extent they would also have to implicitly raise rightness claims that pertain to speech acts, as Habermas spells out. This seems to me not to hold true, however, insofar as the "hardliners" can limit their rightness claim to the motivating power of the *reasons* advanced by appeal to an openly strategic, power-backed use of language aimed to move the addressees to accept what is said (e.g., about demands). Only if the "hardliners" were to defend their truth claims in an argumentative discourse as validity claims capable of consensus could one show in principle that they are also therewith constrained to acknowledge the moral equality of the addressees and give up their restriction of mutual communicative understanding to strategic, power-oriented purposes.

To avoid misunderstanding, when I argue that the methodological presupposition of the transcendental pragmatics of argumentative discourse has primacy for grounding the validity of *TCA,* in no way do I intend to deny that factually existing mutual linguistic understanding among human beings shows how much *all* forms of sociocultural life are "at least implicitly geared to maintaining communicative action by means of argument" (Habermas, "Discourse Ethics," p. 100). In fact, I share this conviction with Habermas, and to that extent I consider the Hobbesian fiction of a "state of nature" made up of purely strategic interactions between human beings to be incompatible with the fact of mutual linguistic understanding. But this conviction is the central hypothesis of a reconstructive theory of cultural evolution and must still for its part be grounded. If understood as being itself a grounding, this hypothesis is transformed into the dogmatic axiom of a speculative metaphysics of history. Nevertheless, there is no urgency to ground the hypothesis, since every act of disputing it necessary moves at the level of argumentative discourse already and to that extent has to violate the principle of self appropriation. One can even assert that lifeworld communication *must* also have already been "implicitly geared to maintaining communicative action by means of argument," and still it would be false to claim one could demonstrate this quasi-sociologically through an empirically testable understanding of lifeworld reality.

61. Oddly enough, in "Discourse Ethics," pp. 99–100, Habermas sees in precisely this circumstance an argument that the skeptic cannot be refuted in debate, as if the skeptic could fully withdraw from discourse and nevertheless somehow advance the skeptical position. In fact, this can be advanced at best by those persons, such as Habermas, who make themselves the skeptic's advocate. Once again, however, one can convict such advocates, as persons engaged in arguing, of performative self-contradiction. On the basis of this discourse-immanent certainty one must have very serious misgivings *about* the condition of the existential skeptic who refuses to argue.

62. Habermas, "Discourse Ethics," pp. 99–101.

63. Habermas, "Discourse Ethics," p. 96.

64. See Apel, "Das Problem der philosophischen Letztbegründung," in *Sprache und Erkenntnis,* pp. 55–82 (see note 34 above).

65. See Apel, "Die Logosauszeichnung der menschlichen Sprache," in *Perspektiven auf Sprache,* pp. 45–87 (see note 32).

66. See Karl-Otto Apel, "Pragmatische Sprachphilosophie in transzendentalsemiotischer Begründung," in Herbert Stachowiak, ed., *Pragmatik: Handbuch pragmatischen Denkens,* vol. 4, part 1 (Hamburg, 1989).

67. See note 61.

68. Habermas, "Discourse Ethics," pp. 95 f.

69. See Apel, *Understanding and Explanation,* pp. 57 ff.

70. If this is subsequently disputed, we get into the *paradox of a fallibilism principle applicable to itself,* something I have discussed in my "Fallibilismus, Konsenstheorie der Wahrheit und Letztbegründung," pp. 174 ff. (see note 9 above).

71. See Gerhard Schönrich, *Kategorien und transzendentale Argumentation* (Frankfurt am Main, 1981), pp. 188 ff. and also Habermas, "Discourse Ethics," pp. 95 ff.

72. See Apel, "Die Herausforderung der totalen Vernunftkritik" (see note 32).

6

What Is a Pragmatic Theory of Meaning? Variations on the Proposition "We Understand a Speech Act When We Know What Makes It Acceptable."[1]

Albrecht Wellmer

Translated by William Rehg

1

What does it mean to understand an utterance? An easy and apparently plausible answer would be, to understand *what* a speaker *says* and *how* he *means* what he says. The sense [*Sinn*] of an utterance is understood here as the resultant of two forces: the meaning [*Bedeutung*] of a sentence and the intention of a speaker who wants to say something (to do something, to make something understood) with this sentence.[2] If in a restaurant I tell a waitress, "I would like a steak," then *what* I say is that I would like a steak (the expression of a wish); what I *mean* is that she should bring me a steak; what I (intentionally) *do* is to order a steak. By contrast, if I tell my friend during a strenuous hike through the mountains, "I would like a steak," I do not order a steak but rather give expression to a strong craving. If I utter the same sentence during a lecture, then in all probability I am giving an example of a statement of desire that can be used in different ways and with different intentions. Finally, if as an actor I utter the same sentence during a performance, then I am not expressing a wish but rather playing someone who expresses a wish. The examples can be multiplied. I mention them to clarify the first, tentative answer to the opening question. Yet the examples already show that this answer is, if not false, then nevertheless misleading, for it introduces the intention or the speaker's intended "meaning" [*Meinung*] as an independent variable, as something that affixes itself to the sentence meaning [*Satzbedeutung*] from the outside, as it were. Once one has taken this step, however, it is easy to go one more and interpret the speaker intention as constitutive for the sense of an utterance, and thereby ultimately *reduce* the sentence meanings to speaker intentions. The above examples, however, point in the opposite direction, showing that actually it is not (independent) speaker intentions that affix themselves to sentence meanings in order to determine the sense of an utterance. Rather, the *situations* and *contexts* of an utterance are what determine how a speaker *can* mean an uttered sentence. The sense of an utterance would consequently be a "resultant" not of sentence meaning and speaker intention but rather of sentence meaning and the utterance *situation.* Suppose a speaker and hearer both understand a situation as having the pragmatically univocal sense of "promising." If in this situation the speaker says, "I promise I'll come tomorrow," he customarily has no choice at all regarding his communicative intention. Although he could be insincere, it is difficult to see how he could *mean* his utterance as other than a promise to come tomorrow. In another situation the same utterance could be meant as an ironic threat, but only in cases where the utterance situation *does not* fix the possible sense of an utterance—or at least does not fix it in all respects, as in the use of deictic expressions—is there *elbow room* for speaker intentions, and hence a possible occasion for the question "*How* do you mean that?" or "*What* (which) do you mean?" etc.

Naturally I am not saying that the latter cases are unimportant or trivial but only that they are *secondary* from the viewpoint of a theory of meaning. By "secondary" I mean that in those cases where a speaker's comprehensible intention goes beyond what the speaker explicitly says (as, for example, in the case of conversational implicatures[3] or indirect speech acts[4]), it must at least be possible for the speaker to make this intention explicit. However, *if* he *actually* wants to make it explicit, he has to move to that level of mutual linguistic understanding [*Verständigung*] where what he can *mean* with an utterance is determined by the meaning of the expressions used and the situation (the "context") of their utterance.[5] Here I am not referring to those cases where a speaker cannot say what he means because he cannot find the linguistic expression that would render an unclear intention clear, both to himself and others. The latter case involves an entirely different relation between implicit and explicit speaker intentions than that assumed above, for here the speaker "means" something in a *determinate* sense only when he has *found* the linguistic expression for *what* he means.

2

What holds for the speaker's intended "meaning" must also hold for the hearer's understanding [*Verstehen*]. Consequently, in order to understand the sense of an utterance, the hearer must be familiar with the meaning of the linguistic expression used and also know what a speaker can mean with an utterance in a given utterance situation. For a hearer correctly to understand the speaker's utterance, i.e., his illocutionary act (and hence his "communicative intention" as well), the speaker's and hearer's *understandings* of the situation [*Situationsverständnisse*] must overlap to a sufficient extent. If this presupposition is not fulfilled, it may be impossible for the hearer to recognize how the speaker's utterance is then and there "situated" and thus what the speaker's communicative intention is. Insofar as that presupposition is fulfilled, the hearer will in many cases understand the speaker's communicative intention, and thus the sense of his utterance, simply as the only one *possible* for a given speech act in this situation. (In cases of doubt he can ask the speaker, what, who, or how he meant it; see above.) In such cases I will, for example, correctly understand a speaker's utterance of "I promise you I'll come tomorrow" as the speaker's promise to come (where I am) tomorrow. It is, of course, no accident that in order to *reproduce* the sense of the relevant utterance, I use essentially the same expressions as the speaker, that is to say, the same sentence scheme "*x* promises *y* to come tomorrow"; I reproduce the sense of his utterance, and thus what I have understood, by transforming a sentence he has used performatively into the corresponding descriptive sentence "He promised me to come tomorrow." That in such cases I use the same expressions as the speaker in order to reproduce the sense of his utterance, and thus in order to say which illocutionary act he carried out, simply by moving from a performative to a descriptive use of the performative verb reflects the fact that we speak a *common* language. I follow Wittgenstein in the view that we mistake the concepts of sentence meaning, intended meaning, and understanding from the start if we do not make the intersubjectivity of a common language the *point of departure* for the analysis. On this presupposition, however, what a hearer can understand as the sense of a linguistic utterance is determined by his knowledge of how he as *speaker* could *mean* such an utterance. If the hearer is therefore to make his understanding of an utterance linguistically explicit, he will ultimately have to fall back on the same linguistic means of expression that the speaker also used, or those the latter *could* use to explain his utterance. In short, the conditions for the possibility of understanding something [*Verstehens*] are identical with the conditions for the possibility of meaning something [*Meinens*].

Of course, this sort of reflection has the prima facie unsatisfying quality of being rather uninformative. In fact, it looks as if we have so far only managed to avoid the issue, shifting our focus inconspicuously from the opening question "What does it mean to understand an utterance?" to two other questions: "What does it mean to understand the meaning [*Bedeutung*] of linguistic expressions and sentences?" and "What does it mean to 'understand' speech (and action) situations?" I proposed the thesis that the speaker's "communicative intention," and thus the sense of an utterance, is largely determined by the meaning of the linguistic expressions employed and the speech situation.[6] Thus in understanding utterances, the hearer's "understanding" of both the sentence meaning and the situation would have to manifest itself. Having recalled that the linguistic competences of speakers and hearers are two complementary manifestations of the *same* competence, I would like in the following to take up the opening question again by going into the *interconnection* between understanding meaning, understanding the situation, and understanding an utterance. Only in this way will I approach the *kind* of considerations underlying Habermas's proposition cited in the title.

3

Utterances are always utterances-in-situations. Sentences, by contrast, are merely potential utterances. Knowing the meaning of sentences or, more generally, linguistic expressions means knowing how one can use them in utterances in order to reach an understanding *with someone about something.* I consider this basic thesis of Habermas, which one can understand as an explication of a basic Wittgensteinian thesis, so evident that rather than justify it at this point, I would like simply to explain it in the further course of my reflections. From now on I will terminologically distinguish between the *understanding* [*Verstehen*] of linguistic *utterances* and the *knowledge* of linguistic *meanings* [*Bedeutungen*]. This terminological distinction recommends itself for distinguishing the general character of the knowledge and ability a competent language user must possess from the *occasional* character of the "knowledge" that a hearer possesses when he understands the sense of a linguistic utterance. It need not be especially emphasized that the two forms of "knowledge" mutually refer to and explain one another: one cannot explain what it means to understand an utterance without recurring to speakers' and hearers' "knowledge of meaning" [*Bedeutungswissen*]. And one cannot explain wherein this "meaning knowledge" consists without recurring to the situations of mutual understanding in which this knowledge manifests itself (i.e., situations in which there is a use of linguistic expressions in utterances and an understanding of utterances). But precisely when one wants to thematize the *interconnection* between a speaker's general knowledge and ability, and his occasional instances of understanding (and intending) meaning, it seems reasonable to terminologically distinguish between the universal and the occasional "knowledge": I *know* the meaning of a linguistic expression and I *understand* the utterance of a speaker who uses this expression. (The expression still *awaits,* so to speak, the understandable intention that fills it with life; i.e., it awaits its *use.*)

The most tangled discussions in the linguistic philosophy of the last decade concern the question about what a competent speaker's/hearer's "meaning knowledge" consists in and how it can be theoretically represented, and thus concern the question about what a "theory of meaning" would have to look like.[7] One of the difficulties confronting such a theory is the fact that a speaker's knowledge of meaning, besides being largely *implicit,* is to a significant degree a *practical* knowledge, an *ability.* This irreducibly practical component in the knowledge of meaning cannot be represented as propositional knowledge without circularity. "Speakers of a language know the meanings of the words belonging to it, but are frequently unable to state them; it is in principle impossible for their knowledge of the language, if it be their mother tongue, to consist in its entirety in knowledge that they could state."[8] On this point the decisive insights are once again due to Wittgenstein.[9] Here I would prefer not to get directly involved in the question of how far and in what sense a competent speaker's "knowledge" does admit of theoretical representation, although I will come back to it in the course of my further reflections. My first concern is simply the categorial connection between knowing meanings and understanding utterances. As is well known, truth semantics is already based on the supposition of an internal connection between meaning and validity (i.e., truth). With his thesis that "we understand a speech act when we know what makes it acceptable," Habermas has generalized the basic idea of truth-conditional semantics, taken as a pragmatic theory of meaning. This formulation contains the program of a pragmatic theory of meaning *in nuce.* Its succinctness is an advantage, even if it must appear as easily misleading in light of my previous reflections: these suggest the knowledge of the acceptability conditions of utterances would have to be, strictly speaking, reckoned at the level of the *general* knowledge that I have designated as the "knowledge of meaning." A speaker who possesses this general knowledge also possesses the capacity for understanding utterances; his (general) linguistic knowledge *manifests* itself in his understanding of (situated) linguistic utterances, among other things, but it is not *identical* with this understanding. The distinction between levels I have in mind is that between a *capacity* and the *manifestation* or *exercise* of this capacity, between competence and performance. Admittedly this distinction may also yet prove to be in need of explanation, but I see no possibility of avoiding it for now.

If one distinguishes between levels as here proposed, the difficulty arises that an acceptability principle in Habermas's sense (I will call it principle A) would not seem to refer *directly* to the understanding of utterances but only to a speaker's/hearer's "knowledge of meaning." To be sure, I see no simple possibility for a *general* reformulation of principle A in this vein, for the following reasons. If, with Habermas, we assume that understanding an utterance means understanding an *illocutionary act,* then this understanding embraces the illocutionary sense of the utterance as much as its specific "content." (In the case of the "standard form" *Mp*, for example, "I promise you I'll come tomorrow," this content is expressed by the dependent clause.) For these two meaning components [*Sinnkomponente*] of illocutionary acts, however, the problem of reformulating principle A poses itself in completely different ways. Its reformulation at first appears comparatively easy as far as the illocutionary component is concerned, if we assume with Habermas that the conditions for using performative verbs, and hence the (general) acceptability conditions for illocutionary acts of a specific type, can be explicitly formulated in statements of "preparatory" and "sincerity conditions" (in Searle's sense[10]) and additional "essential" acceptability conditions (for example, determinate normative conditions in cases of regulative speech acts[11]). The knowledge expressed in such a formulation of acceptability conditions concerns the meaning (the conditions of use) of performative verbs such as "promise," "assert," "guess," "request," etc.; one could also call such knowledge the "knowledge of illocutionary meaning." In relation to *this* knowledge of meaning, principle A could perhaps be reformulated thus:

Principle A′ We are acquainted with the meaning of a performative verb when we know what makes utterances of a corresponding illocutionary type acceptable.

Here the knowledge of acceptability conditions refers to an illocutionary type as such, and not to types of illocutionary acts together with their propositional contents. By contrast, if we turn to the meaning component of utterances represented by dependent clauses, we find that any attempt we might undertake to extend principle A′ to whole performative sentences does not take us very far, as can be shown with a simple example. Take the performative sentence "I assert that all philosophers since Plato have misunderstood his allegory of the cave." In the sense of principle A′, one would have to say that we know the meaning of this sentence when we know what makes the (assertive) use of this sentence acceptable. If we now follow Habermas and take as an "essential" acceptability condition for assertions the condition that a speaker "has good grounds [*Gründe*] to undertake a warrant that the conditions for the truth of the asserted proposition are satisfied," then we have thereby formulated what makes assertions (generally speaking) acceptable.[12] But what makes assertions *in general* acceptable also makes them acceptable in *individual cases.* Therefore, what makes the (assertive) use of our example sentence acceptable is what makes assertions at all acceptable, namely that the speaker has good grounds to undertake a warrant, etc. But precisely this is not, of course, an explanation of what it means to know the meaning of the relevant sentence. But that means, as soon as one's focus *also* includes the "propositional contents" of illocutionary acts, a simple reformulation of principle A no longer suffices.

One could also formulate this result as follows: so long as the focus stays on utterance *types* (in the sense of illocutionary types), principle A has a comparatively clear sense; however, as soon as one brings in the specific propositional contents of utterances, thus as soon as the focus broadens to the meaning of, for example, assertoric sentences, the object of traditional truth semantics, a "pragmatic generalization" of the truth-semantic idea of connecting meaning and validity lacks the resources for outperforming truth semantics on its own turf. Habermas makes allowance for this circumstance by expressly specifying principle A for empirical assertions (see section 5). As it turns out, however, if one attempts to take the basic Habermasian intuition—that a speaker's knowledge of meaning may be interpreted as "knowledge of the acceptability conditions" for utterances—and extend it to illocutionary acts as a whole (in this case assertions), then another sort of difficulty crops up, in fact one that has already troubled truth semantics to some extent.[13] In the first place, it is clear that the knowledge of acceptability conditions cannot in this case be completely represented in a nontrivial or noncircular fashion as propositional knowledge. Second, it is not clear how the boundaries would be drawn between what can be represented as a speaker's propositional "knowledge of meaning" and his "knowledge of the world," such as his knowledge of causes.[14] *Both* types of knowledge could indeed be relevant for evaluating the acceptability of utterances, something especially clear in the case of empirical assertions. However, given that they vary independently of one another to a certain degree—and *must* so vary if learning in the dimension of world knowledge is to be possible—it seems prima facie clear that a speaker's "knowledge of meaning" cannot contain a *complete* or *definitive* knowledge of the acceptability conditions for utterances. Third and finally, to approach this same difficulty from another angle, there is an indissoluble dialectical tension in the very concept of acceptability conditions. This becomes clear in the relation between "assertability" and "truth": if a speaker has good grounds for asserting that p, then he has good grounds—he is entitled[15]—"to undertake a warrant that the conditions for the truth of the asserted proposition are satisfied." Truth conditions (in a nontrivial sense) are only accessible to us through the grounds we can have for or against a proposition's assertion. *To this extent* the knowledge of assertability conditions includes the knowledge of a proposition's truth conditions. However, to the extent that a proposition's assertability conditions are conditions we must be able to *know,* they can also differ from the proposition's truth conditions, for in most cases we cannot *in principle* exclude the possibility that in the future *new* arguments and counterarguments will turn up. Consequently, assertability conditions are both more and less than truth conditions: they are more because not *only* the truth conditions but (in addition) the assertability conditions have to be fulfilled for a speaker to be entitled to assert that p. And they are less, because even grounded truth claims stand under a proviso: this is how we *understand* the idea of truth. As is well known, there have been no lack of attempts to soften the peculiar and unavoidable tension between assertability and truth by interpreting truth as assertability (or "rational assertability") under ideal conditions (Putnam[16]) or as the contents of a discursive consensus that could be reached under ideal conditions (Habermas[17]). I consider such attempts problematic.[18] In my view, a *fallibilistic* interpretation of that tension between assertability and truth is sufficient and the only one possible.[19]

In alluding to the third of the above-mentioned difficulties in the concept of a "knowledge of acceptability conditions," I wanted to make it clear that the problems of truth semantics, worked out by Dummett in the article cited in note 7, do not simply disappear with the transition from a "semantic" to a "pragmatic" theory of meaning. This must not be taken as an objection to Habermas's basic intuition (which I consider correct). It should rather be seen as an indication of the difficulties standing in the way of a sufficiently precise and unmistakable explication of this basic intuition. These difficulties, to repeat, pose themselves first of all with respect to the "dependent propositional contents" of illocutionary acts, and not with respect to the illocutionary meaning of utterances. In what follows, I would therefore like to go first into these difficulties, putting off for later discussion the broader speech-act-theoretic context of Habermas's "acceptability principle."

4

The last section was a kind of excursus intended to prepare the transition from my opening reflections to the discussion of Habermas's thesis that "we understand a speech act when we know what makes it acceptable." We can get an intuitive idea of this transition from Wittgenstein's central concept of a rule: a speaker's knowledge of meaning concerns the *right* usage (i.e., that corresponding to the rule) of expressions and sentences in the language. Habermas's concept of the "acceptability" of utterances can be taken as a validity- and justification-theoretic differentiation and explication of Wittgenstein's concept of using language "according to rules." So considered, there is something immediately obvious about the idea that what a speaker can *mean* with an utterance, and what a hearer can *understand* as the sense of this utterance, is determined by the knowledge of the acceptability conditions of utterances. Conversely, it suggests a direct link with Wittgenstein's reflections, at least with regard to the "practical" aspect of this meaning knowledge.

I call those aspects of meaning knowledge "practical" that, because they designate a specific *ability*, cannot be completely represented as an implicit propositional knowledge. As Wittgenstein says, where we follow the rule "blindly," we do not have a *choice* between words, interpretations, or ways of acting.[20] We run out of reasons. Our understanding of the rule *shows* itself in our application of the rule.[21] This practical aspect of the knowledge of meaning not only lies at the basis of our capacity for having perceptions and experiences [*Erfahrungen zu machen*] but also comes into play in the communicative use of language and in communicative experience, namely in cases where we do not have to *choose* the words in order to "fit" them to our intentions or where we do not have to *interpret* utterances in order to grasp a speaker's intention. Dummett too has cases of the latter type in view when he criticizes Davidson's overdrawn use of the word "interpretation."[22] In this context Dummett refers to Wittgenstein's remark in *Philosophical Investigations,* sec. 201: "that there is a way of grasping a rule which is *not* an *interpretation,* but which is exhibited in what we call 'obeying the rule' and 'going against it' in actual cases." To paraphrase this in relation to a hearer's linguistic understanding, there is a "grasping" of utterances that is not an "interpreting," but rather a "blind," immediate understanding ("but we ought to restrict the term 'interpretation' to the substitution of one expression of the rule for another," sec. 201). Understanding is immediate when it is an immediate expression of our own capacity to use the expressions and sentences employed by the speaker for our own purposes and in a manner appropriate to the situation.

The practical aspect of the knowledge of meaning especially interests me here insofar as the corresponding "ability" [*Kön-*

nen] underlies a speaker's capacity for having perceptions and experiences and for grasping situations. The latter capacity refers directly to the holistic character of natural languages: if utterances are always utterances-in-situations, then the execution and understanding of linguistic utterances is inconceivable where the exercise of the given thematic aspects of linguistic competence, for example, making and understanding a promise, is not embedded in the nonthematic coactivation of a broad spectrum of the speaker's and hearer's knowledge of meaning. Only as a holistically composed *and* practical knowledge can this knowledge of meaning also include within itself the conditions of its own application in concrete situations. Although we occasionally take situations in "with a single glance," we do not actually perceive situations but rather find ourselves *in* them and understand or "grasp" them rightly or wrongly. *In* situations we have perceptions and experiences (through which our understanding of the situation may change). Conversely, our capacity for having perceptions and experiences is a presupposition for our being able to understand situations. Situations *as such* are holistically composed. We can describe, explain, clarify them, etc., but we cannot "state" them like facts, although we can, of course, render what is important or controversial in a situation thematic in the form of statements or assertions.

While a sufficient understanding of the situation is the *general* presupposition for understanding linguistic utterances, the capacity for having perceptions or for being convinced about something on the basis of perception is the *special* presupposition for understanding empirical assertions. Hence if one wishes to speak of a "knowledge of acceptability conditions" in regard to specific empirical assertions, then an important part of such knowledge, however great its propositionally explicable portion, consists in the capacity to use the given perceptual predicates correctly in perceptual situations (for example, in order to report a perception). Only in this way is it conceivable that a hearer can understand simple assertions, such as those about the past or about inaccessible places, possibly even accepting these on the basis of reasons without being in a position to check the assertions themselves (namely through perception). *Were* he (or had he been) in the position of the speaker who "saw it himself," then the hearer would have to be (or to have been) in a position to perceive what the speaker perceived. This type of counterfactual conditional, one could say, expresses the decisive acceptability condition for utterances of the type "I saw it (myself)," i.e., utterances that are used to *ground* an empirical assertion. And *because* this is so, in cases of doubt we occasionally put ourselves in the speaker's perceptual situation, if possible, in order to check an assertion.

Naturally there is nothing ultimate about perceptual certainties. They amount to ultimate certainties from time to time only in the pragmatic sense of removing a doubt, founding a conviction, making more assured action possible, in which case the perceptions themselves are always already embedded in action contexts of the most diverse nature. Yet there is nothing "absolutely" final about perceptual certainties, because perceptions, taken here not in a psychological but in a "grammatical" sense, are saturated with anticipations, extrapolations, and causal interpretations. Moreover, they are dependent on situational understandings and background assumptions of a more or less general nature. The ability manifested in the use of perceptual predicates or perceptual sentences is a fallible (and otherwise more or less acquired) ability in that the perceptual judgment normally contains implications that cannot be redeemed *in* the act of perception. Thus to understand correctly the relation between perception and justification or, more generally, between experience and justification, two things must be *conceived together:* the "blindness" of obeying a rule, such as that manifested in perceptual certitude, and the fallibility of perception. For although perceptual judgments are not justified (but merely "founded" in perceptions), they do not transcend the *universum* of possible justifications inasmuch as they can be challenged *on the basis of reasons* (or new perceptions). Conversely, it is also true that argumentation, even where it is a matter of theoretical discourse, cannot get rid of its internal reference to possible perceptions (possible experience): arguments cannot substitute for experience. For this reason one cannot, strictly speaking, have a "discursive redemption" of empirical truth claims, for either the "redemption" is not *dis-*

cursive (but rather comes through experience), or it is not a matter of a discursive *redemption* (but rather of a convincing justification).

5

Let us turn now to the question of what it means to *know* just *what it is* that makes an assertion *acceptable*—not an assertion in general but a specific assertion. Habermas's specification of this "acceptability principle" for assertions, which I have already cited in part, reads in its complete form as follows:

Principle B To understand an assertion is to know when a speaker has good grounds to undertake a warrant that the conditions for the truth of the asserted proposition are satisfied.[23]

If one takes into account our earlier distinction between the levels of (general) knowledge of meaning and (occasional) instances of understanding, then a better formulation might be,

Principle C To know the meaning of an assertoric sentence is to know when a speaker has good grounds to use this sentence as an assertion.

In the spirit of principle B one could add,

Principle D To make an assertion is to undertake a warrant that the conditions for the truth of the asserted proposition are satisfied.

To understand an assertion *as* an assertion is, then, to understand *that* the speaker is undertaking a warrant, etc. To be sure, the reference to truth conditions in principles B and D appears problematic once one presupposes, as Habermas does, that Dummett's objections against a truth-conditional semantic are valid. For then the formulation "the conditions for the truth of proposition *p* are satisfied" can really only mean "proposition *p* is true." The knowledge of "when a speaker has good grounds . . ." practically takes the *place* here of a "knowledge of the truth conditions," with the result that the term "truth conditions" loses its meaning-theoretic explanatory function, i.e., it becomes redundant. Hence principle D would actually have to read,

Principle D′ To make an assertion is to undertake a warrant that the asserted proposition is true.

Another prima facie difficulty in principle B is that it is not entirely clear how broadly its claim to generality should be understood. It is obviously not applicable to *predictions*, for example. At this point peculiar problems of demarcation arise. On the one hand, Habermas apparently wants to use principle B to distinguish the illocutionary core of a class of speech acts; on the other hand, though, the distinction between predictions and statements about the past is one of semantic contents, i.e., one that concerns the different manner in which the question of truth respectively comes into play. (Principle B does not apply to predictions, because the understanding of predictions first of all involves a knowledge of the "satisfaction conditions" or, if you will, the knowledge of the grounds that would entitle a speaker to ascertain that a prediction has come to pass or has not come to pass (has "come true" or not). Only secondarily does it involve a knowledge of the grounds entitling a speaker to *make* a prediction. One can easily see this in daily weather forecasts: *how* meteorologists manage to forecast the weather is something most of us do not know, but *that* they are making a forecast and *what* they are forecasting we nevertheless understand quite well.) For present purposes I would like to assume this problem is only an ephemeral one of formulation or demarcation, i.e., I will limit myself in what follows to a type of assertion for which the kind of difficulties discussed above do not arise. More precisely, I would like to limit myself largely to a discussion of problems that crop up in connection with grammatically "elementary" assertions of a nonfuturistic type. The reason for this is that with regard to complex propositions—counterfactual conditionals, lawlike propositions, modal propositions, causal propositions, etc.—I consider the transition from a semantics of truth conditions to a pragmatics of assertability conditions immediately convincing. Naturally, by this I do not mean it would be a simple matter to say exactly *what* "acceptability conditions" pertain to each of the types of propositions above. It is certainly no accident that volumes have been written over each of these propositional types. I merely want to say I think it convincing that a speaker's knowledge of meaning, so far as the above types of propositions are concerned, be characterized by the knowledge of those *kinds of grounds* that are relevant or can be relevant for the justification or critique of the corresponding propositions. Naturally this knowledge is predominantly an implicit knowledge; here I would prefer to leave open to what extent, and in what sense, it is a "systematizable" knowledge. At any rate, principle B is formulated with enough generality to avoid hasty commitments.

In contrast to the above, the contents and cogency of principle B are less clear as soon as one focuses on those grammatically elementary empirical propositions whose comprehensibility is always already presupposed whenever discussion turns to the logic of the justification and critique of causal, modal, or counterfactual conditional statements. I use the expression "grammatically elementary empirical propositions" in a loose sense. Essentially, I am thinking of the kind of statements by which one reports simple or complex perceptions and experiences. What I thus have in mind are either statements that a speaker has become convinced with "his own eyes" are true or those for which one may reasonably assume that *some* speaker has been, would have been able to be, or still could be, convinced with his own eyes are true. My involved formulation shows how difficult it is to come to a somewhat clear demarcation; it includes such diverse statements as "Yesterday it rained all afternoon in Oslo," "The rifle was discharged at a distance of approximately 50 cm from the victim's head," "The demonstration proceeded peacefully," "I played piano today for two hours," "After Pericles had finished his speech a storm of protest broke out," "The gardener has still not trimmed the hedge," "Mr. *X* shot Mrs. *Y*," "This apple is worm-eaten," "The village was almost completely destroyed," etc. Besides this, however, I am also thinking of those classes of statements where one finds fluid transitions between statements that can be founded in direct perception and those where this simply can no longer be the case. Compare, for example, "I just put the souffle in the oven," "The souffle has been in the oven for an hour," "The baby is now one day old," "Mr. *X* is forty years old," "This tree is two hundred years old," "This skeleton is at least 10,000 years old," etc. The world is full of corresponding assertions, not only in daily life but also in science. Therefore, it seems evident that a principle such as principle B would *also* have to prove itself with such assertions. On the other hand, I can illustrate all the problems referred to in section 3 with examples of such "elementary" empirical assertions. I would like to show this in three steps.

1. The understanding of an assertion that could be founded in simple or complex perception certainly presupposes, on the hearer's side, the knowledge that the speaker has good grounds for asserting that *p* if he has seen (become convinced through perception) that *p*. If the hearer has no grounds for doubting the speaker's sincerity or the reliability of his perception, then for his part he has a good, although admittedly "indirect," reason for making the corresponding assertion to a third person. As justification he could then mention whence, from whom, he knows that *p*. In cases of doubt this could lead to a discussion over the witness's sincerity or reliability. From courtroom procedures and historiography we know what sorts of complex argumentation and verification procedures this can involve. This kind of knowledge is certainly part of the meaning knowledge (the linguistic competence) of a hearer who understands empirical assertions. But this is just *one side* of such knowledge. The knowledge of the acceptability conditions for empirical assertions involves in addition the hearer's practical capacity to use correctly the given empirical predicates or corresponding sentences as a *speaker*—for reporting perceptions and experiences, for example. Since the idea of a logical construction of empirical concepts [*empirischen Begriffen*] out of elementary perceptual predicates is an empiricist myth, this practical capacity cannot simply be reserved to a sphere of elementary perceptual judgments whose boundaries are somehow clearly marked off. Rather, it is constitutive for the use of

experiential concepts [*Erfahrungsbegriffen*] *as a whole* (just as much as for the use of mathematical concepts, etc.). The mistake of the classical as well as the logical empiricists was that they tried to locate this practical ability, so to speak, in a stratum of elementary perceptual predicates in order thereby to draw a clear line between a sphere of founding perceptions and a sphere of logical operations (or possible justifications). In spite of its revitalization in theories of artificial intelligence, this project today appears irrevocably discredited, at least as a philosophical undertaking. But this means that—to reformulate the problem in linguistic-philosophical terms—the practical aspects of meaning knowledge must be taken into account at all levels of the mastery of a natural language; they are internally connected with the highly diverse capacities for action we acquire along with the acquisition of language. Hence there is no clearly definable boundary between the propositional part (which, for example, can be *formulated* as rules) and the practical part of our knowledge of meaning. Consequently, the idea that one has to make a speaker's linguistic knowledge *completely* explicit in the form of a theory or system of rules, i.e., that one has to be able to reconstruct that knowledge as an implicit propositional knowledge, seems to me to be a new version of the empiricist myth mentioned above. But if that is the case, then an expression such as, "to know when a speaker has good grounds . . . ," which occurs in principle B, must embrace entirely different kinds of knowledge: the propositional knowledge of meaning in the narrower sense (for example, the explanations of meaning a speaker could give), practical knowledge (the capacity to use empirical predicates correctly), the knowledge that a speaker has good grounds for asserting that *p* if he has seen that *p*, etc., and usually in addition to this, a mass of *empirical* knowledge [*Erfahrungswissen*] (e.g., causal knowledge) presenting speakers and hearers with available potential reasons for or against determinate empirical assertions (see step 2).

2. Part of the just-mentioned empirical knowledge actually constitutes at the same time a part of the knowledge of meaning. The simplest example of this is the knowledge of causal

criteria for the existence or nonexistence of simple empirical states of affairs. Every use of empirical predicates includes a certain causal knowledge: a knowledge of causal possibilities, causal conditions, causal criteria, causal probabilities, etc. In addition to this, institutional and social knowledge come into play as soon as one has to do with assertions about social phenomena. But not every part of this "knowledge of the world" can at the same time be part of the knowledge of meaning, for that would make it impossible to acquire new experience and *learn* from experience. To be sure, the boundaries between knowledge of the world and knowledge of meaning are not sharp, let alone fixed once and for all. Nonetheless, every kind of general knowledge claiming to be *empirical,* that is, founded or confirmed in experience, presupposes such a boundary. Only in this way is it at all conceivable that there can be a social distribution of knowledge (Putnam) that does not *coincide* with a social distribution of linguistic competence. Even if one admits, for example, that scientists, winegrowers, criminologists and physicians develop "special languages," in which their special competences and knowledge find expression, these special languages still remain semantically bound to the language of a common lifeworld, although at the price of gradually changing this common language. This means that there must also be a social distribution of the "knowledge of the acceptability conditions" for empirical assertions, since the potential of reasons available to an expert differs from that available to the average speaker. But given that the knowledge of experts is also always incomplete, fallible, and provisional, strictly speaking a hearer can never entirely and definitively know when a speaker has good grounds to undertake a warrant that the proposition he has asserted is true (if one assumes sufficiently complex cases of singular empirical assertions—for example, compare the determination of the age of skeletal remains with statements about the ages of children). This does not mean we cannot know the acceptability conditions for empirical assertions. Rather, it implies that a speaker's knowledge of *meaning* cannot take in the knowledge of *all* possible arguments and counterarguments that possibly or in the future could be brought to bear for or against an empirical assertion.

Were linguistic knowledge not at once both a practical and a world knowledge, it would be blind; were it not *different* from both practical and world knowledge, we could neither practically nor cognitively *learn.*

3. I have designated the "knowledge of when a speaker has good grounds" as "knowledge of the acceptability conditions" for assertions. Since the positions of speaker and hearer are exchangeable and thus symmetrically related to each other, one could also speak of a "knowledge of the assertability conditions" of propositions. If the truth conditions for propositions are only accessible to us via the grounds we can adduce either for or against such propositions—here I disregard our capacity to employ empirical predicates in concrete situations [*Erfahrungssituationen*]—then the "dialectical tension" I identified earlier between assertability and truth is due not least to our *necessarily* incomplete knowledge of these assertability conditions. So considered, a "knowledge of the truth conditions" in a nontrivial sense would be synonymous with a complete and definitive knowledge of the assertability conditions of propositions.

But even if one could make good sense of this idea (which I doubt), the tension between assertability and truth would not thereby relax. The idea of truth contains an unavoidable surplus over and beyond the concept of a grounded truth *claim,* in fact even beyond that of a discursively achieved consensus over truth claims. This is due to the fact that *no* justification of empirical truth claims can secure its resistance to *future* experience and the corresponding counterarguments. That should not be taken to mean that supposedly good reasons can always prove to be bad ones. Rather, it means that even a good justification cannot itself redeem the anticipation of future *confirmation* contained in truth claims. In itself, this is not an objection to principle B. Rather it explains the necessity of a fallibilistic interpretation—something Habermas himself has pointed out.[24]

The "surplus" that the idea of truth contains with respect to our claim to have grounded knowledge at a given time refers neither to the possibility of a complete and definitive future knowledge nor to the possibility of a definitive redemption of empirical truth claims under ideal conditions. Nor does it harbor the promise of a future language no longer in need of revision. This surplus refers rather to the ever present possibility of our being rationally compelled to step beyond and criticize the knowledge and language available to us at a given time. Truth is not a regulative idea in the sense that it refers us to some perhaps even unattainable telos, such as that of an end to the search for truth, a definitive consensus, or simply a "final" language. It is rather a regulative idea in the *critical* sense that it places all knowledge, each rational consensus, and even our agreement [*Übereinstimmung*] *in* language under a proviso: with the idea of truth, language submits itself to a standard that reaches beyond every particular language, every particular knowledge. But such a standard, as always transcending our reach, becomes *tangible* only where we are compelled to revise our convictions in the light of new experience and arguments.

Thus if one wants to explain *what* a speaker warrants (with good grounds) whenever he makes an assertion—namely, that the conditions for the truth of the asserted proposition are satisfied, i.e., that the asserted proposition is true—it is actually this: that the claim he raises will stand up in the face of future experience and arguments or that, as Dummett has put it, "the speaker will not be proved wrong."[25] To be sure, I agree with Habermas that this cannot mean setting up a "falsificationist" theory of meaning in place of a "verificationist" one.[26] That is, verification and falsification are in a certain sense related to each other symmetrically: the falsification of a proposition implies the verification of a falsifying proposition. Put another way, even the assertion of a "falsifying" proposition must be supported by experience and reasons. Only if one interprets the relation between verification and falsification as the early Popper did, in the sense of the logically asymmetrical relation between strictly universal propositions and singular basic propositions, does an essential asymmetry result, i.e., an epistemological priority of falsification over verification (for lawlike propositions). But an asymmetry thesis in *this* form is surely indefensible, containing as it does a wholly fictitious picture of what one might call the "falsification" of scientific theories. Not only are falsifying propositions as a rule *general* propositions (inasmuch as they report the results of repeatable experiments).[27] What is more, designating a theory as "falsified" usually presupposes the development of theoretical alternatives.[28] Hence I do not think a "priority of negation" can be justified in the form of an epistemological or logical-semantic priority of falsification over verification. In contrast to this, the difference between assertability and truth suggests a *fallibilistic* interpretation: we can never exclude the possibility of *new arguments* or new problems coming up, which could *compel* us to look for new answers (without already having to contain these answers). In such cases we discover that the assertability conditions of certain propositions are not really satisfied, or at least not in the degree previously assumed. This makes the truth of these propositions *problematic,* but it does not (necessarily) demonstrate their falsity. "Fallibilism" is a consciousness of the fact that our grounds can prove to be insufficient, the interpretations of our experience problematic; fallibilism spells out, as it were, the difference between assertability and truth. Whereas falsificationism is an antithesis to verificationism, fallibilism is not the *negation* but rather an *interpretation* of the linguistic-pragmatic thesis of the connection between assertions and justifications. In any case, this is how I would like to understand Habermas's proposal (against Dummett) that the discursive redemption of validity claims be interpreted fallibilistically.[29]

6

The reflections in the last section were intended as a partly explanatory and partly critical commentary on Habermas's principle B. In its claim, its formulation, and its universality, this principle is comparable to such principles as "To understand a proposition means to know what is the case if it is true."[30] The analogy is even clearer in the case of the general principle A: "We understand a speech act when we know what makes it acceptable." The problem with such principles is that it is so extraordinarily difficult to explicate what *they* say (and that means to know what makes *them* true or acceptable). The Wittgenstein of the *Tractatus* was naturally aware of this difficulty: on the one hand, he counted his principle of meaning [*Sinnprinzip*] as one of those "nonsense" sentences making up the whole *Tractatus* (as he notes at the end of that work); on the other hand, one can read the *Tractatus* as the *explanation* of this principle of meaning. In what concerns the meaning of his own principle, or principles, of meaning, Habermas is less scrupulous than the early Wittgenstein. Nonetheless, one can also read Habermas's speech-theoretic works, especially since the first of the "Intermediate Reflections" in *The Theory of Communicative Action,* as explanations of these principles of meaning. Only on this basis is it at all possible to understand to what degree the early Wittgenstein, Dummett, and Habermas are talking about the same *problems,* even though each of the explanations goes in an entirely different direction. Habermas is interested above all in the *illocutionary* "binding/bonding forces" [*Bindekräften*] of language, or in the corresponding knowledge of speakers and hearers; there is already, in the formulation of his principle of meaning, a shift in emphasis from the level of logical-semantic analysis to that of a pragmatic ("formal-pragmatic") analysis. Connected with this, of course, is the fact that Habermas is hardly interested in those details of a logical-semantic construction of assertoric sentences, something at the heart of the theories of the early Wittgenstein, Dummett, or Davidson. His principle of meaning for assertions is not the basic constructive principle for an incipient theory of meaning still to be worked out but rather indicates the manner by which insights of truth semantics should be "taken up" [*aufgehoben*] in a pragmatic theory of language. At the same time, the peculiar incommensurability of formal pragmatics and truth semantics finds its source here, inasmuch as formal pragmatics seeks to reconstruct a different *kind* of linguistic knowledge than does truth semantics. In fact, one might say it does not meddle at all in the problematic details of truth semantics but simply says in a general way what *place* these problems have within a pragmatic theory of language. Principle B contains in a pithy formula a convincing counterthesis against the basic idea of truth semantics, but, as we have seen, its polemical sense is clearer than its constructive contents. Perhaps this is how it is with all principles of meaning, in the final analysis: they attempt, by way of summary or anticipation, to explain a central aspect of the connection between meaning and truth, between meaning and validity, or between meaning and understanding; the art of employing them consists in not taking them too literally.

7

As a first approximation, we can now characterize speakers' and hearers' "knowledge of meaning"—at least for an important class of cases—as the knowledge of the acceptability conditions for utterances *of a kind.* This knowledge of acceptability conditions is a presupposition for understanding situated utterances, but it is not *identical* with this understanding. To understand an utterance I have to know *how* a speaker means (or can mean) an utterance, in which sense he uses a linguistic expression, whom or what he means, etc., and knowing *these things* presupposes that I also understand enough of the situation in which the utterance occurs. A knowledge of meaning and an understanding of the situation *together* determine how utterances are understood, and indeed in such a way that I normally understand utterances as they *could* be meant in a concrete situation. Something analogous to the "principle of charity" comes into play here, namely that speakers and hearers reciprocally suppose of one another a linguistic competence. Because knowing meaning and understanding the situation come together in the understanding of utterances, the latter frequently contains not only the knowledge of what *would* make this utterance acceptable but also the knowledge of what *does make* it acceptable. Consider, for example, the directive the stewardess gives before landing to stop smoking; a request for salt, uttered by a guest at breakfast; the remark made by my daughter as we both look out the window, "It's snowing again": I understand these *as* acceptable, as justified [*berechtigt*] or true, because the pertinent grounds in each case are concomitantly supplied by the situation (insofar as I grasp the situation in its relevant features). To this extent, the Habermasian "principle of meaning" holds, in its (unqualifiedly) strong form, for a limited class of cases: to understand a speech act is to know what *makes* it acceptable. In general, however, we have to distinguish analytically between the knowledge of the acceptability *conditions* and understanding an utterance, since otherwise it would be impossible to understand an utterance and nevertheless, on the basis of reasons, *not* accept it. Still, it is exactly the point of Habermas's "acceptability principle" that it explains the sense of linguistic utterances out of the horizon of the possible yes/no responses a hearer can rationally adopt.

Habermas's strong, indicative formulation of his acceptability principle admittedly has, as we have seen, yet another sphere of application. What I called above a speaker's/hearer's "knowledge of illocutionary meaning" likewise permits of such an indicative formulation, and in fact in relation to "illocutionary types." What makes an assertion acceptable? That the speaker has good grounds to undertake a warrant, etc. What makes a directive acceptable? That the speaker has good (normative) grounds to expect the hearer to carry out the enjoined action, etc. The knowledge of these *general* acceptability conditions cannot, however, already represent that knowledge a speaker needs to carry out and understand various types of concrete illocutionary acts. The formulation of those *general* acceptability conditions would be, to use Habermasian terminology, a formal pragmatics in the *narrow* sense, namely a theory of the meaning of pragmatic indicators, which are, roughly speaking, performative verbs. Such a formal pragmatics would not necessarily compete with a truth semantics; one could rather view them as complementary, as Dummett has also proposed.[31] I think that Searle's speech act theory too can be understood in this sense. Habermas has on occasion chosen formulations—among which I also include the formulation of his general acceptability conditions—that point to the idea of a formal pragmatics in this narrow sense. However, the fact that his theory makes a more radical claim results not least from his specification of acceptability conditions for *assertions*. For if understanding an assertion should involve knowing *when* a speaker has good grounds to warrant that the conditions for the truth of the asserted proposition are true, then the knowledge of the acceptability conditions refers not only to the illocutionary mode as such but also to assertions with definite propositional contents. What follows from this for the general case, say for the case of regulative speech acts?

One of Habermas's most important insights in comparison to traditional speech act theory is that the illocutionary sense of "imperative" speech acts—such as requests, summons, directives, commands—also involves a reference to a background of social or moral norms. This background first of all determines the acceptability of the corresponding utterances. From a formal-pragmatic standpoint one could first take this reference as a relation such utterances have—presumably depending on the type of imperative—to a *category* of (normative) grounds that are still indeterminate. Accordingly, one could imagine the understanding of an imperative utterance, for example, a directive, as though it were "put together" from the knowledge of the satisfaction conditions for the propositional contents in the dependent clause and the right grasp of the illocutionary meaning of the utterance in its characteristic relation to a category of normative grounds. A hearer has to understand the directive's *content* (be acquainted with its satisfaction conditions), and he has to understand that he is dealing with a *directive,* the authorization [*Berechtigung*] of which the speaker could, if necessary, substantiate with the help of normative-type grounds. Since the potential grounds, in contrast to the case of assertions, obviously do not result directly from the meaning of the dependent clause, that is, from the utterance's propositional contents, imperative speech acts cannot determine a specific potential of grounds in the same sense as constative speech acts. If, in analogy with the truth claims made with assertions, one wants to speak of a normative validity claim of imperative utterances, then this validity claim cannot refer to particular norms but only to the fact *that* the speaker in the utterance situation has a right to give a particular command or a particular directive, to utter a particular request, etc.

In fact, the authorization of a command, directive, request, etc. depends quite a bit on its propositional contents. The normative background to which the speaker refers with imperative utterances decides *who* in *which* situation is authorized for *what type* of commands, directives, requests, etc. Hence in this case there is both an *analogy* and a *disanalogy* with respect to the case of empirical assertions. The analogy consists in the fact that in both cases the knowledge of the acceptability conditions for an utterance depends on its propositional content. The disanalogy consists in the fact that the knowledge of the acceptability conditions in the case of imperatives—disregarding for the moment a speaker's *general* illocutionary meaning knowledge—is not a knowledge of meaning but a *normative* knowledge. This normative "knowledge" enters into the interpretation of concrete situations: since situations are always already normatively "structured," the understanding of a situation involves a grasp of its normative structure. Conversely, a hearer can often decide solely on the basis of his "normative" understanding of the situation whether an imperative utterance—thus whether a particular directive, a particular request, etc.—is justified [*berechtigt*] or not. A hearer can understand a stewardess's or director's directive, a guest's request, or an officer's command as legitimate [*berechtigt*] or not with respect to the respective propositional content insofar as he rightly understands the utterance situation, including its normative "structure." Here the term "rightly" stands for the right interpretation of a situation in light of a normative background, as well as for the rightness of the norms in the light of which the interpretation occurs. Correspondingly, the practical discourses imaginable in controversial cases can bear on both the right application of presumably legitimate [*legitim*] norms and the legitimacy of these norms themselves.[32] On the other hand, those cases in which a hearer does *not* know whether an imperative utterance is acceptable or not are usually cases in which his interpretation of the situation is fuzzy or uncertain. In this too an asymmetry between imperative utterances and empirical assertions shows up: in the case of assertions a doubt concerns the existence of the fact expressed in the propositional content, whereas in the case of imperative utterances it concerns the character of the *utterance situation*. Hence in the case of imperative utterances the "understanding" of utterances and the knowledge of acceptability conditions also stand in a different relation to each other than in the case of empirical assertions: I *understand* an imperative utterance if

I know its illocutionary sense and its satisfaction conditions, but whether the utterance is *acceptable* depends on the givens, both normative and nonnormative, of the utterance *situation*. The hearer's normative "knowledge," which determines his understanding of the utterance situation, in other words, his knowledge of the acceptability conditions, is a condition for the possibility of understanding only in the sense in which a right situational understanding is the condition for the possibility of understanding. The hearer's situational understanding more or less contains the decisive indication as to *whether* the speaker's utterance is acceptable or not (and thus it often indicates how the utterance can be meant as an illocution). In the case of empirical assertions, on the other hand, a hearer's knowledge of meaning is more or less intermeshed with his knowledge of acceptability conditions; only in this way is it possible that the grounds authorizing an utterance do not (necessarily) have to do with features of the utterance situation, and hence that the validity claim at stake can be decoupled from the situation in which it was uttered. To be sure, every kind of intersubjective validity claim is open to the possibility of being decoupled from the situation of its utterance; this is precisely one of the reasons why I will later call Habermas's classification of speech acts into question (see section 8 below).

According to the above, imperative utterances differ from empirical assertions in that the knowledge of "acceptability conditions" for the latter is first and foremost *meaning* knowledge, whereas for the former it is primarily a *normative* "knowledge." One could, no doubt, argue that a speaker would not be able to learn the difference between various imperative modes such as asking, commanding, etc. without being introduced into a *determinate* moral culture; to this extent the illocutionary meaning of the corresponding performative verbs would always have a *determinate* normative content attached to them as well. However, it seems obvious that the meaning of performative verbs cannot change with a change of normative convictions in the same way that the meaning of empirical predicates can change with a change in causal knowledge. Precisely for this reason one must understand the knowledge of acceptability conditions in the case of imperative utterances as a *normative* knowledge that varies more or less independently of the meaning of the sentences employed. The connection between meaning and validity in the case of imperative utterances is not the same as that in the case of empirical assertions. In the case of imperative utterances, not the meaning knowledge of speakers and hearers but their normative "knowledge" forms the bridge between the "validity claims" of illocutionary acts and possible justifications.

Admittedly an ambiguity still has to be cleared up concerning the normative validity claim connected with imperative utterances. I go on the assumption that not only requests, directives, summons, and orders can be uttered in an imperative form but also, with some frequency, pieces of advice, recommendations, proposals, warnings, invitations, and other regulative speech acts as well. ("Take a seat," "Try it this way," "Don't go too far," "Take a vacation," etc.) Now in many cases it is easy to relate the normative validity claim of imperative utterances *directly* to the propositional content of a corresponding, explicitly formulated regulative speech act. The normative validity claim would then be the claim that the action requested of the hearer—or that to which he is counseled or ordered or invited or stimulated, or which is recommended or proposed to him, or from which he is warned, etc.—that such action is, for the situation, right or best or commanded or permitted or not permitted. In such cases the imperative form of the utterance could be replaced by a normative form. To stay with the above examples, "You may sit down," "You should try it this way," "You shouldn't go too far," "You should take a vacation," etc. Or to come back to the case of a directive, a conductor who requests [*auffordert*] a heedless passenger in the nonsmoking section to stop smoking could instead also say, "You may not smoke here." Now if one understands the normative validity claim of imperative utterances (or more generally, regulative speech acts) in this sense, then it is clear that the term "normative" must be understood in a *broad* sense: an action can be "right" or "false" on moral, technical, aesthetic grounds; it can be commanded, problematic, objectionable, false, or "the best" in view of the addressee's goals, well-being, moral obligations, or the internal logic of his undertaking (as in aesthetic problem contexts). In other words, if one directly relates the normative validity claim of regulative speech acts to their propositional contents, one can no doubt substantiate in this way the close connection between regulative speech acts and normative validity claims. But one cannot, as Habermas would like, correlate the class of regulative speech acts with normative validity claims in the *narrower* sense, namely with *moral* validity claims.

Such a correlation results without forcing things only if one relates the normative validity claim of regulative speech acts not, or not directly, to their propositional contents but rather to the illocutionary act as a whole. Then the paradigmatic cases would be not those where an imperative utterance can be replaced by a normative utterance (as in the conductor example) but rather those where the propositional content only becomes normatively loaded through being uttered, and thus where rights and/or duties for the hearer and/or speaker are *generated through* the act of utterance. Requests, commands, invitations, promises, permissions, offers, "acceptances" (of offers or invitations) usually have this character: a soldier is not obligated—he does not even have the right—to attack unless the officer commands him to do it; no one is obliged to tell me what time it is unless I ask for it; no one is authorized to take up quarters in my house unless I allow it; no one is authorized to present a paper at such and such a colloquium unless invited; and assuming he has been invited, he would not be obligated to come unless he had accepted the invitation or had promised to come; etc.

In cases such as these, the normative validity claim tied to regulative speech acts can only refer to the illocutionary act itself. To be precise, the claim is that, given the "normative structure" of the utterance situation, the speaker is *authorized* to ask the hearer for . . . , to command him to . . . , to promise him that . . . , etc. Validity claims of this sort are normative in a *narrower* sense: they contain a necessary relation to the normative structure of the utterance situation not in the sense of an *additional* validity claim but rather in that of a normative understanding of the situation that the speaker *relies* on without *thematizing* it. Consequently, the normative validity claims (implicitly) raised with such speech acts refer to the illocutionary acts *by which* they are raised in the situation *in which* they are raised. Only this peculiar, normative relation [*Rückbezug*] of regulative speech acts back to themselves and the situation in which they are uttered—a normative self-reference [*Rückbezug*] that is just as implicit as the normative validity claims connected with such speech acts—explains the particular performative character of these speech acts. That is, when valid, they have the "force" to *generate* rights and/or obligations on the part of the hearer and/or speaker (or on the part of a third person). Their real *point* is not the assertion of existing rights, obligations, or reasons for action (although they can also be employed for this) but the generation of new rights, obligations, and reasons for action—rights, obligations, and reasons for action that would not exist without the execution of the corresponding speech acts. Again, this normatively understood *productive* force of regulative speech acts flows from their (implicit) normative relations to themselves and the situation, for only if the normative validity claims connected with them are justifiably raised do they have the "force" to *generate* rights, obligations, or reasons for action.

If the illocutionary point of regulative speech acts, insofar as they are connected with normative validity claims in the narrower sense, is not first and foremost the assertion of existing rights and/or obligations but rather the generation of new rights and/or obligations, then one may well doubt that the connection between regulative speech acts and raising a (special kind of) normative validity claim is sufficient reason for taking such speech acts as the paradigm for understanding what raising normative validity claims involves. Open to question here is Habermas's classification of speech acts into constative, regulative, and expressive ("representative") speech acts, which corresponds to the three validity dimensions of truth, rightness, and sincerity. In the following section of my reflections I would like to deal with this classification problem.

8

Habermas's well-known thesis holds that with each speech act a speaker raises (at least) three "universal" validity claims: that of truth, that of (normative) rightness, and that of sincerity or truthfulness. I find this thesis convincing and would like to discuss the question whether or in which sense it can provide us with a principle for the classification of speech acts. Habermas's answer to this question singles out three classes of speech acts, each of which respectively "thematizes" just *one* of the three validity dimensions of speech acts: in *constative* speech acts *truth* claims are raised, in *regulative* speech acts *normative* validity claims, and in *expressive* (or "representative") speech acts *truthfulness* claims.[33] In the case that validity claims become controversial, for constative speech acts a transition to *theoretical* discourse is available; for regulative speech acts a transition to *practical* discourse. Expressive speech acts, however, do not have a corresponding form of discourse, for truthfulness claims cannot be *justified* but can only *prove their worth* in the consistency of a set of actions.

The thesis that every kind of speech act involves normative validity claims can first be taken to mean that for any speech act, one can ask whether the speaker—assuming he is sincere and the truth claim he makes or "presupposes" is justified—was normatively *authorized* for his speech act as a social *action.* This is true at least for "public" speech acts, and thus for cases of communicative action. I go on the assumption, therefore, that one has to distinguish the normative authorization of speech acts in general from the *epistemic* authorization of (grounded) assertions and from the (special) *moral* rightness of sincere utterances. To be sure, one could also understand the thesis of the universality of normative rightness claims in such a way that the "rightness" of an "authorized" assertion and the "rightness" of a sincere utterance are already understood as normative rightness in the sense of the thesis (Apel seems to tend in this direction). In this case one could say that truth and sincerity claims are normative validity claims *sui generis,* to be distinguished from those normative validity claims (implicitly) raised in regulative speech acts. One would thus distinguish truth, rightness, and sincerity claims according to the *kind* of "entitlement basis" [*Rechtsgründe*] they have or according to the kind of normative validity claim connected with them. This version of the thesis certainly has its attraction. In no way, though, does it take us beyond our point of departure, the constellation paraphrased in the first version of the thesis. For if all three types of validity claim are supposed to be connected with every type of speech act, then it must additionally be true that normative validity claims in the sense of regulative speech acts are *also* connected with truth and sincerity claims. With this we would once again find ourselves with the first version of the thesis of the universality of normative rightness claims.

Recalling what I said earlier about regulative speech acts, we can now take this thesis as saying that with every kind of speech act, the speaker, proceeding on his understanding of the normative structure of the utterance situation, raises the (implicit) claim that his utterance is (normatively) authorized *as* a social action—as an intervention in a social space, as it were. This thesis continues to make sense even after we acknowledge the fact that in real communication contexts there are complex interdependencies and interferences between the different validity dimensions. Here it suffices to point out that we can at least distinguish analytically between the different validity dimensions, *and* that up to a certain point these are also de facto independent of one another: a sincere and true communication can be morally false; a consciously untrue assertion (and thus a lie) can be morally right.

Now from a purely intuitive standpoint, the attempt simply to line up constative and regulative speech acts, as *illocutionary* types, with the *validity* dimensions of truth and normative rightness is undermined by the fact that the concept of a regulative speech act, in Habermas's sense as well, *presupposes* the concept of an explicit normative validity claim that is not itself a regulative speech act in turn. We can show this by way of a simple example, which even corresponds to a rather favorable case for Habermas. In this example an imperative utterance has a direct normative content (i.e., with respect to the propositional content of a corresponding complete and explicit illocutionary act). The girl friend of a student assistant tells him, "Don't put up with that," which in this case amounts to (or even implies), "You don't *have* to (or *shouldn't*) put up with that." The sore point here is his doing the professor's weekly shopping. Perhaps the student has complained (the other assistants have a better deal) but without a really clear idea of his obligations and rights. Yet if the friend now continues by way of justification, "He (i.e., the professor) has *no right* to send you shopping," she raises a normative validity claim that is *not* a regulative speech act. (That it is a normative *validity* claim is evident in the fact that it could in principle issue in a quarrel, even between the two friends.) In other words, normative validity claims, however closely connected with regulative speech acts, do not always appear in the form of regulative speech acts, nor *can* they always so appear if a practical discourse is to be possible.

Of course, if one wanted, one could conceive regulative speech acts at once both broadly enough (to handle our example above) and narrowly enough (to handle my reflections in section 7) that they *analytically* coincided with "raising a normative validity claim" (in the narrow sense). In the process one would no longer be lining up classes of speech acts, at least in a loose sense, with classes of performative verbs: the only criterion of alignment left then would be the given type of "thematic" validity claim. Admittedly, such a "by definition" solution to the problem would be rather forced and unsatisfying as measured against an Austinian understanding of the speech-act-theoretical project. Even aside from that, however, the question would immediately arise as to whether one would not also have to posit classes of speech acts for aesthetic and nonaesthetic value judgments (which do not fit in any of the three classes), possibly even a class for predictions (it is certainly debatable whether predictions are truth claims), perhaps also one for metaphorical utterances, one for philosophical statements, etc. In a word, Habermas's short-cut from *validity dimensions* to *illocutionary classes* remains unconvincing. Rather, it seems to me—to pinpoint where our intuitions diverge—that the differentiation according to *modes* and the differentiation according to *validity dimensions* should be understood as at least partially independent of each other.

Take, for example, advice giving. Here the speaker, if sincere, has his eye on what is best for the hearer, whether the advice is moral, technical, practical, or aesthetic. Or requests. Here the speaker wants or desires something from the hearer, even if his desire might refer to the hearer's well-being, including his moral well-being ("I'm asking you to stop drinking," "I'm asking you to give him the stolen money back"). One notices here immediately, by the way, why requests but not pieces of advice belong to the "productive" regulative speech acts as spelled out in section 7: if the request is justified [*berechtigt*], the speaker's desire "generates" an obligation for the hearer; in contrast, the opinion of a speaker who gives good advice does not generate an obligation for the hearer in the same sense. The latter may be acting irrationally to ignore a good piece of advice, but he does not (necessarily) injure another's well-being or right. Precisely this shows why it is above all normatively "productive" regulative speech acts that display internal connections with moral validity claims.

On the other hand, consider assertions. Here the speaker raises an explicit validity claim opposite a hearer. As long as we stay with the everyday use of the term "assertion," a speaker is able to make entirely different kinds of assertions: he can make any sort of empirical, mathematical, or theoretical assertions, he can assert that he has found the solution to a problem, he can assert that a certain book is exciting, he can assert that all previous philosophers have misunderstood Plato's allegory of the cave, and he can even assert that the professor does not have the right to send students shopping. Naturally, the question is, *Ought* we stay with the everyday use of the term "assert"? In favor of this is the fact that these are all cases of *explicit intersubjective* validity claims and *nothing else* (this is how we consider them, anyhow, when we call them assertions). Here the raising of a validity claim is more or less viewed in *isolation* from those other pragmatic functions that can also be connected with validity claims: acts of informing, pointing something out, descriptions, protests, complaints, objections, justifications, etc. We use the word "assert"—more often descriptively than performatively, as is also the case with many other performative verbs—when we want to designate the pure act of "raising an intersubjective validity claim." The word "assert" marks something like the point of transition from communicative action to discourse: it is controversial assertions, i.e., validity claims as such, that ignite discourses. On this view, the word "assert" involves an abstraction from the specific pragmatic functions of communicative action similar to that found in the traditional term "judgment." This is the sense in which I also understand Austin's original distinction between a performative and a constative use of language. Of course, Austin discovered that the constative use of language is also a special kind of performative language use. I would suggest, however, that its special feature lies not in the fact that the validity dimension of truth is thematized but rather in the fact that validity claims are thematized *as* validity claims.

Another word whose everyday use displays a similar lack of differentiation as that of "assert," albeit in a pragmatically different function, is the word "say." A speaker "says" to a hearer that it is time to go, that there's no more bread in the house, that he's anxious, that he had an affair, that the concert was wonderful, that he (the hearer) should return the book, that the talk was boring, that he (the speaker) cannot swim, that one can't do it *that* way, etc. Here we have all the validity modes gathered peacefully together. Admittedly, we have relaxed the stress on the "raising of a validity claim," focusing instead on the point of "informing" or "pointing something out"; in addition, under certain conditions the point is that of "assuring someone." I consider it speech-act-theoretic dogmatism to maintain that in all those cases a fitting performative verb is available, tailored to the given type of validity claim at stake, that the speaker could use to make it *entirely* clear *how* the utterance was intended. ("I only wanted to say to you that . . ." or "I say to you . . ." is completely grammatically correct and often leaves nothing more to be desired.)

Ought we criticize everyday speech because it throws different sorts of validity claims all together in such an undifferentiated fashion? I am inclined rather to criticize speech act theory when it tries to reprimand everyday speech on *this* point. If one does not associate illocutionary types by definition with validity dimensions, it is hard to see why they should not occasionally be usable across the modes of validity. Consider the word "admit." Some of the above-mentioned utterances *could* be admissions, such as that the speaker is anxious, that he had an affair, that he cannot swim, that there is no more bread in the house, and even that the talk was boring (for example, if he is talking about a good friend). A speaker admits something that is unpleasant for him to say (to acknowledge) and that he "knows" but which the hearer cannot know. That the speaker's (hidden) feelings, wishes, and intentions are especially qualified for this is obvious, since the speaker has a privileged access to them. But the speaker may also have a privileged access, for the time being, to ordinary facts: that he cannot swim, that he's had an affair, that there's no more bread in the house. On the other hand, it can be a matter of informing, say, a doctor that I have a pain in a certain place: what is information in conversation with the doctor might be an admission or a complaint in another context. In the same way we can give *descriptions* not only of everyday scenes or pictures but also of dispositional states and anxiety conditions.

What follows from these rather associative reminders of our intuitive understanding of everyday linguistic communication? I began with the conjecture that to a certain extent the different modes of illocutionary force must be conceived independently of the distinction between validity dimensions. Universal validity dimensions, in Habermas's sense, are sincerity, (moral) rightness, and (empirical) truth. Now one certainly cannot call these the *only* validity dimensions: there are also mathematical, hermeneutical, philosophical, and evaluative validity claims (of an aesthetic or nonaesthetic nature). We can distinguish validity dimensions according to the kind of justification or the form of discourse connected with the corresponding validity claims (or in the case of pure sincerity claims, by the lack of a characteristic form of justification). Distinctions between speech act types are, by contrast, distinctions between communicative functions that utterances can have in situations, between the kinds of relationship a speaker can take up or produce with a hearer, between different ways of generating or asserting obligations, rights, or reasons for action through valid speech acts of a determinate type. However, that the distinction between communicative functions *has* to be at least partly independent of the distinction between validity dimensions results from the fact that the validity claim a speaker raises with his utterance can be isolated from the special relationship he enters into with a hearer *through* his utterance, whether it is thematized *as* a validity claim or put into other communicative functions. Which special validity claim a speaker raises depends solely on *that* [*content*] *for which* he raises it; what kind of communicative function the raising of this validity claim has depends on the relationship *between* speaker and hearer produced or expressed through an illocutionary act. This relationship can only be characterized by considering the positions of speaker *and* hearer: the communicative function of an utterance depends not (only) on which kind of validity claim is dominant but (also) on to whom and with what illocutionary intention a speaker makes this utterance. Conversely, as long as one stays with the performative verbs really available, illocutionary intentions determine the kinds of validity claims only within certain limits and in different ways for different cases. (The doctor should *know* that and where I have pains, and so I inform him. If necessary, I *describe* my complaints as precisely as possible.)

To return to the example of advice giving, I would like to show once more that illocutionary [modes] and validity types cannot be paired up with each other in a one-to-one correspondence. In Habermas's classification, advice giving counts as a regulative speech act, which makes good sense so long as one understands regulative speech acts as utterances whose functions are to supply hearers with reasons for actions. But one can scarcely maintain that with advice giving a *moral* validity claim stands in the foreground or is thematic (unless it is a matter of *moral* advice). As with all other utterances, giving advice can indeed be authorized or unauthorized in a moral sense: not just anyone has the right in any situation to give someone else good advice. But if pieces of advice contain a *thematic* or *dominant* validity claim, it is the claim that what the speaker advises the hearer to do is best or right for the hearer. If the speaker is right in raising this (implicit) validity claim, then it is a *good* piece of advice. Naturally, in giving advice the speaker also expresses the conviction that he himself would, in the hearer's situation, follow the advice he gives the hearer. Accordingly, pieces of advice occasionally take the form, "If I were you I would do *p*." The *specific* illocutionary force of advice giving seems to result precisely from the combination of both of those validity claims: that following a certain course of action is best or right for the hearer *and* that the speaker would act the same way in the hearer's situation. The second validity claim makes the point of the first one plain, so to speak. That is, the speaker tries to look at the situation from the hearer's perspective, i.e., *his* aims, interests, life plans, possibilities, desires, etc., for only in this way can he tell the hearer what *for him* is best or right. The latter is certainly a normative validity claim but, as we have already seen, not necessarily a *moral* validity claim. On the other hand, this validity claim is in no way bound to the situation of advice giving: the question as to what would be the best course of action for someone, as well as the corresponding answers to this question, can also come up in the absence of that person, for example, in a conversation between two friends, a child's parents, two doctors, etc., just as the affected person himself can express the conviction that this or that course of action is best for him. In these instances the corresponding validity claim, if it were uttered, would not be a piece of advice anyhow.

Hence in a certain sense I would proceed in just the opposite way from Habermas. That is, I would go from explicit validity claims of the most varied sort, and thus from validity claims that can be asserted, if necessary, *as* pure *validity* claims for a hearer. The concept of a pure validity claim involves an abstraction from the manifold pragmatic functions of communicative action. This allows us to consider speakers and hearers as already in the role of potential discussion partners whose theme is the validity of a propositional content asserted as valid. Certain validity claims become, or come to the aid of, special illocutionary acts by being inserted into pragmatically characteristic situation relations. For example, the claim that doing *p* is the best course of action for *a* becomes a *piece of advice* or a *recommendation* when I say it to *a* in a situation where a decision still has to be made. The claim that the government or the parliament has no right to restrict basic democratic liberties becomes a *protest* if I address this validity claim to the government or parliament (as in a public demonstration). The claim that it is best to go home or to postpone a meeting becomes a *proposal* when I raise this validity claim opposite an affected person. The claim that I hate *x* or that I cannot swim becomes an *admission* in a situation where uttering it is unpleasant for me. The claims that the weather was bad, the snow miserable, that because of the traffic noise I could not sleep and felt miserable the whole time may each be elements of a *report* I give of my last vacation. The claim that someone behaved impossibly or inconsiderately can become an accusation or a protest if I say it to the one who so behaved, an act of complaining if I say it to a third party, lodging a complaint if I say it to the boss or the responsible party (the teacher, the parents), but also a disparaging remark if I am not myself the one affected by the inconsiderateness.

In none of the above do I mean to maintain that the use of explicitly performative verbs has no other function than that of making explicit the situation relation a speaker intends or supposes with the validity claims he raises. Regulative speech acts in the narrower sense (and thus speech acts that are productive in a normative sense) would already be a clear counterexample to this: what a speaker *does* with them cannot as a rule be accomplished through the (explicit) raising of a normative validity claim. Even making a proposal involves more—and in a certain sense, something else—than saying to the persons affected that it is best (for us, for them) to do *p*. To protest involves something more and something different than saying to someone that he has no right to, etc. One can also express this by saying that the validity conditions [*Gültigkeitsbedingungen*] of a speech act are not identical with the validity conditions [*Geltungsbedingungen*] of the given dominant validity claim contained in the speech act. The former concern the illocutionary act as a whole, and thus the totality of the validity claims raised, implied, or presupposed in an illocutionary act. To a certain extent this brings us back to the thesis of Habermas that I took as a point of departure. Only now, I would like to give this thesis a somewhat different sense than it has with Habermas.

In the following, I would like to put aside those validity conditions of speech acts that can be formulated as "preparatory conditions" in Searle's sense. The speaker's supposition that these preparatory conditions are satisfied can be largely formulated as presuppositions of truth and existential presuppositions (which can prove to be false).[34] Furthermore, I would like to speak of normative *rightness* conditions in the sense explained previously: these rightness conditions concern the authorization of the illocutionary act as a speech action in a normatively structured social space. (As mentioned earlier, this validity dimension is frequently not independent of other validity dimensions.) As far as *sincerity* conditions are concerned, their specific content manifestly differs according to the type of speech act, a fact clearly showing that speech acts can really only be characterized through *specific constellations* of validity claims. By a request a speaker expresses his desire that the hearer do what he requests. By an invitation the speaker expresses his readiness to fulfill the obligations (such as those of a host) resulting from the hearer's acceptance of the invitation. With a proposal the speaker expresses not only his view that the proposed action is best or right but also his readiness, *ceteris paribus,* to act accordingly upon the acceptance of his proposal. In giving advice, the speaker expresses his view not only that a certain course of action is best or right but also that he, the speaker, would act likewise in a similar situation. It seems to me that one cannot explain the illocutionary force of requests, invitations, proposals, or even promises if one does not consider in each case the entirely specific constellations of normative validity claims (which display yet further variety) together with sincerity claims having a completely different content, sincerity claims that, as we see, do not have to refer only to the dominant *normative* validity claim. Only in simple cases, in particular those I have labeled "pure" validity claims, does the sincerity condition refer straightaway to the propositional content of the utterance: the speaker must himself believe what he says.

Now according to my reconstruction, what still remains after the rightness and sincerity claims is not necessarily a "truth claim" in Habermas's sense but rather validity claims having to do more or less with the *essential* validity conditions [*Gültigkeitsbedingungen*] of speech acts: pieces of advice and proposals have to be good in the sense that what is advised or proposed really is best or right for the affected person or persons, information has to be true, and assertions (in the generalized sense given here) have to be epistemically authorized in the given relevant sense (I distinguish between the moral authorization of an *action* and the epistemic authorization of a moral *validity* claim). As to those "regulative" speech acts that I have labeled "productive" in the normative sense, it seems that their essential validity conditions *coincide* with their sincerity and rightness conditions. Precisely in this one sees yet again their tight connection to moral validity claims.

To the extent that illocutionary types can be differentiated with the help of performative verbs, they tend to designate not only a characteristic relationship that a speaker assumes toward a hearer but also, by the same token, a complex constellation of characteristic validity claims. Such validity claims, in being implicitly or explicitly raised by the speaker toward the hearer, determine the specific illocutionary force—a "rationally motivating force"—that the utterance is able to have for this hearer. (I would correspondingly distinguish between the *validity* [*Gültigkeit*] of a speech act, taken "multidimensionally," and the *validity* [*Geltung*] of that for which a given *specific* validity claim is raised.) Special performative verbs and other mode indicators as well become ever more necessary the less an explicitly raised validity claim alone is able to do unequivocally what the speaker *does* with an utterance. This circumstance is closely related to the great variety of *regulative* performative verbs and especially those verbs whose performative use is productive in the normative sense. (Most institutional speech acts fall into this category as well.) However, the more what a speaker does with an utterance reduces to raising a univocal and explicit validity claim, the less need there is for specific performative verbs. "Assert," "assure," "say," and a few others will do the job, indeed, more or less independently of what kind of validity claim is raised. When I say to someone that his gift or his success makes me happy, that I'm afraid, or that I don't believe *x* will still come today, I do not need a special performative verb announcing that I am *giving expression* to something; this is to be seen directly in the sentence employed. On the other hand, a special performative verb would also not add anything useful, since an insincere statement of feeling does not in addition become an expression of feeling in virtue of my adding, "I herewith express that. . . ." We use means of expression such as these only in slightly ritualized contexts, in which case it no longer depends unconditionally or primarily on the speaker's sincerity: we condole, congratulate, or thank someone, and these are special illocutionary acts precisely because I can express my sympathy to someone, wish him happiness or thank him without having the corresponding feelings or desires. Giving expression to a feeling becomes a special illocutionary act, paradoxically, the very moment the speaker's sincerity ceases to be the decisive criterion for the performance of the act (although this does not have to mean that sincerity is unimportant).

Something similar holds for other validity claims: that an utterance is an empirical assertion, a hermeneutical appraisal, a moral judgment, an aesthetic or nonaesthetic evaluation, or a mathematical thesis can be read off from the meaning of the corresponding sentences without needing a performative vocabulary specialized for validity types. Internal connections (such as that between "is" and "ought"), as well as gradual transitions *between* various validity dimensions, also become easier to comprehend on the basis of such an "illocutionary continuum" stretching across the various validity dimensions. Gradual transitions are especially to be found between purely expressive utterances and moral, aesthetic, or otherwise evaluative statements (and even between expressive utterances and empirical statements). It is obvious that the expressive use of language in the form of evaluative statements is variously connected with intersubjective validity claims: affects have a world-disclosing function that precipitates in value statements, while value statements as a rule have an affective component that more or less presents itself with a cognitive function. That a concert is overwhelming, a woman enchanting, an action abhorrent can only be said with good reason by the one overwhelmed by the concert, enchanted by the woman, or filled with abhorrence at the action. Conversely, the one who wants to express his feelings of being overwhelmed, of enchantment, or of abhorrence frequently reaches, in a wholly natural way, for those "objectivating" sentence forms: indeed, it is his feeling itself that evaluates reality. Of course, the line of sight can change and the feeling as such become thematic (for example, when the "appropriateness" [*Berechtigung*] of the feeling is questionable), in which case a purely expressive utterance takes the place of the expressive-evaluative one.[35] On the other side of the spectrum, gradual transitions are to be found between expressive utterances and empirical statements: "I love you," for example, is an utterance standing on the boundary between mere sincerity claims and truth claims.

9

"We understand a speech act when we know what makes it acceptable." As we have seen, in its strong indicative sense this thesis is correct only if we relate it merely to a speaker's/hearer's "knowledge of illocutionary meaning." Then it says what it is to know the meaning of a performative verb, with the help of which speech acts of an illocutionary type can be carried out. However, when we want to get at how we understand situated utterances, inclusive of their propositional contents, we have to conceive the knowledge of the *general* acceptability conditions (defined by the illocutionary type) as completed by a more comprehensive kind of knowledge, namely, the general "knowledge of meaning" together with the speaker's/hearer's empirical, normative, and practical knowledge. For only on the basis of this more comprehensive knowledge of language and world are speakers and hearers able to know the relevant kinds of reasons that can authorize a speaker to raise various sorts of validity claim. A knowledge of "acceptability conditions" in this more comprehensive sense is the presupposition for understanding *situated* utterances. Habermas himself has formulated a corresponding extension of his acceptability principle for the case of empirical assertions. As it turns out, though, this extension of the acceptability principle, i.e., its specification for empirical assertions, can only be taken with a grain of salt, because in the knowledge of the acceptability conditions for empirical assertions "knowledge of meaning" and "knowledge of the world" can come together in complex ways. Frequently we can also understand an empirical assertion when we are not familiar with all the reasons that could authorize a speaker to make it. Accordingly, one must be cautious about extending Habermas's acceptability principle for assertions to cover all kinds of validity claims generally (not "all kinds of speech acts"). One could at least *begin* with a formulation something like this: to understand a validity claim is to know when a speaker has good grounds to warrant that the conditions for the validity of the "asserted" proposition are satisfied. Naturally, one would have to provide such a formulation with commentaries of the sort I have tried to give for empirical assertions. For example, there would have to be investigations of the analogies (and disanalogies) to be found in moving from the connection between empirical truth claims and the logic of causal discourse, on the one hand, to the connection between moral validity claims and the logic of moral discourse on the other. Here an analogy seems to exist not only between the causal and the moral "must," in other words, causal and moral necessity but also to a certain degree between the connections respectively linking a speaker's causal and moral knowledge to his knowledge of meaning. For example, that snow melts upon warming is at once meaning knowledge and causal knowledge. In an analogous sense, it is both a moral knowledge and a meaning knowledge that reckless driving is not right. Accordingly, a change in moral convictions, in a way similar to the extension of causal knowledge, will be reflected by a change in linguistic meanings and modes of description. Nevertheless, in both cases the causal or normative knowledge must also be conceived—presumably in entirely different ways—as more or less independent of a speaker's knowledge of meaning.

The here-proposed generalization of Habermas's acceptability principle for assertions concerns *validity claims* of various sorts, as already pointed out, and not *speech acts* of various sorts. A speaker's communicative competence really involves *both:* the knowledge of the respective speech-act-typical *general* acceptability conditions for utterances *and* the at least partial knowledge of the respective *special* "assertability conditions" for propositions of a certain content. A pragmatic theory of meaning must therefore tie the analysis of the illocutionary dimension of language to a generalized understanding of the internal connection between the meaning of validity claims and the possibility of their justification. On the other hand, the pragmatic approach does *not* need to take shortcuts between validity dimensions and illocutionary types. We are dealing here with two distinguishable components of a "competent" speaker's linguistic knowledge, even if they do reciprocally refer to one another. Only if we correctly relate these two components to each other can we know what makes Habermas's suggestive generalization of the basic principle of truth semantics acceptable, and thus the proposition that was the basic theme of my reflections.[36]

Notes

1. Jürgen Habermas, *The Theory of Communicative Action,* 2 vols., trans. Thomas McCarthy (Boston, 1984, 1987), vol. 1, p. 297 (cited as *TCA*).

2. [The terms *Sinn* and *Bedeutung* have been translated in various ways since Frege put them to work as a pair for his own philosophical purposes. In the present context, "meaning" could probably work for both. In order to alert the reader to Wellmer's usage, however, I reserve "sense" for *Sinn* unless noted otherwise.—Translator]

3. See H. Paul Grice, "Logic and Conversation," in P. Cole and J. L. Morgan, eds., *Syntax and Semantics,* vol. 3, *Speech Acts* (New York, 1975), pp. 41–58.

4. See John R. Searle, "Indirect Speech Acts," in Cole and Morgan, eds., *Speech Acts,* pp. 59–82.

5. I assume with Wittgenstein, Habermas, and Dummett a "normal case" of undistorted mutual linguistic understanding [*Verständigung*] in a common language, which we can mark by the fact that the understanding [*Verstehen*] does not require an act of "translation" (and in this sense, interpretation) on the side of the hearer. See the remarks Dummett directs against Davidson in Michael Dummett, "A Nice Derangement of Epitaphs: Some Comments on Davidson and Hacking," in Ernest LePore, ed., *Truth and Interpretation: Perspectives on the Philosophy of Donald Davidson* (Oxford, 1986), p. 472.

6. To prevent misunderstandings, I am not saying that speech situations determine a speaker's communicative intentions (here one could at most speak of *normative* restrictions and obligations). Rather, what I am saying is that speech situations (extensively) determine those communicative intentions a speaker can *connect* with what he says.

7. See Michael Dummett, "What Is a Theory of Meaning? (II)," in G. Evans and J. McDowell, eds., *Truth and Meaning* (Oxford, 1976), pp. 67 ff.

8. See M. Dummett, "A Nice Derangement of Epitaphs," p. 472.

9. See Albrecht Wellmer, "Intersubjectivity and Reason," in L. Hertzberg and J. Pietarinen, eds., *Perspectives on Human Conduct* (Leiden, 1988).

10. John R. Searle, *Speech Acts* (Cambridge, 1969).

11. On this point, see section 7. See Habermas, *TCA,* vol. 1, pp. 401, 405 ff.; also his "What Is Universal Pragmatics?" in Habermas, *Communication and the Evolution of Society,* trans. Thomas McCarthy (Boston, 1979), pp. 1–68.

12. Habermas, *TCA,* vol. 1, p. 318. [I have changed McCarthy's translation of *Aussage* as "sentence" to "proposition"; in other contexts I have also used "statement."—Translator]

13. I refer here again to Michael Dummett's discussion of these difficulties, esp. in "What Is a Theory of Meaning? (II)."

14. For the distinction between "linguistic knowledge" and "world knowledge," see Jürgen Habermas, "Zur Kritik der Bedeutungstheorie," in his *Nachmetaphysisches Denken* (Frankfurt am Main, 1988), p. 128; English translation forthcoming, MIT Press.

15. ["Entitled" renders the German *berechtigt.* Although this could be translated simply as "justified," it also has the connotation of rightfulness or having a right [*Recht*] to do something. In view of Wellmer's use of this term later in the article, I have, unless noted otherwise, rendered it either as "entitled" or "authorized," thereby keeping it distinct from forms of *begründen,* for which I have reserved forms of "to ground" or "justify."—Translator]

16. See Hilary Putnam, *Reason, Truth and History* (Cambridge, 1981), p. 55.

17. See J. Habermas, "Wahrheitstheorien," in H. Fahrenbach, ed., *Wirklichkeit und Reflexion* (Pfullingen, 1973).

18. See my critique of the consensus theory of truth in Albrecht Wellmer, *Ethik und Dialog* (Frankfurt am Main, 1986), pp. 69 ff.; English translation in Wellmer, *The Persistence of Modernity* (Cambridge, Mass., 1990), pp. 113–231.

19. Habermas has since tended towards this view as well. See *TCA,* vol. 1, p. 318.

20. Ludwig Wittgenstein, *Philosophical Investigations,* trans. G. E. M. Anscombe (Oxford, 1958), sec. 219.

21. See Wittgenstein, *Philosophical Investigations,* sec. 146.

22. Dummett, "A Nice Derangement of Epitaphs," pp. 464 f.

23. Habermas, *TCA,* vol. 1, p. 318.

24. Habermas, *TCA,* vol. 1, p. 318.

25. Dummett, "What Is a Theory of Meaning? (II)," p. 126.

26. Habermas, *TCA,* vol. 1, p. 318.

27. See Albrecht Wellmer, *Methodologie als Erkenntnistheorie: Zur Wissenschaftslehre Karl R. Poppers* (Frankfurt am Main, 1967), p. 118.

28. To name just one example, this was the point of Imre Lakatos's critique of the early Popper's "naive" falsificationism. See Imre Lakatos, "Falsification and the Methodology of Scientific Research Programmes," in I. Lakatos and A. Musgrave, eds., *Criticism and the Growth of Knowledge* (Cambridge, 1970), p. 119.

29. Habermas, *TCA,* vol. 1, p. 318.

30. Ludwig Wittgenstein, *Tractatus Logico-philosophicus,* trans. D. F. Pears and B. F. McGuinness (New York, 1961), par. 4.024.

31. See Dummett, "What Is a Theory of Meaning? (II)," p. 74.

32. There are, of course, other acceptability conditions for imperative utterances. A directive, for example, should also be "right" in the sense that it is *sensible* in relation to the goals presupposed in a given context of interaction or action. There are, however, situations in which the addressee of a directive is obligated, within certain limits, to carry out (what appear to him) senseless or false directives as well. "You are the boss," is what one often says then. This does not mean the speaker would be (rationally) authorized to give senseless or false directives as well as correct ones; it means rather that his "right to directives" includes (or can include) the right to decide *whether* a directive is, or is not, sensible or "right."

33. See Habermas, *TCA,* vol. 1, pp. 308–309.

34. I disregard here conditions of "grammatical correctness" in the narrower sense, for example, that a promise must concern the speaker's *future* actions, etc.

35. In the case of purely expressive (or better, representative) utterances, thus those utterances where a speaker expresses or gives expression to his feelings, desires, intentions, or convictions, the claim to the validity of what is said *coincides* with a sincerity claim on the speaker's part. In *this* sense one can understand expressive utterances also as a class of *speech acts,* for whose execution there is admittedly no need for a *special* performative verb in that the coincidence of validity claim and sincerity claim results from the meaning of the sentences employed. The validity claim raised in such expressive utterances can be disjoined from the sincerity claim insofar as the speaker claims validity for what is *said* ("*She* feels terribly miserable"). But insofar as the essential validity condition of his speech act is the speaker's sincerity, its specific validity claim can *not* be separated from the sincerity claim bound to the first-person form [of expression]. Perhaps we could say that here we have at once a specific kind of *validity claim* (and to this extent, a specific validity dimension) *and* a specific way of *raising* a validity claim (and to this extent, a type of speech act).

36. I am inclined to understand illocutionary force in general from the standpoint of the paradigm of regulative speech acts (in the narrower sense). In this sense I would also attempt to reconstruct a thesis Habermas proposes in volume 2 of *The Theory of Communicative Action* according to which "the concept of a criticizable validity claim derives from an assimilation of the truth of statements to the validity of norms (which was, to begin with, not criticizable)" (p. 70). Habermas's thesis appears in connection with his reflections on the "linguistification of the sacred," through which, as Habermas tries to show, the (original) "authority of the holy is gradually replaced by the authority of an achieved consensus" (p. 77). Now in fact it is easy (as shown not only in Habermas but also in the rhetoric of relevant argumentation) to interpret the illocutionary force of, say, *asserting* in analogy to that of guaranteeing [*Gewährleistens*] or of warranting, and hence in analogy to those regulative speech acts that are productive in a normative respect (see section 7 above). A difference, though, is that here a speaker's right to a speech act is of a special, namely epistemic, nature, whereas the obligations he gen-

erates through his speech act concern the grounding of problematic validity claims or the recognition of grounded validity claims. What the speaker warrants is that the asserted proposition *is valid* (that the conditions of its validity [*Geltung*] are satisfied), where the connection between validity and grounding is to be so understood that the concept of validity designates the context-transcending claim to recognition for a statement, while the concept of grounding designates the context-immanent obligations of speakers and hearers. But if *even* the illocutionary force of asserting can be understood by a certain analogy to that of promising, betting, or vouching for, then it is easy to spell out the concept of illocutionary force as such through the example of those performative verbs whose usage is connected with the *generation* of rights and/or duties, just as Austin did originally. For something like the kernel of meaning in the term "performative" is thereby designated, i.e., the kernel of what we mean when we say that with the use of a performative verb a speaker *does* what he says by saying what he does. If one accepts such an interpretation of illocutionary force, which comes quite close to Austin's original interpretation, then one is practically forced to distinguish further between the "illocutionary force" and the "pragmatic function" of utterances. Illocutionary forces designate, as a rule, special pragmatic functions, but not all the pragmatic functions of utterances correspond to illocutionary forces: describing, reporting, telling, arguing, etc. are linguistic ways of action (complex speech actions) for which there are no performative verbs. By describing, reporting, telling something, by arguing for or against something, a speaker performs some particular thing more or less well. He can, through the use of corresponding verbs, *announce* this performance, but he cannot, as in the case of promising or asserting, also *achieve* it through the use of the corresponding verbs. The decisive reason for this lies not in the complexity of the speech actions involved but in the grammar of the verbs involved: by using them in the first person present, the speaker does not already do what he announces through the use of those verbs. "I tell [*erzähle*] things how they were," is not a narration [*Erzählung*].

7

Art and Rationality: On the Dialectic of Symbolic and Allegorical Form[1]

Peter Bürger

Translated by William Rehg

Art is in this contradiction with itself: if it is independent, then it must be extended to allegory, in which case it has vanished as individuality and the significance brought down to individuality is then itself not expressed.
Hegel[2]

1

Of all the paradoxes involved in processes of linguistically mediated understanding [*Verständigung*], not least is the fact that even philosophical thought cannot dispense with certain concepts that are something like jokers in a card game. They make processes of understanding and self-understanding possible precisely because they admit of opposed semantic contents. Thus Enlightenment philosophy is based on a concept of nature that designates an irretrievable original state as well as an ideal it is necessary to realize. In it the opposites of instinctive drive and ethical life [*Sittlichkeit*] come together, opposites that Sade's demonstrations will finally bring to light. Aesthetic theory too cannot get by without such joker concepts, and where it imagines it can, it misses something essential to the aesthetic experience [*Erfahrung*[3]]. The most important of these concepts is that of form, which embraces the notions of intervention in material and mimetic impulse, i.e., something rational and something preceding all rationality. Adorno once called it the "blind spot of aesthetics."[4] The theoretician who must insist upon the rational determination of conceptual meanings admits in this way that something about his conduct is inappropriate, though without advocating that we abandon concepts altogether.

If one wishes to specify the position of art vis-à-vis rationality, taken as the dominant paradigm of action in bourgeois society, one will have to avoid prior commitments at the analytic level and instead get into the contradictions in those concepts (such as form) emerging from the subject matter itself.[5] In contrast to the unity of sign and significance [*Bedeutung*], particular and universal in the symbol, the concept of form aligned with allegory is based precisely on the separation of sign and significance. In view of the fact that modern society rests on the principle of division [*Entzweiung*], it seems reasonable to consider the allegory as the modern form par excellence but to see the symbol, on the other hand, as merely the remnant of a premodern attitude.[6] The plausibility of this alignment is admittedly based on an abstract, classificatory approach. If, by contrast, one enters into the movement of form, one will not be able to stop at the simple opposition between (modern) allegory and (premodern) symbol but will have to investigate the relational motif they form with each other.

Scarcely any twentieth-century author has pursued the incorporation of literature into the modern paradigm of rationality so consistently as Brecht. In the Keuner stories, however, we can examine how the allegorical fixing of significance fails and, precisely in this failure, opens our eyes to a content in the text no longer covered by the author's intention. What elevates the *Geschichten vom Herrn Keuner* (Tales of Mr. Keuner) above didactic literature is the fact that it shows someone teaching, thereby giving back to the reader the freedom it seemed to take from him in its rush to instruct. For the lessons Mr. K. presents are precisely not to be equated with the content of the stories. Had Brecht wished only to illustrate social-theoretic convictions in allegorical images, then those critics would be right who see his plays and short stories as merely illustrating a political doctrine. By making the teaching itself the object of presentation, however, he sets in motion the dialectic of symbolic and allegorical form. The reader sees more than the allegorist shows him. He sees not only the image illustrating the lesson but at the same time the process of showing, which is in turn subject to interpretation. "In truth," writes Adorno, "Brecht's intended primacy of lesson over pure form becomes one of the form's moments."[7]

"Der Gesandte" (The Envoy), for example, undoubtedly wants to impart a message: the reader is supposed to grasp the necessity of revolutionary discipline. After his return from a hostile foreign land, the envoy is severely reprimanded, even though his mission was a great success. Mr. K. explains: "He has probably gotten used to good eating, trafficked with criminals, and become unsure of judgment."[8] Yet the reader of the Keuner stories has long since learned to ask questions, including precisely those the narrator does not raise here: Is good eating something bad? Is friendliness in one's dealings no virtue? Isn't Mr. K. himself teaching doubt? The dialectic thus drives beyond the established significance, indeed by dint of the form.

The individual short story follows the allegorical principle of form. Its sensuous, concrete shape and significance, forced together only through the act of the allegorist, in fact remain external to each other. The concrete does not display a life of its own but exists merely to signify something else. The story does not concern the envoy and his life circumstances; he is simply a figure by which a constellation can be elucidated. But that also means he is not interesting of himself. The figure is flattened out into a sign. If despite this "Der Gesandte" does not ossify into an abstract learning story, then this is due not so much to the exchange between the first-person narrator and Mr. K.—decided in favor of Mr. K.—as to the context provided by the other stories, in which the teacher assumes a contradictory symbolic shape. The truth content that becomes visible in this way would not be possible without the allegory, yet it also surpasses it.

A short comparison of "Die Denkaufgabe" (The Thought Problem) with the Keuner story "Freundschaftsdienste" (Services of Friendship) can show what the allegorical form of the parable accomplishes in Brecht. Both of these have to do with arbitrating an inheritance dispute among a farmer's three sons. Specifically, the father has left seventeen head of livestock and a will prescribing a complicated formula for dividing the inheritance. A friend of the deceased solves the problem by letting the brothers "borrow" his only animal for the purpose of reckoning; after dividing the inheritance it is left over and returned to the friend. In "Die Denkaufgabe" the matter is organized in a series of short scenes—the search for the will, the arrival of the mourners, the sons' useless attempts to manage the division, the growing irritation of all involved—until finally the friend of the deceased makes the helpful proposal. The story's parabolic character is concealed here by the scenic presentation and seemingly realistic details.[9] This is not the case in "Freundschaftsdienste." The plural in the title already announces the exemplary character of Mr. K.'s story, which he tells explicitly as an example. Correspondingly, Brecht abstains here from any organization of the material, strictly limiting himself to what is necessary for comprehension. To make the reader's identification with the figures wholly impossible, he shifts the event to an Arabian country and uses camels in place of cattle. The allegory that results in this way even includes the explanatory note "Mr. K. designated this a proper service of friendship because it demanded no particular sacrifice."[10] Shown here is not the arbitration of an inheritance dispute but rather Mr. K. the lesson giver, who presents an unimpassioned, businesslike notion of friendship. Yet the fixing of content fails precisely because it appears so apodictic. Since there is apparently nothing in the story to interpret, the reflective reader refuses to rest with the significance first proffered him. The allegorical project shipwrecks on the very closure with which it is realized. In this shipwreck, however, there arises a new, equivocal structure, the result of the opposition of individual Keuner stories as well as of the contradictions visible in the character of Mr. K. The figure of the teacher who presents himself as identical becomes questionable in its identity. The split between allegorical image and the posited significance forcibly closing the individual story becomes open to question once again. Yet the critique of *engagement,* a critique that looks only at the message instead of concerning itself with the movement of form, is also invalidated by this reversal of allegorical intention.

Brecht's text works at two contrapunctually related levels. At the first level the individual story is introduced as a parable conveying a univocally interpretable message. At the second level, however, the interference between stories emerges and the teacher K.'s contradictory stance is registered. The significance imposing itself on the reader at the first level becomes questionable again at the second level, though without simply being negated. In this way, however, the meaning [*Sinn*] is set in motion. In other words, the individual parable is put into a symbolically structured interpretive space in which the sign has no fixed significance but rather is handed over to an indefinite process of reflection. The truth lies not in what Mr. K., the narrator, or the author says but rather in what becomes visible in the interplay of stories.

2

Brecht's return to allegory is part of a comprehensive project of "converting art into a pedagogical discipline."[11] In order to attain this, he relies not on the immanent critique of a metaphysical concept of art but rather on the "transformative power of the commodity character"[12] and the surrender of art to technical apparatus. The *Dreigroschenprozeß* (Threepenny Lawsuit) reports on a sociological experiment in which the "notion of an inviolable phenomenon of art"[13] confronts the utilitarian interests of capital. The right to artistic involvement in fashioning the film version of the *Threepenny Opera,* a right Brecht reserved to himself by contract, did not stand up in court. This led him to conclude that artistic autonomy is empty. The reality of capitalist society has apparently assumed the task of critique. More than fifty years after he wrote this polemic, we know that the commodity character of art products in no way destroys the notion of artistic autonomy but rather finally makes it visible. Neither has Brecht's second assumption proven true, that technical apparatus such as film could contribute to overcoming auratic art.

If the conversion of art into a pedagogical discipline has not materialized as Brecht hoped, then no doubt this is primarily because he applies his critique at a level where art turns out to be resistant. That an art appropriate to modernity would have to renounce elements affiliating it with religious ritual is certainly a plausible idea, but the fact that its transformation has thus far not succeeded suggests that a metaphysical attitude survives in the institution of art. The scandal this gives to the enlightened consciousness always becomes virulent where the program of rationalizing art is taken as a serious project. The fascination still surrounding Benjamin's "Work of Art" essay attests to the quasi-objective force of the problem.

Benjamin accepted and radicalized the Brechtian thesis that the technical media could "be employed to overcome the old 'glowing' 'art' associated with the religious."[14] Where Brecht sees a prospect of application, Benjamin discovers a process of emancipation that should result directly from technical development. "For the first time in world history, mechanical reproduction emancipates the work of art from its parasitical dependence on ritual."[15] By destroying the uniqueness of the work of art, reproduction brings about the decline of the work's aura, the unapproachableness that constitutes it as a work and makes it an object of a quasi-religious meditation. The concept of aura designates more than a specific type of reception; with it Benjamin seeks to invalidate central categories of idealistic aesthetics (autonomy and illusion). The leading idea guiding Benjamin's approach lies not in the thesis of emancipation through the technical media but in the insight that art in bourgeois society is institutionalized in a way that displays structural commonalities with the institution of religion. Coupled with this insight is his insistence on the historically changeable character of experience [*Erfahrung*].

Jürgen Habermas's contribution has been to emphasize the fact that Benjamin "was always ambivalent about the loss of aura."[16] Thus in the studies on Baudelaire, likewise written at the end of the 1930s, Benjamin conceives the decline of aura not as an emancipation process but as a "crisis of artistic reproduction." The camera, he argues, though expanding the range of images one can intentionally record, by the same token limits one's room for phantasy. "If the distinctive feature of the images that rise from the *mémoire involontaire* is seen in their aura, then photography is decisively implicated in the phenomenon of the 'decline of the aura.'"[17] In contrast to the "Work of Art" essay, he now defines the aura as investing the inanimate with a gaze of its own. "To perceive the aura of an object we look at means to invest it with the ability to look at us in return."[18] The cultic character of the auratic reception, whose destruction appeared freeing in the "Work of Art" essay, is here considered the constitutive moment in aesthetic experience.

Jürgen Habermas has proposed an elegant resolution of the "ambiguity" in Benjamin's thesis. According to Habermas, one should separate the "cultic moments" in the aura concept (esoteric access to the art work, the viewer's cultic distance, his contemplative immersion) from the "universal moments" (the "transformation of the object into a counterpart"). In this way the happiness experienced [*Glückserfahrung*] through contact with works of art can be universalized and stabilized.[19] Habermas himself points out the danger lurking in his proposal: in deritualized art the work could fall prey to banality.

In the concepts determining the self-understanding of the institution of art or describing how that institution functions, philosophical thought runs into something at cross purposes to the rationality principle. More specifically, in the symbolic form, philosophical thought comes up against the substantial unity of sign and significance, precisely what modern linguistics beginning with Saussure has called into question. In the concept of aura it runs into a mode of quasi-cultic contact with works of art. Just as the symbolic form proved peculiarly resistant to Brecht's project of redirecting art into a pedagogical discipline, so Benjamin's ambivalence toward the (necessary) decline of aura indicates that aesthetic experience cannot fully dispense with the auratic moment. It should give one pause that an artist as reflective as Tàpies speaks emphatically in favor of an auratic contact with works of art. "The Japanese know quite well that in order for an art object to fulfill its function it must be surrounded by a certain solemnity, a certain deferential mystery."[20] Tàpies describes in detail how the Japanese veil the work of art in multiple ways, thereby creating a distance between the object and its viewer. The objection that this exposes auratic contact for what it is, namely humbug, cannot be refuted. One can argue, however, that such a praxis is modern to the extent it admits its own groundlessness. That the work of art is not something in itself but is rather first constituted as work only by institutionalized contact with it—that is a thoroughly modern insight presupposing that substantial worldviews have lost their validity.

3

Benjamin's ambivalence toward the aura and its decline corresponds to a comparable indecisiveness in his *Origin of German Tragic Drama* regarding the evaluation of allegory and symbol. For in his efforts to rehabilitate baroque allegory as a form of expression, he runs into a difficulty: the majority of German baroque dramas no longer provide the modern reader with any enjoyment. Even Benjamin cannot simply disregard this fact. He criticizes its "elaborate surrounding framework," as well as the "range of the products, their intentional bulkiness and lack of mystery."[21] The criteria he lays down in the process (autonomy of the work, conciseness, mystery) belong to the aesthetics of the symbolic form. The same is true of the attitude of reception he finds missing in the baroque, the "gaze that would have been able to find satisfaction in the object itself."[22] Evidently the modern viewer tends to adopt a symbolic attitude to allegorical works as well.

Yet Benjamin takes still a further step. At the end of the book he sketches a theological critique of allegorical procedure as an objectionable striving for knowledge.

> For something can take on allegorical form only for the one who has knowledge. But on the other hand, if contemplation is not so much patiently devoted to truth as bent unconditionally and compulsively on absolute knowledge in direct meditation, then it is eluded by things in the simplicity of their essence, and they lie before it as enigmatic allegorical references, they continue to be dust.[23]

The antitheses are precisely marked: on the one side is a theologically loaded concept of truth as revealing itself to the one who patiently considers things according to their simple essence; on the other side the sacrilegious striving for knowledge that subjugates things, imposing an alien significance on them and finally destroying them. In designating allegory here as "the triumph of subjectivity and the onset of an arbitrary rule over things," Benjamin characterizes it as a rational form of expression.[24] At the same time, however, he appraises it theologically as evil. For "knowledge, not action, is the most characteristic mode of existence of evil."[25] The rediscovery of allegory as a form of expression finally empties into its theological criticism. Even though this line of thought admittedly undergoes yet a further reversal on the last pages of *The Origin of German Tragic Drama,* when "manifest subjectivity becomes the formal guarantee of the miracle,"[26] its critical turn is at least indirectly symptomatic of Benjamin's unwillingness to abandon the symbol precisely on account of its theological origins.

Rightly impressed by the rehabilitation of allegory, one previously took little notice of Benjamin's argumentation in the opposite direction. In fact, the chapter on allegory in *German Tragic Drama* starts with a sharp condemnation of talk of the symbolic. In Benjamin's view, affirming the "indivisible unity of form and content" only conceals an inability to exhibit their dialectical mediation in the work of art itself. Beyond this, the formula is an instrument for depicting the aesthetic and ethical worlds as always already reconciled. However, Benjamin first of all contrasts this not with allegory but with "the unity of the material and the transcendent object that constitutes the paradox of the theological symbol."[27] It is not the symbol as such that falls victim to his critique but only "this surreptitious talk of the symbolic" from which all traces of the tension of opposites—a tension mounting to paradox in the theological—is removed.[28] Thus instead of simply abandoning the concept and thereby repressing the problem encoiled therein, one should focus on making that paradoxical structure visible even in the aesthetic symbol.

That Benjamin did not intend to replace the symbolic form with allegory is also clear from a posthumous fragment in which he designates allegory as the corrective of art itself.[29] Evidently he considers the symbolic form the constitutive moment of art. Conversely, he speaks at one point of the "antiartistic subjectivity" at work in all baroque allegory,[30] an idea quite compatible with Goethe's remark that all allegorical works "destroy interest in the presentation itself and drive the spirit back into itself, so to speak."[31] Just as Benjamin's rehabilitation of allegory includes its critique, so his critique of the symbolic form includes its rehabilitation. Naturally, this form no longer coincides as such with the image of organic totality that drew on the classical concept of individuality for its mediation of ethical life and beautiful *physis*. Form must rather be defined as a metaphysical principle of unity that conditions even the reading of the allegory as fragment.

Another fragment on *German Tragic Drama* reads,

> The indissoluble correlation between fundamental metaphysical concepts and primal phenomena [*Urphänomenen*] of art. Each can only be explained in light of the other, insofar as fundamental metaphysical concepts of unity are relevant for the answer, and insofar as the question concerns the *ratio* of aesthetic primal phenomena (in form and content).[32]

If metaphysical concepts of unity (ultimately the subject-object of idealistic philosophy) underlie modern aesthetics, then the attempt to locate art inside the paradigm of rationality encounters a boundary that can only be crossed at the price of missing the thing itself [*die Sache selbst*]. Formulated in another way, the critique of idealistic aesthetics calls for a metacritique that would have to sublate [*aufzuheben*] the results of the first critique. Such a venture admittedly runs into the problem that the conventional talk of the symbolic criticized by Benjamin likewise presumes unity, so that the object of legitimate critique seems to coincide with the basic fund of metacritique. This appearance arises because form is conceived as something objective and not as an active principle that constitutes aesthetic experience in the first place.[33] Should we wish to pursue the trail uncovered for us by Benjamin's treatment of allegory and symbol, we will have to view these not as fixed or thinglike but as moving principles of reflection.

4

If one defines symbolic form in terms neither of organic totality nor of the individual's sensuous-ethical wholeness, then there remains as a basis for definition the unity of the sensuous-concrete and significance. Allegory, on the other hand, becomes the site where the break between sensuous sign and significance is located.[34] At the same time, however, establishing this by definition misses something in the object [*Sache*]. This point is illuminated by a passage in the Goethe and Schiller correspondence that Benjamin refers to in the first chapter of his treatise *Goethes Wahlverwandschaften* (Goethe's Elective Affinities). Goethe reports from Frankfurt that certain objects [*Gegenstände*] awaken "a kind of sentimentality" in him. He explains his characteristic reaction through the symbolic properties of these objects. But this only means, first of all, that they impose themselves on him as significant; in their concrete particularity they seem at the same time to point beyond their particular being-such [*Sosein*]. Goethe makes up his mind to direct his attention in the further course of his travel "not so much to what is strange, but to what is significant."[35] Benjamin comments, "the human being is paralyzed in the symbol's chaos and loses the freedom unknown to the ancients. He falls into acting according to signs and oracles."[36] Goethe obstinately experiences [*erlebt*] the world as a universe of significant signs, an obstinacy Benjamin interprets as a premodern attitude in which Goethe takes refuge for fear of his life. This attitude first becomes aesthetically available in an epoch in which the gods have withdrawn from nature.

In his reply to Goethe, Schiller, a Kantian, suggests that the sensuously self-revelatory, "objective" experiences of significance [*Bedeutungserlebnisse*] of which Goethe writes can also be conceived as "subjective" investments of significance and consequently as an allegorist's positings. The relevant passage reads, "They express themselves in such a way as though it here quite depended on the object . . . , and so it seems to me that emptiness and plentitude lie more in the subject than in the object."[37] Here a movement of reflection becomes visible that goes back and forth between the objective and subjective moments of signifying.

Experiencing [*Erleben*] the symbolic object is tied to the temporal moment, revealing itself as significant in the now [*im Jetzt*]. As Benjamin puts it, "the measure of time for the experience of the symbol is the mystical instant in which the symbol assumes the meaning into its hidden and, if one might say so, wooded interior."[38] Under the gaze of one viewing the world in a symbolic attitude, a piece of reality unexpectedly becomes the bearer of an admittedly inexhaustible and unnameable meaning. Proust described such moments in *Remembrance of Things Past,* thereby recording the happiness brought to the experiencer [*Beglückung des Erlebenden*] as well as the latter's disappointment over the fact that the piece of reality does not yield the significance it seemed to promise. Insofar as the experiencer stubbornly clings to the sensuous-concrete, he cannot assign any stable significance to what he perceives. For this he would have to step out of the immediacy of experiencing. Thus he knows significance only as an indeterminate promise of meaning.

Aesthetic reflection, however, does not thereby stand still but rather establishes relationships; it discovers that the concrete is something particular precisely in view of another concrete. In this way the pure immanence of aesthetic experiencing is forced open. The subject who was entirely absorbed in the object of his consideration now comes to experience himself as one separated from the object, who through his own formative conduct is able to answer the experience that brings happiness [*Erlebnis der Beglückung*], an experience that first seemed to condemn him to passivity. The protagonist of Proust's *Remembrance* acquires the experience [*macht die Erfahrung*] that the meaning he sought in the church towers of Martinville must first of all be brought forth by his recording his experiences [*Erlebnis*]. As author, he negates these experiences, steps out of the speechless oneness with them, and gives them a significance, i.e., a new form. For the reader there are in turn two possible stances toward this form. He can fasten his gaze on the sensuous-concrete in its particularity or he can go beyond it to apprehend its significance. In other words, he can adopt either a symbolic or an allegorical attitude.

If he resolves the dialectic of form and content wholly on the side of form, there remains for him at the end only the speechless expression of his experiencing, the outcry of admiration or ecstasy. However, if he resolves the dialectic of the created object wholly on the side of the content, the work in its concrete shape becomes for him a matter of indifference. As sensuous-concrete, it is annihilated by the allegorical gaze aimed at knowledge. For this reason Benjamin speaks of the "anti-artistic subjectivity" of the (baroque) allegory.

Inasmuch as the work of art is set up for the articulation of significance, aesthetic experience [*Erfahrung*] is not wrapped up in the immediacy of momentary experiencing, whose essential quality lies in arresting the passage of time. Nor can it be reduced to registering a content against which the work as concrete always proves resistent. Aesthetic consciousness is thus driven from place to place. It must wholly give itself over to the individual moment in its concretion, yet it must not stop there if the work is not to ossify into a fetish for it. It registers a significance in the work and then comes to experience this in turn as abstraction as soon as it turns once again to the work. It thus accomplishes a movement of reflection, concerned with the extremes of symbolic immediacy and allegorical mediation, without in the process ever arriving at a closure that would be more than a breaking off.

It is precisely contemporary art that also brings out the antithesis of symbolic and allegorical form, as a glance at Norbert Schwontkowski's *Uhrenwürger* (The Clock Strangler) should show. The picture immediately presents itself as allegorical. The act of violence against the clock, a reaction to the unbearable passing of time, only brings forth terror at that infinitude into whose sign the strangled clock metamorphoses. Yet as soon as the viewer returns to the sensuous-concrete impression, he cannot remain satisfied with this stable assignment of significance. If the figure's expressivity, reminding one of Munch's *Scream*, can still be integrated into the allegorical reading of the image, the same is not true of the mystifying correspondence of forms between the head and upper part of the clock.

Figure 1
Uhrenwürger (The Clock Strangler), Norbert Schwontkowski, 1985

Nor is it true of the "misrepresentation" of the arms, evidently necessary because of the parallelism with the lower part of the clock. If the expressive configuration of an allegorical subject of presentation already forces the antitheses of symbolic and allegorical together, then the correspondences just mentioned bring a constructive moment into the image, which returns in the hands of the clock. The viewer again feels required to interpret in turn the elements of form not covered by the allegorical significance. The infinitude generated by the clock strangler's act of violence is infused in the strangler himself and makes his body duplicate the sign that instills him with horror. Yet scarcely has consciousness thus brought what it perceives into a context of significance when its gaze falls on other remaining elements of form, such as the cross on the arm. Read as a patch, this cross impresses on the image a moment of cumbersome realism at cross purposes to the picture's allegorical sign character and expressivity. In this way the image forces the viewer to confront the antitheses built into it. He can stay neither with the impression's immediacy, an immediacy insistent on elucidating its own mediated character, nor with an established (allegorical) meaning whose abstract character becomes recognizable in the turn back to the object at hand. If only one of the two attitudes is maintained, then either the aesthetic object is fetishized in the being-such of its particularity or negated in abstract significance. In both cases aesthetic experience is missed. So it is that art in the modern epoch proves to be an institutionalized praxis that takes the antitheses whose unreconcilability determines modernity and forces them into an unending process of reciprocal negation. It thereby becomes the privileged place for an experience [*Erfahrung*] deserving the name because it does not happen to us but rather is *made* by us.

Notes

1. This chapter is part of the attempt at a new definition of aesthetic modernity that I took up in my book *Prosa der Moderne* (Frankfurt am Main, 1988). It presupposes the earlier study "Institution Kunst und Modernisierungsprozeß," in P. Bürger, ed.,

Zum Funktionswandel der Literatur (Frankfurt am Main, 1983), pp. 9–32, and sketches a metacritique of my study *Zur Kritik der idealistischen Ästhetik* (Frankfurt am Main, 1983).

2. G. W. F. Hegel, *Jenaer Systementwürfe III,* ed. Rolf-Peter Horstmann, in *Gesammelte Werke,* vol. 8 (Hamburg, 1976).

3. [In the course of this article the distinction between *Erfahrung* (*erfahren*) and *Erlebnis* (*erleben*) will become quite important. *Erfahrung* can have an active sense that includes the idea of learning; in German, one not only "has" but also "makes" [*macht*] an experience in this sense. *Erlebnis* connotes a more passive, immediate kind of experiencing. Besides noting the German in brackets, I have tried to capture the distinction by reserving the plural "experiences" or gerundive "experiencing" for *Erlebnis;* with forms of *Erfahrung,* on the other hand, I have sometimes tried to bring out the processual dimension with expressions such as "come to experience."—Translator]

4. Theodor W. Adorno, *Aesthetic Theory,* trans. C. Lenhardt, ed. Gretel Adorno and Rolf Tiedemann (London, 1984), p. 203 [translation slightly altered—Translator].

5. If aesthetic theory does not wish to disappoint our interest in the things it takes for its subject matter, it must "make certain its categories are appropriate to the object," as Jürgen Habermas has required of the social sciences in the *Positivismusstreit,* in *Zur Logik der Sozialwissenschaften* (Frankfurt am Main, 1970), p. 11.

6. See also Paul de Man, "The Rhetoric of Temporality," in his *Blindness and Insight: Essays in the Rhetoric of Contemporary Criticism,* 2nd ed. (Minneapolis, 1983), pp. 187–228, here esp. p. 226, and Heinz Schlaffer, *Faust zweiter Teil: Die Allegorie des 19. Jahrhunderts* (Stuttgart, 1981), esp. chapter 1.

7. Theodor W. Adorno, "Engagement," in T. W. Adorno, *Noten zur Literatur* (Frankfurt am Main, 1965), vol. 3, p. 120. This insight, of course, did not lead Adorno to reclaim Brecht.

8. Bertolt Brecht, "Der Gesandte," in *Geschichten vom Herrn Keuner,* in B. Brecht, *Prosa* (Frankfurt am Main, 1967), vol. 2, p. 393.

9. Bertolt Brecht, "Die Denkaufgabe," in B. Brecht, *Prosa* (Frankfurt am Main, 1967), vol. 1, pp. 234 f.

10. Bertolt Brecht, "Freundschaftsdienste," in *Geschichten vom Herrn Keuner, Prosa,* vol. 2, p. 390.

11. Bertolt Brecht, *Schriften zur Literatur und Kunst,* 2 vols. (Berlin, 1966), vol. 1, p. 180.

12. Brecht, *Schriften zur Literatur und Kunst,* vol. 1, p. 193.

13. Brecht, *Schriften zur Literatur und Kunst,* vol. 1, p. 246.

14. Brecht, *Schriften zur Literatur und Kunst,* vol. 1, p. 180.

15. Walter Benjamin, "The Work of Art in the Age of Mechanical Reproduction," in W. Benjamin, *Illuminations,* ed. with an Introduction by Hannah Arendt, trans. Harry Zohn (New York, 1969), p. 224.

16. Jürgen Habermas, "Walter Benjamin: Consciousness Raising or Rescuing Critique," in Habermas, *Philosophical-Political Profiles,* trans. Frederick G. Lawrence (Cambridge, Mass., 1985), p. 145.

17. Walter Benjamin, "On Some Motifs in Baudelaire," in *Illuminations,* p. 187.

18. Walter Benjamin, "On Some Motifs in Baudelaire," p. 188.

19. Habermas, *Philosophical-Political Profiles,* pp. 146 f.

20. Antoni Tàpies, *La Pratique de l'art,* Coll. Idées 374 (Paris, 1974), p. 269.

21. Walter Benjamin, *The Origin of German Tragic Drama,* trans. John Osborne (London, 1977), p. 181. [At a number of points in the subsequent citations of this text I have altered the translation to fit the present context.—Translator]

22. Benjamin, *German Tragic Drama,* p. 181.

23. Benjamin, *German Tragic Drama,* p. 403.

24. Benjamin, *German Tragic Drama,* p. 233.

25. Benjamin, *German Tragic Drama,* p. 230.

26. Benjamin, *German Tragic Drama,* p. 234.

27. Benjamin, *German Tragic Drama,* p. 160.

28. Benjamin, *German Tragic Drama,* p. 160.

29. Walter Benjamin, *Gesammelte Schriften,* vol. 1, ed. Rolf Tiedemann and Hermann Schweppenhäuser (Frankfurt am Main, 1972), p. 951.

30. Benjamin, *German Tragic Drama,* p. 233.

31. Goethe, "Über die Gegenstände der bildenden Kunst," in Goethe, *Werke,* ed. K. Heinemann (Leizig, n.d.), vol. 22, p. 74.

32. Benjamin, *Gesammelte Schriften,* vol. 1, p. 915.

33. "Matter is determined as indifferent: it is the *passive* as against Form as active," according to Hegel's *Science of Logic,* trans. W. H. Johnston and L. G. Struthers (New York, 1929), vol. 2, p. 79.

34. Insofar as something sensuous points to significance, both forms coincide in the comprehensive concept of symbol developed by Ernst Cassirer: "By 'symbolic form' is understood every energy of intellect through which an intellectual meaning content is tied to a concrete sensuous sign," *Wesen und Wirkung des Symbolbegriffs* (Darmstadt, 1956), p. 175.

35. Letter of Goethe to Schiller, August 16, 1797, in *Der Briefwechsel zwischen Schiller und Goethe,* vol. 1, ed. Hans Gerhard Gräf and Albert Leitzmann (n.p., 1955), pp. 377 ff., here p. 379.

36. Walter Benjamin, "Goethes Wahlverwandschaften," in *Gesammelte Schriften,* vol. 1, p. 154.

37. Letter of Schiller to Goethe, September 7, 1797, in *Briefwechsel,* vol. 1, p. 399.

38. Benjamin, *German Tragic Drama,* p. 165. The privileging of the moment in the aesthetic epiphany returns in the notion of the necessity of the form of the symbolic work of art, the concrete shape of which is nonetheless due solely to the fact that an indefinite process of forming has been fixed. Valéry insisted on this with the incorruptible purity of the rationalist: "A poem is never finished; it's always an accident that puts a stop to it—i.e., gives it to the public," in *Analecta,* trans. Stuart Gilbert, vol. 14 of *The Collected Works of Paul Valéry,* ed. Jackson Mathews (Princeton, N.J., 1970), p. 104. To the extent that the symbolic attitude denies the work's indefinitely open character, it stands at cross purposes to the principle of rationality.

III

Postenlightenment Challenges

8

Philosophy and Social Practice: Avoiding the Ethnocentric Predicament

Thomas McCarthy

In 1967 Richard Rorty congratulated Anglo-American philosophers for having made it around "the linguistic turn"; fifteen years later he urges us to get on "the literary-historical-anthropological-political merry-go-round" subsequently set in motion.[1] These disparate images mark the rise and fall of the most recent attempt to set philosophy on the path of a science. The more or less neo-Kantian aspirations of analytic philosophy have been subverted from within by criticisms of the repeated attempts to establish and exploit some basic distinction between form and content: analytic/synthetic, conceptual/empirical, meaning/experience, scheme/content, and so on. And they have been challenged from without by the invasion of post-Kantian Continental philosophy, with its ideas of the historical variability of structures of thought and action and their embeddedness in lifeworlds and traditions, of the conventionality of criteria of rationality and their entanglement with power and interest, of rational subjects as embodied and practically engaged with the world—ideas, in short, of the impurity of "pure reason." All of this has served to produce a metaphilosophical tumult in which the leading parties have called for everything from the end of philosophy or its radical transformation to less radical, holistic and coherentist alterations of the analytic program.[2] It is not my intention here to survey the contemporary philosophical scene but to explore two proposed paths beyond it.

For better and for worse, philosophical thought has repeatedly been influenced by its close dealings with the specialized sciences. In the decades following World War II, the predominant influence on American philosophy came from the formal and physical sciences. There have since been more or less intimate relations with linguistics, and there presently is a torrid love affair with neuroscience and artificial intelligence. Even the humanities and art criticism have recently managed, through the mediation of hermeneutics and literary theory, to establish relations with segments of the Anglophone philosophical community. My concern here is with history and the human sciences. Since their rapid development in the nineteenth century, these disciplines have had an enormous influence on Continental philosophy, an influence that carried into American Pragmatism but not much beyond it. Analytic philosophers could easily view Peirce as concerned chiefly with familiar problems of logic, language, and science; if it was not always possible to overlook James's and Dewey's appropriation of the human sciences, they could themselves be ignored; Mead was no problem, for he had very early on been put up for adoption by the social psychologists.

The end result of this (and other factors too complex to guess at) was the very peculiar postwar spectacle of mainstream Anglo-American philosophy flowing along for decades with virtually no influx from the human sciences. This was peculiar in both senses of the term. Not only was it distinctive of analytic philosophy that after a century of development of specialized modes of inquiry tailored to comprehending sociocultural phenomena, it all but ignored them except for persistent attempts to assimilate them to the natural sciences. It was also very queer. Since philosophy itself is a form of reflection on human thought and action, it might naturally be assumed to have especially close relations to those sciences that have developed other reflective approaches to the same domain. And in fact, in those limited areas in which sociohistorical research has seeped into the mainstream, its potential to alter the course of philosophical reflection has been evident. In philosophy of science, for instance, taking the history of science seriously spelled the end of logical empiricism, and current work in the sociology and ethnography of science promises to alter yet again our understanding of that paradigmatically rational practice.

Wittgenstein's later philosophy, with its suggestion of a quasi-ethnographic approach to "conceptual relations," seemed for a while to offer a promising point of entry for social research into the inner chambers of philosophy. Unfortunately, it was never much used in that way. Peter Winch did offer a thought-provoking Wittgensteinian account in *The Idea of a Social Science and Its Relation to Philosophy,* but he took scarce notice of the other side of the same coin, namely, the idea of philosophy and its relation to social science. More recently, however, the idea that the trajectory of linguistic philosophy leads to historical and anthropological studies of social practices has gained ground. It is, in fact, one of the chief impulses behind the "new historicism" in Anglo-American philosophy. It is worth recalling that today is not the first time in which philosophy has seen itself forced to renounce previous claims to absoluteness. This recurred with some regularity in the 150 years after Hegel—in the wakes of Marx and Darwin, Freud and Nietzsche, Historicism and Pragmatism—before its more recent occurrence in the wakes of Heidegger and Wittgenstein. If we keep that in mind, we are less likely to be overcome with vertigo at the rapid downfall of the latest regime of objectivism after its improbable restoration here in the decades following World War II. And we are less likely to suppose that the only alternative to objectivism is some form of relativism.[3] In what follows I want to contrast two very different ways of taking seriously the turn to social practice, so as to bring into sharper focus some of the basic issues it raises.

1

In *Philosophy and the Mirror of Nature* Richard Rorty criticizes the idea of the mind as a special field for philosophical investigation and the associated quest for foundations in various forms of self-knowledge.[4] He is equally hard on the "successor subject" of traditional epistemology, the "impure" philosophy of language in which philosophical concerns are recast as questions to be dealt with through "the logical analysis of language." Invoking the names of Dewey, Wittgenstein, and Heidegger, he proposes instead a turn to social practice, which will bring us down from the clouds back to earth, that is, back to the concrete, situated actions and interactions in which our working notions of reason, truth, objectivity, knowledge, and the like are embedded. He interprets this turn as leading to an "epistemological behaviorism" that uncompromisingly resists "the urge to see social practices of justifications as more than just such practices."[5] He means by this to emphasize the temporal rather than the atemporal, the contingent rather than the necessary, the local rather than the universal, the immanent rather than the transcendent features of the practices in questions, or more precisely, to deny the latter in the name of the former.

The key to Rorty's epistemological behaviorism is viewing justification as a social phenomenon, so that understanding knowledge becomes a matter of understanding the social practices in which we justify beliefs. The traditional philosophical investigation of "the nature of human knowledge" becomes the study of certain modes of action and interaction, prominently among them those that "count as justification within the various disciplinary matrices constituting the culture of the day."[6] Studies of this sort do not require special philosophical methods but draw instead upon "the usual empirical-cum-hermeneutic methods" of cultural anthropology and intellectual history.[7] Explicating rationality and epistemic authority is, then, a matter not of coming up with transcendental arguments but of providing thick ethnographic accounts of knowledge-producing activities: "If we understand the rules of a language game, we understand all that there is to know about why the moves in that language game are made"[8]—all, that is, except for a historical account of how the rules of the game came to have the shape they do and other "nonepistemological" lines of inquiry.

As an expression of opposition to the traditional quest for foundations, this is all to the good. But Rorty goes beyond that to a radically historicist account—he denies it is a theory—of reason, truth, objectivity, knowledge, and related notions. This account is spiced with such formulas as "what our peers will let us say" and "conformity to the norms of the day."[9] Less epigrammatically, Rorty defends the currently widespread view that "truth and knowledge can only be judged by the standards of the inquirers of our own day. Nothing counts as justification except by reference to what we already accept. . . . There is no way to get outside our beliefs and our language so as to find some other test than coherence."[10] There is a way of understanding this on which it is unexceptionably but uninterestingly true: we can't get outside our own skins, we have to start from where we are, we have to judge things by our own lights—in short, we have to make do without a God's-eye point of view. Rorty's way is more interesting but also easier to take exception with. It amounts to flattening out our notions of reason and truth by removing any air of transcendence from them. He allows that Socrates and Plato introduced into our culture "specifically philosophical" uses of terms which, like Kant's ideas of pure reason, were "designed precisely to stand for the Unconditioned—that which escapes the context within which discourse is conducted and inquiry pursued."[11] But, he adds, these are nothing like the "ordinary" uses of these terms, the "homely and shopworn" uses with which we make do outside of philosophy, where there is no divide between what can be justified by the resources of our culture and what is rational, true, real, objectively known, and so forth. It is the specifically philosophical uses that cause all the trouble, and the remedy is a familiar form of therapy: we are to get rid of the philosophical cramps caused by any such transcendent ideas by restricting ourselves to the commonsense notions immanent in our culture.

This move is not as unproblematic as it might and, given its widespread acceptance, apparently does seem. To begin with, it runs counter to the general thrust of epistemological behaviorism by seeking not to describe but to reform (some of) our practices. Rorty acknowledges this but thinks that we have little to lose from dropping ideas that were invented by philosophers and have never been of much use outside philosophy. It would be possible, I think, to show that other, "non-Platonic" cultures also have context-transcending senses of truth and reality, but I won't attempt to argue that here. It would also be possible to open the Bible and show that its authors regularly assumed senses of truth and reality (and, of course, justice) beyond conformity to the norms of their culture and that these senses entered into the pores of our culture together with the religions of the Bible, but I won't attempt that either. What I would like to argue is that, as a matter of fact, our ordinary, commonsense truth talk and reality talk is shot through with just the sorts of idealizations that Rorty wants to purge. In everyday talk we normally mean by "true" nothing like "what our society lets us say" but something closer to "telling it like it is—like it *really* is." And by "real" we normally mean nothing like "referred to in conformity with the norms of our culture" but something closer to "there anyway, whether we think so or not."

When Rorty describes truth talk in *Philosophy and the Mirror of Nature,* he singles out, in addition to the disquotational uses of "true," its use as a term of praise to commend to others beliefs we approve of. Even as late as 1985, in "Solidarity and Objectivity," he writes that the word "true" is "merely an expression of commendation" for beliefs we hold to be justified, so that "there is nothing to be said about truth save that each of us will commend as true those beliefs which he or she finds good to believe."[12] It is only more recently that Rorty pays attention to what he calls the "cautionary" uses through which we remind ourselves that things may turn out not to be the way that the beliefs we accept as justified say they are.[13] But this acknowledgment comes too late, for his epistemological behaviorism is built on a site from which the situation-transcending, idealizing elements of culture have been cleared.

What results from this is the not inconsiderable irony that a project designed to promote a frank self-acceptance of our culture through curing its philosophical ills is metamorphized into a deflationary revisionism supported primarily by philosophical arguments. Part of the problem is Rorty's tendency to give the same treatment to Plato's and Kant's very different attempts to articulate aspects of context transcendence in philosophical terms. On his account, both attempts issue in "transcendentalia" that, unlike their "commonsense counterparts," float free of actual practices of justification.[14] He doesn't take seriously enough the fact that Kant introduced his regulative ideas precisely by way of contrast to the constitutive ideas of the Platonic tradition. Nothing in experience can correspond to regulative ideas. They are representable not in and of themselves but only in relation to the practices they regulate. Thus Rorty's constant worry about our not being able to conceive of an ideal limit point of inquiry or ideal conditions of acceptability or an ideal speech situation is beside the point. What he should be concerned with is how such idealizations actually function in structuring our practices in the various departments of life—how, for instance, the idea of an objective world structures the way we deal with factual disagreements in everyday life and science by directing our attention to subjective sources of error, or how the idea of a common humanity structures the way we deal with justifications of injustice and oppression based on class, racial, or gender differences. Rorty will say, "But these just are *our* practices." That response does indeed take us to the heart of the matter. Our culture is everywhere structured around transcultural notions of validity, and that means that Rorty's "frank ethnocentrism" lands him in just the universalist position he is trying to escape.

This is obviously not what he intends. He has in mind the ways in which historical, social, and cultural studies have gradually but inexorably eroded our cultural self-confidence, shaken to the roots our universalist self-understanding, and made us ever more aware of our own particularities and limitations. The real question is what to make of the historical self-awareness that has been developing in the West for more than 150 years now and of the antirationalist forms in which it has been brought to philosophical expression. One of the ways in which Rorty tries to deal with it is by adapting the Kantian notion of the two standpoints to his purpose. "To be a behaviorist in epistemology," he tells us, is to look at inquiry in our culture "bifocally," both as "the achievement of objective truth" and as "patterns adopted for various historical reasons." From the former standpoint the results of inquiry are "the best idea we currently have about how to explain what is going on"; from the latter standpoint they are "just the facts about what a given society, or profession, or other group takes to be good grounds for an assertion of a certain sort."[15] These are incompatible points of view in the sense that we cannot occupy both simultaneously. But there is no need to do so; we may shift from one point of view to the other.[16] On this model, the standpoint of the observer of cultural practices is not the viewpoint of God but of, say, the historian of ideas or the anthropologist, and that, as we now realize, is not a view from nowhere. Interpreters inevitably bring with themselves the perspectives and concerns of their own cultures; they cannot avoid relying upon the taken-for-granted assumptions built into the languages and practices that comprise their own cultural identities. In the case at hand, this means that we can distance ourselves from certain of our cultural practices only by taking the others for granted. We can never be "observers" without being "participants."

It is only in the sense that we are always situated within a culture before, while, and after we distance ourselves from any of its particular elements that the participant's standpoint is prior to the observer's; we cannot possibly adopt an exclusively third-person attitude toward our culture, only mentioning but never using the resources it offers for reasoning. For instance, the very practice of describing "the facts about what a given group takes to be good grounds" is itself a normatively structured activity that involves appealing to good grounds. Rorty sometimes writes as if it were only when we are engaged in such dubious enterprises as epistemology that we endorse established patterns of normal inquiry rather than simply treating them as a "pattern adopted for historical reasons," but of course we endorse them whenever we are engaged in the types of inquiry in question. And while he does characterize the two standpoints as complementary, he has a marked tendency to ignore the participant's standpoint when he is promoting his own brand of historicism. In general, it is not *because* we agree that we grant an assertion to be true; rather, we agree because we have good grounds for granting its truth. Particularly in practices of reflective inquiry, it is the reasons or grounds offered for a claim that comprise its warrant and, when conditions are right, lead to agreement in the relevant community. Thus it is, for instance, that Rorty cannot convince us to accept his claims about knowledge, morality, politics, and the rest by adducing community agreement or cultural approval or anything of the sort. Participating in recognizable forms of practice of rational justification, he attempts to get us to agree with his views by presenting, in his own voice, a variety of supporting reasons, chief among them, it should be noted, some very solid philosophical arguments against the received forms of foundationalism. We are clearly meant to respond to these as "participants," to accept them as good grounds, grounds that warrant the position he espouses.

Related difficulties arise in Rorty's account of the scope of justification. Adopting the detached third-person standpoint of an observer of culture, he points out that what effectively counts as a warrant is always relative to some particular historical community. In the end, justification must rely on "something relatively local and ethnocentric—the tradition of a particular community, the consensus of a particular culture," something "relative to the group to which we think it necessary to justify ourselves." He then goes on to draw from this, in the first-person, the lesson that "the question of whether justifiability to the community with which we identify entails truth is simply irrelevant."[17]

For many types of question the intended audience of justification may indeed be the restricted audience of one's family, friends, professional associates, community, culture, or the like. But such restrictions are clearly not intended when, for example, we put forward and try to justify claims about *the* objective world. Claims that conflict with what we take to be established truths are not treated as true of another, different, objective world or allowed to stand on the same footing as the accepted claims, perhaps with some sort of index for the group to whom they are justified. If they are conflicting claims, they cannot all be true—cannot, as Kant might way, all be valid for consciousness in general or, as Peirce glossed this, valid for the community of rational inquirers. It is this universalizing move that Rorty, by opposing solidarity to objectivity, wants to block. While he does allow that the "desire for objectivity" might be viewed as the "desire for as much intersubjective agreement as possible," he vigorously resists any ideal extension of this to "humanity as such" via some notion of a "transcultural rationality."[18] While this might make sense as a detached observation on the historical situatedness of human reason, it does not make sense in the first-person attitude of someone participating in rational argumentation or critique where it is supposed that there is a truth of the matter.

Rorty's "ethnos" is heir to centuries of distinguishing between appearance and reality, doxa and episteme, prejudice and reason, and so forth. To justify his beliefs to us, he cannot simply appeal to communal agreement, established conventions, and the like. And it is, of course, telling that he never attempts to do so. Instead, he presents us with just the sorts of reasons we are accustomed to receiving for claims such as he makes, reasons meant to support their validity not just for us but *simpliciter.* When we enter what Rorty, following Sellars, calls "the logical space of reasons," agreement depends on our assessment of the arguments and evidence, or as Rorty says, on our confidence, based on experience with arguments in such matters, that nobody will find an objection. For many matters, "nobody" means just that, nobody, and not merely no member of my group. In these cases my description of my community's agreement represents them as accepting validity claims on grounds that I, as a party to the agreement, also regard as good grounds. The detached third-person description does not *replace* the engaged first-person endorsement but *reports* it. And it is not the reported areement that warrants the claim but the warrant for the claim that grounds the agreement.

2

The paradoxes and contradictions that beset neohistoricist reactions to the desublimation of reason make it imperative to explore alternative responses. Max Horkheimer's attempt in the early 1930s to inaugurate an "ongoing dialectical interpenetration" of philosophy and empirical social research provides a convenient point of departure, for he found himself in a situation similar to ours in one important respect: it was marked by a reactive pendulum swing away from previously dominant forms of rationalism and toward exaggerated forms of antirationalism. In opposition to both, Horkheimer called for a continuation-through-transformation of the critique of reason, a materialist elucidation of the nature, conditions, and limits of reason in the interest of rendering it effective in human relations. If the subjects of knowledge and action could no longer be viewed as solitary, disengaged, and disembodied, and if the structures of reason could no longer be viewed as timeless, necessary, and unconditioned, then the transformation required would take the self-critique of reason in the direction of sociohistorical inquiry. As reason is tied to action, mediated by language, and rooted in forms of life, its structures have to be grasped mediately in the acts and products, symbols and systems, practices and institutions in which it is embodied. Self-reflection and self-understanding take on a historical, hermeneutical, and social-theoretical cast as they proceed through the interpretation and critique of the sociohistorical world.

This line of thought is continued and refined in Habermas's theory of communicative action. It offers an alternative to neohistoricism not by denying the situatedness of reason but by illuminating features of our situation that are invisible from the historicist perspective. In what follows, I will focus on several points of instructive contrast to Rorty's epistemological behaviorism. They can be characterized generally and rather loosely as social-practical analogues to the Kantian notion of regulative ideas. Habermas relocates the Kantian opposition between the ideal and the real within the domain of social practice itself. He argues that communicative interaction is everywhere permeated by idealizing pragmatic presuppositons concerning reason, truth, and reality.[19] Strictly speaking, these idealizations are neither constitutive of reality in the Platonic sense nor merely regulative in the Kantian sense. As suppositions we cannot avoid making while engaged in processes of mutual understanding, they are actually effective in structuring communication, and at the same time they are typically counterfactual in ways that point beyond the limits of actual situations. As a result, our ideas of reason, truth, objectivity, and the like are both "immanent" and "transcendent" to the practices, norms, and standards of our culture and our day.

Presented in this abstract manner, these countertheses no doubt seem to be so many unsupported claims with a very low degree of initial probability. To help dispel that air of insubstantiality, I would like in the remainder of this chapter to look briefly at practical embodiments of several of Habermas's reconstituted "ideas of reason." To sharpen the issue with contemporary contextualists, I will consider three ideas that run directly counter to Rorty's epistemological behaviorism: the accountability of subjects, the objectivity of the world, and the truth of statements.

The Accountability of Subjects

It is not only the reception of post-Heideggerian and post-structuralist thought that has led to the "twilight of subjectivity" in Anglo-American philosophy. Various currents within analytic philosophy have also worked to marginalize questions of agency. To mention only one recent example, in *Wittgenstein on Rules and Private Language* Saul Kripke gives an account of rule following, and hence of meaning and rationality, in terms of a speaker's responses "agreeing with those of the community," of his or her behavior "exhibiting sufficient conformity" to the shared practices of the community.[20] The stress of Rorty, Kripke (or Kripke's Wittgenstein), and others on agreement and community is reminiscent in certain ways of the stress on consensus in sociological action theory following World War II. In the then dominant Parsonian paradigm, social order was explained through the internalization and institutionalization of cultural values and norms. Correspondingly, social actors were represented as by and large committed, in consequence of socialization, to prescribed or expected courses of action, while social action was conceptualized as normatively regulated behavior such that deviation from established patterns would regularly enough be sanctioned. This model was effectively criticized in the 1960s by approaches to social action developed in the symbolic interactionist tradition stemming from George Herbert Mead and in the phenomenological tradition of sociology stemming from Alfred Schutz. Particularly in the sociologies of everyday life constructed by Erving Goffman and

Harold Garfinkel and their followers, the picture of social actors as unreflective rule followers was rendered implausible beyond repair. Here I want only to note certain features of the ethnomethodological critique.[21] This will serve two purposes simultaneously: first, it will indicate more precisely just why consensus and conformity models of rationality are mistaken, even at the descriptive level, and second, it will itself illustrate how philosophical lines of questioning can fruitfully be pursued in the medium of social research. This will make evident, I hope, that the turn to social practice gets cut short in its historicist versions.

In his "Studies of the Routine Grounds of Everyday Activities," Garfinkel inveighs against models that portray the social actor as a "judgmental dope" who acts "in compliance with preestablished and legitimate alternatives of action that the common culture provides."[22] Such models treat as epiphenomenal the actor's own knowledge of social structure and his or her reflexive use of the resources for making sense that the culture makes available. It is primarily to counter this portrayal that ethnomethodology focuses on practical reasoning in everyday settings and treats the "rational properties of practical activities" as the "ongoing accomplishment" of actors themselves.[23] What emerges from this is an account of social practice that gives subjects an active role in creating and sustaining the shared meanings that structure and define situations of interaction. It is not possible to go into all the details of that account here or to assess its general strengths and weaknesses. I want instead to highlight a few of its features that are ignored in the oversimplified conformity models of social practice that are now, philosophically transfigured, enjoying a renaissance.

To begin with a point of apparent similarity, Garfinkel's "breaching experiments" bring out very nicely the ways in which we use our commonsense knowledge of social structure to make situations of interaction both intelligible and accountable. This shared knowledge informs the normative expectations we bring to social situations, and thus it serves simultaneously as a cognitive and a normative background to interaction. We orient our behavior to these shared schemes of interpretation and expectation, mutually attributing knowledge of them to one another and holding each other accountable in terms of them. Unwarranted deviations from background expectations are sanctionable by everything from negative affective responses and breakdowns of cooperation to explicit reprimands and punishments. Our awareness of this differential accountability for behavior that departs from, versus that which conforms to, socially standardized expectations is a primary source of the motivated compliance that characterizes routine interaction.

Up to this point Garfinkel's account seems to support conformity models. But he goes on to stress the reflexivity that characterizes the ways in which we use our knowledge of what is required in situations to analyze, manage, and transform those very situations. We are usually aware of what's going on and what's expected of us, we have an idea of what we can and cannot get away with, and we realize that our actions can reconstitute the very situation of which they are a part. We know how to play off established definitions of a situation to get our point across, to put our partners at ease, to make them feel uncomfortable, or whatever. The intersubjectivity of mutual understanding is something that we ourselves accomplish, and we do so in ever changing situations and "for all practical purposes."

This account highlights the irreducible activity of agents in sustaining the mutual intelligibility of their interactions. They do not simply say "what society lets them say" or act "in conformity with the norms of the day." They are competent actors who have mastered the necessary cultural knowledge and the required social skills to deal with situations as they arise. Nor is this a matter of following set rules in predefined situations, for social rules are neither fully spelled out nor algorithmically applicable, and social situations are not predefined but themselves actively constituted by the participants' own activities. What is normally called for is not mere conformity, but competent practical reasoning to deal with the contingencies that arise. There is always an element of the discretionary, elaborative, and ad hoc about how we apply rules and schemes, for they do not define their own applications. Each new application requires judgment in the light of the specifics of the situation.

Moreover, there are always unstated conditions and qualifications—what Garfinkel calls "et cetera clauses"—to balance the unavoidable simplification of social complexity that attaches to any general rule. Thus if we want to make sense of social situations, we cannot help but relate reflexively to background schemes of interpretation and expectation, and draw actively on our capacities for practical reasoning in concrete situations. In any case, as competent actors we shall be held accountable for doing so. That is to say, we believe ourselves to be, and take others as being, knowledgcable subjects confronted by real choices, for which we and they will be held accountable.[24] In normal social interaction, we reciprocally impute practical rationality to interaction partners, credit them with knowing what they are doing and why they are doing it, view their conduct as under their control and done for some purpose or reason known to them, and thus hold them responsible for it. Although this pervasive supposition of rational accountability is frequently—strictly speaking, perhaps even always—counterfactual, it is of fundamental significance for the structure of human relations that we deal with one another as if it were the case.

The accent here certainly falls differently than it does in models that stress "agreement in responses," "conformity to the norms of the day," "community approval," and the like. What they give us are pictures of social practice without a subject, where the determining factors are language, tradition, society, rules, criteria, norms, and the like. Garfinkel's thicker description of making sense in everyday settings, with its emphasis on the agents' own practical reasoning, brings the subject back into social practice. But how does that help us with the question of historicism raised above? It seems to leave us with essentially the same picture of mutually exclusive, self-contained lifeworlds, even if we grant that under the ethnomethodological microscope there is more going on in placid scenes of "community agreement" than appears to the naked eye. The hinge on which my critique of epistemological behaviorism turned was the idea that social practice is structured by context-transcending notions of truth and reality. I want to return to that point now and examine it more closely. For this purpose Melvin Pollner's study "Mundane Reasoning" offers a convenient point of departure.[25]

The Objectivity of the World

The phenomenon that attracts Pollner's interest is the practices by which we maintain the supposition of an objective world known in common, in the face of discrepant reports about just what belongs to that world. He finds in studying them that conflicts of experience and testimony are typically dealt with in ways that themselves presuppose, and thus reconfirm, the intersubjective availability of an objectively real world. For example, discrepancies are attributed to errors in perception owing to poor visibility, physical obstacles, deficient eyesight, lack of proper equipment, optical illusions, hallucinations, and so forth; or to errors in interpretation due to the fact that the observer is a novice, doesn't have the whole story, is telling the story from a particular, restricted vantagepoint, and the like; or to errors in reporting ranging from unclarity and imprecision to outright lying. It is an interesting feature of such "error accounts" that we are held sanctionably accountable for producing them in the appropriate circumstances. That is to say, the maintenance of an intersubjectively available objective world is normatively required by the network of expectations structuring everyday interaction. We are held accountable, and in turn hold our interaction partners accountable, for treating the transcendent objectivity of the world as invariant to discrepant reports. We do this by drawing on a repertoire of procedures for resolving conflicts of experience and testimony, procedures that are themselves based upon the very presupposition they maintain. Thus the objectivity of real-world events—their validity for "consciousness in general," as Kant would say, or as we can say in a more sociological mode, their intersubjective validity—is the *presupposition and product* of social practices for which we are held accountable. We are expected to employ only explanations of discrepancies that are predicated upon that presupposition. Moreover, we are sanctioned for failure to do so—and with good reason: it is the basis of our cooperative activities.[26]

This provides us with at least a starting point for empirically substantiating Habermas's view of the objective world as an "idea of reason" or idealizing supposition of social interaction. Pollner's work gives us a feel for how that idea regulates our everyday practices of resolving conflicts about what is really the case so as to leave the world's objectivity intact. If there were space, I might go on to examine how it regulates scientific practice as well. The recent flow of ethnographic studies of science by Latour and Woolgar, Gilbert and Mulkay, Collins and Pickering, and others provides ample material for that purpose. To be sure, such authors are frequently caught up in the same flush of antirationalism that motivates the contextualist reaction in other fields. And so they present their thick descriptions of laboratory life in radically antiobjectivist terms, stressing above all the contingent, local, contextual, ad hoc features of scientific practice in opposition to the overrationalized images that dominated our imaginations for all too long. Scientists too, it turns out, are practical reasoners in Garfinkel's sense, and not judgmental dopes following rules and applying criteria in predefined situations. They too operate with schemes of interpretation and expectation that are irremediably vague and loose fitting, and as in everyday life, this vagueness and loose fit are not a defect but a functional necessity if general schemes are not to be applied to an unpredictable variety of particular situations. All of this is a valuable antidote to the received view of scientific rationality, but it need not push us to embrace the simple antithesis of that view. As ethnographers of science are coming to realize, there is a very wide middleground to be staked out between the extremes of straightforward scientific realism and pure social constructionism.

The Truth of Statements

As the repeated attempts to define truth in terms of idealized rational acceptability, warranted assertability under ideal conditions, and the like indicate, idealizing presuppositions of rational accountability and intersubjective validity figure in our conception of truth as well. There is no need to insist on *defining* truth in this way (thus courting a naturalistic fallacy). What is important for our purposes is the internal relation between truth and idealized rational acceptability that is embedded in our practices of truth-telling so that, for instance, it makes perfectly good sense to say things like "We have good reason to believe that *p*, and we are all agreed that it is so, but of course we may be wrong, it may turn out to be false after all." Any adequate account of our practices of truth will have to attend not only to the situated, socially conditioned character of concrete truth claims and of the warrants offered for them but also to their situation-transcending import as well. While we have no idea of standards of truth wholly independent of particular languages and practices, "truth" nevertheless functions as an "idea of reason" with respect to which we can criticize not only particular claims within our language but even the very standards of truth we have inherited. Though never divorced from social practices of justification, from the rules and warrants of this or that culture, it cannot be reduced to any particular set thereof. We can and typically do make contextually conditioned and fallible claims to unconditional truth (as I have just done). It is this moment of unconditionality that opens us up to criticism from other points of view. Without that idealizing moment there would be no foothold in our accepted beliefs and practices for the critical shocks to consensus that force us to expand our horizons and learn to see things in different ways. It is precisely this context-transcendent, in Kantian terms, "regulative," surplus of meaning in our notion of truth that keeps us from being locked into what we happen to agree on at any particular time and place, that opens us up to the alternative possibilities lodged in otherness and difference, which have been so effectively invoked by postmodernist thinkers.

Rorty's emphasis on the particular, changeable, and contingent is an understandable reaction to the traditional preoccupation with the universal, timeless, and necessary. But it is no less one-sided for that, nor any less questionable in its practical implications. To dispense with the ideal in the name of the real is to throw out the baby with the bathwater. Idealized notions of accountability, objectivity, and truth are pragmatic presuppositions of communicative interaction in everyday and scientific settings. They are at the basis of our shared world, and they are the motor force behind expanding its horizons through learning, criticism, and self-criticism. In the encounter with other worlds, they represent a major alternative to resolving differences through coercion, the alternative of reasonable dialogue. Replacing rational accountability with conformity to established patterns, ideal acceptability with de facto acceptance, and objectivity with solidarity, as Rorty does, undercuts that alternative. It entraps us in an ethnocentric predicament that, while somewhat roomier than its egocentric prototype, is no more liveable.[27] An alternative is to recognize the idealizing elements intrinsic to social practice and build on them.

Notes

1. See his introductions to R. Rorty, ed., *The Linguistic Turn* (Chicago, 1967) and R. Rorty, *Consequences of Pragmatism* (Minneapolis, 1982).

2. For an overview of this metaphilosophical situation, see K. Baynes, J. Bohman, T. McCarthy, eds., *After Philosophy* (Cambridge, Mass., 1987).

3. See R. Bernstein, *Beyond Objectivism and Relativism* (Philadelphia, 1983).

4. R. Rorty, *Philosophy and the Mirror of Nature* (Princeton, 1979). Hereafter cited as *PMN*.

5. *PMN*, p. 390.

6. *PMN*, p. 340, n. 20.

7. *PMN*, p. 385.

8. *PMN*, p. 174.

9. See *PMN*, pp. 175 ff. and 357 ff. Rorty characterizes his position as a "frank ethnocentrism" in "Solidarity or Objectivity," in J. Rajchman and C. West, eds., *Post-analytic Philosophy* (New York, 1985), pp. 3–19.

10. *PMN*, p. 178.

11. *PMN*, p. 309.

12. "Solidarity or Objectivity," p. 6.

13. R. Rorty, "Pragmatism, Davidson, and Truth," in E. Lepore, ed., *Truth and Interpretation: Perspectives on the Philosophy of Donald Davidson* (New York, 1986), pp. 333–355, here pp. 334–335.

14. *PMN,* pp. 281–282.

15. *PMN,* p. 385.

16. *PMN,* p. 386.

17. R. Rorty, "The Priority of Democracy to Philosophy," in M. Peterson and R. Vaughan, eds., *The Virginia Statute for Religious Freedom* (Cambridge, 1988), p. 259.

18. "Solidarity and Objectivity," pp. 4, 5, 15.

19. I am emphasizing the cognitive dimension here. Habermas also discusses idealizations more directly relevant to the moral-practical side of interaction. See, for example, J. Habermas, "What Is Universal Pragmatics?" in Habermas, *Communication and the Evolution of Society* (Boston, 1979), pp. 1–68; J. Habermas, "Philosophy as Stand-In and Interpreter," in *After Philosophy,* pp. 296–315; J. Habermas, *The Theory of Communicative Action* (Boston, 1984), vol. 1, chapters 2, 3.

20. S. Kripke, *Wittgenstein on Rules and Private Language* (Cambridge, Mass., 1982), pp. 96 ff.

21. I shall be relying principally upon Garfinkel's earlier studies, collected in *Studies in Ethnomethodology* (Englewood Cliffs, N.J., 1967), republished by Polity Press (Cambridge, 1984). My interpretation of them draws on the excellent account by John Heritage, *Garfinkel and Ethnomethodology* (Cambridge, 1984).

22. H. Garfinkel, "Studies in the Routine Grounds of Everyday Activities," in *Studies in Ethnomethodology,* pp. 35–75, here p. 68.

23. H. Garfinkel, "What Is Ethnomethodology?" in *Studies in Ethnomethodology,* pp. 1–34.

24. See J. Heritage, *Garfinkel and Ethnomethodology,* pp. 75 ff., 115 ff.

25. M. Pollner, "Mundane Reasoning," *Philosophy of the Social Sciences* 4 (1975): 35–54.

26. To acknowledge a constructivist dimension in our relation to the objective world is not, I hasten to add, ipso facto to endorse a sociocultural idealism.

27. Hilary Putnam draws this analogy in "Why Reason Can't Be Naturalized," in *After Philosophy,* pp. 222–244, here pp. 230 ff.

9

The Debate over Performative Contradiction: Habermas versus the Poststructuralists

Martin Jay

Of the many laudable aspects of Jürgen Habermas's remarkable career, none is perhaps as strking as his consistent willingness to engage in constructive debate with a wide variety of critical interlocutors. There can, indeed, be few thinkers whose theoretical development has been so powerfully marked by public encounters with opponents over a lifetime of intense intellectual interaction. From his earliest debates with the German student movement in the 1960s and his participation in the "positivism dispute" with the followers of Karl Popper, through his exchanges with Hans-Georg Gadamer over hermeneutics and Niklas Luhmann over systems theory, up until his spirited involvement in the current controversies over postmodernism and the "normalization" of the German past, Habermas has been a courageous and responsible "public intellectual" of the kind rarely found in contemporary Western culture. He has, moreover, been patiently willing to learn from others involved in the collective project he has done so much to launch.[1] Although anyone who knows first-hand the passionate intensity with which he argues would hesitate before calling him a cold-blooded "saint of rationalism," as Gladstone once did John Stuart Mill,[2] Habermas is certainly one of the most cogent examples of the power of the communicative rationality he so fervently espouses.

This fit between Habermas's ideas and his actions is a particularly important one, for it draws our attention to an issue that is itself at the heart of his theory. I refer to the value of performative consistency, which is one of the reigning regulative ideals of his universal pragmatics. There can, in fact, be few more withering rebukes in his vocabulary than the charge of "performative contradiction," which he uses again and again to challenge the validity of his opponents' positions.

There is, however, to my knowledge, no sustained examination of the implications of this concept in his work, despite its central importance. Attempting such a task is especially urgent, because the very same issue has been explicitly raised in much poststructuralist thought, but with radically different conclusions. Without hoping to arrive at a definitive resolution of a long-standing philosophical dispute, I want to use this opportunity to explore the multiple implications of the theme of performative consistency and contradiction. For in so doing, a central dimension of Habermas's achievement may become clearer.

A useful point of entry into the issue is the traditional dialectical notion of contradiction, which was still powerfully present in the work of Habermas's mentors in the Frankfurt School. Hegel's critique of Aristotelian logic as too formal and ahistorical has, of course, always had a strong, if at times controversial, impact on Marxist thought.[3] Although dividing over the questin of whether contradictions exist in nature and society or merely in society—Engels exemplified the former position, Lukács the latter—most Marxists have insisted that contradiction is an ontological reality, not merely a logical one. Thus, for example, Herbert Marcuse contended in *One-Dimensional Man* that "if dialectical logic understands contradiction as 'necessity' belonging to the very 'nature of thought' . . . , it does so because contradiction belongs to the very nature of the *object* of thought, to reality, where Reason is still Unreason and the irrational still rational."[4] Similarly, Theodor Adorno claimed that "dialectical contradiction expresses the real antagonisms which do not become visible within the logical-scientistic system of thought."[5] Rejecting the charge that suspending the logic of noncontradiction leads inevitably to irrationalism, classically leveled by Karl Popper in his "What Is Dialectic?"[6] he insisted that "if one contaminates by association dialectics and irrationalism then one blinds oneself to the fact that criticism of the logic of noncontradiction does not suspend the latter but rather reflects on it."[7]

In subtle ways, however, Adorno distanced himself from the more straightforward Hegelian-Marxist position represented by Marcuse. He did so by viewing as problematic the normative alternative presupposed by the critique of contradiction—a perfectly positive dialectical sublation. Rather than embracing such a normative vantage point, Adorno came to see it as itself an expression of a potentially oppressive identity theory. Thus in *Negative Dialectics* he warned against the hypostatization of noncontradictoriness as the complete overcoming of all tensions and differences in a grand synthesis: "It is precisely the insatiable identity principle that perpetuates antagonism by suppressing contradiction. What tolerates nothing that is not like itself thwarts the reconciliation for which it mistakes itself. The violence of equality-mongering reproduces the contradiction it eliminates."[8] Reconciliation, for Adorno, thus paradoxically includes a moment of preserved contradiction, which is not merely an evil to be overcome. "The task of dialectical cognition is not, as its adversaries like to charge, to construe contradictions from above and to progress by resolving them—although Hegel's logic, now and again, proceeds in this fashion. Instead, it is up to dialectical cognition to pursue the inadequacy of thought and thing, to experience it in the thing."[9]

Whether or not Adorno was correct in his critique of Hegel, the significance of his position is clear.[10] By arguing against the goal of a perfectly noncontradictory world, in which logical and ontological categories would be seamlessly united, he opened the door for a more modest notion of contradiction, which would be meaningful for only certain aspects of social reality. As we will see shortly, Habermas was to walk through that door.

In another respect, however, Adorno defended a notion, or rather a practice, of contradiction that Habermas would tacitly reject. Continuing to use the tools of critical reason, Adorno nonetheless denounced the tyranny of the Enlightenment because of its totalitarian imposition of reason on a recalcitrant world. According to Habermas, "Adorno was quite aware of this performative contradiction inherent in totalized critique.

Adorno's *Negative Dialectics* reads like a continuing explanation of why we have to circle about within this *performance contradiction* and indeed even remain there."[11] Unlike those who seek to escape the paradox of a rational critique of totalizing reason by denouncing reason *tout court,* Adorno, Habermas claims, "wishes to endure in the performative contradiction of a negative dialectics, which directs the unavoidable medium of identifying and objectifying thought against itself. Through the exercise of endurance, he believes himself to be remaining most nearly faithful to a lost, noninstrumental reason."[12]

However much Habermas admired Adorno for refusing to force his way out of this dilemma or seek false consolations, however much he shared Adorno's reluctance to posit an ultimate unity of concept and reality, he nonetheless has sought to shift the terms of the argument about contradiction in a new direction, which would lead out of the aporias of the dialectic of enlightenment in its classical Frankfurt School formulations. Whereas Adorno remained terrified of the imposition of logical consistency on a world that should be nonidentical to its concept, insisting that conceptual representations can never be fully adequate to their objects, Habermas focused instead on the relations among subjects. The most extensive exposition of this change appeared in a passage from *Legitimation Crisis,* which bears quoting in its entirety:

> The concept of contradiction has undergone such attrition that it is often used synonymously with "antagonism," "opposition," or "conflict." According to Hegel and Marx, however, "conflicts" are only the form of appearance, the empirical side of a fundamentally logical contradiction. Conflicts can be comprehended only with reference to the operatively effective rules according to which incompatible claims or intentions are produced within an action system. But "contradictions" cannot exist between claims or intentions in the same sense as they can between statements: the system of rules according to which utterances—that is, the opinions and actions in which intentions are incorporated—are produced is obviously different in kind from the system of rules according to which we form statements and transform them without affecting their truth value. In other words, the deep structures of a society are not logical structures in a narrow sense. Propositional contents, on the other hand, are always used in utterances. The logic that could justify speaking of "social contradictions"

> would therefore have to be a logic of the employment of propositional contents in speech and in action. It would have to extend to communicative relations between subjects capable of speaking and acting; it would have to be a universal pragramatics rather than logic.[13]

For Habermas, in other words, contradictions exist less on the level of social *ontology*, as they did for Hegelian Marxists like Marcuse, than on that of intersubjective *communication*. Class societies have fundamental contradictions, he claims, only because "their organizational principle necessitates that individuals and groups repeatedly confront one another with claims and intentions that are, in the long run, incompatible."[14] *Legitimation Crisis* is devoted to explaining how such fundamental class contradictions can be displaced from the economic to other levels of social interaction. The plausibility of its argument is less important for us here than the link Habermas forges between contradiction and communication. He does, to be sure, also acknowledge that contradictions can be meaningfully applied to incompatibilities in the system-maintenance mechanisms of societies, but he clearly prefers using the term to indicate competing claims to the truth by actors in the society, claims whose validity can be discursively weighed.

Despite his adherence in *Legitimation Crisis* to the notion of "dialectical contradiction," it may seem that Habermas has quietly returned to a more conventional Aristotelian alternative. Thus, for example, in his recent critique of deconstructionist ideas about contradiction, he claims, "There can only be talk about 'contradiction' in the light of consistency requirements, which lose their authority or are at least subordinated to other demands—of an aesthetic nature, for example—if logic loses its conventional primacy over rhetoric."[15] What takes this argument beyond being a mere restatement of traditional logic, however, is its emphasis on the performative dimension of language, the *use* of arguments in communicative interaction rather than the consistency of statements or propositions per se. A performative contradiction arises not when two antithetical propositions (*A* and not *A*) are simultaneously asserted as true but rather when whatever is being claimed is at odds with the presuppositions or implications of the act of claiming it. To use the terminology of J. L. Austin and John Searle, to which Habermas is indebted, it occurs when the locutionary dimension of a speech act is in conflict with its illocutionary force, when what is said is undercut by how it is said. For instance, according to Habermas, the communicative use of language harbors an immanent obligation to justify validity claims, if need be. When the claims one makes on a locutionary level deny the very possibility of such a justification, then a performative contradiction is committed.

A particularly strong version of this argument, going somewhat beyond Habermas's more cautious formulations, can be found in the work of Karl-Otto Apel, who has claimed that like it or not, humans are necessarily socialized into a transcendental-pragmatic language game from which they withdraw at the peril of autistic isolation or even suicide. One cannot make a "decision" to join or abstain from participating in this language game, he contends, "since any choice that could be understood as meaningful already presupposes the transcendental language game as its condition of possibility. Only under the rational presupposition of intersubjective rules can deciding in the presence of alternatives be understood as meaningful behavior."[16]

Although uncomfortable with the transcendental basis of Apel's position, which entails a foundationalism he feels is untenable, Habermas often adopts a similar strategy against certain of his opponents. Those whose ideas derive from Nietzsche are especially inviting targets, for their illocutionary practice seems most radically in tension with their locutionary assertions. That is, they employ methods of argumentation that tacitly entail intersubjective validity testing to defend a position that denies communicative rationality its legitimacy. As Habermas puts it with reference to Adorno's negative dialectics and Derrida's deconstruction, "The totalizing self-critique of reason gets caught in a performative contradiction since subject-centered reason can be convicted of being authoritarian in nature only by having recourse to its own tools."[17]

Other examples of Habermas's reliance on the critical leverage of the performative contradiction argument might be given, but by now its importance for his position should be clear. He uses it first to criticize inconsistencies in his opponents' argumentative practice and second to provide a standard by which social contradictions can be judged now that the older Hegelian-Marxist model of ontological contradiction is no longer viable. How successful, we must now ask, has he been in defending its effectiveness for these purposes? How, in particular, has his defense functioned as an antidote to the post-structuralist critique of communicative rationality? To answer these questions requires giving that critique a careful reading. Although there are several possible versions from which to chose, let me focus on three in particular, those offered by Michel Foucault, Rodolphe Gasché, and Paul de Man.[18]

Foucault's critique appeared in his 1966 encomium to the critic and novelist Maurice Blanchot, "The Thought from Outside."[19] Its opening section is devoted to the theme "I speak, I lie." Foucault begins by evoking the ancient Greek liar's paradox, a self-contradictory assertion by Epimenides, a Cretan, that "all Cretans are liars." In condensed form, it is the statement "I lie," which Foucault contrasts with the apparently self-consistent statement "I speak." But surprisingly, he contends that the latter is more problematical than the former. That is, the liar's paradox can be solved if we recognize that a distinction can be made between two propositions one of which is the object of the other.[20] For there is no logical contradiction involved if the two propositions are on different levels.

"I speak," which at first glance seems to be lacking even a superficial paradoxical tension, in fact raises more fundamental problems, according to Foucault. "'I speak' refers to a supporting discourse that provides it with an object. That discourse, however, is missing; the sovereignty of 'I speak' can only reside in the absence of any other language."[21] Such an absence seems to grant the speaking subject an enormous originary power, but, so Foucault claims, it is really the opposite that is true. For the supposed void surrounding "I speak" is really "an absolute opening through which language endlessly spreads forth, while the subject—the 'I' who speaks—fragments, disperses, scatters, disappearing into that naked space. . . . In short, it is no longer discourse and the communication of meaning, but a spreading forth of language in its raw state, an unfolding of pure exteriority."[22] It is precisely modern literature, such as that of Blanchot, which best registers this exteriority of language to the speaking subject.

The challenge Foucault presents to the cogency of performative contradiction thus arises from his positing of the exemplary character of a literary language that is wholly exterior to the intentionality of a speaking subject. If in this use of language there is no meaningful actor responsible for the speech acts whose locutionary and illocutionary responsible dimensions can be consistent or contradictory, then it makes little sense to employ performative criteria to judge the value of arguments or to characterize social tensions.

What, moreover, if the very idea of contradiction is a misnomer when applied to all varieties of linguistic interaction? This is the troubling question asked by the second poststructuralist critic whose work bears on the question at hand, Rodolphe Gasché. Whereas Foucault posits a linguistic level exterior to pragmatic interaction but doesn't really flesh out its implications,[23] Gasché develops Derrida's richly articulated analysis of the aporetic workings of language on all its levels. In *The Tain of the Mirror* he argues that deconstruction "starts with a systematic elucidation of contradictions, paradoxes, inconsistencies, and aporias constitutive of conceptuality, argumentation, and the discursiveness of philosophy. Yet these discrepancies are not logical contradictions, the only discrepancies for which the philosophical discourse can account. Eluded by the logic of identity, they are consequently not contradictions properly speaking."[24] If they are not to be understood as logical contradictions, then what are they? Gasché answers that "deconstruction attempts to 'account' for these 'contradictions' by 'grounding' them in 'infrastructures' discovered by analyzing the specific organization of these 'contradictions.'"[25] These basic infrastructures are what Derrida variously calls archetraces, *differance*, supplementarity, iterability, re-marking, dissemination, etc. Whatever one makes of these terms, they are not to be understood as equivalent to "contradiction." For they can never be resolved in a dialectical way through some kind of higher synthesis. They always subtend any more logical use of language, which can never efface their disruptive effects. Even as a regulative ideal, a noncontradictory sublation would entail the restitution of what Gasché claims was the traditional philosophy of speculative reflection, what Adorno would have called identity theory.

According to Gasché, Austin's attempt to transcend a mentalist philosophy of reflection by turning to speech acts "amounts to nothing more or less than the surreptitious reintroduction of the problem of reflection in order to solve the problems left in the wake of logical positivism. His revolution consisted of hinging the entire representational function of langauge, with which Russell and Whitehead were exclusively concerned, on a constituting self-reflexivity of the linguistic act."[26] Insofar as Habermas has adopted an Austinian notion of performance, he too falls prey to a philosophy of identitarian reflection, despite his repudiation of the mentalist fallacy.[27] If we abandon reflection philosophy, Gasché concludes, we must also cease trying to apply logical categories like contradiction to linguistic performance, which can never be disentangled from the heterological infrastructures "beneath" or "behind" the level of pragmatic utterances.

Still another way to conceptualize this noise in the logical system entails accepting the existence of something called contradictions but denying the possibility of ever overcoming them. One of the most influential versions of this strategy appears in Paul de Man's analysis of Nietzsche in *Allegories of Reading*.[28] Here de Man defends in Nietzsche precisely what Habermas criticizes: his willing embrace of performative contradiction, which resulted from his appreciation of the undecidable dimensions of linguistic performance. "Already in *The Birth of Tragedy*," de Man claims, "Nietzsche advocates the use of epistemologically rigorous methods as the only possible means to reflect on the limitations of these methods. One cannot hold against him the apparent contradiction of using a rational mode of discourse—which he, in fact, never abandoned—in order to prove the inadequacy of this discourse."[29] Why can't one hold it against him, as Habermas clearly does? De Man begins his answer by approvingly citing Nietzsche's own observation, showing his debt to Kant (filtered through Schopenhauer), that "great men, capable of truly general insight, were able to use the devices of science itself in order to reveal the limits and relativity of all knowledge, thus decisively putting into question the scientific claim to universal validity and purpose."[30] In other words, there is nothing problematic in using the scientific method to show the limits of scientific knowledge. Here, however, one might reply that what is being challenged is only an overinflated claim to knowledge, which was never a necessary implication of the scientific method properly understood.

De Man's second answer is more substantial. It entails a careful reading of the tensions between the thematic and rhetorical implications of *The Birth of Tragedy.* As might be expected, he finds the work divided against itself: "For all its genetic continuity, the movement of *The Birth of Tragedy,* as a whole as well as in its component parts, is curiously ambivalent with regard to the main figures of its own discourse: the category of representation that underlies the narrative mode and the category of the subject that supports the all-pervading horatory voice."[31] These and other ambivalences in Nietzsche's work are not, however, to be taken as signs of weakness, as Habermas would probably contend. "Have we merely been saying that *The Birth of Tragedy* is self-contradictory and that it hides its contradictions by means of a 'bad' rhetoric?" de Man asks. "By no means: first of all, the 'deconstruction' of the Dionysian authority finds its arguments within the text itself, which can then no longer be called simply blind or mystified. Moreover, the deconstruction does not occur between statements, as in a logical refutation or in a dialectic, but happens instead between, on the one hand, metalinguistic statements about the rhetorical nature of language and, on the other hand, a rhetorical praxis that puts these statements into question."[32] In short, for Nietzsche and de Man, there is an inevitable disparity between the content of an assertion and the rhetoric of its expression.

This conclusion is at odds with the tradition of defining and then decrying contradictions in two ways. First, against the older Aristotelian tradition, it rejects the imposition of logical categories onto the world. De Man endorses Nietzsche's contention that our reluctance to affirm and deny one and the same thing "is a subjective empirical law, not the expression of any 'necessity' *but only of an inability.*"[33] That is, the apparent truth of logical propositions is only the result of an arbitrary human fiat. "In fact," Nietzsche continues, "*logic* (like geometry and arithmetic) applies only to *fictitious truths* [*fingierte Wahrheiten*] *that we have created.*"[34] Like Adorno with his anxiety about the domination of nature by concepts, de Man follows Nietzsche in rejecting the belief that the world can be made commensurate with logical categories.

De Man's second target is the more performative notion of contradiction that we have seen Habermas defend. Now that we know logic is a subjective imposition, he asks, can we then assume that "all language is a speech act that has to be performed in an imperative mode"?[35] Nietzsche's text appears to make precisely this argument, at least on a locutionary level. But the text "acts" in a different way; it "does not simultaneously affirm and deny identity but it denies affirmation. This is not the same thing as to assert and to deny identity at the same time. The texts deconstructs the authority of the principle of contradiction by showing that this principle is an act, but when it acts out this act, it fails to perform the deed to which the text owed its status as act."[36] That is, Nietzsche may think he is rejecting the unequivocal affirmation of identity that is at the basis of the logic of noncontradiction, but his text does only one thing, deny that affirmation. To be performatively consistent, it would have to both deny and affirm simultaneously. De Man claims that this dilemma is not peculiar to Nietzsche, for "the deconstruction states the fallacy of reference in a necessarily referential mode. There is no escape from this, for the text also establishes that deconstruction is not something we can decide to do or not to do at will."[37]

For de Man, therefore, the lesson is no less universal than Apel's, though its content is quite different: the tension between the constative and performative modes of language is permanent and irreducible. Indeed, "the differentiation between performative and constative language (which Nietzsche anticipates) is undecidable; the deconstruction leading from the one model to the other is irreversible but it always remains suspended, regardless of how often it is repeated."[38] It makes no sense, therefore, to charge someone with performative contradiction when such a crime is the original sin of all language.

This permanent condition is itself an expression of another undecidable aspect of language, which de Man attributes to rhetoric itself. Rhetoric can either apply to the skills of persuasion, which involve intersubjective interaction, or to the figural tropes, which are best located on that infrastructural level noted by Gasché. For de Man, "Rhetoric is a *text* in that it allows for two incompatible, mutually self-destructive points of view, and therefore puts an insurmountable obstacle in the way of any reading or understanding. The aporia between performative and constative language is merely a version of the aporia between trope and persuasion that both generates and paralyzes rhetoric and thus gives it the appearance of a history."[39]

These, then, are some of the main challenges presented by poststructuralism to Habermas's reliance on the concept of performative contradiction as a cornerstone of his universal pragmatics. Foucault locates language entirely outside of a sovereign subject who can be held responsible for its effects. Gasché describes that "outside" in terms of infrastructures that are irreducibly heterological and thus never equal to logical contradictions that can be overcome. De Man endorses Nietzsche's contention that consistency and contradiction are merely subjective projections onto a world whose complexity humans are unable to fathom. And he further argues that while Nietzsche's constative assertion of this very argument is at odds with the performative effects of his text, this tension is emblematic of the always undecidable status of rhetoric, at once a technique of conscious persuasion and an expression of what might be called the linguistic unconscious of tropes and figures.

How might Habermas respond to these arguments? Or rather, what have his responses been to those he has already tried to meet? Against Foucault's emphasis on the exteriority of language, which was, of course, a standard structuralist assumption of the 1960s, he has maintained the possibility of a reconstructive science applicable to the level of communicative utterance. In "What Is Universal Pragmatics?" he admitted that "this abstraction of *language* from the use of langauge in *speech* (*langue* versus *parole*), which is made in both the logical and the structuralist analysis of language, is meaningful." Nevertheless, he went on, "this methodological step is not sufficient reason for the view that the pragmatic dimension of language from which one abstracts is beyond formal analysis."[40] This argument is directed against the classical structuralist binary opposition, which privileges *langue* over *parole*. But it is important to note that Habermas did not quarrel with the opposition, urging us to efface the boundary in poststructuralist fashion, but rather simply reversed the hierarchy.

The issue between Habermas and the poststructuralists, then, is the extent to which one level can be analytically distinguished from the other in order to map out its workings. It is always easy to demonstrate that such a procedure does violence to the inevitably mixed quality of linguistic phenomena. But so does virtually every human effort to understand the infinitely complex reality we call the world. Although it certainly is worthwhile being aware of the inevitably partial quality of our results when we chose to isolate one dimension of a phenomenon for analysis, refusing to analyze at all leads to cognitive and practical paralysis. While it may well be the case that performative utterances are always made against the backdrop, or better put, through the medium, of a language that is at once *langue* and *parole,* Habermas's development of a universal pragmatics, however one may judge all of its implications, demonstrates the power of choosing to isolate the one from the other. Essentially reducing language to only its "deepest" level and bracketing the other as insignificant is as impoverished as assuming no meaningful distinction can be made between levels at all.

This impoverishment is especially evident if we emphasize, with Gasché, the domination of the deepest level by heterological infrastructures. Although useful as a reminder that not every linguistically embodied opposition or tension can be reduced to logical contradictions, Gasché's argument seems too quickly to assume that none can. Nor is it necessarily the case that every attempt to defend consistency is an expression of a discredited philosophy of reflection, in which difference is reduced to sameness. Habermas, in fact, has been very careful to emphasize that intersubjective communication is necessary when the parties involved are *not* identical. Consensus or consistency means not perfect unity but merely an always provisional willingness to agree on the basis of a process of validity testing that can be revised later. On the level of individual speech acts, performative consistency does not completely obliterate the distinction between locutionary meaning and illocutionary force. To rule nonreflective consistency out of court on a priori grounds is thus to impose a foundationalist transcendentalism of the most blatant kind.

De Man's Nietzschean emphasis on the self-limiting status of scientific inquiry, which acknowledges its own insufficiency, need not, as we have seen, pose a problem for anything but the most extravagant versions of science. Habermas, with his strongly hermeneutic understanding of science, needs no reminder of its limits. For by shifting the argument from the insufficiency of a monologic scientific grasp of the world (the Nietzschean and indeed Kantian premise of de Man's critique) to the intersubjective validity testing of arguments about the world, he has made it possible to restore a meaningful dimension to the charge of contradiction, which no longer refers to the gap between concepts and objects. Instead, it has been recast in the performative mode, pitting locutionary and illocutionary dimensions of interactions against each other.

De Man's second argument is, of course, directed against this move. By contending that we can never unravel the constative from the performative dimensions of speech acts, that the two are in fact always in conflict, and finally that "rhetoric" means both techniques of persuasion and language's tropic unconscious, he wants to deny the possibility of any noncontradictory consistency. Habermas's reply has been to claim that this argument levels the genre distinction between literature, dominated by rhetoric in the second sense, and philosophy, beholden to it in the first. His basic point is that the latter is grounded in a normal use of language in which"all participants stick to the reference point of possibly achieving a mutual understanding in which the *same* utterances are assigned the same meaning."[41] More generally, he chastizes deconstructionists for failing to register the distinction between the "world-disclosing" functions of literature and the "problem-solving" functions of theoretical discourse that have been differentiated out in modern societies.

Rejoinders to these arguments doubtless exist, but I will allow others less drawn to Habermas's position than I to contrive them. Let me, however, finish with a few questions of my own that concern the relation between the individual and the social dimensions of his argument. It is one thing to accuse Nietzsche, Adorno, Derrida, etc. of getting caught in performative contradictions that undercut the power of their arguments. It is another to redescribe, as we've seen Habermas do in *Legitimation Crisis,* social contradictions in terms of a public clash of incompatible claims and intentions.

First of all, this argument may put too much weight on those aspects of language that Habermas has concentrated his energies on exploring: the pragmatic rather than the structural (or infrastructural) level and "normal" understanding-oriented speech rather than world-disclosing speech. What we usually see as social conflicts are just as likely to be generated by the clash between these levels or modes as by a tension only within the former. Although it may be possible for some of these conflicts to be translated into discursively adjudicable claims, it is by no means clear that all or even most can. Habermas perhaps tacitly concurs with this insight when he allows the term contradiction to be used for dysfunctional system-maintenance mechanisms as well as utterances. In a way, this concession implies that contradictions can exist on the nonpragmatic level of language too. If so, Habermas needs to explore their implications more carefully than he has hitherto done; in particular, he needs to articulate the linkages between the two types of contradiction more explicitly.

Second, Habermas's strong rejection of "consciousness philosophy," that equation of thought with the interiority of a sovereign subject we have also seen Foucault criticize, raises the question of the location of the responsible speaker who is able to perform consistently. How can Habermas, for example, accuse Nietzsche, Derrida, or Adorno of performing contradictions, unless he attributes to them the ability to decide whether or not they will?[42] What is perhaps needed is a more explicit differentiation between what we might call the "subject" and the "agent" that does not abandon the responsibility of the latter even as it robs the former of its putative sovereignty.[43]

Third, the model of performative contradiction may be inadequate to explain the clash between different social groups who may be communicating perfectly, doing all they can to reach an understanding, but in fact have different, perhaps even irreconcilable, interests. Here it might be not the procedural level that is generating contradictions but rather the substantial level of what is being discussed. Habermas, to be sure, argues that "conflicts that are described independently of communications theory or systems theory are empirical phenomena without relation to truth. Only when we conceive of such oppositions within communications theory or systems theory do they take on an immanent relation to logical categories."[44] But such empirical phenomena are often far more powerful motors of political and social practice than those immediately accessible to discursive adjudication. Are they not to be construed as having any relation to truth and logic until they are made available for such theoretical consideration?

Finally, the lesson of Adorno's reluctant willingness to endure the state of performative contradiction may be worth pondering. His decision is perhaps defensible as a recognition that the current social reality (but not something called "language") renders abnormal the state of performative consistency Habermas wants to instantiate. What speech act theorists like to call the "happy" or "felicitous" outcome of illocutionary acts may be hard to come by in a world not conducive to fulfilling other kinds of happiness. And a fortiori, the intersubjective overcoming of contradiction is even less likely to occur.

Still, the incontrovertible examples that we do have in everyday life of such happy outcomes may perhaps be seen as the prefigural traces of the more utopian possibility that Habermas, despite all his reservations about redemptive utopias, has never fully abandoned. Our dogged tendency to see tensions, conflicts, and aporias as contradictions amenable to resolution, rather than as mere epiphenomena of an eternally exterior linguistic system of heterological infrastructures or tropic displacements, bears witness to the irradicability of this hope. In fact, it may be one of the central lessons of Habermas's remarkable oeuvre that only when conflicts become performative contradictions can their resolution be possible at all.

Notes

1. See, most notably, John B. Thompson and David Held, eds., *Habermas: Critical Debates* (Cambridge, Mass., 1982), and Richard J. Bernstein, ed., *Habermas and Modernity* (Cambridge, Mass., 1985).

2. Cited in Michael St. John Packe, *The Life of John Stuart Mill* (New York, 1970), p. 455.

3. A salient exception to this rule is the Italian Marxist Lucio Colletti. See, for example, his "Contraddizione dialettica e non-contraddizione," in *Tramonto dell'ideologia* (Rome, 1980).

4. Herbert Marcuse, *One-Dimensional Man: Studies in the Ideology of Advanced Industrial Society* (Boston, 1964), p. 142.

5. Theodor W. Adorno, Introduction, *The Positivist Dispute in German Sociology,* trans. Glyn Adey and David Frisby (London, 1976), p. 26.

6. Karl Popper, "What Is Dialectic?" *Conjectures and Refutations* (London, 1962).

7. Adorno, Introduction, p. 66.

8. Theodor W. Adorno, *Negative Dialectics,* trans. E. B. Ashton (New York, 1973), pp. 142–143. Translation emended.

9. Adorno, *Negative Dialectics,* p. 153.

10. For a critical analysis of Adorno's argument, see Michael Rosen, *Hegel's Dialectic and Its Criticism* (Cambridge, 1982), pp. 160 f.

11. Jürgen Habermas, *The Philosophical Discourse of Modernity: Twelve Lectures,* trans. Frederick Lawrence (Cambridge, Mass., 1987), p. 119.

12. Jürgen Habermas, "A Philosophico-political Profile," in *Habermas: Autonomny and Solidarity,* ed. Peter Dews (London, 1986), p. 155.

13. Jürgen Habermas, *Legitimation Crisis,* trans. Thomas McCarthy (Boston, 1973), pp. 26–27.

14. Habermas, *Legitimation Crisis,* p. 27.

15. Habermas, *The Philosophical Discourse of Modernity,* p. 188.

16. Karl-Otto Apel, "The Problem of Philosophical Foundations in Light of a Transcendental Pragmatics of Language," in *After Philosophy: End or Transformation?* ed. Kenneth Baynes, James Bohman, and Thomas McCarthy (Cambridge, Mass., 1987),

p. 281. This argument attempts to avoid the decisionist underpinnings of Apel's earlier position criticized by Thomas McCarthy in *The Critical Theory of Jürgen Habermas* (Cambridge, Mass., 1978), p. 321.

17. Habermas, *The Philosophical Discourse of Modernity,* p. 185.

18. I might have also pursued a similar critique in the hermeneutic tradition. See, for example, Hans-Georg Gadamer, *Truth and Method* (New York, 1986), p. 308, where he concludes that "however clearly one demonstrates the inner contradictions of all relativist views, it is as Heidegger has said: all these victorious arguments have something about them that suggests they are attempting to bowl one over. However cogent they may seem, they finally still miss the main point. In making use of them one is proved right, and yet they do not express any superior insight of any value." I am indebted to Joel Whitebrook for drawing my attention to this passage.

19. Michel Foucault, "Maurice Blanchot: The Thought from Outside," trans. Brian Massumi; Maurice Blanchot, "Michel Foucault as I Imagine Him," trans. Jeffrey Mehlman. Both works are found in *Foucault/Blanchot* (New York, 1987).

20. Foucault, "Maurice Blanchot," pp. 9–10. Foucault is perhaps drawing here on Bertrand Russel's theory of types, as Thomas McCarthy has suggested to me, or possibly on the distinction he would later make in *The Archaeology of Knowledge* between *énoncé* and énonciation (usually translated as "statement" and "enunciation"). In any event, Foucault's acceptance of this answer to the liar's paradox is not shared by all poststructuralist thinkers. See, for example, Jean-François Lyotard, *Rudiments païens* (Paris, 1977), pp. 229–230. He claims the paradox is not refutable. In fact, in his later work *The Postmodern Condition: A Report on Knowledge,* trans. Geoff Bennington and Brian Massumi (Minneapolis, 1984), Lyotard defines postmodern science by its willing embrace of paradox and its disdain for consensus. Thus, although he uses speech-act theory to introduce the notion of "performativity," he never takes the issue of performative contradiction seriously.

21. Foucault, "Maurice Blanchot," p. 10.

22. Foucault, "Maurice Blanchot," p. 11.

23. Foucault does, to be sure, have a discussion of contradictions in discursive formations in *The Archaeology of Knowledge,* trans. A. M. Sheridan Smith (New York, 1972), pp. 149 f. He concludes that archaeological analysis "erects the primacy of a contradiction that has its model in the simultaneous affirmation and negation of a single proposition" (p. 155).

24. Rodolphe Gasché, *The Tain of the Mirror: Derrida and the Philosophy of Reflection* (Cambridge, Mass., 1986), p. 135.

25. Gasché, *The Tain of the Mirror,* p. 142.

26. Gasché, *The Tain of the Mirror,* p. 76.

27. Gasché, to be sure, acknowledges that Habermas, along with Herbert Schnädelbach, has provided the best defense of a reflection philosophy by jettisoning vain attempts to distinguish metacommunicative from communicative versions of the argument. But he clearly thinks that the deconstructionist rejection of all versions of it is superior. See his discussion on p. 78.

28. Paul de Man, *Allegories of Reading: Figural Language in Rousseau, Nietzsche, Rilke, and Proust* (New Haven, 1979).

29. De Man *Allegories of Reading,* p. 86.

30. Cited from *The Birth of Tragedy,* in de Man, *Allegories of Reading,* p. 86.

31. De Man, *Allegories of Reading,* p. 94.

32. De Man, *Allegories of Reading,* p. 98.

33. Nietzsche cited in de Man, *Allegories of Reading,* p. 119.

34. Nietzsche cited in de Man, *Allegories of Reading,* p. 121.

35. De Man, *Allegories of Reading,* p. 124.

36. De Man, *Allegories of Reading,* pp. 124–125.

37. De Man, *Allegories of Reading,* p. 125.

38. De Man, *Allegories of Reading,* p. 130.

39. De Man, *Allegories of Reading,* p. 131.

40. Habermas, *Communication and the Evolution of Society,* trans. Thomas McCarthy (Boston, 1979), p. 6.

41. Habermas, *The Philosophical Discourse of Modernity,* p. 198.

42. That Habermas tacitly holds on to the existence of a sovereign subject, despite his critique of consciousness philosophy, might be discerned from his own rhetorical style, which certainly projects a powerful authorial presence behind it.

43. For a recent attempt to draw such a distinction, see Paul Smith, *Discerning the Subject* (Minneapolis, 1987).

44. Habermas, *Legitimation Crisis,* p. 28.

10

Foucault: Critique as a Philosophical Ethos

Richard J. Bernstein

Our age is, in especial degree, the age of criticism, and to criticism everything must submit.

Kant, Preface to The Critique of Pure Reason

One of the last essays that Foucault wrote before his untimely death is the short text "What Is Enlightenment?"[1] It is a remarkable text for many reasons. When we recall Foucault's sharp critique of Kant and Kantian problematic in *The Order of Things,* it may seem surprising that he turns to a reading of Kant's famous essay, published in November 1784, in order to show the thread that connects his work with the "type of philosophical interrogation" (p. 42) that Foucault claims Kant initiated. But as any close reader of Foucault knows, his writings are filled with surprises and novel twists. It is almost as if Foucault started each new project afresh, bracketing what he had written previously, constantly experimenting with new lines of inquiry. This is one reason why reading Foucault is so provocative, disconcerting, and frustrating. For just when we think we have grasped what Foucault is saying and showing, he seems to dart off in new directions (and even seems to delight in frustrating attempts to classify and fix what he is doing). But Foucault's essay is much more than a reflection on the question What is enlightenment? and its relation to the "attitude of modernity." It is, in the classical sense, an *apologia,* a succinct statement and defense of his own critical project. It is also an *apologia* in the sense that Foucault seeks to answer (at least obliquely) the objections of many of his critics. During the last decade of his life Foucault was being pressed about the normative status of his own critical stance. It becomes clear that he is defending himself against what he calls the "blackmail" of the Enlightenment. Although he emphasizes the importance of Kant's texts for defining a certain manner of philosophizing that is concerned with the present, one that also reflects on the *relation* of philosophizing to the present, this

> does not mean that one has to be "for" or "against" the Enlightenment. It even means precisely that one has to refuse everything that might present itself in the form of a simplistic and authoritarian alternative: you either accept the Enlightenment and remain within the tradition of its rationalism (this is considered a positive term by some and used by others, on the contrary, as a reproach); or else you criticize the Enlightenment and then try to escape from its principles of rationality (which may be seen once again as good or bad). And we do not break free of this blackmail by introducing "dialectical" nuances while seeking to determine what good and bad elements there may have been in the Enlightenment. (P. 43)

The last sentence is an allusion to the German tradition of critical theory, and specifically to Habermas. For perhaps the most formidable critic of Foucault is Habermas, for whom the question of critique and its normative foundations has been one of the central issues of his corpus.[2] Habermas, who acknowledges the insight and force of Foucault's brilliant critical analyses of modernity, nevertheless argues that Foucault "contrasts his critique of power with the 'analysis of truth' in such a fashion that the former becomes deprived of the normative yardsticks that it would have to borrow from the latter."[3] In short, Habermas thinks that Foucault's critical project, for all its insight, is nevertheless enmeshed in serious "performative contradictions." But from Foucault's perspective, Habermas, like others who develop similar lines of argument, is engaged in Enlightenment blackmail.

The question that I want to probe here is, What does Foucault mean by critique, especially when he speaks of an attitude, "a philosophical ethos that could be described as a permanent critique of our historical era" (p. 42)? I want to focus on what precisely is *critical* in this "permanent critique." This question is not only crucial for understanding Foucault but has a much more general significance. For the question of critique, especially a critique of the present historical era, has become one of the most important issues of our time. To use a Wittgensteinian expression, the very "grammar" of critique seems to presuppose some measure or standard, some basis for critique. And yet there has been so much skepticism about any and all appeals to standards and "foundations" that one is compelled to reflect on the very intelligibility of the concept of critique. The issue is especially poignant in regard to Foucault because he has been read as calling into question and undermining any privileged discourse or "position" from which we can engage in critique. For Foucault, talk about "normative foundations" elicits "normalization," which he takes to be one of the primary dangers of the "disciplinary society." To phrase it in a slightly different way, we want to know whether it makes sense to speak of critique without implicitly or explicitly presupposing some "basis" for the critique, a "basis" that in *some* sense is defended, warranted, or affirmed. Foucault's critics argue that his concept of critique is confused and/or incoherent. Yet Foucault and many of his defenders appear to claim that Foucault has developed a new type of critical stance that does *not* implicitly or explicitly appeal to any basis, ground, or normative foundations.

The question of the status, character, and meaning of critique has already received a great deal of attention both by critics and defenders of Foucault. Much of the recent prolific literature on his thought has gravitated toward "an effort to think through the practical or political consequences of Foucault's genre of critical thinking."[4] But what precisely is this "genre of critical thinking"? To answer this question, I will proceed in three stages. First, I want to highlight some of Foucault's key claims in "What Is Enlightenment?" as they pertain to the question of critique. Second, I want to consider the strong case that has been made against Foucault, one that seeks to expose his confusions, contradictions, and incoherence. Third, I will consider the ways in which Foucault and his defenders have sought to defuse and answer these objections. Proceeding in this manner will enable me to return to the question, What is this "philosophical ethos that could be described as a permanent critique of our historical era"?

1

Foucault begins his essay with a thought experiment. "Let us imagine that the *Berlinsche Monatschrift* still exists and that it is asking its readers the question: what is modern philosophy? Perhaps we could respond with an echo: modern philosophy is the philosophy that is attempting to answer the question raised so imprudently two centuries ago: *Was ist Aufklärung?*" (p. 32). According to Foucault, this is the question that philosophers have been confronting ever since Kant, "a question which modern philosophy has not been capable of answering and yet which it has never managed to get rid of, either" (p. 32). Foucault claims that Kant confronted this question in a novel way, that he initiated a new way of thinking about philosophy and its relation to its historical present. For Kant, enlightenment "is neither a world era to which one belongs, nor an event whose signs are perceived, nor the dawning of an accomplishment. Kant defines *Aufklärung* in an almost entirely negative way, as an *Ausgang*, an 'exit,' a 'way out.' He is not seeking to understand the present on the basis of a totality or a future achievement. He is looking for a difference: what difference does today introduce with respect to yesterday?" (p. 34).

Foucault is already anticipating the thread that connects him with Kant. For Foucault's experiments with writing a "history of the present" are directed to highlighting what is different in the present without any appeal to a "totality or a future achievement." He ruthlessly excludes any appeal to teleology or the progressive development of history. Foucault tells us that Kant thinks of enlightenment as a "way out," but this doesn't mean we have any basis for hope or looking forward to a future achievement that will redeem us. Enlightenment is a process, a task, an obligation that releases us from immaturity—an immature status for which man himself is responsible.

Enlightenment means achieving mature responsibilty (*Mündigkeit*). Enlightenment is "the moment when humanity is going to put its own reason to use, without subjecting itself to any authority. . . . And it is precisely at this moment that the critique is necessary, since its role is that of defining the conditions under which the use of reason is legitimate in order to determine what can be known, what must be done, and what may be hoped" (p. 38).[5]

But if we are to understand how Kant's text is located "at the crossroads of critical reflection and reflection on history" (p. 38), then we need to examine the other key term that Foucault introduces in his thought-experiment: "modernity." Foucault disclaims any attempt to give a full-scale analysis of modernity or enlightenment. Nevertheless, drawing upon Baudelaire, Foucault tells us that "modernity" is not primarily a term for denoting a period or epoch of history. Rather, he wants to speak of modernity as an attitude, "a mode of relating to contemporary reality," an *ethos*. It is "a mode of relating to contemporary historical reality where there is an ironic heroization of the present" (p. 40). "For the attitude of modernity, the high value of the present is indissociable from a desperate eagerness to imagine it, to imagine it otherwise than it is, and to transform it not by destroying it but by grasping it in what it is" (p. 41). Summing up, Foucault tells us, "Modern man, for Baudelaire, is not man who goes off to discover himself, his secrets and his hidden truth; he is the man who tries to invent himself. This modernity does not "liberate man in his own being'; it compels him to face the task of producing himself" (p. 42).

Here too Foucault is at once anticipating and defending his own attitude to the present, his own ethos. For Foucault relentlessly and scathingly attacks the very idea that human beings have some hidden essence that we can presumably discover and that, once revealed, enables us to achieve freedom and autonomy. There is *no* hidden essence to be discovered; there is no hidden *depth* revealing what we truly are; there is only the task of producing or inventing ourselves. This is what Foucault calls 'ethics' in his late writings.

It is these converging reflections on enlightenment and modernity that provide the background for Foucault's central claim that Kant initiated a new type of philosophical interrogation, "one that simultaneously problematizes man's relation to the present, man's historical mode of being, and the constitution of the self as an autonomous subject" (p. 42). The legacy of Kant that Foucault stresses "is not faithfulness to doctrinal elements, but rather the permanent reactivation of an attitude—that is, of a philosophical ethos that could be described as a permanent critique of our historical era" (p. 42).

In characterizing this ethos, Foucault first gives a negative characterization stressing two points. The first I have already anticipated. For this permanent reactivation means a refusal of enlightenment blackmail, a refusal to get trapped in declaring oneself to be "for" or "against" enlightenment. The second point is to distinguish sharply between enlightenment and humanism. Throughout his writings Foucault has always set himself against humanism (although the meaning of "humanism" and the precise target of Foucault's attack changes in the course of his writings).[6] In this context, however, by "humanism" Foucault means a set of themes that reappear in the most diverse contexts ranging from Christian humanism to Nazi humanism where there is an unexamined reliance on dubious conceptions of man "borrowed from religion, science, or politics" (p. 44). Enlightenment must not be confused with humanism. Indeed, Foucault's point is even stronger. Enlightenment as a principle of critique and a permanent creation of ourselves is *opposed* to humanism.

But still, even if we are careful about avoiding enlightenment blackmail and sharply distinguishing enlightenment from humanism, we need a "positive" characterization of this philosophic ethos of critique of the historical present. It is at this point in Foucault's own "little text" that we can most clearly discern the sense in which it can be read as an *apologia*. Foucault begins his positive characterization by telling us that this philosophic ethos is a "limit attitude." This, of course, has Kantian resonances. But here Foucault sharply distinguishes his understanding of a limit attitude from Kant's view. In a succinct but dense passage, Foucault gives one of the most complete statements of what he means by critique.

Criticism is no longer going to be practiced in the search for formal structures with universal value, but rather as a historical investigation into events that have led us to constitute ourselves and to recognize ourselves as subjects of what we are doing, thinking, saying. In that sense criticism is not transcendental, and its goal is not that of making metaphysics possible: it is genealogical in its design and archaeological in its method. Archaeological—and not transcendental—in the sense that it will not seek to identify the universal structures of all knowledge or of all possible moral action, but will seek to treat the instances of discourse that articulate what we think, say, and do as so many historical events. And this critique will be genealogical in the sense that it will not deduce from the form of what we are what is impossible for us to do and to know; but it will separate out, from the contingency that has made us what we are, the possibility of no longer being, doing, thinking what we are, do, or think. It is not seeking to make possible a metaphysics that has finally become a science; it is seeking to give new impetus, as far and wide as possible, to the undefined work of freedom. (P. 46)[7]

Such a "historical-critical attitude must also be an experimental one," and it must be local and specific, always pressing specific limits in order to grasp "the points where change is possible and desirable, and to determine the precise form this change should take" (p. 46). Anticipating the objection that he caught within a self-referential inconsistency, Foucault tells us we have "to give up hope of our ever acceding to any complete and definitive knowledge of what may constitute our historical limits" (p. 47). The possibility of moving beyond these limits is always itself limited. This is why we are always in the position of beginning again. This is why a critique of the present requires *permanent reactivation.*

Foucault reiterates his main points and indicates his affinity with Kant's interrogation when he declares, "The critical ontology of ourselves has to be considered not, certainly, as a theory, a doctine, nor even as a permanent body of knowledge that is accumulating; it has to be conceived as an attitude, an ethos, a philosophic life in which the critique of what we are is at one and the same time the historical analysis of the limits that are imposed on us and an expeirment with the possibility of going beyond them" (p. 50).[8]

2

Now the problem or rather the cluster of problems that has drawn the fire of some of Foucault's sharpest critics is already suggested in this last passage. For Foucault tells us that "the critique of what we are is at one and the same time the historical analysis of the limits that are imposed on us and an experiment with the possibility of going beyond them." But precisely how are these "moments" interrelated? In what ways are Foucault's "interpretive analytics" critical?[9] To sharpen the relevant issues, I want to consider how three critics have pressed their objections to show that Foucault's understanding of critique is confused, incoherent, or contradictory. All three acknowledge the incisiveness of Foucault's historical analyses for interpreting modernity, but each seeks to locate what they take to be serious confusions/contradictions.

The title of Nancy Fraser's paper "Foucault on Modern Power: Empirical Insights and Normative Confusions" indicates the problem she is concerned with.[10] Fraser gives a sympathetic account of Foucault's genealogical method, showing how he seeks to bracket questions concerning legitimacy of normative validity and how his novel analysis of power, especially modern biopower, problematizes modernity and even has important political implications.[11] But the problem she locates is, How can we reconcile Foucault's attempt to suspend *all* questions of "normative foundations" with his engaged critique of biopower? Her conclusion, after working through several unsuccessful possibilities for reconciling these tensions, is that Foucault vacillates between two equally inadequate stances.

> On the one hand, he adopts a concept of power which permits him no condemnation of any objectionable features of modernity. But at the same time, and on the other hand, his rhetoric betrays the conviction that modernity is utterly without redeeming features. Clearly what Foucault needs and needs desperately are normative criteria for distinguishing acceptable from unacceptable forms of power. As it stands now, the unquestionably original and valuable dimensions

of his work stand in danger of being misunderstood for lack of an adequate normative perspective.[12]

Fraser never defines what she means by "normative" or even what an "adequate normative perspective" might look like. Care is needed here because "normative" is a term of art that suggest to many some sort of permanent ahistorical universal standards of evaluation. And it is clear that Foucault rejects any such standards. But we can drop the explicit reference to normative standards or foundations and still see the force of Fraser's critique. For she notes, "Foucault calls in no uncertain terms for resistance to domination. But why? Why is struggle preferable to submission? Why ought domination to be resisted?"[13]

It is clear from the way in which Charles Taylor begins his article on Foucault that he is concerned with a problem similar to the one posed by Fraser. For he says, "Certain of Foucault's most interesting historical analyses, while they are highly original, seem to lie along already familiar lines of critical thought. That is, they seem to offer an insight into what has happened, and into what we have become, which at the same time offers a critique, and hence some notion of a good unrealized or repressed in history, which we therefore undersand better how to rescue."[14] Taylor suggests that one might think there are two goods which need rescuing: freedom and truth. These two goods are deeply linked because "the negation of one (domination) makes essential use of the negation of the other (disguise)."[15] But as Taylor notes, "Foucault himself repudiates this suggestion. He dashes the hope, if we had one, that there is some good we can affirm, as a result of the understanding these analyses give us."[16]

In short, what Taylor is claiming is that the force and indeed the intelligiblity of Foucault's "genre" of critique seem at once to affirm some good and repudiate any appeal to such a good. Unlike Fraser, who takes a more agnostic stance on the question of whether it is possible to supply an "adequate normative perspective" that is compatible with Foucault's "empirical insights," Taylor claims that Foucault's unstable position is "ultimately incoherent."[17]

Taylor seeks to justify this charge by sketching three successive analyses of Foucault, each of which is progressively more radical in the sense that while each may initially lead us to think that Foucault is affirming some good, the final consequence to be drawn is that there is no such good to be affirmed. The first analysis (taken from *Discipline and Punish*) opposes the classical liturgical idea of punishment to the modern "humanitarian one," but refuses to value the second over the first because "humanitarianism" is seen as a growing system of discipline and control. The second analysis seems to give "an *evaluational* reason for refusing the evaluation which issues from the first analysis."[18] Foucault calls into question the very idea that we have a hidden nature that is being controlled and repressed. The ideology of "expressive liberation" turns out to be just a strategy of disciplinary power. This might lead us to think that we need to be liberated from *this* illusion—a liberation that is "helped by our unmasking falsehood; a liberation aided by the truth."[19] This is the third analysis. But according to Taylor, Foucault refuses this value position as well. He refuses to affirm the goods of freedom and truth. This is what Taylor calls Foucault's Nietzschean stance—and it is incoherent. Why? Because, Taylor claims, "'power' belongs in a semantic field from which 'truth' and 'freedom' cannot be excluded."[20] The very concept of power, even in Foucault's reformulation, does not make sense unless there is at least an implicit appeal to liberation from dominating forms of power. Furthermore, it requires an appeal to "truth" because the imposition of control "proceeds by foisting illusion upon us; it proceeds by disguises and masks." Consequently, Foucault's critical stance is incoherent because "the Foucauldian notion of power not only requires for its sense the correlative notions of truth and liberation, but even the standard link between them, which makes truth the condition of liberation. And yet Foucault not only refuses to acknowledge this, but appears to undermine anything except an ironical appeal to 'freedom' and 'truth.'"[21]

Fraser and Taylor limit themselves primarily to what they take to be the "confusions/contradictions" in Foucault's critique of modern forms of biopower. But Habermas in his *Philosophical Discourse of Modernity* is much more ambitious. He seeks to give a reconstruction of Foucault's intellectual development from *Madness and Civilization* to the first volume of the *History of Sexuality.* It is a rich and broad canvas on which Habermas wants to show that despite the twists and turns of Foucault's development, he is trapped within the *aporias* of the "philosophy of the subject," which is now reaching exhaustion. But for my purposes I want to highlight only those aspects of Habermas's analysis that bear on the question of critique. I have already indicated the central theme, a variation of the theme developed by Fraser and Taylor. It is the claim that Foucault constrasts his critique of power with the "analysis of truth in such a manner that the former becomes deprived of the normative yardsticks that it would have to borrow from the latter." Fleshing out what Habermas means, we can say that Habermas accuses Foucault of sliding down the slippery slope of "totalizing critique." Critique, even genealogical critique, must preserve at least one standard by which we engage in the critique of the present. Yet when critique is *totalized,* when critique turns against itself so that all rational standards are called into question, then one is caught in a performative contradiction.[22]

"Genealogy," according to Habermas, "is overtaken by a fate similar to that which Foucault had seen in the human sciences." "To the extent that it retreats into the reflectionless objectivity of a nonparticipatory, ascetic description of kaleidoscopically changing practices of power, genealogical historiography emerges from its cocoon as precisely the *presentisic, relativistic, cryptonormative* illusory science that it does not want to be."[23] Let me explain what Habermas means. By "presentistic" Habermas is referring to the "felicitious positivistic" stance that Foucault claimed for himself in describing the contingent power/knowledge regimes. This is the "cool façade of a radical historicism."[24] But this stance requires withholding or bracketing any evaluative judgment of the kaleidoscopically changing practices. Such pure "ascetic description" leads to relativism in the sense that there is no basis or position from which one can evaluate or judge this passing array of power/knowledge regimes. It is like adopting the panoptical gaze. But Foucault does not consistently assume such a "position," nor is it even possible. He exhibits "the passions of aesthetic modernism."[25]

He assumes a position of "arbitrary *partisanship* of a criticism that cannot account for its normative foundations."[26] Foucault, Habermas claims, is "incorruptible enough to admit these incoherences," but this doesn't mean that he escapes from them.[27]

Although Fraser, Taylor, and Habermas differ in their lines of attack, the cumulative force of their criticisms is to show that Foucault's understanding of a philosophic ethos as "a permanent critique of our historical era" is confused, incoherent, and enmeshed in performative contradictions.

3

Now the questions arise, Is this enlightenment blackmail? Are Foucault's critics forcing him into a grid that distorts his critical project? Are they wedded to a set of distinctions and binary oppositions, e.g., normative/empirical, liberation/domination, universal/relative, rational/irrational, that Foucault subverts? Foucault himself suggests that this is so, and this is precisely what many of Foucault's defenders have claimed. Indeed, if we juxtapose the portrait of Foucault sketched by his critics with what Foucault says in "What Is Enlightenment?" we are struck by glaring disparties. Foucault doesn't defend a stance of "felicitious positivism"; he defends the permanent reactivation of critique of our historical era. He shows his awareness that a "limit attitude" is itself always limited. He doesn't bracket the question of freedom and liberation. He even speaks of the need "to grasp the points where change is possible and desirable, and to determine the precise form this change should take" (p. 46). Now, of course, many responses are possible to these discrepancies between what Foucault says and the charges his critics bring against him: he is changing his mind once again; he is adopting a more conciliatory tone; he is rewriting his own history; he is making claims that contradict what he says in other places; etc. But we might also entertain the possibility that something has gone wrong here. Perhaps we can give a different, more sympathetic reading of what Foucault is doing that makes sense of his genre of critique and escapes from the harsh criticisms of those who claim his position is incoherent. This is the possibility that I want to explore by probing a number of interrelated themes in his work. In each case I want to show how they enable us to get a better grasp of his critical intent and yet still leave us with difficult unresolved problems.

The Rhetoric of Disruption

Throughout his writings Foucault not only returns again and again to the multiple uses of language; he is himself an extraordinary and skillful rhetorician. The question arises, To what end or purpose does he use rhetoric, and how does it work? The answer is complex. But the main point is nicely brought out by William Connolly when he says, "The rhetorical figures, to use a phrase of Nietzsche's, incite us to 'listen to a different claim' rather than to accept the findings of an argument."[28] In part, Foucault seeks to break and disrupt the discourse that has preoccupied so much of modern philosophy, a discourse in which we have become obsessed with epistemological issues and questions of normative foundations. And he does this because he wants to show us that such a preoccupation distracts us and even blinds us from asking new kinds of questions about the genesis of social practices that are always shaping us and historically limiting what we are. Foucault deploys "rhetorical devices to incite the experience of discord or discrepancy between the social construction of self, truth, and rationality and that which does not fit neatly within their folds."[29] He seeks "to *excite* in the reader the experience of discord between the social construction of normality and that which does not fit neatly within the frame of these constructs."[30] In this respect we can draw parallels with Nietzsche's multiple styles and also with that other great skeptical gadfly, Socrates, who also sought to disrupt the conventional and comforting convictions of his interlocutors. Viewed in this way, we can make sense of Foucault's attraction to metaphors of strategy and tactics. It is this rhetoric of disruption that is the source of Foucault's critical sting. There are even those, like Dreyfus and Rabinow, who claim that "Foucault uses language to articulate an understanding of our situation which moves us to action."[31] (Later I want to return to this claim.)

But how does Foucault *do* this? How do his rhetorical strategies work? A full-scale answer would have to examine his own micro- and macropractices, i.e., his *specific* use of rhetorical devices and figures as well as the way in which he carefully crafts his works.

> The Foucauldian rhetorical strategy works, for instance, through displacement of . . . unifying or mellow metaphors by more disturbing ones; and by conversion of noun forms giving solidity to modern conceptions of truth, subject, and normality into verbs that present them as constructions; and by the posing of questions left unanswered in the text; and by the introduction of sentence fragments that communicate even though they do not fit into the conventional form that gives primacy to the subject.[31]

We can even grasp Foucault's use of that favored rhetorical device of Nietzsche, hyperbole. One might think, for example, that Foucault is heralding the death of the subject, that he is claiming that the subject itself is *only* the result of the effects of power/knowledge regimes, that he completely undermines and ridicules any and all talk of human agency. There is plenty of textual evidence to support such claims. But is is also clear, especially in his late writings when he deals with the question of the self's relation to itself and the possibility of "the man who tries to invent himself," that he is not abandoning the idea that "we constitute ourselves as subjects acting on others."[33]

Or again, especially in his essays in *Power/Knowledge,* it looks as if Foucault is abandoning any appeal to truth or reducing truth to a mere effect of power/knowledge regimes. But Foucault also sharply criticizes the polemicist who "proceeds encased in privileges that he possesses in advance" and refuses to recognize his adversary as "a subject having the right to speak." The polemicist objective "will be, not to come as close as possible to a difficult *truth,* but to bring about the triumph of the just cause he has been manifestly upholding from the beginning" (emphasis added).[34]

Or still again, for all of Foucault's skepticism about expressive notions of freedom and liberty, we have seen that in "What Is Enlightenment?" he claims his type of critique "is seeking to give new impetus, as far and wide as possible, to the undefined work of freedom."

Now instead of claiming that Foucault is flatly contradicting himself on the question of the subject, truth, and freedom, we can read him in a different way—as deliberately using hyperbolic rhetorical constructions in order to compel us to disrupt and question our traditional *understandings* of these key concepts. And he effectively does this by showing us the dark ambiguities in the construction of these concepts and the role they have played in social practices.[35]

Now I think it is correct to read Foucault in this way. It enables us to understand the critical sting of his writings, a critical sting that results from disrupting cherished convictions and raising new sorts of questions about the historical contingencies that shape our practices. But there are problems that arise when we seek to think through how Foucault's rhetoric of disruption works. Let me illustrate this by considering an example of the macrorhetorical level of his works. Here we can review the analyses that Taylor gave in order to expose Foucault's incoherence.

When Foucault begins *Discipline and Punish* with the detailed, graphic execution of Damiens (which he immediately juxtaposes with the timetable drawn up eighty years later in the rules for the house of young prisoners in Paris), it is a stunning rhetorical device for eliciting conflicting disruptive reactions in the reader. For Foucault knows the reader will react with a sense of the horror to what initially *appears* to be the barbaric spectacle of gratuitous torture. We are seduced in taking comfort in the realization that "our" methods of punishment, whatever their defects, are much more humane, even though a doubt may be planted by the perplexing juxtaposition of the timetable. It is only gradually that our confidence begins to be undermined as we see what the process of "humanization" involves. For we come to see how "the birth of the prison" is virtually an allegory for the birth of the disciplinary society, the panoptic society of surveillance that makes such effective use of the disciplines that control our bodies. So we might say that the rhetorical power of his analysis depends upon skillfully eliciting and at the same time undermining the evaluative reactions of the reader. And as we react in horror against what strikes us as so constraining and repressive about the disciplinary society, we are tempted to think there is some good here that is being repressed and needs to be liberated, expressed, and affirmed. But again this elicits in us the expectation of some positive theory of liberation from domination and repression. Foucault has set us up for the critical analysis of *The History of Sexuality,* an analysis that is not simply restricted to the historical genesis of contemporary discourses of sexuality but seeks to show us that standard understandings of the dynamics of liberation and repression are distortive and misleading. He also seeks to show us that the will to know the truth about ourselves turns out to be a "specific form of extortion of truth," the invention of specific types of discourse that do not liberate us from repression but rather subject us to a new, more subtle control of our bodies. And this analysis leaves us again in an ambiguous situation. For to the extent that we accept Foucault's unmasking of the "repressive hypothesis," we are compelled to question traditional narratives of liberation and domination. We are compelled to rethink what these concepts mean. Foucault, as he so frequently does at the end of his books, ironically tantalizes us with new possibilities: "Moreover, we need to consider the possibility that one day, perhaps, in a different economy of bodies and pleasures, people will no longer quite understand how the ruses of sexuality, and the power that sustains its organization, were able to subject us to what that austere monarchy of sex, so that we became dedicated to the endless task of forcing its secret, or exacting the truest of confessions from a shadow."[36]

Now the point that I want to emphasize is that Foucault's rhetoric of disruption works because it at once presupposes and challenges an ethical-political horizon. He deliberately seeks to elicit conflicting responses in us, exposing fractures in "our" most cherished convictions and comforting beliefs. I speak of an "ethical-political *horizon*" because this horizon keeps receding. Foucault never quite thematizes this ethical-political perspective, and yet it is always presupposed. Without it the rhetoric of disruption would not work. One may well be skeptical of any talk of ahistorical normative standards. But this does not make the question of what one is for or against disappear. The rhetoric of disruption and genealogical critique does not escape from the implicit affirmation of some "good," some ethical-political valorization. Even the rhetorical sting of the analyses in *History of Sexuality* depends upon our revulsion against the idea that the will to knowledge exhibited in contemporary discourses of sexuality does not liberate us from repression but rather furthers the normalization of our docile bodies; they result in new techniques of control. Even if one thinks that *philosophical* attempts to face this issue have led us into dead ends, one can't escape the question of what it is that we are *affirming*, and why "we" affirm it. One can only go so far in clarifying what is distinctive about this new genre of critique by employing the devices of negative theology: stating what it is *not*. Foucault is a master in using these devices.[37] But the more effective he is in employing them, the greater the urgency becomes to give a positive characterization of the ethical-political perspective that informs his critique and enables his rhetoric of disruption to work. This is the issue that Foucault never squarely and unambiguously confronts.

Dangers

In 1983 Foucault was interviewed about his work in progress on the genealogy of ethics. He was asked, "Do you think that the Greeks offer an attractive and plausible alternative?" Foucault answered emphatically,

> No! I am not looking for an alternative; you can't find the solution of a problem in the solution of another problem raised at another moment by other people. You see, what I want to do is not the history of solutions, and that's the reason why I don't accept the word *alternative*. I would like to do the genealogy of problems, of *problématiques*. My point is not that everything is bad, but that everything is dangerous, which is not exactly the same as bad. If everything is dangerous, then we always have something to do.[38]

This claim is not only applicable to Foucault's late work in progress concerning the genealogy of ethics but also is relevant to all his genealogical studies. And it is a theme running through all his work. His archaeological-genealogical analyses of *problématiques* are intended to specify the changing constellation of *dangers*. This is what critique as a philosophic ethos is intended to expose. And this theme has been highlighted by many of Foucault's defenders. Thus Dreyfus and Rabinow assert, "His aim has never been to denounce power *per se* nor to propound truth but to use his analysis to shed light on the specific dangers that each specific type of power/knowledge produces."[39] Again, they tell us, "Nor did he consider it his main task to offer alternative possibilities for acting. He was simply trying to diagnose *the* contemporary danger" (emphasis added).[40] David Hiley also stresses the danger theme when he says, "Yet while everything may be thought to be dangerous, he nevertheless believed that there was something uniquely dangerous about modernity."[41] What is uniquely dangerous is "the fact that everything becomes a target for normalization."[42] Now initially this does seem to be an attractive and illuminating way of understanding Foucault. And again, it does accord with the stance he takes in his genealogical critical analyses. If one wants to speak of alternatives, the first task is to grasp the dangers we confront. But when we think out this concept of danger, we also face some hard problems. For we might say that the very notion of danger is itself *value-laden*: Dangers for whom? Dangers from whose perspective? Why are these dangers "dangerous"? There is something comparable to an interpretative or hermeneutical circle here. For the very specification of what are taken to be dangers or the unique dangers of modernity only makes sense from an interpretative perspective, one that involves an *evaluation* of our situation, not just a "neutral" description but an evaluative description. After all, there are conflicting and perhaps even incommensurable claims about what are the specific dangers of modernity. Think, for example, of Heidegger's very different interpretation of the "supreme danger" we confront—the danger that arises from enframing (*Gestell*): "Thus where enframing reigns, there is *danger* in the highest sense."[43] So the talk of "dangers" or being responsive to what is intolerable only shifts the question to the adequacy or perspicuity of the evaluative-interpretative perspective from which one specifies dangers. This is why it is simply evasive or begging the question to say, as Dreyfus and Rabinow do, "What makes one interpretative theory better than another on this view has yet to be worked out, but it has to do with articulating common concerns and finding a language which becomes accepted as a way of talking about social situations, while leaving open the possibility of 'dialogue,' or better, a conflict of interpretations, with other shared discursive practices used to articulate different concerns."[44] What are these "common concerns"? Do they include common *evaluations* of dangers? Who shares these common concerns? Here too I think there is danger of failing to see that what gets pushed out the front door is smuggled in through the back door. One might say that "quite consistent with his interpretative stance, Foucault . . . has abandoned the attempt to legitimate social organization by means of philosophical grounding" and that he refuses "to articulate normative principles."[45] But we still want to understand what makes something dangerous. Or if everything is dangerous, what is it that makes some dangers more intolerable than others. Here too there is an evaluative ethical-political bias that is operative and indeed is the basis for the very intelligibility of the talk of dangers that never becomes fully explicit or thematized.

Specificity and Subjugated Knowledges

It may be objected that to speak of an "ethical-political" perspective that is at once presupposed and secreted by Foucault's interpretative analyses is itself misleading. For it invites us to think in the very global terms that Foucault wants to avoid. Indeed, it may be argued that we can grasp the point of Foucault's genre of critique only when we fully appreciate his extreme nominalism and his insistence on specificity.[46] Despite what at times has the ring of global claims about discourses, social practices, power/knowledge regimes, Foucault is always directing our attention to what is local, specific, and historically contingent. He emphasizes this over and over again when seeking to explicate what he means by a philosophical ethos as "a permanent critique of our historical era." Insofar as such a critique is directed to opening new possibilites for thinking, acting, and grasping the points where change is possible and desirable, it must be appropriated by those who have been marginalized and subjected. In short, all effective criticism must be *local.* This theme dovetails with Foucault's claim about the changing role of the intellectual and with Foucault's deep aversion to the "inhibiting effect of global, *totalitarian theories.*"[47] He tells us, "In contrast to the various projects which aim to inscribe knowledges in the hierarchical order of power associated with science, genealogy should be seen as a kind of attempt to emancipate historical knowledge from that subjection, to render them, that is, capable of opposition and of struggle against the coercion of a theoretical, unitary, formal and scientific discourse."[48] Once again I think there is something important about this emphasis in Foucault, although it also raises some hard problems.

One of the many good reasons why Foucault's rhetoric of disruption is so effective and has been so fertile for novel researches is because he at once captures and shapes a pervasive mood (*Stimmung*) of our time. He is not only a master of revealing the dark constraining side of the "humane" practices that shape our lives and our bodies, he is always showing us how discursive practices exclude, marginalize, and limit us.[49] He develops devastating critiques of global solutions to specific problems and exposes the treacherous ambiguities of loose talk about total revolution. We live in a time when it appears that only specific types of resistance, opposition, and revolt seem to make any sense. Contrary to the reading of Foucault that exaggerates the strain in Foucault that shows how what we are, do, and think is *only* the precipitate or result of anonymous historically contingent practices, Foucault can be read as always seeking to expose instabilities, points of resistances, places where counterdiscourses can arise and effect transgressions and change. It is the nexus of specific limits and transgressions that is his primary concern. Nevertheless, even if we stick to the specific and local, to the *insurrection of subjected knowledges,* there is an implicit valorization here that never becomes fully explicit and yet is crucial for Foucault's genre of critique.[50] For there are the subjected knowledges of women, blacks, prisoners, and gays, who have experienced the pain and suffering of exclusion. But throughout the world there are also the subjected knowledges of all sorts of fundamentalists, fanatics, and terrorists, who have their own sense of what are the unique or most important dangers to be confronted. What is never quite clear in Foucault is why anyone should favor certain local forms of resistance rather than others. Nor is it clear why one would "choose" one side or the other in a localized resistance or revolt.

Foucault insists, "Where there is power, there is resistance."[51] The existence of power relationships "depends on a multiplicity of points of resistance; these play the role of adversary, target, support, or handle in power relations."[52] But "adversary" and "target" are reversible and symmetrical in the sense that if *a* is *b*'s adversary or target, *b* may be *a*'s adversary or target. But when we transfer this way of speaking and place it within the context of the type of power relations that Foucault analyzes, we are compelled to face the evaluative questions, Which point of resistance is to be favored? By whom? And why? This is why the claim that Foucault's rhetoric is intended to incite us to action is so unsatisfactory. For it is never clear, even in a specific local situation, how one is to act and why. So the appeal to specificity and locality doesn't help us to elucidate the ethical-political question of how one is to act. It only relocates this issue on a specific and local level.[53]

Freedom and Skepticism

"Foucault is the great skeptic of our times. He is skeptical about dogmatic unities and philosophical anthropologies. He is the philosopher of dispersion and singularity." "To question the self-evidence of a form of experience, knowledge, or power, is to free it for our purposes, to open new possibilities for thought or action. Such freedom is the ethical principle of Foucault's skepticism."[54] This line of interpretation, this reading of Foucault, is extremely appealing, and it has been developed in different ways by commentators on Foucault who seek to defend him against "enlightenment blackmail." Foucault does seem to be working in a tradition that has analogies and parallels with Sextus Empiricus and the Pyrrhonian skeptics. This is even another reason why Foucault is at once so provocative and disconcerting. For his distinctive strength is in a radical questioning and a withholding and suspending of judgment. Nothing is to be taken for granted, not even our predisposition to demand that a thinker must "take a position." David Hiley is right when he argues that we misunderstand the tradition of skepticism and Foucault's own skeptical stance if we fail to realize that it is an ethical stance.[55] For it is only by viewing it in this manner that we can appreciate the relationship between skepticism and freedom. Freedom, then, is not to be understood as the liberation of some human essence that is repressed or the affirmation and actualization of some good that is locked up in what we "essentially" are. Freedom is a type of detachment or suspension of judgment that opens new possibilities for thought and action. This does accord with the theme in "What Is Enlightenment?" that enlightenment is an exit, a way out, and with Foucault's claim that the critique of what we are is at one and the same time the historical analysis of the limits imposed on us and an experiment with the possibility of going beyond them. But skeptical freedom, as Hegel so brilliantly showed in the *Phenomenology of Spirit,* is radically unstable. It is always in danger of becoming merely abstract, i.e., it "ends up with the bare abstraction of nothingness or emptiness and cannot get any further from there, but must wait to see whether something new comes along and what it is, in order to throw it too into the empty abyss."[56] We can see how the radical instability of skepticism shows up in Foucault. For Foucault is not simply adopting a position of detachment and skeptical suspension of judgment. He is constantly tempting us with his references to new possibilities of thinking and acting, of giving new impetus to the undefined work of freedom, of the need to grasp the points where change is possible and desirable, and of determining the precise form these changes should take. But the problem is that these references to desirable new possibilities and changes are in danger of becoming empty and vacuous unless we have some sense of which possibilities and changes are *desirable* and why. We can accept Foucault's claim that a permanent reactivation of the philosophical ethos of critique does not require the critic to lay out blueprints for the future or "alternatives." Foucault himself is in that tradition that stresses that the primary function of the critic is to analyze the present and to reveal its fractures and instabilities, the ways in which it at once limits us and points to the transgression of these limits. But we must be extremely wary of sliding from references to new possibilities of thinking, acting, and being to a *positive* evaluation of such possibilities.

No one has revealed the dark possibilities that can erupt in history better than Foucault. So the same type of problem that we encountered before arises again here. Foucault's rhetoric—even the attraction of the distinctive type of skeptical freedom he adumbrates, the appeal of "the possibility of no longer being, doing, or thinking what we are, do, think"—is itself dependent or parasitic upon an ethical-political valorization. What does it even mean to say that some possibilities are desirable? Without thematizing this question, it is difficult to discern what precisely is critical about his genre of critique. It is *not* Foucault's critics that have imposed this problem on him. It emerges from Foucault's own insistence that there are changes that are desirable and that critique enables us "to determine the precise form this change should take." A skeptical freedom that limits itself to talk of new possibilities for thinking and acting but heroically or ironically refuses to provide any evaluative orientation as to which possibilities and changes are desirable is in danger of becoming merely empty, or even worse, it witholds judgment from those catastrophic possibilities that *have* erupted or *can* erupt.

Ethics

Foucault in his last works turned to the question of ethics, although typically he uses the term "ethics" in a novel and apparently idiosyncratic manner: "The kind of relationship you ought to have with yourself, *rapport à soi,* . . . and which determines how the individual is supposed to constitute himself as a moral subject of his own actions."[57] And if we again turn to the essay "What Is Enlightenment?" we can see how important this motif is for Foucault. It is evident in his analysis of Baudelaire's conception of modern man as the "man who tries to invent himself," who seeks to make his own life a work of art. This kind of ethics is an aesthetics of existence.

As Dreyfus and Rabinow clearly stress, Foucault's critical ontology has two separate but related components: "work on oneself and responding to one's time."[58] In his interview concerning his work in progress on the genealogy of ethics, Foucault asks, "But couldn't everyone's life become a work of art?"[59] Does Foucault's turn to such an aestheticized understanding of ethics help us to understand his critical stance? One might be inclined to respond affirmatively, at least insofar as Foucault is giving some content to the type of changes he thinks would be desirable. But for a variety of reasons I think we need to be extremely cautious in assessing this turn to ethics. Foucault himself is extremely tentative and resists the idea that his experimental studies of the genealogy of ethics yield any alternatives to our present situation. Even sympathetic commentators have noted the many problems that he leaves unresolved.[60] Not the least of these is that the very way in which Foucault talks about ethics in terms of the self's relationship to itself *seems* to presuppose a way of speaking about the self that he had previously so effectively criticized. What precisely is a "self"? How is the "self" related to what Foucault calls a "subject"? Who is the "I" that constitutes "itself" as a moral agent? It is difficult to see how Foucault himself escapes the radical instabilities that he exposed in "Man and His Doubles." And there are other problems. For this way of speaking of ethics, which is now sharply distinguished from politics, *seems* to be radically individualistic and voluntaristic with no consideration of anything or any other beyond one's relationship to oneself.[61]

What is perhaps most ironic about Foucault's talk of ethics and freedom as it pertains to our historical situation is that its intelligibility presupposes the notion of an ethical or moral agent that *can* be free and that can "master" itself. But Foucault not only fails to explicate *this* sense of agency, his genealogical analyses seem effectively to undermine any talk of agency that is not a precipitate of power/knowledge regimes. Who or what is left to transgress historical limits?

The most generous comment to make about Foucault's tentative probings of ethics is that they are "suggestive," opening new lines of inquiry. But they do not significantly further our grasp of his genre of critique. Even if one were to grant that Foucault is tentatively exploring possibilities and changes that would be desirable, he never clarifies why an ascetic-aesthetic mode of ethical life *is* desirable.

I can now return to the question of critique as a philosophical ethos that is a permanent critique of our historical era, critique that is practiced as "a historical investigation into the events that have led us to constitute ourselves and to recognize ourselves as subjects of what we are doing, thinking, saying" (p. 4). I do think, as I have tried to show, that it is possible to give a more sympathetic reading of Foucault that at least blunts the criticism of those who argue that he is confused, contradictory, and incoherent. I think we can see that he is inciting us to "*listen* to a different claim." He does disconcert and disrupt. He forces us to ask hard questions about our most cherished beliefs and comforting convictions. He shows us novel ways in which our bodies are controlled and made docile. He consistently refuses to allow us the illusion of easy solutions and alternatives. He has a remarkable ability to compel us to ask new sorts of questions and open new lines of inquiry. He unmasks illusions. To read him as *only* revealing the way in which global power/knowledge regimes supplant each other and completely determine what we are is to misread him. For it is to screen out the many ways in which Foucault is always focusing on instabilities, points of resistance, specific points where revolt and counterdiscourse are possible. We can evaluate his hyperoscillations positively, i.e., we can see them as showing us how difficult "the undefined work of freedom" is and how much patient labor is required "to give form to our impatience for liberty."

But nevertheless, as I have also tried to show, when we think through what Foucault is saying and showing, we are left with hard issues that are not resolved. These all cluster about the question of the ethical-political perspective that informs his critique. And these problems do not arise from imposing an alien grid or set of demands upon Foucault. On the contrary, they arise from his *own* practice of critique. Foucault never thematizes these problems; he never treats them with the rigor that they demand, a type of rigor he exemplified in his genealogical analyses. At best, we have only hints and suggestions, not all of which seem compatible. And at times Foucault seeks to deny us the conceptual resources for dealing with the very issues his analyses force us to confront. This is one reason why his critics find him confused, contradictory, and incoherent. Foucault's own inciting rhetoric of disruption forces us to raise questions and at the same time appears to deny us any means for effectively dealing with these questions.

Ironically, the current polemic about enlightenment blackmail tends to boomerang. It is a diversionary tactic that obscures more than it illuminates. It tends to close off issues rather than open them up. It seduces us into thinking that we are confronted with only two possibilities: either there are universal ahistorical normative foundations for critique or critique is groundless. This specious "either/or" closes off the topos that needs to be opened for discussion, the topos toward which so much of the polemic of modernity/postmodernity gravitates. How can we still today in our historical present find ways of significantly clarifying and warranting the ethical-political perspectives that inform a critique of the present? This is *the* question that Foucault's genre of critique requires us to raise, a question he never quite answered.

Let me conclude with a statement that Foucault made in an interview conducted in May 1984 just before his death, where Foucault sounds like some of those he accused of enlightenment blackmail.

> I insist on this difference [between discussion and polemics] as something essential: a whole morality is at stake, the morality that concerns the search for the truth and the relation to the other.
>
> In the serious play of questions and answers, in the work of reciprocal elucidation, the rights of each person are in some sense immanent in the discussion. They depend only on the dialogue situation. The person asking the questions is merely exercising the right that has been given him: to remain unconvinced, to perceive a contradiction, to require more information. . . . As for the person answering the questions, he too exercises a right that does not go beyond the discussion itself; by the logic of his own discourse he is tied to the questioning of the other.[62]

I can think of no better description of the type of discussion and dialogue that is now required to probe the ethical-political perspective that informs Foucault's genre of critique.

Notes

1. Michel Foucault, "What Is Enlightenment?" in *The Foucault Reader,* ed. Paul Rabinow (New York: Pantheon Books, 1984). Page numbers in this paper refer to this text.

2. Habermas did not publish his full scale critique of Foucault until after Foucault's death. This appears in *The Philosophical Discourse of Modernity,* trans. by F. Lawrence (Cambridge, Mass.: MIT Press, 1987). The German text was published in 1985. In two earlier articles Habermas referred to Foucault and made some critical remarks about him. These remarks and Habermas's discussion of Foucault in *The Philosophical Discourse of Modernity* have set off a storm of controversy. See Habermas's "Modernity versus Postmodernity," in *New German Critique* 22 (1981): 3–14, and "The Entwinement of Myth and Enlightenment: Re-reading *Dialectic of Enlightenment,*" in *New German Critique* 26 (1982): 13–30. After Foucault's death, Habermas wrote an obituary, "Taking Aim at the Heart of the Present," which is reprinted in *Foucault: A Critical Reader,* ed. by David Hoy (Oxford: Basil Blackwell, 1986).

3. Jürgen Habermas, "Taking Aim at the Heart of the Present," p. 108. In this obituary Habermas relates what most impressed him when he first met Foucault in 1983: "the tension, which resists easy categorization, between the almost serene scientific reserve of the scholar striving for objectivity on the one hand, and, on the other, the political vitality of the vulnerable, subjectively excitable, morally sensitive intellectual" (p. 103).

4. Michael S. Roth, "Review Essay" of recent literature on Foucault, p. 71, in *History and Theory* 1987: 70–80. This is an excellent review of recent discussions of Foucault.

5. Foucault also tells us, "It is necessary to stress the connection that exists between this brief article and the three *Critiques*" (p. 37).

6. For a discussion of what Foucault means by humanism and the distinction between humanism and enlightenment, see David R. Hiley, *Philosophy in Question: Essays on a Pyrrhonian Theme* (Chicago: University of Chicago Press, 1988), pp. 101–104. The chapter in Hiley's book "Knowledge and Power" presents a lucid but different reading of the issues raised by Foucault's essay "What Is Enlightenment?" Hiley defends Foucault against the blackmail of enlightenment. Nevertheless he concludes his chapter by showing how Foucault's account "that identifies normalization and unfreedom, and that connects liberation with transgression and connects maturity with self-creation—remains deeply problematic for other reasons" (p. 110). These reasons are related to Foucault's ambivalent attitude toward the relation of an "aesthetics of existence" and its relation to a "notion of community."

7. Several commentators have debated the precise relationship between Foucault's understanding of archaeology and genealogy and whether the move to genealogy represents a break or change in his intellectual development. For different interpretations of Foucault's development, see Hubert L. Dreyfus and Paul Rabinow, *Michel Foucault: Beyond Structuralism and Hermeneutics,* second edition (Chicago: University of Chicago Press, 1983); Jürgen Habermas, *The Philosophical Discourse of Modernity,* lectures

9 and 10. See also Arnold I. Davidson's essay "Archaeology, Genealogy, Ethics," in *Foucault: A Critical Reader,* ed. by David Hoy.

8. Foucault takes up a number of other themes in his essay that I have not discussed, e.g., Kant's distinction of the private and public use of reason. He also briefly explores how the work on our historical limits has "its generality, its systematicity, its homogeneity, and its stakes" (p. 47).

9. "Interpretative analytics" is the term used by Dreyfus and Rabinow to characterize Foucault's distinctive orientation beyond structuralism and hermeneutics. See *Michel Foucault: Beyond Structuralism and Hermeneutics.*

10. Nancy Fraser, "Foucault on Modern Power: Empirical Insights and Normative Confusions," in *Praxis International* 3 (1981): 272–287. One should also see her two subsequent articles on Foucault: "Foucault's Body Language: A Post-humanist Political Rhetoric?" in *Salmagundi* 61 (1983): 55–70, and "Michel Foucault: A Young Conservative?' in *Ethics* 96 (1985): 165–184.

11. Fred Dallmayr has argued that Fraser and others have given too simplified and undifferentiated an analysis of Foucault's understanding of power. He shows the complexity and the changing nuances of Foucault's understanding of power in "Pluralism Old and New: Foucault on Power," in *Polis and Praxis: Exercises in Contemporary Political Theory* (Cambridge, Mass.: MIT Press, 1984).

12. Nancy Fraser, "Foucault on Modern Power," p. 286.

13. Fraser, "Foucault on Modern Power," p. 283.

14. Charles Taylor, "Foucault on Freedom and Truth," reprinted in *Foucault: A Critical Reader,* ed. David Hoy, p. 69.

15. Taylor, "Foucault on Freedom and Truth," p. 70.

16. Taylor, "Foucault on Freedom and Truth," p. 69.

17. Taylor, "Foucault on Freedom and Truth," p. 83.

18. Taylor, "Foucault on Freedom and Truth," p. 80.

19. Taylor, "Foucault on Freedom and Truth," p. 80.

20. Taylor, "Foucault on Freedom and Truth," p. 91.

21. Taylor, "Foucault on Freedom and Truth," p. 93. Taylor also develops a number of other criticisms, which I have not discussed, including the claim that Foucault's conception of "power without a subject" is also incoherent.

22. This is the line of criticism that Habermas first indicated in his brief reference to Foucault in "The Entwinement of Myth and Enlightenment: Re-reading *Dialectic of Enlightenment.*"

23. Jürgen Habermas, *The Philosophical Discourse of Modernity,* pp. 275–276.

24. Habermas, *The Philosophical Discourse of Modernity,* p. 275.

25. Habermas, *The Philosophical Discourse of Modernity,* p. 275.

26. Habermas, *The Philosophical Discourse of Modernity,* p. 276.

27. Habermas, *The Philosophical Discourse of Modernity,* p. 276. Habermas argues that Foucault's "putative objectivity of knowledge is itself put in question (1) by the involuntary *presentism* of a historiography that remains hermeneutically stuck in its starting situation; (2) by the unavoidable *relativism* of an analysis related to the present that can understand itself only as a context-dependent practical enterprise; (3) by the arbitrary *partisanship* of a criticism that cannot account for its normative foundations" (p. 276). He then seeks to reveal the unresolved aporias and contradictory impulses involved in each of these three areas. See *The Philosophical Discourse of Modernity,* pp. 276–286.

28. William E. Connolly, "Taylor, Foucault, and Otherness," in *Political Theory* 13 (August 1985): 368. Connolly's article is a response to Charles Taylor, "Foucault on Freedom and Truth," which also originally appeared in *Political Theory* 12 (May 1984): 152–183. For Taylor's reply to Connolly, see "Connolly, Foucault, and Truth," in *Political Theory* 13 (August 1985): 377–385. Connolly is one of Foucault's most sympathetic commentators, but he also presses a number of important criticisms. See his *Politics and Ambiguity* (Madison: University of Wisconsin Press, 1987).

29. Connolly, "Taylor, Foucault, and Otherness," p. 368.

30. Connolly, "Taylor, Foucault, and Otherness," p. 368.

31. Hubert L. Dreyfus and Paul Rabinow, "What Is Maturity? Habermas and Foucault on 'What Is Enlightenment?'" in *Foucault: A Critical Reader,* ed. by David Hoy, p. 114.

32. Connolly, "Taylor, Foucault, and Otherness," p. 368.

33. Michel Foucault, "On the Genealogy of Ethics: An Overview of Work in Progress," in *The Foucault Reader,* ed. by Paul Rabinow, p. 351. See also Ian Hacking's discussion of this interview, "Self-Improvement," in *Foucault: A Critical Reader,* ed. by David Hoy.

34. Michel Foucault, "Polemics, Politics, and Problemizations," in *The Foucault Reader,* p. 382. Throughout this interview Foucault speaks of "the search for the truth" and gaining "access to the truth."

35. Maurice Blanchot makes a similar point about Foucault in his subtle appreciative essay "Michel Foucault as I Imagine Him," in *Foucault/Blanchot* (New York: Zone Books, 1987). He writes,

> And were not his own principles more complex than his official discourse, with its striking formulations, led one to think. For example, it is accepted as a certainty that Foucault, adhering in this to a certain conception of literary production, got rid of purely and simply, the notion of the subject: no more oeuvre, no more author, no more creative unity. But things are not that simple. The subject does not disappear; rather its excessively determined unity is put in question. (P. 78)
>
> Similarly, when one ascribes to Foucault a quasi-nihilistic distrust of what he calls the will to truth (or the will to serious knowledge), or, additionally, a suspicious rejection of the idea of reason (possessing universal value), I think one is underestimating the complexity of his concerns. The will to truth, to be sure, but at what cost? What are its guises? What political imperatives are concealed beneath that highly honorable quest? (P. 79)

There is another aspect of Foucault's rhetoric that should be noted. In several of Foucault's interviews given for English-speaking audiences, he adopts a more moderate, reasonable, "democratic" tone as compared to some of his more extreme "Nietzschean" pronouncements in French. Many of Foucault's American champions tend to portray him as a "radical democrat," a domesticated Nietzschean without Nietzsche's antidemocratic biases.

36. Michel Foucault, *The History of Sexuality,* vol. 1, *An Introduction* (New York: Vintage Books, 1980), p. 159. See also Nancy Fraser, "Foucault's Body Language: A Posthumanist Political Rhetoric?"

37. Blanchot notes how the formulas of negative theology are already effectively employed in *The Archaeology of Knowledge* "Read and reread *The Archaeology of Knowledge* . . . and you will be surprised to rediscover in it many a formula from negative theology. Foucault invests all his talent in describing with sublime phrases what it is he rejects: 'It's not . . . , nor is it . . . , nor is it for that matter . . ,' so that there remained almost nothing for him to say in order to valorize what is precisely a refusal of the notion of 'value'" ("Michel Foucault as I Imagine Him," p. 74). Foucault continued to work and overwork these formulas throughout his writings. Unfortunately, many of Foucault's sympathetic commentators also tend to overwork these devices, informing us what he does *not* say, believe, or intend.

38. Michel Foucault, "On the Genealogy of Ethics: An Overview of Work in Progress," in *The Foucault Reader,* p. 343.

39. Dreyfus and Rabinow, "What Is Maturity?" p. 116.

40. Dreyfus and Rabinow, "What Is Maturity?" p. 118.

41. David Hiley, *Philosophy in Question,* p. 94.

42. Hiley, *Philosophy in Question,* p. 103.

43. Martin Heidegger, "The Question Concerning Technology," in *Martin Heidegger: Basic Writings,* ed. by David F. Krell (New York: Harper and Row, 1977), p. 309. One may argue that the concept of danger is not necessarily "value-laden." It is being used merely as a nonevaluative *functional* expression. But this line of defense loses plausibility when one speaks of the dangers of modernity or the dangers of the displinary society.

44. Dreyfus and Rabinow, "What Is Maturity?" p. 115.

45. Dreyfus and Rabinow, "What Is Maturity?" p. 115. Even Dreyfus and Rabinow say that Foucault "owes us a criterion of what makes one kind of danger more dangerous than another." See the 1983 afterword to *Michel Foucault: Beyond Structuralism and Hermeneutics,* p. 264.

46. John Rajchman emphasizes Foucault's historical nominalism in his book *Michel Foucault: The Freedom of Philosophy* (New York: Columbia University Press, 1985).

47. Michel Foucault, *Power/Knowledge* (New York: Pantheon Books, 1980), p. 80.

48. Foucault, *Power/Knowledge,* p. 85.

49. Blanchot acutely perceives that even in *Madness and Civilization* the primary theme is "the power of exclusion." See "Michel Foucault as I Imagine Him," p. 65.

50. Habermas notes an interesting parallel between Foucault's appeal to specific *insurrections of subjugated knowledges* and Lukács more global argument about the "privileged" possibilities of knowledge by the proletariat. See *The Philosophical Discourse of Modernity,* p. 280.

51. Foucault, *The History of Sexuality,* vol. 1, p. 95.

52. Foucault, *The History of Sexuality,* vol. 1, p. 95.

53. John Rajchman characterizes Foucault's politics as a postrevolutionary "politics of revolt." But he never answers the question Why revolt? or In the name of what? See chapter 2, "The Politics of Revolt," in *Michel Foucault: The Freedom of Philosophy.*

54. John Rajchman, *Michel Foucault: The Freedom of Philosophy,* pp. 2, 4.

55. Like Rajchman, Hiley approaches Foucault by situating him in the tradition of skepticism. See "Knowledge and Power," in *Philosophy in Question.* This is not a new theme in Foucault. In an interview with J. K. Simon in *Partisan Review* 38 (1971), he said, "What I am trying to do is grasp the implicit systems which determine our most familiar behavior without our knowing it. I am trying to find their origin, to show their formation, the constraint they impose upon us. I am therefore trying to place myself at a distance from them and to show how one could escape."

56. G. W. F. Hegel, *The Phenomenology of Spirit* (Oxford: Oxford University Press, 1977), p. 51.

57. Michel Foucault, "On the Genealogy of Ethics: An Overview of Work in Progress," p. 352.

58. Dreyfus and Rabinow, "What Is Maturity?" p. 112.

59. Michel Foucault, "On the Genealogy of Ethics," p. 350.

60. See, for example Mark Poster, "Foucault and the Tyranny of Greece"; Arnold I. Davidson, "Archaeology, Genealogy, Ethics"; and Ian Hacking, "Self-Improvement." These essays are in *Foucault: A Critical Reader.* See also Reiner Schürmann, "On Constituting Oneself as an Anarchistic Subject," in *Praxis International* 6 (1986): 294–310.

61. See David Hiley's discussion of this problem in "Knowledge and Power," pp. 110–114.

62. Michel Foucault, "Polemics, Politics, and Problemizations: An Interview," in *The Foucault Reader,* p. 381.

11

The Face in the Sand: Foucault and the Anthropological Slumber

Herbert Schnädelbach

Translated by William Rehg

The rumor has been spreading and can now be heard on all sides: man's hour has come.[1] In announcing the death of God, Nietzsche supposedly became the first to insinuate the death of man; his echo resounds in the chorus of voices renouncing humanism and urgently recommending that man finally bid himself farewell. "Farewell to man" means the end of the notion that man is the center of the world, the author of his history and the foundation of all knowledge, including the knowledge of himself. This modern antihumanism says that man should no longer make himself into a principle but should realize he is merely an epiphenomenon of subhuman and superhuman powers and processes. It demands his abdication as monarch of all being and his conversion from cosmological narcissism, that absolute paranoia in which everything merely revolves around him.

This does not mean man's death in a literal sense but is only a somewhat dramatic metaphor for his decentering. No doubt its current voguishness has more than a little to do with this melodramatic quality. However, the tidings that man is dead get amplified in other ways as well, the first of which is the shock that an openly propagated antihumanism deals to our moral sensibility. We are assured here that this has nothing to do with a partisanship for the inhuman but is rather a theoretical position able to show that depriving *the* human being of power, in a practical respect as well, is the necessary condition for human *beings* at last finding their way to themselves and to a life of human dignity. The concordance of opinion on this is astounding. Heidegger explains the point as follows:

> The highest determinations of the essence of man in humanism still do not realize the proper dignity of man. To that extent the thinking in *Being and Time* is against humanism. But this opposition does not mean that such thinking aligns itself against the humane and advocates the inhuman, that it promotes the inhumane and deprecates the dignity of man. Humanism is opposed because it does not set the *humanitas* of man high enough. Of course the essential worth of man does not consist in his being the substance of beings, as the "Subject" among them, so that as the tyrant of Being he may deign to release the beingness of beings into an all too loudly bruited "objectivity."
>
> Man is rather "thrown" from Being itself into the truth of Being, so that ek-sisting in this fashion he might guard the truth of Being. . . . Man is the shepherd of Being.[2]

Only the decentered human being can live in a human fashion, i.e., according to his true makeup. Even B. F. Skinner says this:

> We are told that what is threatened is "man *qua* man," or "man in his humanity," or "man as Thou not It," or "man as a person not a thing." These are not very helpful expressions, but they supply a clue. What is being abolished is autonomous man—the inner man, the homunculus, the possessing demon, the man defended by the literatures of freedom and dignity.
>
> His abolition has long been overdue. . . . Science does not dehumanize man, it de-homunculizes him, and it must do so if it is to prevent the abolition of the human species.[3]

Precisely this concern about the self-abolition of man through his hybrid striving for autonomy also motivates the modern critique of anthropocentrism in ethics, as well as all the contemporary attempts to resituate the grounding of norms in pre-Kantian soil. Hans Jonas describes his *Imperative of Responsibility* this way: "The old questions concerning the relation of 'is' and 'ought', cause and end, nature and value are reopened from an ontological perspective in order that, going beyond value subjectivism, the newly manifest duty of human beings might be anchored in being."[4] Jonas asks that for the sake of the physical and moral survival of humanity, we finally vacate the normative center [of the universe] and realize that "the anthropocentric confinement of former ethics no longer holds."[5]

As the above examples indicate, a further reason for the success of theoretical antihumanism lies in its ability to address—from metaphysical, technological, and ethical points of view—the concern about the human and human dignity. This allows it quickly to pacify and even win to its own side the sentiments stirred up by its antihuman rhetoric. However, the noteworthy unclarity of the catch words it employs also contributes to its resonant power: "death of man," of the "subject," or of the "individual" (whose death are we talking about, anyhow?).[6] *Man,* or what we have considered such up to now, could die under the pressure of interpretations and arguments speaking against his continued survival without his ever having been a subject. The *subject* would in turn be capable of continued existence, even after the "death of man," as long as one does not confuse it with man as he actually exists. The philosophy of the subject and anthropology are not by definition identical, for subjectivity is a set of general determinations that real human beings may or may not exemplify. Social relations are conceivable in which human beings have ceased being subjects because this property has entirely passed on to institutions and machines. Conversely, Marx and Engels hoped that in the postrevolutionary future, human beings would finally become subjects of their own history and destiny, whose objects they were hitherto. "The end of the *individual*" refers to yet a third thesis. A platitude of cultural critique since the twenties, it is quite compatible with an anthropological and subject-philosophical orientation and was almost always presented this way as well. According to the conservative version, the new collectivism threatens precisely when man insists on being the world's center and sole point of orientation, or in Heidegger's words, the "substance of beings, as the 'Subject' among them."[7] This makes decentering of the subject "man" appear as the necessary presupposition of true individuality. Consequently, as the motto of theoretical antihumanism, "the death of man" means that what dies or has to die is man as subject of himself and of the human world, and in this sense it is also reasonable to speak of "the death of the subject."[8]

The thesis of the end of the subject "man" gains its greatest impetus, however, from the contemporary scientific knowledge of human beings. Here man himself has become, after God and nature, an anthropomorphism.[9] We find it ever more difficult to connect what we reliably know about ourselves from empirical science with what we immediately know about ourselves in lifeworld contexts. Conversely, the anthropomorphic self-image [acquired in the lifeworld] is the first thing one must give up if one wants to talk about the human being in a scientific fashion. Such prescientific acquaintance with ourselves prepares us to be neither subjects nor objects of science.[10] The decentering of the human being this engenders in the human sciences not only has a methodological side, however. The fact that today no single discipline can really answer the question What is the human being? has the same effect. This is just as true of the natural sciences as of the social sciences and humanities. Their experts find nothing more embarrassing than the remark, "You know so much; why don't you tell us this, then: what is the human being?" While they can always make some response to this, the question is too much for all of them. Thus when the human being strives for a most reliable, i.e., scientific, knowledge about himself, he must in today's scientific civilization piece together his self-image from purely heterogeneous bits of information. He is a highly complex organism, a caprice of evolution, a disruptive exception in the earth's biosphere, a historical configuration, a point of intersection in the social ensemble—and in each case one always notices that such information merely applies what the dominant sciences of the day (biology, theory of evolution, ecology, history, sociology) happen to know much more precisely in their respective domains. The necessity compelling human beings first of all to look away from themselves in order to make objective science possible makes the human being appear as a mere epiphenomenon of something much more reliably investigated elsewhere. For this reason the humanities are continually afflicted by doubts about their scientific character, or else they understand themselves as secondary disciplines that digest and apply [scientific results]. This also holds for philosophical anthropology.[11] As its name indicates, if anthropology were per se philosophical, it would not need the supplement "philosophical." At the same time, this supplement is obviously meant to indicate the self-referential character of this discipline, without which anthropology is "objective" science, human biology. The radical solution is the total abolition of the human being in the territory governed by the traditional human sciences: psychology without psyche (Skinner), history without a subject (Lübbe), the theory of social systems without actors (Luhmann), linguistic science without speakers (Saussure), and finally as a provisional halting point, even anthropology without human beings (Lévi-Strauss).

Thus the philosophical critique of humanism and a deanthropologization carried to completion in the human sciences have merged together in our century and powerfully reinforced each other. Only in this way can one really understand the current journalistic power that decentering enjoys. Michel Foucault's *Order of Things* joins the philosophical and empirical-scientific dimensions of this thesis with a third, the epistemological. "Man will disappear"[12]—Foucault makes this prognosis only on the basis of "archaeologically" identifiable changes in the depths of forms of knowing and discursive practices already guiding the philosophy and science of an epoch. Hence such archaeology is not supposed to be reducible to either philosophy or science: "As the archaeology of our thought easily shows, man is an invention of recent date. And one perhaps nearing its end."[13] Thus he is merely "a new wrinkle in our knowledge," and one can be sure "that he will disappear again as soon as that knowledge has discovered a new form."[14] These forms of knowing (*episteme*) do not depend on man, but he depends on them. Indeed, he is nothing more than the product of a linguistic fault line located at the transition from the classical age to modernity in 1800:

> In classical thinking man did not exist. What did exist in the place where we now discover man was the capacity—peculiar to discourse and language—to represent things. . . . At the end of the 18th century discourse ceased to play the organizing role it possessed in classical thinking. . . . In contrast, in the lacuna discourse left behind man constituted himself. . . . Man existed where discourse fell silent.[15]

If today we must reckon with changes of *episteme* similar to those that brought on the modern age in the wake of the classical—changes Foucault sees intimated by the "return of language," through which "man will return to that serene nonexistence in which he was formerly maintained by the imperious unity of Discourse"[16]—if such changes are presently afoot, then "one can certainly wager that man [will] be erased, like a face drawn in sand at the edge of the sea."[17]

1

"Man had been a figure occurring between two modes of language."[18] This news of the end of man, broadcast from an anticipated posthumanist perspective, also determines Foucault's version of a history of the philosophical discourse of modernity. Its point is that precisely at the moment when man stepped onto the stage of knowledge and the "human sciences" came into being, philosophy fell into the "anthropological slumber (*sommeil*)," though it had scarcely been awakened from its dogmatic slumber by Kant.[19] Foucault also describes the break with precritical metaphysics as due to the collapse of the order of things in the sign of representation. Man then steps into this vacuum as the only possible guarantor of cognitive order in general. As a result, he also moves into the center of things philosophically. Foucault understands Kant's Copernican revolution as an anthropological turn, as the genesis of an "epistemological consciousness of man as such."[20] This epistemological turn to man "became necessary at the moment when representation lost the power to determine, on its own and in a single movement, the interplay of its syntheses and analyses."[21] The dilemma in this solution, however, consists, according to Foucault, in a conflation of two spheres that previously were clearly separated. On the one side, knowledge of the actual human being took the form of a knowledge of human nature or the human essence on the same level as the knowledge of nature. On the other side, metaphysics existed as the epitome of "transcendental" knowledge, i.e., the conditions first making knowledge of man and nature possible, though these were not supposed to have anything to do with man. According to Foucault's presentation, both cognitive levels collapse into one another as a result of the crisis in representation.

There is an empirical-transcendental short circuit whose sparks spawn "man," a sensible-intelligible hermaphrodite completely overburdened by the task of henceforth producing by himself achievements that the old order of things would have taken from his shoulders. Foucault plays off Kant's terminology when he speaks of anthropology as the "analytic of man." It is, in addition, an analytic of finitude, because man is actually known only as an empirical being, his transcendental heightening notwithstanding.[22] However, this ambiguous empirical-transcendental bipolarity in the knowledge of man remains dogmatic: "The anthropological configuration of modern philosophy consists in doubling over dogmatism, in dividing it into two different levels each lending support to and limiting the other: the pre-critical analysis of what man is in his essence becomes the analytic of everything that can, in general, be presented to man's experience."[23]

According to Foucault, anthropology is the key to the philosophical discourse of modernity. This discourse is ruined by its own aporias, which necessarily result from the problematic of an analytic of finitude. In Foucault's view, they fit together to form an "anthropological 'quadrilateral'"[24] whose baseline is laid down by the "repetition of the positive within the fundamental [*Fundamentalen*],"[25] for precisely the crux of anthropocentrism is its concern with a foundation [*Fundament*] that is supposed to be just as positively available as what has need of the foundation to begin with. In epistemology this "repetition" signifies the "reduplication" of the empirical in the transcendental, from which man emerges as a "strange empirico-transcendental doublet," since he appears there as a being in which "knowledge will be attained . . . of what renders all knowledge possible."[26] Foucault joins the epistemological repetition of that "repetition" with its object-theoretic and metaphysical segments, thereby closing the quadrilateral of aporias with "the perpetual relation of the *cogito* to the unthought" and the "retreat and return of the origin."[27] This perpetual oscillating of knowledge between primary and derived, original and originated, *principium* and *principiatum,* ultimately signifies the collapse of the discourse of modernity, the "end of man" as "return of the beginning of philosophy" and the "return of language," which again moves to center stage.[28] Consequently, Foucault sees the entire philosophical discourse of modernity as simply an anthropocentric intermezzo in the history of thought. "Anthropology" thus appears as "the fundamental arrangement that has governed . . . the path of philosophical thought from Kant until our own day,"[29] reigning during the brief lifespan of man, who supposedly has been only "a figure occurring between two modes of language."[30]

While this tableau is impressive, it does not correspond to the facts. It is not the case that modern philosophy as a whole is anthropocentric. In fact, it is not even the only anthropocentric episode in the history of philosophy. (Naturally, one could defend Foucault at this point by arguing that he defines the expressions "modern" and "anthropocentric" in precisely such a way that they apply to the epochs he analyzes, but this would render the expressions out-and-out circular and thus destroy the explanatory value Foucault wants them to have in his analyses.) In the first place, we can identify at least three figures of anthropocentric philosophizing that "grand" philosophy always took as provocations deserving of vehement response: Sophist philosophy, Enlightenment empiricism, and left Hegelianism. Protagoras' "The human being is the measure of all things" provoked Plato to react with his enraged "Why not the pig or the baboon?" and the counterclaim "God is the measure of all things."[31] The Platonic theory of Ideas represents the first decentering of the human being in the history of philosophy, and one can write the entire history of metaphysics as a series of attempts to stabilize this [decentering] in ever new ways against the danger of Sophist skepticism constantly looming on the horizon. Enlightenment empiricism is anthropocentric because after the rejection of Cartesian innate ideas, it finds the site of the *cogito* empty of anything that would point beyond the human. Kant opposed this return of skepticism with his transcendental program. The third type of anthropocentrism is Feuerbach's and hence that of left Hegelianism: "The new philosophy makes man—with the inclusion of nature as the foundation of man—the unique, universal and highest object of philosophy. It thus makes anthropology, with the inclusion of physiology, the universal science."[32] Thus only this third form of philosophy reduced ad hominem satisfies the conditions Foucault considers characteristic for the philosophical discourse of modernity as a whole, whereas the other two forms can be easily associated with the discourse of similarity and representation, i.e., with ancient (predominant up to the Renaissance) and classical *episteme.* My thesis, then, is the following: Foucault's picture of the philosophical discourse of modernity is the result of an untenable left Hegelian projection; his archaeology of the human sciences—whose explanatory power will not be disputed here—cannot be satisfactorily applied to the most recent history of philosophy.

The Hegelian projection becomes clearer in Foucault's closer description of the very "anthropological quadrilateral" he seeks to destroy. The universal mediation of the positive and the fundamental, the empirical and the transcendental, the thought and the unthought, and the primary and the derived—this was the gigantic program of Hegelian dialectic. Only the thinking that sticks to this program, in however modest a form, oscillates back and forth between those poles without awakening from the anthropological slumber, for that slumber, Foucault writes, is "so deep that thought experiences it paradoxically as vigilance, so wholly does it confuse the circularity of a dogmatism folded over upon itself in order to find a basis for itself within itself with the agility and anxiety of a radically philosophical thought."[33] A "circularity of a dogmatism folded over upon itself in order to find a basis for itself within itself" is a precise epistemological description of the basic motif guiding all dialectical systems, be they idealistic, materialistic or whatever: the Absolute internally differentiating itself, alienating itself from itself, and thereby rediscovering itself as unity and stabilizing itself.[34] Foucault holds this basic motif responsible for philosophy's sterile arousal in its anthropological slumber. However, he projects not the genuinely Hegelian but rather the left Hegelian version of this motif on philosophy, for he considers this philosophy as a whole anthropological. "From Kant until our own day" he sees only circular dogmatism or dogmatic circularity bearing the label "man."

This view of things, however, is plausible only if one considers the dialectical anthropology founded by Feuerbach and sociologized by the young Marx to be the rational kernel of Hegelianism and then goes on to refer this back to Kant. In the process, the Hegelian critique of Kant, simply presumed to be finished and legitimate, functions as a bridge. If Hegel is to Kant as Feuerbach is to Hegel, then transcendental philosophy must appear in the light of a Hegelian and left Hegelian double projection as an "analytic of finitude," and Kant's Copernican revolution as an anthropological turn. In *The Order of Things* Foucault cites Kant's famous questions What can I know? What ought I do? What may I hope? What is man? And he takes Kant's remark "At bottom all this could be reckoned to be anthropology, because the first three questions are related to the last" as reason for dating the birth of Feuerbachian man back to Kant.[35] But even if Kant's philosophy is anthropological in the sense that the individual philosopher is oriented to a "pragmatic point of view"—"Physiological knowledge of man investigates what *nature* makes of him: pragmatic, what *man* as a free agent makes, or can and should make, of himself"[36]—Foucault's dating procedure overlooks its nonanthropological foundations. The question What is man? guides the critical enterprise only from a pragmatic point of view. At the same time, this question does not precede that enterprise but rather enters only at the conclusion, when the question of ends arises. Only as a being that posits goals itself [*selber zweckesetzendes*], and not as a natural being, is man a final end [*Endzweck*]. Not anthropology but only a metaphysics of morals grounded in critical reason can show that this is the case. Kant's philosophy is not anthropocentric—his exchanges with empiricism and popular German philosophy show this only too well. For in his view intersubjectively valid science and universal morality are possible only on the condition that the actual, empirical human being is decentered.[37] For Kant, transcendental subjectivity is a set of principles that first constitute individual identity, personality, and moral autonomy in general. To understand this as anthropological would mean pushing Kant's philosophy straight into the whirlpool of bisected dogmatism, whereupon one can throw in Hegel or Nietzsche, depending on one's position, as a life preserver.

The objections to this interpretation of Kant are well known: Did he not unite the empirical and the transcendental in the human essence and banish man to the diremption [or division: *Entzweiung*] of a split self-consciousness? Is this hardship that comes with finitude not that of which Adorno used to speak, i.e., that of the strict separation between thing-in-itself and appearance? These questions have always already adopted that Hegelian perspective that Adorno foisted upon Kant: Kant the philosopher of subjective consciousness, of abstract understanding [*Verstandes*], of finitude, of diremption. Thus Kant's work must appear as the document of a tragic dualistic ontology, and the tradition running through Hölderlin, Schelling, Hegel, and Marx as a promising, even if unfinished, solution. A dialectic between the empirical and the transcendental in Kant could obtain only if both were located at the same ontological level. But Kant wrote the paralogism chapter in the *Critique of Pure Reason* in order to exclude such an ontologization of the transcendental; it was Descartes's error, not Kant's, to mistake "I think" for "I" or the *res cogitans*. There is simply no possibility that the "I think" *exists* as the I, i.e., as I exist, but rather I can always only *say* "I think" as an addition to my mental involvement with my representations.[38] What nonetheless sounds in Kant like a two-world theory of the subject acquires a reasonable meaning only if one understands the whole of the transcendental as the competence of empirical human beings for following determinate rules and principles in thought, knowledge, and action. Such rules first make science and morality, in the emphatic sense of these terms, at all possible. That the human being can do this makes him a rational being. At the same time, this does not imply a primary anthropological proposition, because he has reason to consider himself rational only where science and morality actually "take place."[39] The human being is precisely not the author of these rules and principles but is rather the place of their application and actualization in specific, strictly limited contexts. To ask about the "modes" of these rules and principles so that one can continue to press charges of anthropological dualism would amount to mixing up discourses, as though the rules of chess and its actual play existed at two levels that could only be mediated dialectically. It makes just as little sense to project the conditions for the possibility of actual science and morality upon just this level of factual occurrence so that an allegedly immanent critique can then identify dogmatic circularities in Kant.

Kant's philosophy is a philosophy of finitude, but not in the sense of the anthropological-anthropocentric "analytic of finitude" that Foucault takes as the crux of the entire philosophical discourse of modernity. In Kant "finitude" means that thinking cannot master the absolute—hence his separation of thing-in-itself and appearance, together with the critique of metaphysics that this separation entails. That this also has consequences for anthropology is no reason for understanding this expression as primarily anthropological, nor is it so intended. Kant's philosophy is not a philosophy of the finite being "man," and the same can be asserted even more emphatically about the whole of German idealism. The latter transforms transcendental philosophy into a philosophy of absolute subjectivity, and to consider this anthropological at heart requires even greater projective straining than does the identification of transcendental philosophy with anthropology. The subject is not man but the Fichtean Ego, Schelling's "Nature" or "primordial act of will," from which it is only a small step to Schopenhauer's "Will" and Hegel's Absolute Idea. What man might be or should be is, in contrast, always something wholly derivative and ephemeral. To this extent the German idealists also keep their distance from a skeptical sophist anthropocentrism. Thus Hegel in the *Encyclopedia* assigns anthropology at most a wholly subordinate place in the system—as the theory of subjective spirit in its immediacy, i.e., as soul or natural spirit.[40] And in the *Philosophy of Right* all his anti-ideological ridicule is poured out on the "composite idea which we call *man*," which he locates in the "system of needs" of civil society. Hegel identifies this "man" as *bourgeois,* therewith implicitly identifying the anthropological thinking of the Enlightenment as *bourgeois* philosophy.[41] However, if the whole of German idealism can only be read as anthropocentric at the price of violent reinterpretation, one must ask oneself which philosophy Nietzsche is supposed to have awakened from the anthropological slumber: Only the left Hegelians? Or Kierkegaard, whom he evidently did not know and whose turn from the ethical to the religious actually constitutes a decentering that sublates [*aufhebt*] the turn to the actually existing human being? If one considers that neither *Lebensphilosophie* since Schopenhauer, value philosophy, Husserl of the *Logical Investigations,* nor Frege thought anthropocentrically, then Foucault's diagnoses hold only for the narrow left-Hegelian and Hegelian-Marxist tradition that joined hands in France with the phenomenology of the late Husserl and finally found its way through the productive misunderstandings of *Being and Time* to Sartre and Merleau-Ponty. Thus it may occasionally strike one that the only rational content to Foucault's theory of the anthropological slumber is his exchange with Sartre and his break with the Hegelian past that he acquired at the feet of Hyppolite and the young Althusser.[42]

Yet such an interpretation would be unsatisfactory for the simple reason that Foucault only marginally adopts the role of historian of philosophy. His theme is the *episteme* of modernity after the collapse of the discourse of representation. At issue is the archaeology of the human sciences, not that of Hegelianism. Foucault's reconstruction of this *episteme* becomes much more plausible if one seeks to illustrate it not so much in prominent philosophies as in the real praxis and self-understanding of science, for it could well be that philosophical systems are reacting against this praxis with the aim of yet making Plato's victory over Protagoras a permanent one. In that case, the attempts by Nietzsche and pragmatism to rehabilitate Sophist philosophy represent more than a symptom.[43] My thesis is this: the fate of modernity is that it must draw [*schöpfen*] not only its normative but also its cognitive foundations out of itself;[44] after the end of metaphysics these foundations, as the a priori of science, lie no longer at a higher level but at the same level as the objects of scientific knowledge. This seems to be the real reason for the circularities Foucault describes between the positive and the fundamental, the empirical and the transcendental, as well as for the problems these subsequently engender. In this perspective the natural, historical, or social man, as he knows himself from the natural, historical, and social sciences, must himself assume the role of transcendental synthesis—as "sensuous being" (Feuerbach), as "historical consciousness" (Dilthey), as "*ensemble* of the social relations" (Marx). No metaphysical Beyond can take this burden from him. It is astonishing that the reflexive couplings this entails—the subject of the natural sciences is itself a natural being, the subject of the historical sciences a historical being, and the subject of the social sciences a social being—were always celebrated in the nineteenth century as advances in enlightenment through demythologization, although they in fact led to mortgages in the philosophy of science that even today are not paid off.[45]

The costs of this epistemological turn to the subject were hardly noticed. This stems from the fact that the turn was executed, as a rule, without the speculative totalization that alone leads to aporias and antinomies in self-referential patterns of thought—there is no need for a dialectic if one does not insist on asking about the whole.[46] The alternative is *practical pragmatism.* By this I mean an attitude of doing science that abstains from transcendental questions of principle and is content to take the plausibility of those anthropocentric couplings at face value and otherwise to proceed pragmatically. One can at some point be quite justified in taking the positive fundamentally, whereas in other contexts this is not recommended. Why should the empirical not also for once play a transcendental role as a relative a priori? The Kantian who staunchly resists this move can then be consoled with the remark that we are just beginning, so perhaps later we can do things differently. If he is still not satisfied, he will be charged with metaphysical foundationalism.[47] Practical pragmatism is the pragmatic way of dealing with Foucault's "anthropological quadrilateral." In the course of time it has learned a variety of justifications from the philosophy of science, even where pragmatism as a theory is expressly criticized. The older positivism still belonged to the philosophy of representation. Its conventionalistic dissolution, already underway in Mach and completed by Popper and Neurath, has left pragmatism with porous boundaries, for after the break with the "myth of the given" everything in science has become purely a question of instrumental expediency.[48] This conventionalism only conceptualizes the fact that modern science is defined no longer ontologically but methodologically, and the norms for this can only be introduced anthropocentrically, i.e., against the background of some "picture of the human being," be it naturalistic, historical, or culturalistic. This corresponds to the fact that the modern sciences no longer have a real use for the concept of truth. The natural and technological sciences work with models that function more or less well, while the so-called humanistic disciplines [*Geisteswissenschaften*] provide more or less convincing narrations and interpretations. But what scientist can claim these are "true" in some emphatic sense? Although such philosophers of science as Popper stubbornly defend the concept of truth, the reality of science shows this to be rather dispensable. Thus the wearying schizophrenia between practical pragmatism and epistemological realism can finally be given up. One need only bid "farewell to matters of principle" (Marquard), even in the philosophy of science, which then would finally correspond to the pragmatic praxis of science.

The *episteme* of modernity is pragmatistic and achieves its philosophical self-awareness in functionalism. It gets by without those totalizing self-closures that speculative philosophy alone found so necessary. In his fascination for Hegelianism, however, Foucault projects these on the philosophical discourse of modernity as a whole, thereby producing the image of the anthropological slumber. The history of twentieth-century philosophy is, above all else, a history of protests against this pragmatism: the latter's anthropocentric unconcern was once again supposed to be met by the Platonic and Kantian decentering of the empirical human being. Here one can mention the struggles against psychologism in logic conducted by Frege, Husserl, and the neo-Kantians, as also the new ontologies and theories of objective value and even Russell's and Wittgenstein's philosophy of an ideal language. Heidegger I have already mentioned. In terms of the history of philosophy, Foucault's *Order of Things* should be included in this series of farewells to man, even if he confuses the domination of practical pragmatism with the speculative dreams of philosophy in its anthropological slumber. For Foucault, as for Heidegger, man must disappear so that thinking might again become possible: "It is no longer possible to think in our day other than in the void left by man's disappearance. For this void does not create a deficiency; it does not constitute a lacuna that must be filled. It is nothing more, and nothing less, than the unfolding of a space in which it is once more possible to think."[49] Heidegger puts it this way: "But if man is to find his way once again into the nearness of Being he must first learn to exist in the nameless."[50] This "nameless" corresponds to Foucault's "void left by man's disappearance," because once man "has strayed into subjectivity," thinking can only reach the nameless through "the descent . . . [in]to the poverty of the ek-sistence of *homo humanus*."[51] This renunciation of reputed humanistic riches decenters the human being as subject and gives back language its primacy over the language user, a process Foucault describes as reinstating the rightful entitlements of discourse.[52]

2

If it is correct that Foucault's archaeology of the human sciences has primarily diagnosed the modern *episteme* emergent in the praxis of practical pragmatism, which is anthropocentric without totalizing self-closure, then how can this be reconciled with the opening claim that the scientific decentering of man is synchronous with the philosophical one? The answer is that precisely practical pragmatism with its anthropocentric plausibilities can afford to abstain from Kant's decisive closing question, one that orients everything else: What is man? Hence such pragmatism readily accords with the theoretical antihumanism of the human sciences. Whatever shocking things such antihumanism might say about man, they will not ruffle the pragmatist in questions of method and morality, for he will deal with those assertions too in a pragmatic manner. Practical pragmatism is a stance so anthropocentric that it can abstain from fundamental reflection on the human being. This attitude, not primarily the philosophy called "pragmatism," is what Heidegger meant when he presented it as the truth of the "*homo animalis* of metaphysics." For him, anthropology and pragmatism are two sides of the same thing.[53]

From this it follows that the mutually reinforcing processes of the scientific and philosophical decenterings of man stem from opposed roots, which does not mean they are incompatible. By contrast, the explicit and consistent anthropocentrism that has not already made every possible pragmatic concession must find itself in a rather hopeless minority position: here I refer to the currently much-reviled tradition of left Hegelianism that stretches from Feuerbach through the young Marx and Lukács down to the older critical theory, Bloch, Sartre, and praxis philosophy. This line still takes seriously the totality motif, borrowed from a materialistically inverted Hegel, of a human species being producing and reproducing itself through social praxis. Foucault was wrong when he simply identified this limited conceptual configuration with the philosophical discourse of modernity. In doing this, he also unintentionally aided and abetted all those who presently consider modernity as a whole a left-Hegelian project and, reaching back to premodern thinking, announce the postmodern era.[54] To consider the anthropological slumber the distinguishing feature of modern philosophy per se is philosophical ethnocentrism, the presence of which in Foucault can probably only be explained in biographical terms.

And yet Foucault's analyses are quite current, for they contain a striking diagnosis not only of modernity's practical-pragmatistic *episteme* but also of the totalizing-anthropocentric philosophy that in our century is mainly found in so-called Hegelian-Marxist circles. Foucault's "anthropological quadrilateral" very precisely describes the configuration of aporias in which such thinking inevitably gets entangled. The "repetition of the positive within the fundamental"—precisely this is the result of bringing together anthropology and epistemology, a combination that becomes attractive after the transition from Feuerbach to Marx. Critical theory, for example, attempts to bring it off as the unity of epistemology and social theory.[55] What results is a grand theory with an empirical-transcendental dual status that, though indeed fascinating for enthusiasts of grand theory, in effect creates more problems than it can solve. Most important, one no longer has the option of falling back on the Hegelian dialectic once one has abandoned the premises of absolute idealism. Despite Adorno's "negative dialectic," every postidealist attempt to reconstruct the dialectic in a manner logically adequate to an empirical-transcendental totality must be judged a failure.[56] On the basis of this two-faced concept of totality, Foucault implicitly explains other basic motifs of Hegelian-Marxist thought as well. On his view, the alleged unity of the empirical and the transcendental implies that a theory construed this way would like to be both empirical and critical, i.e., it attempts to orient itself simultaneously toward the truth of the facts and toward the truth of the discourse disclosing the facts. As a result, we find ourselves in a discourse that wants to be at once positivistic and eschatological, though in fact it simply oscillates between two poles, which Foucault sees personified in Comte and Marx.[57] Thus in a theory of this type man must appear "as a truth both reduced and promised."[58] From this standpoint we can also understand the genesis of the theory of alienation and its significance for the Marxist-inspired followers of Hegel. The presupposed unity of the empirical and the transcendental cannot be redeemed in the world of actual human beings. Since Hegel the theory of alienation has functioned to explain the obvious discrepancy between the species being Man, which conditions everything, and empirical-historical human beings. The speculative-theological motif taken up by Hegel, i.e., an Absolute that alienates itself and reconciles itself with what has been alienated, assumes in Feuerbach and Marx an anthropologically and historico-philosophically secularized form. Hence even here the idea of alienation corresponds to an eschatology of reconciliation, i.e., a condition in which Man and the human being will finally correspond to each other. Until then, however, the human being no longer exists and does not yet exist. Anthropology thus becomes negative,[59] and the philosophy of history receives the task of solving the puzzle this poses. The solution lies in utopian thinking. If, against all empirical evidence, one wants to hold on to Man as the "empirical-transcendental doublet," then after the break with theology and metaphysics one can no longer project this into the Beyond. However, if one is to save at least the idea of this doublet, one must also remove it from the presence of the present that one criticizes.[60] But this unity is also not supposed to be a "mere" idea, for that would clash with the dual empirical-critical character of the theory and its basic concepts. Thus as the unlocated location of its redemption, the indeterminate albeit rationally anticipated future offers its services. This "concrete" utopia (Bloch) attempts to solve the empirical-transcendental dilemma by means of temporalization.

Foucault presents a further aspect of this dilemma under the title "The '*Cogito*' and the Unthought."[61] Even from an object-theoretic point of view, the anthropocentric totalization leads the theory to oscillate constantly between the poles of thinking and what is thought, for only their absolute unity could satisfy the theory's totalizing claims. The no longer Cartesian but modern *cogito* must be connected in an evident way with its own and the world's being, indeed, at the place where the empirical-transcendental double essence Man constitutes himself and his world. The constant confrontation of the *cogito* with the unthought is, according to Foucault, a mechanism that necessarily results from that anthropocentric totalization. Everywhere it turns, the *cogito* encounters something empirical that at the same time means the transcendental without being able to represent it. Thus, both on the side of the subject and of the object, what is unthought in thought constantly recedes, reproducing itself as a constant task. In the context of his concise explanations Foucault mentions Husserl, but it is not difficult to relate this to Sartre, Adorno, and Freud—the theoreticians of the "être-pour-soi," the nonidentical, and the unconscious. Adorno returned to utopian thinking as a way out of the epistemological dilemma of the *cogito* and the unthought: "To want substance in cognition is to want a utopia."[62]

Even in Foucault's fourth motif of the "anthropological quadrilateral," "The Retreat and Return of the Origin," one can find diagnostic allusions to Hegelian Marxism. Although no one subscribes to the Enlightenment myths of the origin of language or the state, this does not mean everyone, like the positivists and pragmatists, has bid farewell to questions of origin in general. Rather, in a manner analogous to the empirical-transcendental fallacy, origins are now viewed as something that is constantly present in the originated without thereby being immediately tangible, for that would negate [*höbe . . . auf*] the difference between origin and originated, or between the transcendental and the empirical. Thus the origin necessarily appears as something that, because constantly obscured in the originated, always reproduces itself as a task. According to Foucault, this distinguishes modern historical thinking from the traditional approach to origins.[63] This could be spelled out by means of the Marxian thesis that human beings, though themselves continually producing and reproducing their life conditions, cannot comprehend this and put it to practical advantage so long as their prehistory lasts. Here again the solution lies in a turn to utopian thinking, i.e., in a future condition of society in which human beings themselves finally consciously make their history. After the end of prehistory their own true origins would no longer evade them, and the task of practically appropriating those origins would be solved. As Foucault describes it, the constant dialectic of origin and originated under anthropocentric conditions is probably no less than the theoretical basis of the problem of alienation itself, a problem apprehended in such a way that it allows nothing but a utopian solution.

Foucault's critical diagnosis of the philosophical discourse of modernity, which he sees only slowly awakening from its "anthropological slumber," essentially concerns only Hegelian Marxism (aside from a few sidelong glances at Husserl). Precisely this is the reason that his diagnosis also has considerable relevance for students of critical theory, a tradition with which Foucault was not very familiar but nonetheless had in mind when he wrote *The Order of Things*.[64] The same holds for the reconstruction of critical theory in the work of Jürgen Habermas. From Foucault's point of view, *Knowledge and Human Interests* still operates entirely within the "anthropological quadrilateral": the unity of social theory and epistemology is maintained and cognitive interests have an empirical-transcendental dual status, for "the achievements of the transcendental subject have their basis in the natural history of the human species."[65] When Habermas writes that "knowledge-constitutive interests take form in the medium of work, language and power,"[66] he hits almost precisely those three domains Foucault sees occupied by the "human sciences," at once empirical and transcendental: "language, life, and labour."[67] From Foucault's perspective, *Knowledge and Human Interests* is also an example of the discourse that would like to be both empirical and critical, at once positivistic and eschatological. Already at this point, and not just after his reception of Peirce prompted by Apel, Habermas attempts to bring the real and the ideal into a more than merely conceptual relation to each other via the motif of counterfactual anticipation. One should note too how Habermas's approach, even before he gave critical theory a "language-analytic turn" (Wellmer), provides a model for that cross-contamination of anthropology and philosophy of language to which Foucault would respond with nothing but a "philosophical laugh."[68] One can see this in the following: "The human interest in autonomy and responsibility is not mere fancy, for it can be apprehended a priori. What raises us out of nature is the only thing whose nature we can know: *language*. Through its structure, autonomy and responsibility are posited for us."[69] Habermas's later linguistic turn is certainly no example of Foucault's "return of language," through which the human being allegedly will again disappear. Hence the fundamental changes Habermas has since undertaken in this concept of critical theory at least seem to indirectly confirm Foucault's analyses in *The Order of Things,* for they follow the trend toward the pragmatic *episteme* constituting the heart of modern anthropocentrism. The basis of grand theory, which now no longer links social theory so much to epistemology as to a theory of rationality, is a universal or formal pragmatics, i.e., a formal theory of action having a quasi-transcendental status but open to the empirical through the method of fallible rule construction. "Pragmatic" and "pragmatism" is not merely a play on words, for Apel's interpretation of Peirce still underlies the concept of formal pragmatics. This interpretation led to a pragmatic, meaning-critical [*sinnkritischen*] transformation of the Kantian a priori, a transformation Habermas takes in a reconstructive-fallibilistic direction (in contrast to Apel).[70] Hence if one sees not primarily Hegelian Marxism but the pragmatism of the modern *episteme* as the true object of Foucault's analysis of the "anthropological quadrilateral," then that analysis must also be applied to Habermas's formal-pragmatic reconstructionism. In that case it too lies in the "anthropological slumber."

To be sure, all this still does not justify any objection against Habermas, for the pragmatic approach, i.e., reconstructive-fallibilistic approach, to the four segments of the "anthropological quadrilateral" keeps his theory from becoming antinomistic, as already shown. Thus the anthropocentrist could peacefully sleep on. Besides, there may in fact be no convincing alternatives to Habermas's theoretical program, including, for example, the one Foucault offers. There is no need to decide this issue here, however. Rather, what must be questioned is simply the claim that Habermas's turn from the philosophy of the subject and of consciousness to the theory of communicative intersubjectivity has taken him beyond the pale of Foucault's diagnosis of modern anthropocentrism.[71] The very opposite is the case: the philosophy of intersubjectivity as well is situated in the "anthropological quadrilateral" and displays the problems identified by Foucault. To show this, one must first dissolve the sweeping equation of human being, subject, and consciousness that Habermas uses in his critique of Foucault. As already indicated, decentering the human being is not the same as decentering the subject. If the actual human being as subject of himself and his world vacates the center, it remains quite possible for another authority to be subject: the Ego, the Absolute Idea, history, progress, evolution, the system, or even society as estranged from individual human beings, as in Marx and Adorno. Furthermore, philosophy of the subject and philosophy of consciousness do not coincide, i.e., the linguistic turn does not automatically finish off the aporias of the philosophy of consciousness in the way Apel and Habermas frequently claim. The expression "philosophy of consciousness" has to do with a philosophical form of language, namely, one that operates with certain expressions (such as "consciousness," "representation," "sensation," "intuition," "thinking," "intention," and so forth) that then present the philosopher the objects of philosophical reflection. I have suggested that this be designated as a "mentalistic paradigm."[72] In my opinion, this term has the advantage of making room for a philosophy of consciousness that is not mentalistic, e.g., the analytic philosophy of mind. This also implies that the philosophy of consciousness need not fall into the aporias of methodological or material solipsism, inasmuch as one can also find mentalistic theories of intersubjectivity, i.e., philosophical approaches that hold that actual intersubjectivity constitutes subjectivity, while nonetheless describing such intersubjectivity mentalistically. As examples I mention Hölderlin, Hegel, Humboldt, Schleiermacher, and Dilthey.

If the above is correct, then Foucault's diagnosis of the "anthropological slumber" is independent of the question of whether one ought to adopt a philosophy of the subject or not, and of the choice between mentalistic and linguistic paradigms. Linguistic formal-pragmatic philosophy of intersubjectivity does not in any case get beyond the anthropocentrism Foucault has in mind. It too remains in the realm of the empirical-transcendental *clair obscure* that shines forth as the stronger theory only as long as one renounces a totalizing theoretical self-closure and is content with a pragmatic approach. Thus it is not the *linguistic*-pragmatic but the linguistic-*pragmatic* turn—not its linguistic aspect but its pragmatistic one—that preserves Habermas's reconstructed critical theory from Foucault's four-sided catastrophe.

The question remains, then, whether there is any reason at all for awakening from the anthropological slumber, or whether it is not rather Foucault who is sleeping. Foucault is justified the moment one's analysis of the philosophical discourse of modernity becomes unduly fascinated by Hegel—as Foucault himself was—and one thereby backs into a left Hegelian and praxis philosophical perspective. If one proceeds on the assumption that Hegel is the first theoretician of modernity and that we still remain in the frame of consciousness shaped by the left Hegelians,[73] then Foucault's farewell to the "face in the sand" is probably unavoidable. Habermas understands modernity as the situation faced by a culture that "has to draw [*schöpfen*] its normativity out of itself."[74] The philosopher of precisely this situation, however, is Kant. He is the first, the genuine philosopher of modernity—not only of its unreconcilable and unbridgeable faults and fissures but also of the constitution of truth and obligatory force from subjective conditions of possibility that philosophers must draw from themselves without confusing them with de facto, i.e., anthropological or even sociohistorical, conditions. Hegel already presupposes all of this, first casting it in the light of the speculative philosophy of unification (Hölderlin) and later in that of an absolute dialectic as dialectic of the absolute. This makes it appear as mere "finitude," as something to be overcome if one is finally to project a solution that heads toward a sublation [*Aufhebung*] of the modern divisions within the state, religion, and philosophy. Hegel's project is not that of modernity but rather that of transcending [*Aufhebung*] modernity, a project that, precisely in its left Hegelian transformations, we can no longer propose or even continue today. Recourse to a materialistically inverted Hegel is likewise an error, because drawing normativity out of oneself [*Aus-sich-Schöpfen*] cannot be the same as creating it out of oneself [*Aus-sich-Schaffen*], i.e., producing the normative. In ethics Kant referred to the fact of pure practical reason, a fact we can certify in reflection even though we may not take ourselves to be its authors. If one disregards for the moment the problem of the naturalistic fallacy,[75] drawing normativity out of oneself can only consist in the grounded recognition of the normative obligatory force of existing normative structures. Those cultures are modern whose human members live in cognitive and normative orders for which they themselves must accept responsibility. This does not mean, however, that everything for which they accept rational responsibility they must first have produced themselves in order to be responsible for it: their traditions, forms of life, worldview, and so on. If generating obligatory force were really the same as generating the content of obligations, then human beings would be either their own subjects and modernity itself, a left Hegelian project in fact, or they would be fully powerless in a normative sense, since everything speaks against the idea of a human self-creation [*Selbstschöpfung*]. Rendering the concept of "modernity" more precise in the indicated sense could essentially defuse the present controversy over the project of modernity, for naturally even the protagonists of pre- and postmodernity are in the business of creating normativity through grounded recognition. They too do not accept traditions as valid merely because they exist but rather have reasons for defending them or not questioning them, whereby they too enter the modern discourse over the rational acceptability of normative structures. On the other hand, modernity becomes a project without prospects if we burden it with the mortgage of having to produce all responsible normativity by itself. For this reason too the project of modernity can be saved from Foucault only if we preserve Kant from all left-Hegelian projections and otherwise stand by him. It is the step from Kant to Hegel that allows philosophy to fall into the "anthropological slumber."

Notes

1. ["Man" is an appropriate translation of Schnädelbach's *Mensch* inasmuch as the philosophical anthropology targeted by Foucault has a sexist dimension (of which Foucault was not unaware). Inasmuch as Schnädelbach's concern with antihumanism goes beyond the issue of sexism, however, I have often found "human being" more appropriate.—Translator]

2. Martin Heidegger, "Letter on Humanism," trans. Frank A. Capuzzi, J. Glenn Gray, and David Farrell Krell, in *Basic Writings,* ed. Krell (New York, 1977), p. 210.

3. B. F. Skinner, *Beyond Freedom and Dignity* (New York, 1971), p. 200.

4. Hans Jonas, *Das Prinzip Verantwortung: Versuch einer Ethik für die technologische Zivilisation* (Frankfurt am Main, 1979), p. 8. This quote from the Preface is not present in the English edition, *The Imperative of Responsibility: In Search of an Ethics for the Technological Age,* trans. Hans Jonas with the collaboration of David Herr (Chicago, 1984).

5. Jonas, *Imperative,* p. 8.

6. On what follows, see Manfred Frank, "Subjekt, Person, Individuum," in Manfred Frank, Gérard Raulet, and Willem van Reijen, eds., *Die Frage nach dem Subjekt* (Frankfurt am Main, 1988), pp. 7 ff.; Helmuth Vetter, "Welches Subjekt stirbt?" in Herta Nagl-Docekal and Helmuth Vetter, eds., *Tod des Subjekts?* (Vienna, 1987), pp. 22 ff.

7. Heidegger, "Letter on Humanism," p. 210.

8. Herta Nagl-Docekal, Introduction to Nagl-Docekal and Vetter, *Tod des Subjekts?* pp. 7 ff.

9. See Gellner's critique of Peter Winch's "Idea of a Social Science," in Ernest Gellner, *Cause and Meaning in the Social Sciences* (London, 1973), pp. 49 ff., esp. p. 52.

10. See also Odo Marquard's variations on a Weberian theme in his well-known article "Über die Unvermeidlichkeit der Geisteswissenschaften," in Marquard, *Apologie des Zufälligen: Philosophische Studien* (Stuttgart, 1986), pp. 103 f. On the following, see also my treatise "Die Philosophie und Wissenschaften vom Menschen," in Clemens Bellut and Ulrich Müller-Schöll, eds., *Mensch und Moderne: Beiträge zur philosophischen Anthropologie und Gesellschaftskritik* (Würzburg, 1989), pp. 19–39.

11. On this, see Jürgen Habermas, "Anthropologie," in Alwin Diemer and Ivo Frenzel, eds., Fischer Lexicon series, *Philosophie* (Frankfurt am Main, 1958), p. 18.

12. Michel Foucault, *The Order of Things: An Archaeology of the Human Sciences* (New York, 1973), p. 385. Hereafter cited as *OT*.

13. *OT*, p. 387.

14. *OT*, p. xxiii.

15. Michel Foucault, "Die Ordnung der Dinge: Ein Gespräch mit Raymond Bellour" (The Order of Things: A Conversation with Raymond Bellour), in Adelbert Reif, ed., *Antworten der Strukturalisten* (Hamburg, 1973), pp. 152 f.

16. *OT*, pp. 303 and 386, respectively.

17. *OT*, p. 387.

18. *OT*, p. 386.

19. *OT*, pp. 340 ff. [Here I have altered the rendering of *sommeil* from "sleep" to "slumber," in order to preserve the parallel with Kant.—Translator]

20. *OT*, p. 309.

21. *OT*, p. 340.

22. See *OT*, pp. 340–341, also p. 312.

23. *OT*, p. 341.

24. *OT*, pp. 341–342.

25. *OT*, p. 315. See also pp. 314 ff. and 335.

26. *OT*, pp. 335, 318, respectively.

27. *OT*, p. 335.

28. *OT*, p. 342, also p. 303.

29. *OT*, p. 342.

30. *OT*, p. 386.

31. This is a paraphrase of Plato, *Theaetetus* 161c and *Laws* 716c. To quote the latter exactly, "Now it is God who is, for you and me, of a truth the 'measure of all things,' much more truly than, as they say, 'man.'" Trans. A. E. Taylor, in *The Collected Dialogues*

of Plato, Including the Letters, ed. Edith Hamilton and Huntington Cairns (New York, 1961), p. 1307.

32. Ludwig Feuerbach, *Principles of the Philosophy of the Future,* trans. Manfred H. Vogel (Indianapolis, 1986), sec. 54, p. 70.

33. *OT,* p. 341.

34. See also my article "Dialektik und Diskurs," in Herbert Schnädelbach, *Vernunft und Geschichte: Vorträge und Abhandlungen* (Frankfurt am Main, 1987), pp. 151 ff., esp. 157 f.

35. Immanuel Kant, *Logic,* trans. by Robert S. Hartman and Wolfgang Schwarz (New York, 1974), p. 29 [Kant's emphasis and dashes have been removed by Schnädelbach.—Translator]. See *OT,* p. 341. Foucault's assessment of Kant is, on the whole, noticeably indecisive. In his monograph on Foucault, Urs Marti reports an unpublished introduction written in 1961 for Kant's *Anthropology from a Pragmatic Point of View,* in which Foucault reads Kant as having maintained the difference between transcendental and anthropological philosophizing. His successors forgot Kant's critical lesson and necessarily fell into what *OT* later calls the "anthropological slumber." See Urs Marti, *Michel Foucault* (Munich, 1988), p. 61. In *OT,* on the contrary, Kant immediately appears as the forefather of anthropological philosophizing, because the Copernican revolution itself is already interpreted as a turn to anthropology. Of course, Foucault acknowledges that Kant at least drew the distinction between the empirical and the transcendental, which in his opinion the question What is man? ends up conflating (see *OT,* p. 341).

36. Immanuel Kant, *Anthropology from a Pragmatic Point of View,* trans. by Mary J. Gregor (The Hague, 1974), p. 3.

37. Contra Heidegger's reading of Descartes and Kant, Jacob Ragozinski shows that Kant's Copernican revolution in fact also decentered the Cartesian ego. Transcendental subjectivity is precisely not the putative absolute subject of modern metaphysics. See Jacob Ragozinski, "Der Aufruf des Fremden: Kant und die Frage nach dem Subjekt," in Frank et al., *Die Frage nach dem Subjekt,* pp. 192–229, esp. p. 199.

38. "Through this I or he or it (the thing) which thinks, nothing further is represented than a transcendental subject of the thoughts = *X*. It is known only through the thoughts which are its predicates, and of it, apart from them, we cannot have any concept whatsoever, but can only revolve in a perpetual circle, since any judgment upon it has always already made use of its representation." Immanuel Kant, *Critique of Pure Reason,* trans. Norman Kemp Smith (New York, 1965), B 404.

39. In the "Transcendental Aesthetic," *Critique of Pure Reason,* B 35, it reads, "These [extension and figure] belong to pure intuition, which, even without any actual object of the senses or of sensation, takes place [*stattfindet*] in the mind *a priori* as a mere form of sensibility." [I changed N. Kemp Smith's "exists" to "takes place."—Translator] This expression ("takes place") is not chosen accidentally but refers to the fact that Kant viewed the subjective conditions for the possibility of science and morality as something one comes across at the place of subjectivity, i.e., as found in the features characterizing the occurrence [*Stattfindens*] of science and morality. This underlines once again the impossibility of equating Kant's "I think" with the actual human being or with Fichte's "I." Put in Foucault's terminology, Kant remains a philosopher of human nature and thus does not leave the realm of classical *episteme.* Not as such is the human being an end-in-itself but only insofar as he shares in the "rational nature" that is end-in-itself. See *Foundations of the Metaphysics of Morals,* trans. Lewis White Beck (Indianapolis,

1959), pp. 46 f. Not the human being but the human being's "rational nature" as it "takes place" in scientific and moral activity is the basis of Kantian philosophy.

40. G. W. F. Hegel, *Enzyklopädie der philosophischen Wissenschaften im Grundrisse* (1830), sec. 387.

41. See *Philosophy of Right,* trans. T. M. Knox (Oxford, 1952), p. 127, sec. 190 note. In his "On the Jewish Question" Marx takes up this Hegelian motif again, naturally without mentioning Hegel, in order to denounce as bourgeois ideology the Rights of Man proclaimed in France in 1793. With this he founded the "left" tradition, i.e., the antibourgeois, ideology-theoretic critique of humanism, to which the older critical theory is also indebted (see note 59 below). The verbal correspondence with the parallel, Nietzsche-inspired tradition of the critique of "humanitarianism" (Gehlen) is often astonishing. In this tradition one also finds Foucault when he celebrates the replacement of humanism as unqualified liberation. See his Interview with Madeleine Chapsal, May 1966, in Günther Schiwy, *Der französische Strukturalismus* (Reinbek, 1969), pp. 203 ff. The specific difference between the Marxist and Nietzschean critiques of humanism probably lies in the theory of alienation. The boundary between humanistic and antihumanistic antihumanism is defined by the idea that, on the basis of social reasons, human beings are no longer, or not yet, themselves. See also Sartre's critique of structuralism in Schiwy, pp. 208 ff.

42. See Marti, *Michel Foucault,* p. 10.

43. On Nietzsche's assessment of the Sophists, see Friedrich Nietzsche, *The Will to Power,* trans. Walter Kaufmann and R. J. Hollingdale, ed. W. Kaufmann (New York, 1967), sec. 429 (March–June 1888), pp. 233 f. Also see F. C. S. Schiller, *Plato or Protagoras?* (Oxford, 1908), and his "Humanism," in Ekkehard Martens, ed., *Texte der Philosophie des Pragmatismus* (Stuttgart, 1975), pp. 18 ff., esp. p. 191.

44. This is a variation of a formulation found in Jürgen Habermas, *The Philosophical Discourse of Modernity,* trans. Frederick Lawrence (Cambridge, Mass., 1987), p. 7. [I have changed Lawrence's translation of *schöpfen* from "create" to "draw" in view of a distinction Schnädelbach will make at the end of this article.—Translator]

45. Evidence for these celebrations could be drawn from the history of physiological, psychological, anthropological, and sociological interpretations of Kant. In each case one thought one had finally gotten beyond Kant through a concrete or "realistic" interpretation of the transcendental a priori.

46. See Arend Kulenkampff, *Antinomie und Dialektik* (Stuttgart, 1971), esp. pp. 60 ff.

47. The protophysics dispute as well as the controversy between Karl-Otto Apel and Hans Albert can serve as examples.

48. See also Herbert Schnädelbach, *Erfahrung, Begründung und Reflexion: Versuch über den Positivismus* (Frankfurt am Main, 1971), esp. pp. 105 ff.

49. *OT,* p. 342.

50. "Letter on Humanism," p. 199.

51. "Letter on Humanism," p. 231.

52. See *OT,* pp. 303 ff. On the primacy of language in Heidegger, see "Letter on Humanism," pp. 206, 239.

53. Heidegger, "Letter on Humanism," p. 231.

54. See, for example, Peter Koslowski, *Die postmoderne Kultur* (Munich, 1987). On Jürgen Habermas as the "project leader" of modernity, see esp. pp. 14 f.

55. See Christel Beier, *Zum Verhältnis von Gesellschaftstheorie und Erkenntnistheorie: Untersuchungen zum Totalitätsbegriff in der kritischen Theorie Adornos* (Frankfurt am Main, 1977).

56. On this point, see also my articles, "Dialektik als Vernunftkritik: Zur Konstruktion des Rationalen bei Adorno" and "Dialektik und Diskurs," in *Vernunft und Geschichte,* pp. 179 ff. and 151 ff.

57. See *OT,* pp. 319 f.

58. *OT,* p. 320.

59. Adorno writes, "We cannot say what man is. Man today is a function, unfree, regressing behind whatever is ascribed to him as invariant. . . . That we cannot tell what man is does not establish a peculiarly majestic anthropology, it vetoes any anthropology." Theodor W. Adorno, *Negative Dialectics,* trans. E. B. Ashton (New York, 1973), p. 124. The term "negative anthropology" is the title of a book by Ulrich Sonnemann, which Adorno mentions approvingly at the end of the Preface to the German edition, *Negative Dialektik* (Frankfurt am Main, 1966), p. 9.

60. Adorno put the human being under the theological prohibition against images in order not to sabotage his historical realization: "To decipher the human essence by the way it is now would sabotage its possibility." *Negative Dialectics,* p. 124.

61. *OT,* pp. 322 ff.

62. Adorno, *Negative Dialectics,* p. 56.

63. *OT,* pp. 328 ff.

64. Foucault first explicitly refers to the Frankfurt School and Habermas in his "Subject and Power," an Afterword to Hubert L. Dreyfus and Paul Rabinow, *Michel Foucault: Beyond Structuralism and Hermeneutics* (Chicago, 1982), pp. 208–226, here p. 210.

65. Jürgen Habermas, "Knowledge and Human Interests: A General Perspective," Appendix to Habermas, *Knowledge and Human Interests,* trans. Jeremy J. Shapiro (Boston, 1971), p. 312. [Habermas's emphasis is removed.—Translator]

66. Habermas, "Knowledge and Human Interests," p. 313. [Habermas's emphasis is removed.—Translator]

67. *OT,* p. 351. [Note that the German rendition of Foucault reads not "life" but "work" (*Arbeit*).—Translator] In his Afterword to Dreyfus and Rabinow, *Beyond Structuralism,* Foucault says, "When Habermas distinguishes between domination, communication, and finalized activity, I do not think that he sees in them three separate domains, but rather three 'transcendentals'" (p. 218, note 1). Here he leaves it open whether or not he still holds his old objection against the empirical-transcendental conflation of spheres. At some point it has to be clarified whether Foucault's later analyses of power, which were supposed to prepare a comprehensive theory of the subject—"Thus it is not power, but the subject, which is the general theme of my

research" (p. 209)—would not themselves be vulnerable to such an objection. Of course, that would not be an objection to the objection.

68. *OT,* p. 343.

69. Habermas, "Knowledge and Human Interests," p. 314.

70. See Jürgen Habermas, "What Is Universal Pragmatics?" in Habermas, *Communication and the Evolution of Society,* trans. Thomas McCarthy (Boston, 1979), pp. 1–68, esp. 21 ff.

71. See Ludwig Nagl, "Zeigt die Habermassche Kommunikationstheorie einen 'Ausweg aus der Subjektphilosophie'? Erwägungen zur Studie *Der philosophische Diskurs der Moderne,*" in Frank et al., *Die Frage nach dem Subjekt,* pp. 346 ff.

72. See the article "Philosophie" in Ekkehard Martens and Herbert Schnädelbach, eds., *Philosophie: Ein Grundkurs* (Reinbek, 1985), pp. 37 ff., esp. 58 ff.

73. See Habermas, *Philosophical Discourse of Modernity,* p. 53.

74. Habermas, *Philosophical Discourse of Modernity,* p. 7.

75. See Karl-Heinz Ilting, "Der naturalistische Fehlschluß bei Kant," in Manfred Riedel, ed., *Rehabilitierung der praktischen Philosophie* (Freiburg, 1972), vol. 1, pp. 113–130.

Contributors

Karl-Otto Apel is Professor Emeritus of Philosophy at the University of Frankfurt. His works translated into English include *Understanding and Explanation: A Transcendental-Pragmatic Perspective* (1984) and *The Transformation of Philosophy* (1980).

Richard J. Bernstein is Professor of Philosophy at the New School for Social Research. Among his recent publications are *Beyond Objectivism and Relativism: Science, Hermeneutics, and Praxis* (1983) and *Philosophical Profiles: Essays in a Pragmatic Mode* (1986).

Peter Bürger teaches in the Department of Linguistics and Cultural Sciences at the University of Bremen. He is the author of *Theory of the Avant-Garde* (1984).

Dieter Henrich is Professor of Philosophy at the University of Munich. Two of his better-known works are *Hegel im Kontext* (1971) and *Fluchtlinien* (1982).

Martin Jay is Professor of History at the University of California at Berkeley. He is the author of *The Dialectical Imagination* (1973) and *Marxism and Totality: The Adventures of a Concept from Lukacs to Habermas* (1984).

Thomas McCarthy is Professor of Philosophy at Northwestern University. He is the author of *The Critical Theory of Jürgen*

Habermas (1978) and *Ideals and Illusions: On Reconstruction and Deconstruction in Contemporary Critical Theory* (1991).

Herbert Schnädelbach is Professor of Philosophy at the University of Hamburg. His *Philosophy in Germany, 1831–1933* (1984) has been translated into English.

Charles Taylor is Professor of Political Philosophy at McGill University. He is the author of numerous articles and books, including *Hegel* (1975) and, more recently, *Sources of the Self: The Making of the Modern Identity* (1989).

Michael Theunissen is Professor of Philosophy at the Free University of Berlin. He is the author of *The Other: Studies in the Social Ontology of Husserl, Heidegger, Sartre, and Buber* (1984).

Ernst Tugendhat is Professor of Philosophy at the Free University of Berlin. His works in English are *Traditional and Analytic Philosophy: Lectures on the Philosophy of Language* (1982) and *Self-Consciousness and Self-Determination* (1986).

Albrecht Wellmer is Professor of Philosophy at the Free University of Berlin. Two of his books have been translated into English: *Critical Theory of Society* (1971) and *The Persistence of Modernity: Essays on Aesthetics, Ethics, and Postmodernism* (1991).

Index

Studies in Contemporary German Social Thought
Thomas McCarthy, General Editor

Theodor W. Adorno, *Against Epistemology: A Metacritique*
Theodor W. Adorno, *Prisms*
Karl-Otto Apel, *Understanding and Explanation: A Transcendental-Pragmatic Perspective*
Seyla Benhabib and Fred Dallmayr, editors, *The Communicative Ethics Debate*
Richard J. Bernstein, editor, *Habermas and Modernity*
Ernst Bloch, *Natural Law and Human Dignity*
Ernst Bloch, *The Principle of Hope*
Ernst Bloch, *The Utopian Function of Art and Literature: Selected Essays*
Hans Blumenberg, *The Genesis of the Copernican World*
Hans Blumenberg, *The Legitimacy of the Modern Age*
Hans Blumenberg, *Work on Myth*
Susan Buck-Morss, *The Dialectics of Seeing: Walter Benjamin and the Arcades Project*
Craig Calhoun, editor, *Habermas and the Public Sphere*
Jean Cohen and Andrew Arato, *Civil Society and Political Theory*
Helmut Dubiel, *Theory and Politics: Studies in the Development of Critical Theory*
John Forester, editor, *Critical Theory and Public Life*
David Frisby, *Fragments of Modernity: Theories of Modernity in the Work of Simmel, Kracauer, and Benjamin*
Hans-Georg Gadamer, *Philosophical Apprenticeships*
Hans-Georg Gadamer, *Reason in the Age of Science*
Jürgen Habermas, *On the Logic of the Social Sciences*
Jürgen Habermas, *Moral Consciousness and Communicative Action*
Jürgen Habermas, *The New Conservatism: Cultural Criticism and the Historians' Debate*
Jürgen Habermas, *The Philosophical Discourse of Modernity: Twelve Lectures*
Jürgen Habermas, *Philosophical-Political Profiles*
Jürgen Habermas, editor, *Observations on "The Spiritual Situation of the Age"*
Jürgen Habermas, *The Structural Transformation of the Public Sphere: An Inquiry into a Category of Bourgeois Society*
Axel Honneth, *The Critique of Power: Reflective Stages in a Critical Social Theory*
Axel Honneth and Hans Joas, editors, *Communicative Action: Essays on Jürgen Habermas's* The Theory of Communicative Action

Axel Honneth, Thomas McCarthy, Claus Offe, and Albrecht Wellmer, editors, *Philosophical Interventions in the Unfinished Project of Enlightenment*

Hans Joas, *G. H. Mead: A Contemporary Re-examination of His Thought*

Reinhart Koselleck, *Critique and Crisis: Enlightenment and the Pathogenesis of Modern Society*

Reinhart Koselleck, *Futures Past: On the Semantics of Historical Time*

Harry Liebersohn, *Fate and Utopia in German Sociology, 1887–1923*

Herbert Marcuse, *Hegel's Ontology and the Theory of Historicity*

Guy Oakes, *Weber and Rickert: Concept Formation in the Cultural Sciences*

Claus Offe, *Contradictions of the Welfare State*

Claus Offe, *Disorganized Capitalism: Contemporary Transformations of Work and Politics*

Helmut Peukert, *Science, Action, and Fundamental Theology: Toward a Theology of Communicative Action*

Joachim Ritter, *Hegel and the French Revolution: Essays on the* Philosophy of Right

Alfred Schmidt, *History and Structure: An Essay on Hegelian-Marxist and Structuralist Theories of History*

Dennis Schmidt, *The Ubiquity of the Finite: Hegel, Heidegger, and the Entitlements of Philosophy*

Carl Schmitt, *The Crisis of Parliamentary Democracy*

Carl Schmitt, *Political Romanticism*

Carl Schmitt, *Political Theology: Four Chapters on the Concept of Sovereignty*

Gary Smith, editor, *On Walter Benjamin: Critical Essays and Recollections*

Michael Theunissen, *The Other: Studies in the Social Ontology of Husserl, Heidegger, Sartre, and Buber*

Ernst Tugendhat, *Self-Consciousness and Self-Determination*

Mark Warren, *Nietzsche and Political Thought*

Albrecht Wellmer, *The Persistence of Modernity: Essays on Aesthetics, Ethics, and Postmodernism*

Thomas E. Wren, editor, *The Moral Domain: Essays in the Ongoing Discussion between Philosophy and the Social Sciences*

Lambert Zuidervaart, *Adorno's Aesthetic Theory: The Redemption of Illusion*